D1797036

Celebrity Memoir

Hannah Yelin

Celebrity Memoir

From Ghostwriting to Gender Politics

Hannah Yelin
Oxford Brookes University
Oxford, UK

ISBN 978-3-030-44620-8   ISBN 978-3-030-44621-5   (eBook)
https://doi.org/10.1007/978-3-030-44621-5

© The Editor(s) (if applicable) and The Author(s) 2020
This work is subject to copyright. All rights are solely and exclusively licensed by the Publisher, whether the whole or part of the material is concerned, specifically the rights of translation, reprinting, reuse of illustrations, recitation, broadcasting, reproduction on microfilms or in any other physical way, and transmission or information storage and retrieval, electronic adaptation, computer software, or by similar or dissimilar methodology now known or hereafter developed.
The use of general descriptive names, registered names, trademarks, service marks, etc. in this publication does not imply, even in the absence of a specific statement, that such names are exempt from the relevant protective laws and regulations and therefore free for general use.
The publisher, the authors and the editors are safe to assume that the advice and information in this book are believed to be true and accurate at the date of publication. Neither the publisher nor the authors or the editors give a warranty, expressed or implied, with respect to the material contained herein or for any errors or omissions that may have been made. The publisher remains neutral with regard to jurisdictional claims in published maps and institutional affiliations.

Cover image: Anna Duffy, aduffydesign.com
Cover design by eStudioCalamar

This Palgrave Macmillan imprint is published by the registered company Springer Nature Switzerland AG
The registered company address is: Gewerbestrasse 11, 6330 Cham, Switzerland

For Arvo

Acknowledgements

Like the texts it discusses, this book has its share of invisible hands that have helped shape its contents. Thank you to every one of them, especially Su Holmes, Milly Williamson, Leander Reeves, Michele Paule, and Laura Clancy. To my UEA cohort, I "salute" you. Angela Royston, my first and most generous reader, thank you. Jack Royston, for so much more, but, yes, also the reading. And Ros Yelin, for everything.

I am grateful for the quirk of history that meant that I was born at a time when I could access good quality, free education: not born so early that I had to fight for my right to be educated as a woman, and not born too late to benefit from free, means-tested university education. I am not sure I would have found my way had I been starting my higher education in the economic climate my wonderful students find themselves in today.

CONTENTS

LIST OF FIGURES

CHAPTER 1

Introduction

The memoirs of female celebrities reveal battlefields of self-determination. In them, famous women tell us their story, in their 'own words'. It is an open secret, however, that constellations of ghostwriters, management and market forces orbit these texts, undermining assertions of authorship or unfettered access to the 'real' woman behind the public image. As a result, the ghostwritten memoir inhabits a complex grey area between biography, autobiography, fact and fiction.

A thorough interrogation of the memoirs of contemporary, female celebrities is urgent and necessary. There is a historical, representational lack when it comes to the recording of the lives of women.[1] Women's erasure is a product of continuing patriarchal gatekeeping of official histories. Feminist philosopher Simone De Beauvoir charts the difficulty for women to define themselves in their own terms from ancient mythology to when she was writing in the mid-twentieth century.[2] More recently, in her stage show *Nannette*, comedian Hannah Gadsby laments of a long list of alleged and convicted sexual predators, including Harvey Weinstein, Bill Cosby, Woody Allen and Roman Polanski, 'these men control our stories' and they 'don't give a fuck about women'.[3]

[1] Judith Butler, *Gender Trouble* (London: Routledge, 1990).

[2] Simone de Beauvoir, *The Second Sex*, trans. H.M. Parshley (London: Penguin Books, 1997).

[3] Hannah Gadsby, *Nannette* (Netflix, 2018).

© The Author(s) 2020
H. Yelin, *Celebrity Memoir*,
https://doi.org/10.1007/978-3-030-44621-5_1

1

As a successful publishing phenomenon centred upon books sold as 'true' female experiences, celebrity memoir, therefore, demands attention. Their enormous popularity, commercial success and resultant cultural impact are grounds for investigation in their own right. Moreover, given the historical incursions upon women's *self*-representational agency, it is crucial that we attend to the fact that some of the most widely read texts authored by women are not necessarily (or at least not solely) authored by women.

The celebrity author in need of a ghostwriter is often a figure of derision. This book is not a straightforward exercise in rehabilitation of the genre per se. Indeed, at points my analysis of these texts, and the gendered power dynamics they represent, is deeply critical. However, celebrity memoir is a productive and complex cultural artefact. Far from being a reason for ridicule, ghostwriting is a fascinating microcosm of the celebrity machine. The ghosts within must be made visible if we are to understand the ways in which women in the public eye are often coaxed or curtailed when giving an account of themselves. The project of this book, then, is to reveal these oft-ignored intermediaries and the power dynamics of their presence.

Ghostwriters trigger intense cultural anxieties about both the power afforded to those who exist in the spotlight and the risk of this power falling into the wrong hands. The ghostwriter for Donald Trump's memoir fears that the myth he created of 'a charmer with an unfailing knack for business' changed history for the worse by helping Trump get elected as the President of the United States.[4] The writer who helped Instagrammer Caroline Calloway pen social media posts and a book proposal exposed her identity to a global media furore, with quality news titles around the world engrossed in the dispute, despite the fact that the memoir was never actually written and the advance on the $500,000 book deal had to be returned.[5] The punitively gendered construction of authenticity surrounding women's autobiographical acts is writ large in the discourses of betrayal which circulated through and around this story, and the gleeful schadenfreude at Calloway's setbacks (albeit setbacks

---

[4] Jane Mayer, 'Donald Trump's Ghostwriter Tells All,' *The New Yorker*, 18 July 2016.

[5] Natalie Beach, 'I Was Caroline Calloway: Seven Years After I Met the Infamous Instagram Star, I'm Ready to Tell My Side of the Story,' *The Cut*, 10 September 2019.

which she was able to parlay into a deal for a new, forthcoming book titled *Scammer*).[6]

The celebrity memoir occupies a nexus of promises of 'access' and 'authenticity'. It combines the 'intimate' revelations that are central to celebrity coverage with autobiography's promise of self-disclosure. Such promises must be interrogated in relation to the fact that these texts are so visibly mediated. Moreover, the assumption that we are capable of revealing our essential selves is based upon problematic Enlightenment ideas of personal sovereignty.[7]

How, then, can we understand the collaborative construction of these texts and its implications for both agency and 'authorship'? The process of attributing meaning to the celebrity life story can be understood as a negotiation, not only between the (various) agents involved in the text's construction, but in terms of how the meaning of these texts is shaped by their wider relationship with extratextual material—that is, the wealth of information we 'know' about a celebrity's life from other sources.

The production of a memoir, collaborative or otherwise, is an act that claims certain forms of agency in self-representation. Yet, as they respond to external criticism from tabloids, gossip blogs or twitterstorms, these memoirs implicitly contain the regulatory narratives levelled at authors in other media. This model of what I will call the *celebrity-as-assemblage* applies not only to the complex mediations of collaboratively authored memoir, but also to celebrity as a whole: the performance of the celebrity self is always in dialogue with, and so constituted of, its paratexts and surrounding materials in a web of conflicting mediation. Thus, celebrity agency in self-representation can be seen to be multiple and negotiated, taking many forms.

Just as the demands of narrative in life writing must impose linear order upon the disorder of lived experience, these texts attempt to impose a singular reading upon the multiplicity of narratives that surround a celebrity. Within the boundaries of these texts, a star identity can be carefully controlled and, as such, they create an opportunity for intervention in a public image that must be constantly reclaimed, rebranded or redressed. However, because the assemblage is non-hierarchical, they

---

[6] Stephanie McNeal, 'Caroline Calloway Says She Is Releasing a Book Called "Scammer",' *BuzzFeed News*, 15 January 2020.

[7] Sidonie Smith and Julia Watson, *Reading Autobiography* (Minneapolis: University of Minnesota Press, 2001), p. 6.

can never replace or obscure the other narratives that circulate around the celebrity. This book is in part a response to calls for a better understanding of the industrial production of celebrity.[8] I offer a framework for reading these texts which accounts for both their collaborative authorship and the industrial conditions of their construction without dismissing them as solely the cynical manufacture of corporate merchandise.

Ghostwritten memoir offers a 'moment' of interaction between celebrity and audience in which the concerns of celebrity culture (such as privacy, authenticity, myth-making, marketing, agency, subjectivity) uniquely coalesce in an interaction between slow, old media and instantaneous, new media. The reader of celebrity memoir is addressed individually in the celebrity's first-person, confessional voice in a performance of constructed intimacy that is experienced as a one-on-one address and sustained for the duration of 300 pages. As such, celebrity memoirs offer a uniquely rich opportunity to interrogate celebrity culture's promise of access to the 'private', 'intimate' self. Celebrity memoirs are constructed around this feeling of intense privacy and yet, simultaneously, are transparent exercises in public image management. Thus, the genre has much to reveal as a way of explicitly reading the bridge between publicity and privacy that is at the heart of celebrity culture.[9]

As such, this book will be useful for literary studies of memoir, feminist media studies work on representational politics, work on the creative industries examining the politics of production, and celebrity studies' understandings of 'authenticity', 'artifice' and the gender dynamics of celebrity culture. As such, this is not solely a book about celebrity memoir. Rather, it is a demonstration that celebrity memoirs are the exemplary texts through which one can understand wider celebrity culture. Such an interrogation necessitates new terms, concepts and tools to interrogate celebrity culture, namely here, the *celebrity-as-assemblage*, the *gendered authenticity contract* and the *economics of access*.

---

[8] Graeme Turner, 'Approaching Celebrity Studies,' *Celebrity Studies* 1 (2010), 11–20; Graeme Turner, Frances Bonner, and P. David Marshall, *Fame Games: The Production of Celebrity in Australia* (Cambridge: Cambridge University Press, 2000).

[9] Leo Braudy, *The Frenzy of Renown: Fame and Its History* (New York: Oxford University Press, 1986); Richard de Cordova, *Picture Personalities: The Emergence of the Star System in America* (Chicago: University of Illinois Press, [2001] 1990); Milly Williamson, 'Celebrity, Gossip, Privacy, and Scandal,' *The Routledge Companion to Media and Gender*, ed. by Cynthia Carter, Linda Steiner, and Lisa McLaughlin (New York: Routledge, 2014).

As 'official' celebrity narratives, memoirs react to their media environ-ment, modelling the ways in which celebrities are always in interaction with the multiplicity of coverage, judgements and readings that circulate around them, and affording a model for understanding the *celebrity-as-assemblage*. The explicit coexistence of industrial brand-building and the revelation of a 'real' self behind the image make ghostwritten memoirs the ideal celebrity texts for consideration of the questions of celebrity authenticity, which have concerned the field.[10] Whilst celebrity texts of all kinds tend to engage with these competing discourses, it is rare to find examples so entirely defined by both visible manipulation and apparent access to essential subjectivity and inner thoughts. This I theorise as a *gendered authenticity contract*: an expectation of impossible access to a 'real' woman behind a public image, which causes anger when this inevitably cannot be delivered. This allows analysis of what I will term the celebrity's *economics of access*: where (the appearance of) access and exposure is traded as vital celebrity currency.

Through the memoirs examined here, we see the space available for female self-representation in public, and the incursions upon it. We see the weight of recurring conventions, despite the diversity of the celebri-ties and the autobiographical forms they deploy. At the same time, we will see that, whilst many of these gendered conventions appear inescapable, there is space for resistance and the possibility for alternative models of femininity. By offering an understanding of celebrity memoir—as ghost-written, as an agentic intervention, as a negotiated terrain which makes its negotiations exceptionally visible on the page and as a microcosmic cultural artefact with much to tell us about celebrity culture at large—I aim to provide new ways of approaching the mediated, collaboratively constructed nature of all celebrity. Only by approaching celebrity thus, and through the diversity of autobiographical forms examined here, can we understand the weight of narrative convention and how very gendered these conventions are.

[10] Richard Dyer, *Heavenly Bodies: Film Stars and Society* (New York: St. Martin's Press, 1986), p. 10; Sean Redmond, 'Pieces of Me: Celebrity Confessional Carnality,' *Social Semiotics* 18.2 (2008), 149–61; Su Holmes, 'Off-Guard, Unkempt, Unready'? Decon-structing Contemporary Celebrity in Heat Magazine,' *Continuum: Journal of Media & Cultural Studies* 19.1 (2005), 21–38.

These memoirs are both a perpetuation of, and an intervention into, harshly gendered celebrity cultures that coax particular subjectivities or models of personhood from women. Surrounding factors that shape, enable or inhibit the ways in which the self can be represented are as important to examine as those resulting representations. For example, social ideas surrounding gender, race and class, sources of authority, cultural hierarchies, currencies of authenticity, intimacy, likeability and sexual appeal, audience appetites and market forces all place pressure on the subject positions available to the celebrity author-subject. Likewise, the specificities of the individual celebrity's existing 'star image',[11] the celebrity's domain or field of work and the form of memoir adopted, all contribute to or curtail the types of life stories that can be told. This is why you will find in this book texts that span a range of auto-biographical modes, such as autobiographical fiction and photo-diary, as well as more 'traditional' memoir forms. These examples show the weight of generic convention at play—conventions of both autobiography and celebrity construction. However, it would be problematic to assume—as the popular press often does—that celebrity memoir is formulaic: the sample included here reveals that celebrity memoir as a genre is far from homogenous in terms of its textual address or mediation of gender politics.

The memoirs of female celebrities variously function to reinscribe and/or counter patriarchal narratives, depending on the particular construction of the memoir in hand. This book, therefore, focuses exclusively on the memoirs of famous women. In the coming case studies, we shall see many examples of the gendered nature of fame. It is hard to imagine, for example, the male equivalent of Anderson's claim, made in a promotional interview for her fictionalised memoir, *Star*, 'my breasts have a career. I'm just tagging along'.[12] Whilst a study of the memoirs of male or non-binary celebrities would reveal its own gendered conventions and their ramifications, this book fills the gap in the study of memoir and mediation in the specific context of patriarchal histories of curtailing,

---

[11] Richard Dyer, *Stars* (London: British Film Institute, 1979).

[12] Mike Sager, 'What I've Learned: Pamela Anderson,' *Esquire Magazine*, 31 December 2004.

coaxing and commodifying women's subjectivities in ways that require their own distinct theorisation from celebrities of other genders. Chapters are organised around the different 'fields' from which the celebrities' fame originates: reality TV stars Jade Goody, Paris Hilton and the Kardashians; YouTubers Zoella, iJustine and JennxPenn; pop-stars Lady Gaga and M.I.A.; and Katie Price, Pamela Anderson and Jenna Jameson under the heading 'glamour girls' (a British euphemism for soft-core pornography). The nature of multiplatform celebrity performance means that these categories cross-fertilise and blur. They nevertheless prove illuminating because of the ways in which hierarchies of cultural value and perceived associations of 'talent' (or lack thereof) shape the subject positions available to a celebrity author.

In terms of scope, I confine my analysis to female celebrities with memoirs published in the twenty-first century, with a high-profile or 'cross-over' success in the celebrity fields of reality TV, YouTube, pop-stardom or porn/glamour modelling. However, within this sample, patterns emerge pointing to wider conventions of female celebrity. In terms of age, at 19, YouTuber Jenn McAllister was the youngest of these celebrities at the time of the release of her memoir, the oldest being porn-star Jenna Jameson, who released her memoir aged 30. In a postfeminist celebrity culture, the commodified subjectivity, feelings and experiences of specifically young, famous women are both norm and ideal.[13] Memoirs by older female celebrities such a Grace Jones, Sharon Osbourne and Toyah Wilcox were released in the period; however, as scholars of ageing celebrity observe,[14] the responses to older famous women, from erasure to hypervisibility, from disgust to celebration of freedom, are distinct and need their own analysis. There is a significant variation in class back-grounds (as discussed in Chapter 4 through the classed identities of Jade Goody and Paris Hilton). Notably, the three 'glamour girl' author-subjects relate their working-class origins, whilst both pop-stars were educated at prestigious universities and endeavour not to be received as middle class. There is less variation in terms of race. Except for M.I.A. and the Kardashians, the authors of the books examined here are all white. Racism in porn consumption, YouTube comments and reality TV

---

[13] *Interrogating Postfeminism*, ed. by Yvonne Tasker and Diane Negra (Durham: Duke University Press, 2007).

[14] Deborah Jermyn, '"Get a Life, Ladies: Your Old One Is Not Coming Back": Ageing, Ageism and the Lifespan of Female Celebrity,' *Celebrity Studies* 3.1 (2012), 1–12.

has been well documented and is likely to have contributed to the fact that the 'cross-over' stars who get book deals are predominantly white.[15] Pop-stardom was the only field in which there was a broad choice of stars with memoirs from different ethnic and racial backgrounds. Further, there is virtually no variation in terms of professed sexual orientation. Whilst Lady Gaga has come out as bisexual and campaigns for LGBT rights, explicit heterosexuality runs throughout the texts and images analysed here, including her photo-memoir.

Within the scope of the selection, these patterns say much about the potency of the conventions that govern upon whom the light of fame is shone—who gets offered a book deal in a structurally racist, ageist, heteropatriarchal society; whose book gets well-promoted once released—and accords with what scholars of celebrity have noted about female celebrity: she is presumed to be young, white and overtly, availably heterosexual.[16]

Chapter 2 situates the contemporary memoirs of female celebrities in their cultural and historical contexts. It shows how celebrity memoir is a hate object in both popular media and academe, as both have overlooked the genre's valuable insights about celebrity culture, female subjectivity and agency. This chapter demonstrates that, whilst selling gendered access to the commodified celebrity private life is nothing new, these books are very much a product of a cultural moment at the turn of the twenty-first century. Key themes in this chapter include: authenticity, artifice, agency, gender, authorship, hierarchies of cultural value and access.

Chapter 3 examines the tensions that arise when life writing—an act of subjectification—is undertaken by an individual with a professional investment in their own objectification. The illustration is especially stark in the examples chosen (Katie Price, Pamela Anderson, Jenna Jameson), as they are sexually inflected through the celebrity author-subjects' career origins in soft-core pornographic modelling or hardcore pornographic films.

---

[15] Mark P. Orbe, 'Representations of Race in Reality TV: Watch and Discuss,' *Critical Studies in Media Communication* 25.4 (2008), 345–352; Xavier Landes and Morten Nielsen, 'Racial Dodging in the Porn Industry: A Case with No Silver Bullet,' *Porn Studies* 5.2 (2018), 115–30; Sabina Perrino, 'Recontextualizing Racialized Stories on YouTube,' *Narrative Inquiry* 27.2 (2017), 261–85.

[16] Sean Redmond, 'The Whiteness of Stars: Looking at Kate Winslet's Unruly White Body,' *Stardom and Celebrity: A Reader*, ed. by Su Holmes and Sean Redmond (London: Sage, 2007); *In the Limelight and Under the Microscope: Forms and Functions of Female Celebrity*, ed. by Su Holmes and Diane Negra (New York: Continuum, 2011).

Despite the predominantly female target audience of celebrity autobiography, women made famous by male-targeted pornography have authored some of the most commercially successful and widely read contemporary texts in the genre. This chapter demonstrates that the ghosting relationship is charged with complex, gendered power dynamics. Given the aforementioned historic representational lack, these books are rare examples giving voice to women's subjectivity, to women's sexual autobiography, and to women in the sex industry specifically. It is significant, therefore, that these texts are often co-authored by men. Examination of the power dynamics of ghosting is especially necessary when these texts narrate (and make palatable) stories of trauma, abuse and sexual violence. I argue that a thematic and formal preoccupation with constructedness interacts with (and potentially undermines) testimonies of trauma survival that make claim to truth status. Key themes in this chapter include the commodification of female experience, constructedness, writing the body, postfeminist sexual empowerment, ghostwriting and trauma.

Using the memoir of Jade Goody, Chapter 4 opens with a consideration of the various capitals the celebrity and ghostwriter bring to the exchange of collaborative authorship. This chapter then contrasts Goody with Paris Hilton, to show that their class origins shape the ways in which they are able/required to represent themselves in their memoirs. Where Goody adopts a model of abjection, seeking exoneration from the audience in return for a thorough confession, Hilton can adopt a strategy of camp play and heightened artifice, refusing to give much away and deliberately undermining the little she does reveal. Chapter 4 ends with an analysis of the similarities between both women's reception as 'white trash'. The invisibility of whiteness within racist celebrity culture is examined in the contrast between Hilton and the Kardashians' ethnic self-representation. That 'white trash' is a class-based insult would suggest that it is Goody's and Hilton's class identities that render them vulnerable to criticism, but their socio-economic backgrounds are diametrically opposed. The nature of reality TV celebrity, with its subjects' lives on continual display, provides a basis for the gendered classing of its female stars as 'trash', a status deriving from the failure to demonstrate acceptably feminine restraint rather than relating to socio-economic status. This analysis reveals that, whilst celebrity culture and its supporting gossip media have been viewed as a 'low' field with tabloid sensibilities, its value system is punitively middle class, policing the appropriateness of its players and shaming those who fall short. Key issues in this chapter include class, race and 'white-trash' celebrity, shame and display, confession and evasion, respectability, camp play and the 'undeserving' rich.

Chapter 5 examines the memoirs of YouTube celebrities Zoella, iJustine and JennxPenn and how these texts relate the abuse and sexual harassment their celebrity author-subjects receive for sharing their lives online. The combination of what I term YouTube's *economics of access* and cultural sexism, which constructs women's sexuality as available for male pleasure, results in a *gendered authenticity contract* which the male audience angrily believes has been reneged upon when the (often sexualised) access they feel entitled to is not granted. I demonstrate how the risk of inspiring further abuse forces these women to normalise online harassment, as they soothe and assuage their audiences whenever mentioning the sexist trolling they experience. The economic need to build audience loyalty to maintain one's status as a YouTuber demands interaction with the audience's comments to stay on the right side of the algorithms that determine their success. Whilst YouTubers may make and upload their own videos, it does not necessarily follow that they have full control of their narratives or are any less embroiled in constellations of 'ghost'-like intermediaries than the celebrities discussed in previous chapters. And yet, digitally enabled, lone-working and insecurely entrepreneurial, theirs is a kind of celebrity of the gig economy. Chapter 5 argues for an understanding of YouTube celebrity through the concept of millennial precarity and questions the consequences of exposure without insulation. Key themes in this chapter are: trolling, cultures of online sharing, digital identity and networked self-representation, gig-economy celebrity, millennial precarity and the risks of exposure without insulation.

At first look, the visual memoirs of M.I.A. and Lady Gaga, the focus of Chapter 6, appear to be quite different texts that break the conventions outlined in the previous chapters. M.I.A.'s anthology of graphic art and Gaga's photographic diary of life on the road appear to be setting themselves up as postmodern masquerades: playful bricolages with performed identities which direct attention to the surface in a genre that is usually concerned with finding 'hidden depths'. Rather than written confessional narratives like those of Katie Price and Jade Goody, which draw upon nineteenth-century realist modes, M.I.A. and Gaga's texts appear to be constructing a self-conscious performance of 'doing' pop-stardom.[17] In a culture determined to know its female celebrities, where celebrity exists in an *economics of access* that coaxes stars to share as much as possible, this focus on the surface image could be read as a resistant move against interpretation, negotiating against these demands. Whilst these books do demonstrate meaningful differences that show that the genre is not homogenous, they ultimately still trade in the same currencies as the texts in previous chapters: for example, authenticity, access, and suffering. Rather than being exceptions, these texts demonstrate the extreme persistence of certain conventions of female celebrity (self)-representation. Although they do not offer the written confessions that are the norm, a form of confession can be extracted, nonetheless. Chapter 6 demonstrates the rare moments when the status of the celebrity author-subject in relation to their ghost can be discerned in the text and how these power relations also shape the meaning of the resultant co-authored work. Key issues in this section include the celebrity photograph, hierarchies of cultural value, claims to artistry and creative agency, directing attention to the surface as a resistant strategy against interpretation, the wider agents of mediation as 'ghosts', the ghost as employee, and the containment of disruptive femininity, consent and sexual assault.

BIBLIOGRAPHY

Braudy, Leo. *The Frenzy of Renown: Fame and Its History*. New York: Vintage, 1997.

Butler, Judith. *Gender Trouble: Feminism and the Subversion of Identity*. London: Routledge, 1990.

de Beauvoir, Simone. *The Second Sex*, trans. H. M. Parshley. London: Penguin Books, 1997.

de Cordova, Richard. *Picture—Personalities: The Emergence of the Star System in America*. Chicago: University of Illinois Press, [2001] 1990.

Dyer, Richard. *Stars*. London: British Film Institute, 1979.

———. *Heavenly Bodies: Film Stars and Society*. New York: St. Martin's Press, 1986.

Gadsby, Hannah. *Nannette*. Netflix.com, 2018.

---

[17] Hannah Yelin, '"I Am the Centre of Fame": Doing Celebrity, Performing Fame and Navigating Cultural Hierarchies in Grace Jones' I'll Never Write My Memoirs,' *Celebrity Studies* (2019).

Holmes, Su. '"Off-Guard, Unkempt, Unready"? Deconstructing Contemporary Celebrity in Heat Magazine.' *Continuum: Journal of Media & Cultural Studies*, 19 (1), 2005: 21–38.

Holmes, Su and Diane Negra, eds. *In the Limelight and Under the Microscope: Forms and Functions of Female Celebrity*. New York: Continuum, 2011.

Jermyn, Deborah. '"Get a Life, Ladies: Your Old One Is Not Coming Back": Ageing, Ageism and the Lifespan of Female Celebrity.' *Celebrity Studies*, 3 (1), 2012: 1–12.

Landes, Xavier and Morten Nielsen. 'Racial Dodging in the Porn Industry: A Case with No Silver Bullet.' *Porn Studies*, 5 (2), 2018: 115–30.

Orbe, Mark. 'Representations of Race in Reality TV: Watch and Discuss.' *Critical Studies in Media Communication*, 25 (4), 2008: 345–52.

Perrino, Sabina. 'Recontextualizing Racialized Stories on YouTube.' *Narrative Inquiry*, 27 (2), 2017: 261–85.

Redmond, Sean. 'The Whiteness of Stars: Looking at Kate Winslet's Unruly White Body.' *Stardom and Celebrity: A Reader*, ed. by Su Holmes and Sean Redmond. London: Sage, 2007.

———. 'Pieces of Me: Celebrity Confessional Carnality.' *Social Semiotics*, 18 (2), 2008: 149–61.

Sager, Mike. 'What I've Learned: Pamela Anderson.' *Esquire Magazine*, 31 December 2004. http://web.archive.org/web/20121217055346/http://www.esquire.com/features/ESQ0105-WIL_Anderson.

Smith, Sidonie and Julia Watson. *Reading Autobiography: A Guide for Interpreting Life Narratives*. Minneapolis: University of Minnesota Press, 2001.

Tasker, Yvonne and Diane Negra. *Interrogating Postfeminism: Gender and the Politics of Popular Culture*. Durham, NC: Duke University Press, 2007.

Turner, Graeme. 'Approaching Celebrity Studies.' *Celebrity Studies*, 1 (1), 2010: 11–20.

Turner, Graeme, Frances Bonner, and P. David Marshall. *Fame Games: The Production of Celebrity in Australia*. Cambridge: Cambridge University Press, 2000.

Williamson, Milly. 'Celebrity, Gossip, Privacy, and Scandal.' *The Routledge Companion to Media and Gender*, ed. by Cynthia Carter, Linda Steiner, and Lisa McLaughlin. New York: Routledge, 2014.

Yelin, Hannah and Jonathan Wise. 'Dave: Now Everyone Has a Mate Called Dave.' *Advertising Works 17: Case Studies from the IPA Effectiveness Awards 2008*, ed. by Neil Dawson. Henley-on-Thames: WARC, 2009.

CHAPTER 2

The Ghostwritten Memoirs of Female Celebrities: Authorship, Authenticity, Agency and Gendered Access

Celebrity Memoir as Broadsheet Hate Object

The wide readership and commercial power of the ghostwritten celebrity memoir are indicative of its cultural significance,[1] yet it remains a critically overlooked, much-derided genre, dismissed by one *Observer* reviewer as 'a literary phenomenon of the non-literate'.[2] This somewhat typical sweeping insult takes in the texts, their readers, and their ghosted celebrity author-subjects. In the case of the latter, it highlights the fact that the denigration comes from a perceived gap between a celebrity subject's literary ability and their ghosted output. Yet the conflicted logics of 'ghosting'—its ambiguous and mediated claims to authorship and access to subjectivity—remain relatively unexplored in relation to celebrity memoir.

---

[1] Ben Yagoda, for example, calculates that 'total sales in categories of Personal Memoirs, Childhood Memoirs, and Parenthood Memoirs increased more than 400 per cent between 2004 and 2008'. Ben Yagoda, *Memoir: A History* (New York: Riverhead Books, 2009), p. 7.

[2] Carole Cadwalladr, 'All Because the Ladies Love Jordan,' *The Observer*, 12 February 2006.

© The Author(s) 2020
H. Yelin, *Celebrity Memoir*,
https://doi.org/10.1007/978-3-030-44621-5_2

13

Every autumn, as the new batch of celebrity memoirs is released in anticipation of the lucrative Christmas gift market, the broadsheet media gleefully predict the death of the genre.[3] And yet, such books continue to be released in great numbers, counting commercial successes amongst them.[4] 'Are we seeing the death of the celebrity memoir?' asked a *Daily Mail* headline, hopefully.[5] These stories pose as quantitative news, hiding behind a smattering of ('notoriously unreliable') Nielsen Bookscan sales data.[6] In reality, they present qualitative judgements laden with discourses of cultural value, with journalists keen to distance themselves from the genre and perform their 'superior' taste: 'As for me', states Iain Hollingshead in the closing sentence of a *Telegraph* article titled 'Is it curtains for the celebrity memoir?', 'I'm going to do my best to hasten its demise by auctioning my collection on eBay – and buying some good novels instead. Especially ones not ghost-written for Katie Price'.[7] Ghostwriting is presented here as further contaminating unapologetically low culture. A *New Statesman* review of Jade Goody's *Catch a Falling Star* opens with a comparable disdainful reference to the invalidating presence of the ghostwriter: 'The last thing you expect to read, on opening the second autobiography by the former *Big Brother* contestant Jade Goody, is an extract from *Prospect* magazine. Like the rest of this book, it's not written by her'.[8] These articles show journalists proudly and performatively distancing themselves from this material, keen to 'distinguish

---

[3] November and December are reportedly responsible for one-third of the annual turnover of bookshop chains. Paul Bignell, 'Decline and Fall of the C-List Female Celebrity Memoirs,' *The Independent*, 23 December 2007.

[4] For example, an article in *The Independent*, titled, 'Celebs Lose Their Sheen for Publishers as Gift-Buyers Spurn Celebrity Biographies,' focusses upon the decline of the genre despite listing commercial successes from the celebrity author-subjects Zoe 'Zoella' Sugg (178,000 copies), Lynda Bellingham (265,000 copies), and Sir Alex Ferguson (850,000 copies). Gideon Spanier, 'Celebs Lose Their Sheen for Publishers as Gift-Buyers Spurn Celebrity Biographies,' *The Independent*, 19 December 2014.

[5] Jack Crone, 'Are We Seeing the Death of the Celebrity Memoir?' *Mail Online*, 20 December 2014.

[6] Jerry Maatta, 'Apocalypse Now and Again: Mapping the Bestselling Classics of the End of the World,' *Hype: Bestsellers and Literary Culture*, ed. by Jon Helgason, Sara Kärrholm, and Ann Steiner (Lund, Sweden: Nordic Academic Press, 2014), p. 160.

[7] Ian Hollingshead, 'Is It Curtains for the Celebrity Memoir?' *The Telegraph*, 9 December 2011.

[8] Lynsey Hanley, 'Reality Cheque,' *New Stateman*, 16 October 2008.

themselves by the distinctions they make'.[9] It is significant that, despite discussing a crop of memoirs by both male and female celebrity authors, and demonstrating contempt for the genre as a whole, both journalists choose to focus upon young, female, sexualised reality-stars in summing up their disparagement. Hollingshead mentions seventeen texts authored by male celebrities (including footballer Paul Gascoigne, reality TV businessman Alan Sugar, and pop boy band One Direction), and two female celebrities (Price and actress Joanna Lumley). And yet, it is Price he points to as typifying the abasement of the genre. It is because of such gendered denigration that this book focusses exclusively on the memoirs of famous women. A 2007 *Independent* headline makes the gender specificity of the disparagement explicit, heralding the 'Decline and fall of the C-list female celebrity memoir', using the heavily gendered benchmark of 'likeability' as a measure for success and claiming this is a problem specifically facing female celebrities.[10] Both these texts and their female (and in the cases of Price and Goody, working-class) author-subjects are 'bad objects'; they are rejected due to the anxieties they stimulate, viewed as inauthentic due to visible mediation and thus denied authority.

The centrality of gender to the derision of the genre is clear and extends to its female readership. Reporting from a Katie Price book-signing, for example, Carole Cadwalladr, characterises the readers as an illiterate, irrational, emotional and out-of-control swarm: 'the crowd surges forward - women with buggies, women with bumps and women with small, slightly confused children. [...] Jordan can't write. And her readers don't like reading'.[11] John Carey argues that such conceptions of the 'masses' as sub-human hordes in thrall to popular culture reveals an elitist desire to 'preserve the intellectual's seclusion from the "mass"' and has been a recurring characterisation since late nineteenth-century educational reforms provoked a 'hostile reaction to the unprecedentedly large reading public'.[12] Milly Williamson has demonstrated that class and gender work together in overlapping denigrations where 'open class

---

[9] Pierre Bourdieu, *Distinction: A Social Critique of the Judgement of Taste* (London: Routledge, 1984), p. 6.

[10] Bignell.

[11] Cadwalladr.

[12] John Carey, *The Intellectuals and the Masses: Pride and Prejudice Among the Literary Intelligentsia* (London: Faber, 1992), p. vii.

prejudice [...] is concealed behind sexism'.[13] These journalistic characterisations of the genre, its star author-subjects, and its audience, suggest
that the dismissal of celebrity memoir is part of a wider contempt for
culture targeting women—especially those of working-class backgrounds.

CELEBRITY MEMOIR AS SCHOLARLY BAD OBJECT

It is significant that even celebrity studies, a field which deliberately
and politically seeks to disrupt such cultural hierarchies, has neglected
celebrity memoirs, treating them as just one of many supplementary texts
that comprise intertextual celebrity identity work. In a scholarly field
concerned with the vexed status of the 'real' amongst obvious mediation,
celebrity memoirs have been held to epitomise the problems of inauthenticity and manufacture.[14] Rather than viewing memoirs as a site for the
interrogation of these central issues of celebrity, analysis of the memoir
has tended to end with the identification (and dismissal) of these texts as
constructions—an omission which, deliberately or otherwise, reproduces
gendered discourses of cultural value.

A small community of scholars such as Leigh Gilmore[15] and Julie
Rak[16] have convincingly examined the contemporary popularity of the
memoir genre. But this has tended to centre upon 'ordinary' authors
without any pre-existing fame.[17] The community of scholars who have
applied critical attention to memoirs by and about famous women is
smaller still. Here, Pamela Fox's work on the memoirs of women in
country music began the important work of questioning the contradictory

---

[13] Milly Williamson, 'Female Celebrities and the Media: The Gendered Denigration of
the "Ordinary" Celebrity,' *Celebrity Studies* 1.1 (2010), 118.

[14] Dyer (1979); Emma Bell, 'From Bad Girl to Mad Girl: British Female Celebrity,
Reality Products, and the Pathologization of Pop-Feminism,' *Genders* 48 (2008).

[15] Leigh Gilmore, 'American Neoconfessional: Memoir, Self Help and Redemption on
Oprah's Couch,' *Biography* 33.4 (2010), 657–79.

[16] Julie Rak, *Boom! Manufacturing Memoir for the Popular Market* (ON: Wilfrid Laurier
University Press, 2013).

[17] For example, James Frey's (2003) account of addiction and recovery, *A Million Little
Pieces*, which, gained bestseller status through support from Oprah Winfrey's TV Book
Club, but was then exposed to be fabricated by website, *The Smoking Gun*, resulting
in a lawsuit enabling readers to demand a full refund. Both Gilmore and Rak discuss
Frey's book in particular and the text has become a go-to example for demonstrating the
problem of truth claims in contemporary memoir.

role of the ghost in manufacturing and undermining authenticity.[18] This work has been continued in Katja Lee's arguments for the possibility of celebrity agency and her endeavours to trace evidence of its presence in the co-authored text.[19] However, with the exception of these attempts to recuperate the genre, celebrity memoir itself has rarely been the focus of analysis.

Celebrity memoir has been equally neglected by literary scholarship. The genre's visible commercial function contributes to academic uneasiness regarding its validity as an object of study. Where other literary forms are understood as genres, memoir is understood as an industry. As Julie Rak suggests, 'the books of the memoir boom are produced by mainstream presses for large audiences, and perhaps that is why critics of autobiography tend to overlook them or not teach them in their classes'.[20] Indeed whether fairly or not, memoir, more than other genres, has been understood as a commodity manufactured for a market. Rak charts this back to eighteenth-century France and the 'scandalous memoirs' produced by former courtesans to pay for their court cases: 'They were written in order to sell and they were bought because they were scandalous'.[21] This intertwining of memoir and capitalism is integral to Ben Yagoda's conception of the genre: 'not only the way stories are told, but the way arguments are put forth, products and properties marketed'.[22] Thus, the contemporary moment is 'unprecedented' in both the 'sheer volume' of the memoir genre and the pervasiveness of its rhetoric under capitalism.[23] The close relationship between memoir and commercial markets that is used to undermine the genre in terms of cultural value simultaneously defines the genre and offers evidence of its enormous reach and cultural power.

The perceived low status specifically of ghostwritten memoir has led to scholarly neglect, and it being 'largely dismissed in favour of the perceived

---

[18] Pamela Fox, 'Recycled "Trash": Gender and Authenticity in Country Music Autobiography,' *American Quarterly* 50.2 (1998), 234–66.

[19] Katja Lee, 'Not Just Ghost Stories: Alternate Practices for Reading Coauthored Celebrity Memoirs,' *The Journal of Popular Culture* 47.6 (2014), 1256–70.

[20] Rak (2013), p. 3.

[21] Ibid., p. 5.

[22] Yagoda (2009), p. 28.

[23] Ibid.

authenticity found in self-generated texts'.[24] G. Thomas Couser is one such scholar who dismisses celebrity memoir out of hand, moralising that 'seeking to immortalize oneself is not necessarily a noble motive; hence the redundancy of celebrity memoir'.[25] Thus, the ghostwritten celebrity memoir becomes doubly discredited. That a book is authored by a sole subject is no guarantee that their words are credible, and yet, if the authorship is collaborative, it is read as a guarantee that their words are *not* credible. The association of the genre with subjects from 'low' culture has contributed to its devaluation. Echoing the synechdocal sexism of the broadsheet press, John Sutherland notes:

> The general rule about ghosting is that the lower the literature, or aspiration, or our esteem for the author, the less we're upset [...] When Katie Price admits that hands other than her own create her bestselling works, we smile indulgently. No one expects a model to write her own books any more than they expect her to sew her own clothes.[26]

So low are society's expectations of such celebrity women that their inability to author their life stories is a presumption, not a disappointment. Falling between scholarly disciplines, ghostwritten celebrity memoir is the genre that no one wants to claim.

The Twenty-First-Century Celebrity Memoir Moment

There is a long tradition of the celebrity memoir form,[27] ghosting is not a new phenomenon,[28] and consumption of the sexual lives of famous women is a historically entrenched public appetite dating back over 200 years.[29] Nonetheless, the turn of the twenty-first century was a

---

[24] Mark Sanders, 'Theorizing the Collaborative Self: The Dynamics of Contour and Content in the Dictated Autobiography,' *New Literary History* 25 (1994), 455.

[25] G. Thomas Couser, *Memoir: An Introduction* (Oxford: Oxford University Press, 2012), p. 14.

[26] John Sutherland, 'Among the Ghosts,' *Spectator*, 11 June 2011.

[27] Yagoda (2009), Rak (2013).

[28] Ernest R. May, 'Ghost Writing and History,' *The American Scholar* 22.4 (1953), 459–65.

[29] Williamson (2014).

moment when news about the 'private' lives of celebrities evolved in new online forms and became a constant feed updated across multiple platforms as if 'in real time'. It is in this context of 'the everywhere of fame' that I analyse celebrity memoirs,[30] and, from this point onward, that I define the contemporary period of the genre, analysing texts published between 2004 and 2015. The contemporary appetites and commercial imperatives for a fantasy of access, celebrity news, and reality products are evidenced as these have resisted the patterns of decline seen in television and print media.

In the late 1990s, women's magazines were declining in circulation, with the exception of weekly celebrity titles, which enjoyed increasing sales figures.[31] The rapid expansion of home Internet use[32] saw the launch of online celebrity gossip sites such as Popbitch in the UK (1999) and Perez Hilton in the United States (2004). With them, came a 'shift to a more malicious or "bitchy" discussion of female celebrities, as well as the heightened profile of the female "train-wreck" celebrity'.[33] The punitive circulation of celebrity scandal has always historically targeted public women,[34] and pejorative celebrity gossip has been integral to the success of historic publications such as 1950s title, *Confidential Magazine*.[35] However, an increasingly vicious tone of celebrity discourse flourished with celebrity gossip blogging, exacerbating the trend towards caustic and highly gendered vitriol.[36]

[30] Sean Redmond, 'Intimate Fame Everywhere,' *Framing Celebrity: New Directions in Celebrity Culture*, ed. by Su Holmes and Sean Redmond (London and New York: Routledge, 2006), p. 27.

[31] Anna Gough-Yates, *Understanding Women's Magazines: Publishing, Markets and Readerships* (London: Routledge, 2003), p. 137.

[32] James Curran and Jean Seaton, *Power Without Responsibility: Press, Broadcasting and the Internet in Britain* (London: Routledge, 2010), p. 238.

[33] Kirsty Fairclough, 'Fame Is a Losing Game: Celebrity Gossip Blogging, Bitch Culture and Postfeminism,' *Genders* 48 (2008).

[34] Williamson (2014).

[35] Nick Muntean and Anne Helen Petersen, 'Celebrity Twitter: Strategies of Intrusion and Disclosure in the Age of Technoculture,' *M/C Journal* 12.5 (2009).

[36] Fairclough (2008).

Where celebrity gossip magazines had previously demanded a cover charge for a weekly despatch, these sites could offer daily updates for free. As Kirsty Fairclough argues, gossip blogs operate at 'such a frenetic pace that traditional celebrity gossip delivery mechanisms are struggling to compete'.[37] Digital media facilitated new fissures in an already (at times deliberately) porous division between public and private. As Richard Berger has observed: this was a 'new media that was largely untouched by the restrictive content regulation of the PCC [Press Complaints Commission] and government legislation'.[38] This discourse from a 'perceived back region',[39] both responded to and encouraged appetites for access, with content from such sites being discussed and recycled across mainstream media platforms.

Meanwhile, the television industry was seeking new formats to attract mass audiences and contend with increasingly fierce market competition. The arrival of digital television in the UK saw 497 new channels introduced in 20 years.[40] The average number of channels watched per person increased[41] while average weekly hours viewed remained static.[42] As a result, average UK viewing per channel declined.[43] In 2000, *Big Brother* was launched in both the UK and United States with contestants giving up their privacy for 3 months to live under 24-hour surveillance, allowing viewers to watch every aspect of their everyday lives, including those considered private, overly intimate, or indecent, and as such normally out of bounds, for example, going to the toilet, having sex or sleeping. This new format provided Channel 4 with an effective return on investment, national news coverage, high viewing figures, corresponding advertising rates and lucrative sponsorship deals. The fantasy of absolute access (which is in reality highly mediated) proved to be

---

[37] Ibid.

[38] Richard Berger, *Framing the Subversive: Journalism, Celebrity and the Web*. Paper presented at *The End of Journalism? Technology, Education and Ethics*, University of Bedfordshire, 18 October 2008.

[39] Ibid.

[40] This is a twelve thousand per cent increase. Hannah Yelin and Jonathan Wise, 'Dave: Now Everyone Has a Mate Called Dave,' *Advertising Works 17: Case Studies from the IPA Effectiveness Awards 2008*, ed. by Neil Dawson (Henley-on-Thames: WARC, 2009), p. 114.

[41] From 4 to 30, ibid.

[42] On average, people spent more time watching TV than in paid employment, ibid.

[43] From 6 hours 18 minutes to 50 minutes—an 87% drop, ibid.

a formula for commercial success at a time when TV channels were struggling for audiences.[44]

This moment, marked by commercial and competitive intensity, online media evolutions, and a cultural preoccupation with accessing the lives of others, saw celebrity memoir sales figures boom.[45] Celebrity gossip was defying the trend towards decline in television and print media, evolving online, and increasingly ubiquitous across all platforms. Added to this, the free-marketisation of the UK publishing industry in 1997 saw the end of the 1899 netbook agreement, which had allowed publishers to set and maintain the retail prices of books. 'When that happened', Jonny Geller, managing director of Curtis Brown's books division, told *The Guardian*, 'the supermarkets came in with huge discounts, and you got a mass market'.[46] This is borne out by the sales figures. Yagoda calculates that 'total sales in categories of Personal Memoirs, Childhood Memoirs, and Parenthood Memoirs increased more than 400 per cent between 2004 and 2008'.[47] By 'making a private history public',[48] celebrity memoir offers credibility to the idea of a 'real' identity that supposedly exists 'behind' a public persona at a time when this very dynamic is unique in its ability to attract mass audiences, adapt to new forms, and shape national media consumption.

This was the moment at which the memoirs in this study were released. They now exist and must compete within a culture that constructs celebrity according to a logic of exposure, where access is perceived to equal authenticity and unauthorised access offers the greatest authenticity of all. There is a rush to analyse new media forms such as social media and their cultural functions as technologies of self-making,[49] and yet this 'old'

---

[44] Channel 4 reported a record financial year after Big Brother's first series and saw audience figures grow steadily over subsequent years: 'Record Year for Channel Four,' *Daily Mail*, 1 May 2001; Nadia Cohen, 'Beep, Beep, Beep ... It's Big Brother!' *The Daily Mail*, May 2002.

[45] Rak (2013).

[46] John Harris, 'Why Celebrity Memoirs Rule Publishing,' *The Guardian*, 13 December 2010.

[47] Yagoda (2009), p. 7.

[48] Rachael McLennan, *American Autobiography* (Edinburgh: Edinburgh University Press, 2013), p. 7.

[49] For example K. Tiidenberg, 'Bringing Sexy Back: Reclaiming the Body Aesthetic via Self-Shooting,' *Cyberpsychology: Journal of Psychosocial Research on Cyberspace* 8.1 (2014).

(yet still thriving) media form remains comparatively unexamined. This book is, therefore, in effect, a study of an old media genre in a moment of change. As Su Holmes argues, celebrity texts must compete with one another as each claims 'to offer a higher form of truth'.[50] Reality TV claims to offer unprecedented direct access while reactive gossip media contradictorily offer accompanying 'behind the scenes' stories in real time. Added to this cycle, a constant stream of celebrity social media 'has been equated with the assertion of the authentic celebrity voice [whilst] the seemingly unrehearsed quality of the communiqués lends the form an immediacy and casualness'.[51] With a high cover price, and a much-delayed (slow media) release date, memoir must work harder to deliver a return for buyers with appetites for the story 'behind' all previous stories whilst reconciling, tallying with or reacting to the wealth of interconnected, pre-existing extratextual narratives.

GHOSTED CELEBRITY AUTHORSHIP

Ghostwritten celebrity memoir occupies a subsection of the autobiography genre. The field has been defined by self-generated autobiography and as a result, when ghostwritten memoir is engaged with, its singularities are often ignored so that texts can be read as if they had been authored by a single individual. This is something that the texts themselves encourage through tone, consistency with extratextual narratives that circulate around the star and, frequently, the invisibility of the ghost. Narrated in the first-person, without quotation marks, the straight authorial address implies frank confession and direct access to subjectivity. These texts frequently actively veil the collaborative production process and seek to collapse the distinctions between narrator, implied author, and actual author.

---

[50] Su Holmes, '"All You've Got to Worry About Is the Task, Having a Cup of Tea, and Doing a Bit of Sunbathing": Approaching Celebrity in *Big Brother*,' *Understanding Reality Television*, ed. by Su Holmes and Deborah Jermyn (London: Routledge, 2004), p. 121.

[51] Muntean and Petersen (2009).

The status of singular author connotes power. Michel Foucault has argued that the 'coming into being of the notion of "author" constitutes the privileged moment of individualisation in the history of ideas'.[52] However, collaborative authorship is not denied legitimacy in all of its forms. From political speechwriters such as Peggy Noonan's writing for American presidents, to literary editors such as Maxwell Perkins' partnership with F. Scott Fitzgerald, forms of authorship exist that show that collaboration can result in culturally celebrated sources of power or authority. Authorship-as-collaboration scholarship ranges from that which argues for the inherently collaborative foundation of all writing due to its socially constructed nature, to those who ask whether the death of the author has been a means to deny certain groups *author*ity.[53]

Lee has identified the critical and popular tendency in the reading of celebrity memoir to 'mute the celebrity and allow the non-celebrity signature to take the credit',[54] a practice based primarily on 'suspicions about the intellectual labors (or lack thereof) of the rich and famous'.[55] Just as agency takes multiple forms, participation in the collaborative writing process may be the result of various practices—for example, conception, oration and authorisation may not fall within traditional definitions of *writing*, but cannot be denied as participatory acts which shape the life story.

It is for this reason that, unless there is some textual evidence to the contrary, I attribute the words in these texts to their celebrity author-subjects, despite the fact that as critical readers we can only ever *infer* who is speaking behind the collectively-produced, first-person 'I'. Whilst the presence of the ghostwriter problematises the promise of the single authorial signature,[56] I nonetheless ascribe quotes to the celebrities involved

---

[52] Michel Foucault, 'What Is an Author?' *Textual Strategies: Perspectives in Poststructuralist Criticism*, ed. by Josue V. Harari (Ithaca: Cornell University Press, 1979), 141–60, p. 141.

[53] Lisa Ede and Andrea A. Lunsford, 'Collaboration and Concepts of Authorship,' *PMLA* 116.2 (2001), 354–69, p. 354.

[54] Lee, p. 1257.

[55] Ibid., p. 1256.

[56] Philippe Lejeune, 'The Autobiography of Those Who Do Not Write,' trans. Katherine Leary, *On Autobiography*, ed. by Paul John Eakin (Minneapolis: University of Minnesota Press, 1989).

more concretely than is strictly possible to discern in the text (e.g. 'Paris Hilton relates' or 'Paris Hilton's memoir relates'). This does not mean I take the text's claims to offer the voice of the celebrity author at face value: far from it. The reader of collaboratively authored memoir can never truly know who is speaking or the nature of the contributions made by each party.[57] But to deliberately seek an alternative terminology that interrupts this claim of authorship (e.g. 'Hilton and/or her ghost relates'), and to ignore the fact that the texts themselves attribute these words to the celebrity author-subject, denies the celebrity selves agency too firmly (a perspective which dovetails with popular and gendered assumptions about the celebrity's intellectual capacities). I invoke their ghostwriters when this is pertinent to what is being said or how— to draw attention to a moment of uncharacteristic self-reflexivity, for example—not as a means to discredit the female, celebrity author-subject.

Ghostwritten celebrity memoir presents many layers of mediation as well as complexities that arise from the explicit promise of access to a 'true' self, in an environment in which the degree of authorship a star has had can only be inferred. This raises questions of the relationship between ghostwriting, the agency of its subjects and the resultant granting or denial of the status of object of authenticity and authority.

The emphasis in twentieth-century literary theory, from New Criticism to postmodernism, has been upon the text as *text*, independent of an extratextual author.[58] However, ghostwritten memoirs are so much a product of the market in which they are produced, and so much in dialogue with their paratexts, that this needs to be addressed for application to a context in which the texts exist in an assemblage of webs of conflicting mediation.

Before the 'life' even reaches the creative and editing processes of the ghostwriter, its first layer of mediation is that of the memory of the subject. The inevitably partial 'imaginative acts of remembering' through which all autobiography is mediated are 'a subjective form of evidence,

[57] G. Thomas Couser, 'Making, Taking, and Faking Lives: The Ethics of Collaborative Life Writing,' *Style* 32.2 (1998), 334–51.

[58] Leroy Searle, 'New Criticism,' *The Johns Hopkins Guide to Literary Theory*, ed. by Michael Groden, Martin Kreiswirth, and Imre Szeman (Baltimore: The John Hopkins University Press, 2005); Roland Barthes, 'The Death of the Author,' *Image/Music/Text*, trans. Stephen Heath (New York: Hill and Wang, 1977), pp. 142–47.

not externally verifiable' but 'asserted on the subject's authority'.[59] If, however, the subject is denied authority to begin with, the layering of inauthenticity as represented by the ghostwriter, compounds the existing invalidation.

In the field of literary criticism, Wayne Booth raises questions that, although developed with reference to fiction, are especially applicable to collaborative life-writing: 'what are the author's responsibilities to those whose lives are used as "material"?', 'what are the author's responsibilities to others whose labor is exploited to make the work of art possible?', and 'what are the responsibilities of the author to truth?'[60] Couser responds to these questions by charting the ethics and power dynamics presented by collaborative life-writing along a continuum 'from ethnographic autobiography, in which the writer outranks the subject, to celebrity autobiography, in which the subject outranks the writer'.[61] Couser's analysis highlights the fact that, whilst they must coalesce for the production of the book, the interests of writer and subject are not necessarily aligned. Whilst this has validity, the presentation of a clear direction to the hierarchy is a reductive, exaggerated distinction. A celebrity may 'outrank' their writer economically; however, this does not straightforwardly translate into agency in the production of their life story. This reading fails to account for non-economic forms of capital and the diversity of markers of status and acts by which one places oneself within a hierarchy.

Couser's analysis functions in terms of economic, and arguably symbolic, capital.[62] However, consider as an example the difference in cultural capitals[63] between Jade Goody and her ghostwriter, Lucie Cave (which shall be discussed in detail in Chapter 4). Now the editorial director of global multimedia conglomerate, Bauer, Cave is a university-educated journalist and broadcaster who at the time of collaborating with Goody was the editor of celebrity gossip magazine, *heat*. Goody, by contrast, was a working-class woman repeatedly excluded from her

[59] Smith and Watson (2001), p. 6.

[60] Wayne C. Booth, *The Company We Keep: An Ethics of Fiction* (Berkeley: University of California Press, 1988), pp. 130–32.

[61] Couser (1998).

[62] Bourdieu (1984).

[63] Ibid.

state secondary school, who became famous, and publicly mocked, for her malapropisms, confusion and lack of education. One therefore cannot assume that Cave is merely an exploited scribe doing Goody's bidding, when it is possible, if not likely, that she had a greater awareness than her subject of the reception that aspects of Goody's life story would receive. As if in acknowledgement of this fact, a foreword by Cave to Goody's fifth and final memoir, *Jade: Fighting to the End*, describes Goody as 'candid' and 'extremely vulnerable'.[64] Goody's agency in the process of her self-representation is therefore problematic.

On occasions when the field of autobiography studies does engage with collaborative construction, it appears to sit at either end of a spectrum. Either it is still very much indebted to its origins in ethnography where, in Philip Lejeune's words, the subject is 'studied from above',[65] a model which does not accord with celebrity memoir due to the star's economic (and in some cases symbolic) status, or, like Couser, the field assumes 'the subject outranks the writer',[66] situating the celebrity at the apex of social hierarchy. Neither of these two models offers a satisfactory account of collaborative construction because each fails to take into account the different capitals that each party may bring to the collaboration; the other processes of mediation that occur through the texts' industrial production; or the ways in which agency in self-representation is, in these texts, multiple and negotiated. Rather than evading or simplifying the challenges ghostwriting presents to interpretation, they are the very subject of this book.

My aim is to account for the autobiographical nature of these books without valorising the author (and thus the coherent self). Given that ghosted authorship involves at least two people, an appropriate conceptual framework for celebrity memoir must also account for the fact that they are produced in industrial conditions, without dismissing the genre as merely disingenuous corporate merchandise. An effective framework must also treat the texts as narratives with unreliable subjectivities that collapse distinctions between narrator, implied author, and actual author, and yet have author-subjects who undeniably exist beyond the text. Whilst the academy often treats these aspects as discrete, the texts offer a reading experience that enables the reconciliation of these paradoxical, coexistent contradictions.

---

[64] Jade Goody, *Jade Fighting to the End* (London: John Blake, 2009), p. vii.

[65] Lejeune, p. 199.

[66] Couser (1998).

Agency and Authorship

Questions of authorship and authenticity necessarily raise questions of agency. The dominant assumption is that celebrities are merely manipulated puppets, seen to exist only through the hegemonic, industrial machinery that produces them. In 1979, Dyer questioned this 'manipulation thesis'[67] and yet such assumptions remain persistent in both popular and scholarly discourse today.[68] Even Dyer engages with memoir primarily as evidence of manipulation.[69] This industrial machinery is undeniably present. Ghosted celebrity memoir is a medium in which this is particularly visible. And yet, a celebrity is one of many agents in the production of the life story. They may not act freely, but they do act. Indeed, in our networked, multiplatform celebrity culture, the celebrity 'life' must interact with a pre-existing field of narratives that circulate around the celebrity, with or without her authorisation. Any framework for analysing the negotiated agency of the celebrity author-subject, therefore, must account for this multiplicity.

Celebrity is a struggle between various interests, agents and narratives, the meaning of which are in constant flux. P. David Marshall recognises this agentic complexity arguing that 'public identity is a peculiar form of power'[70] which operates in what he calls 'negotiated "terrain"'.[71] Whilst Marshall creates an important space for a negotiation between multiple agents, including audiences, in our understanding of celebrity selfhood, he defaults to the idea of celebrity as manufactured rather than being one of those agents.[72] His 'collective' conception of celebrity has the identified forces operating upon or around the celebrity, rather than theorising the active participation of the celebrity herself.

---

[67] Dyer (1979), p. 13.

[68] For a discussion of the persistence of assumptions of celebrity manipulation see Lorraine York, 'Star Turn: The Challenges of Theorizing Celebrity Agency,' *The Journal of Popular Culture* 46.6 (2013), 1330–47.

[69] Richard Dyer, 'Lana: Four Films of Lana Turner,' *Movie* 25.4 (1977–8), 30–54.

[70] P. David Marshall, 'Personifying Agency: The Public–Persona–Place–Issue Continuum,' *Celebrity Studies* 4 (2013), 369–71.

[71] P. David Marshall, *Celebrity and Power: Fame in Contemporary Culture* (Minneapolis: University of Minnesota Press, 1997), p. 47.

[72] Ibid.

Joe Moran builds on Pierre Bourdieu's 'field' theory, with its account of the negotiation between structure and agency,[73] by proposing a model of 'situated agency'.[74] In this reading, the celebrity author is a self-reflexive agent of their own fame, negotiating their own celebrity within and alongside whatever structural or industrial constraints may also be operating upon them. Moran seeks to demonstrate that commercial success does not equal vulgarity by showing that many of the bestselling authors in America are also literary prize winners with cultural capital. This, he somewhat sneeringly claims, counters or balances accusations of the vulgarity or taint of commercial success. He is keen to separate these 'high brow' celebrity authors from 'the pervasiveness of "entertainment celebrity"'.[75] Therefore, whilst Moran's theory of situated agency offers immense potential for reimagining the celebrity-as-agent, he precludes so-called low culture, entertainment celebrity forms, such as the memoirs investigated in this book.

How, then, should one approach a framework for understanding agency across a broader range of celebrity forms and modes of cultural production? For Lorraine York, celebrity agency is a complex and open-ended set of exchanges with stakes in various industrial relations: 'it need not be determined to be either present or absent, just as the celebrity need not be determined to be either powerful or powerless. Instead, one may investigate the differential levels of agency that a celebrity may have or lose at any stage'.[76] Understanding who determines the meaning of celebrity, then, is not simply a case of celebrity versus manipulative industry fabrications,[77] nor is it is a case of hegemonic producers versus the consuming audience,[78] nor need it be restricted by genre or hierarchies of cultural value.[79]

---

[73] Pierre Bourdieu, *Outline of a Theory of Practice* (Cambridge: Cambridge University Press, 1977).

[74] Joe Moran, *Star Authors: Literary Celebrity in America* (London: Pluto, 2000), p. 67.

[75] Ibid., p. 1.

[76] York (2013), p. 1341.

[77] Dyer (1979).

[78] Marshall (1997).

[79] Moran, p. 67.

Another consideration is the way that celebrities can perform their agency (or its lack). Rebecca Williams cites actress Drew Barrymore's active choice in the on-screen roles she takes-on as an opportunity to participate in a 'performed agency', inviting audiences to view her as 'author' of her own image.[80] Similarly, the celebrity author-subjects discussed in this book construct their star images in relation to ideas of the 'empowered' woman and, in almost all cases, endeavour to intertwine their on- and off-screen personas to do so. These celebrity author-subjects can be seen to be, quite literally, 'authoring' their own images in ways that both subvert and reinforce dominant gender norms.

Whilst the memoirs examined here do not always demonstrate progressive gender politics, there are definite moments of textual resistance: speaking back to an industry that hounds and exposes these women, and finding strategies to either resist the demands of the genre to expose themselves further, or to set the terms of their exposure. These resistant gestures within the texts, however, are frequently co-opted by larger, regressive narrative and thematic trends and, instead, become moments that reveal the pressures which coax the telling of the life story in particular directions.

In their consideration of autobiographical convention, Smith and Watson argue for the way in which one is 'coax[ed], coach[ed] or coerce[d]' into giving an account of oneself because pre-existing 'discursive patterns both guide and compel us to tell stories about ourselves in particular ways'.[81] As Judith Butler argues, 'conditions do not "act" in the way that individual agents do, but no agent acts without them'.[82] The industrial conditions which collectively produce the mediated life stories examined here do not negate the author-subjects' agency in self-representation. However, their agency must be understood as operating 'alongside and even within structural forces and constraints'[83] which are also working to shape the celebrity life story.

These structural forces and constraints are necessarily gendered. The conflict and contortions that arise from the texts' attempts to negotiate such constraints reveal the contradictory pressures upon the space

---

[80] Rebecca Williams, 'From Beyond Control to in Control: Investigating Drew Barrymore's Feminist Agency/Authorship,' *Stardom and Celebrity* 111–126 (2007), 111.

[81] Smith and Watson (2001), pp. 32, 51.

[82] Judith Butler, *Precarious Life: The Powers of Mourning and Violence* (London: Verso, 2004), p. 11.

[83] York (2013), p. 1339.

available to any woman who wishes the account she gives of herself to be received favourably. Efrat Tseëlon's understanding of femininity as a paradox is useful here: a woman is 'an impossible creature who is given space and no space at all, who is offered a position while being denied that position'.[84] The social, psychological and visual roles that are available to women create this paradoxical 'impossible position'.[85]

Thus, agency in the celebrity memoir is complex: negotiated, situated, performed and gendered. As the texts simultaneously intervene in and capitulate to competing and contradictory demands, they demonstrate how their female authors both have agency and yet are still constrained in circumstances not of their choosing. The production of a memoir is an act that claims certain forms of agency in self-representation. One can use a memoir to speak back to extratextual criticism levelled through commentary upon the celebrity life, yet even this entrenches and canonises those punitive discourses as part of the star's story. In a multiplatform, networked media landscape, where memoir is one of many texts that constitutes a star's life story, this can never be fully controlled.

MEMOIRS AND THE MISOGYNY OF CELEBRITY CULTURE

In the coming case studies, we shall see many examples of the gendered nature of fame. Sexism runs throughout celebrity culture. 'Quite blatantly', argues Misha Kavka, 'female celebrities are judged more harshly' than male celebrities.[86] The 'stark differences'[87] in the way men and women are treated in celebrity culture manifests in the representations of women's bodies, the policing of 'acceptably' feminine behaviour, the discourses of intimacy and sexual insinuation targeted at female stars, and the feminised trivialisation of celebrity culture in general.

[84] Efrat Tseëlon, *The Masque of Femininity: The Presentation of Woman in Everyday Life* (London: Sage, 1995), p. 2.

[85] Ibid., pp. 2–3.

[86] Misha Kavka, 'Hating Madonna and Loving Tom Ford: Gender, Affect and the "Extra-Curricular" Celebrity,' *Celebrity Studies* 5.(1–2) (2014), 59–74, p. 71.

[87] Holmes and Negra, 'Introduction' (2011), p. 1

Celebrity culture operates as a 'theatre of punishment'[88] policing 'cultural consensus about "out of bounds" behaviours for women'[89] in an 'affective condition that brings into play gender norms [to] determine what is "appropriate"'.[90] For example, the pathologisation that proscribes certain celebrity behaviours as unacceptably unfeminine is revealed through the therapised confessional apologies of Jade Goody's memoir, the negotiation of stigma in the memoirs of porn stars, and the conventions of middle-class femininity that many of the celebrity author-subjects are eager to represent themselves as fulfilling.

The memoirs examined throughout this book are full of detailed accounts of the female celebrity body—its appearance and the 'beauty work' performed to 'perfect' it—that are offered as integral elements of the female celebrity life story (again in ways which are not the case for male stars). As Su Holmes and Diane Negra argue, the body is '*the* key terrain upon which discourses surrounding female celebrity are mapped'[91] [original emphasis]. This operates as a form of governance of women's bodies as the female celebrity body is offered up to their female audience with an invitation to women to judge both stars and themselves.[92]

An affective, and heavily gendered, condition of celebrity culture is the centrality of discourses of intimacy and sexuality. These texts operate as 'women's culture', a commodified genre of intimacy which constructs, as Lauren Berlant theorises, 'intimate publics' that enact a fantasy of universal female experience predicated on intimacy and revelation.[93] Williamson charts the direct links between the contemporary celebrity condition and the late eighteenth-century fame of women in the theatre, noting the gendered 'illusions of public intimacy that began with insinuations of prostitution' and continue to this day.[94] This is clearly discernible in the construction of intimacy offered by the memoirs of Jameson, Price,

[88] Imogen Tyler and Bruce Bennett, '"Celebrity Chav': Fame, Femininity and Social Class," *European Journal of Cultural Studies* 13.3 (2010), 375–93, p. 380.

[89] Holmes and Negra, 'Introduction' (2011), p. 2.

[90] Kavka (2014), p. 60.

[91] Holmes and Negra, 'Introduction' (2011), p. 7.

[92] J. A. Wilson, 'Star Testing: The Emerging Politics of Celebrity Gossip,' *The Velvet Light Trap* 65 (2010), 30.

[93] Lauren Berlant, *The Female Complaint: The Unfinished Business of Sentimentality in American Culture* (Durham, NC: Duke University Press, 2008).

[94] Ibid.

and Anderson in Chapter 3, which is perhaps not surprising as they are all stars who have crossed over to achieve mainstream cultural impact from their work in either the soft- or hardcore porn industries. However, the same dynamic of punitive sexual insinuation surrounds the memoirs of Goody and Hilton discussed in Chapter 4, interacting as they do with extratexts such as Hilton's leaked sex tape and Goody's sex acts filmed in the *Big Brother* house.

Repeatedly through these case studies, we see the construction of intimacy through the sexualised exposure of (and harm to) the female celebrity body or, in Helen Hester's terms, 'the body in a state of intensity'.[95] These range from images of Gaga's bloodstained body collapsed backstage, to Jameson's testimony of surviving a violent gang rape. There is both 'a gendered dynamic of popular interest and pleasure in the misfortunes of female celebrities'[96] and a postfeminist celebrity culture which lets men 'off the hook' with regard to male violence against women[97] and, indeed, sells women's harm for its own entertainment appeal.[98]

The derision directed at celebrity culture more widely is implicitly gendered in its designation as 'trivial', 'gossipy' and concerned with the feminised 'private' sphere.[99] On those rare occasions when male celebrities are called upon to present themselves in comparable ways, the derision of the feminine remains intact as 'the process of fame can have a certain "feminising" effect when setting up men as the object of the gaze'.[100] Christine Geraghty argues for the intrinsically gendered nature the very term celebrity, given that women are 'particularly likely to be seen as celebrities whose working life is of less interest than their personal life'.[101]

---

[95] Helen Hester, *Beyond Explicit: Pornography and the Displacement of Sex* (Albany: State University of New York Press, 2014), p. 65.

[96] Holmes and Negra, 'Introduction' (2011), p. 1.

[97] Natasha Patterson and Camilla A. Sears, 'Letting Men Off the Hook? Domestic Violence and Postfeminist Celebrity Culture,' *Genders* 53 (2011).

[98] Karen Boyle, 'Producing Abuse: Selling the Harms of Pornography,' *Women's Studies International Forum* 34 (2011), 593–602.

[99] Holmes and Negra, 'Introduction' (2011), p. 14.

[100] Tim Edwards, 'Medusa's Stare: Celebrity, Subjectivity and Gender,' *Celebrity Studies* 4.2 (2013), 155–68, p. 158.

[101] Christine Geraghty, 'Re-examining Stardom: Questions of Texts, Bodies and Performance,' *Stardom and Celebrity*, p. 99.

In many ways, the memoirs in this sample support Geraghty's observations: they offer up details of the celebrity's private life and work towards the specularisation of their celebrity author-subjects. It is significant, however, that every memoir in this study, without exception, positions the author as demanding to be taken seriously as workers. They emphasise the professional skills and physical labour that go into becoming a successful model,[102] the creative vision that goes into a sell-out arena tour,[103] the talent that goes into winning singing competitions,[104] and the graft of responding to the gruelling posting schedule required to stay on the right side of YouTube algorithms.[105] They demonstrate the business acumen and judgement that goes into navigating contracts in the porn industry,[106] selling your own branded merchandise,[107] and setting up a music label.[108] These memoirs, therefore, do not only or straightforwardly uphold the common characterisation of female celebrity. Rather they both compound and contest models of celebrity femininity—offering the opportunity to respond to the vicissitudes of gendered celebrity culture whilst negotiating one's performance within it.

Postfeminist Celebrity Memoirs

The memoirs in this sample exist within, and contribute to, a postfeminist cultural context. The conventions of the memoir genre and the 'postfeminist sensibility'[109] share a significant thematic overlap in their potential to

---

[102] Pamela Anderson, *Star Struck* (London: Pocket, 2006); Katie Price, *Being Jordan* (London: John Blake, 2005).

[103] Lady Gaga and Terry Richardson, *Gaga x Richardson* (London: Hodder & Stoughton, 2011).

[104] Goody (2009).

[105] McAllister, Jenn, *Really Professional Internet Person* (London: Scholastic, 2015).

[106] Jenna Jameson, *How to Make Love Like a Porn Star: A Cautionary Tale* (New York: It Books, 2010).

[107] Paris Hilton, *Confessions of an Heiress: A Tongue-in-Chic Peek Behind the Pose* (New York: Fireside Books, 2004); Kourtney Kardashian, Kim Kardashian, and Khloe Kardashian, *Kardashian Konfidential* (New York: St. Martin's Press, 2011).

[108] Mathangi "Maya" Arulpragasm, *M.I.A.* (New York: Rizzoli, 2012).

[109] Rosalind Gill, 'Postfeminist Media Culture Elements of a Sensibility,' *European Journal of Cultural Studies* 10.2 (2007), 147–66, p. 147.

be 'both sexist and transformative'.[110] For example, the 'emphasis upon self-surveillance' which is constitutive of postfeminist media culture[111] is equally foundational to the confessional conventions of the memoir genre. Whilst postfeminism demands constant monitoring of the self, autobiography is necessarily a form of self-surveillance as the author's identity and life experiences are scrutinised, accounted for, analysed and given meaning through discursive regimes. Moreover, the interrelated themes that underpin the postfeminist sensibility are found throughout these memoirs in particular, namely the focus on individualism, choice and empowerment, the 'girling' of adult women, the imperative for self-improvement through beauty work, and the suggestion that sex is the locus of women's power.[112]

These memoirs directly invoke questions of personal power, and frequently offer their celebrity author-subjects as examples of 'empowered' femininity, issuing such advice as 'it's your choice who you are'[113] and 'know how to work it'.[114] Despite discussion of social issues that affect women—for example, the experiences of sexual assault and partner violence discussed in the memoirs of Anderson, Jameson and Price—none of the memoirs invoke feminism as a collective movement with a shared goal of improving the situation of women as a social group. Instead, such structural inequalities are 'reprivatised', and presented as challenges to be overcome in an individual path to empowerment.[115] Thus, individual solutions are offered in place of coherent responses to structural, social problems. This accords with the understanding of postfeminism as part of a 'backlash'[116] against the gains of second wave feminism in which

[110] Jessica Ringrose, *Postfeminist Education: Girls and the Sexual Politics of Schooling* (London: Routledge 2013), p. 121.

[111] Ibid.

[112] Gill (2007).

[113] Anderson, (2006), p. 212.

[114] Price (2005), p. 7.

[115] Lois McNay, *Foucault and Feminism: Power, Gender and the Self* (Cambridge: Polity, 1992), p. 106.

[116] Susan Faludi, *Backlash: The Undeclared War Against American Women* (New York: Anchor Books, 1992).

feminism is 'taken into account' only 'in order to emphasise that it is no longer needed'.[117]

The depoliticisation of women's concerns under postfeminism is accompanied by a declawing of the threat of the capable, independent, adult woman through a process of 'girling'.[118] This characterisation of the girlish woman works in tandem with an emphasis upon consumerist 'beauty work'[119] in which 'consumption as a strategy... for the production of the self'[120] intertwines with the imperative for self-improvement.[121] This encourages costly and labour-intensive practices to produce the desirably feminine body which are justified as unproblematic 'pleasures'.[122] Whilst the nature, framing and degree of emphasis varies from text to text, these acts of 'girling' and/or 'beauty work' are seen, without exception, in every one of the memoirs examined here. Postfeminist celebrity culture may not be the only factor. These girlish, non-threatening personas may also be constructed to appear 'likeable' and non-threatening so readers can relate.[123] Furthermore, showing the work that goes into constructing the celebrity image is a common strategy for making claims to authenticity. It is significant, however, that although these traits appear across the celebrity memoirs analysed here, postfeminist dictats are most fervently adhered to, and insisted upon, in the memoirs of 'glamour girls' Price, Anderson and Jameson: those who originate from (and in some cases sustain) careers with the greatest professional investment in male desire and pleasure.

Unsurprisingly, this is also true of another key motif of postfeminism: the presentation of sexual pleasure as the source of women's

---

[117] Tasker and Negra (2007), p. 28.

[118] Ibid., p. 43

[119] Adrienne Evans and Susan Riley, 'Immaculate Consumption: Negotiating the Sex Symbol in Postfeminist Celebrity Culture,' *Journal of Gender Studies* 22.3 (2013), 268–81, p. 276.

[120] Tasker and Negra (2007), p. 2.

[121] Angela McRobbie, 'Postfeminism and Popular Culture,' *Interrogating Postfeminism*, p. 35.

[122] Avelie Stuart and Ngaire Donaghue, 'Choosing to Conform: The Discursive Complexities of Choice in Relation to Feminine Beauty Practices,' *Feminism & Psychology* 22.1 (2012), 98–121.

[123] Abigail Gosselin, 'Memoirs as Mirrors: Counterstories in Contemporary Memoir,' *Narrative* 19.1 (2011), 133–48.

power. As Joel Gwynne argues of postfeminist sexual memoir, readers are 'expected to perceive [the sexual practices related] as empowering simply because the authors/narrators claim to enjoy' them.[124] Enthusiastic self-sexualisation, variously termed 'raunch culture'[125] and 'compulsory sexual agency',[126] celebrates models of feminine sexuality markedly similar to those promulgated in sexist, male-targeted media, however, this time under the guise of female sexual empowerment. This combination of apparent sexual freedoms and intensified incitements to perfect the feminine body produce a 'new sexual contract' in which hyper-sexualised emphasis upon feminine sexuality is required as a sort of compensation for the adoption of masculine traits in the entry of women into civic society.[127] Whilst this constitutes a central narrative theme across the 'glamour girl' memoirs, it is also integral to the photo-memoir of Lady Gaga, a research subject originally chosen for this book with the assumption that her seemingly resistant, oppositional persona might offer a point of contrast.[128]

These imperatives (interpellating the female subject as conventionally feminine, girlish, hyper-sexual, consuming, and always perfecting the body) are heralded as empowering under the rhetoric of choice.[129] However, it is an exaltation of choice and women's freedoms in which regressive gender roles are celebrated and 'chosen' above all others. The mutually reinforcing relationship between postfeminism and neoliberalism can be seen in its endorsement of individualism, consumption and choice, as well as the depoliticisation of collective social movements and perpetuation of conservative social roles. This is equally true of purportedly

[124] Joel Gwynne, *Erotic Memoirs and Postfeminism: The Politics of Pleasure* (Basingstoke: Palgrave Macmillan, 2013), p. 118.

[125] Ariel Levy, *Female Chauvinist Pigs: Women and the Rise of Raunch Culture* (London: Free Press, 2006).

[126] Rosalind Gill, 'Culture and Subjectivity in Neoliberal and Postfeminist Times,' *Subjectivity* 25 (2008), 432–45, p. 440.

[127] Angela McRobbie, 'Top Girls? Young Women and the Post-Feminist Sexual Contract,' *Identity in Question*, ed. by Anthony Elliott and Paul du Gay (London: Sage, 2009), p. 79.

[128] David Annandale, 'Rebelais Meets Vogue: The Construction of Carnival, Beauty and Grotesque,' *The Performance Identities of Lady Gaga*, ed. by R. J. Gray (Jefferson, NC: McFarland Publishing, 2012).

[129] Rosalind Gill, 'Critical Respect: The Difficulties and Dilemmas of Agency and "Choice" for Feminism,' *European Journal of Women's Studies* 14.1 (2007), 69–80.

countercultural female celebrities such as Lady Gaga. In 'cool postfeminism', a stance characterised by ironic distance and even nihilism does not exempt a star from embodying postfeminist values of girlishness, self-sexualisation and unthreatening femininity.[130] Thus, just as memoirs coax a performance of subjectivity, postfeminist media culture coaxes certain subjectivities from the contemporary, female subject.

CELEBRITY AUTHENTICITY

Celebrity culture and the autobiography genre both appeal to their audiences by promising to reveal the 'real' person. As a result, critical understandings of both celebrity and memoir focus on problematising such claims and highlighting the inherently constructed nature of authenticity. From the field of literary criticism, Jakki Spicer has observed that 'since its inception as a formalised field of study, autobiography studies has been preoccupied with whether an autobiographical text can communicate to its readers the reality of its author's experiences'.[131] As well as the difficulties of converting lived experience into written narrative, these texts are compromised by the limits of the subject's self-knowledge, memory, or ability to conceive of themselves outside culturally designated subjectivities. As Mary Evans writes, 'contemporary auto/biography cannot in any sense "reveal" because the author has internalised the norms and conventions' of their era.[132] It is possible, of course, that the explicit incursions into the authenticity of the celebrity memoir are an open secret that can be taken into account by the reader, who is able to simultaneously search for insight into a 'real' person and for discrepancies, without necessarily undermining the functioning of the text. Despite the ghostwriter's known position occupying much of the authorial space, readers look to the 'I' of the narrator for insight into the life of a different author, the celebrity author-subject.

---

[130] Caitlin Yunuen Lewis, 'Cool Postfeminism: The Stardom of Sofia Coppola,' *In the Limelight*.

[131] Jakki Spicer, 'The Author Is Dead, Long Live the Author: Autobiography and the Fantasy of the Individual,' *Criticism* 47.3 (2005), 387–403, p. 388.

[132] Mary Evans, *Missing Persons: The Impossibility of Auto/Biography* (London: Routledge, 1999), p. 138.

As I have suggested, this situates the ghostwritten memoir in a complex grey area between biography, autobiography, fact and fiction. Dan Shen argues that the memoir reader is always 'consciously or half-consciously comparing the textual world with the extratextual reality'.[133] Thus, when Paris Hilton's memoir states 'I have pretty much grown up in public and I've done some pretty immature things along the way',[134] the public circulation of her leaked sex tape or news coverage of her jail time for driving under the influence operate as extratextual discourses directing readers' inferences as to what she may be alluding.[135] These intertexts help to hide the ghostwriter and ease readers into the collusive suspension of disbelief that the woman they know from the web of celebrity gossip is directly relating her life story to them. Whilst the memoir is an intervention into the multiple versions of the celebrity subject, it cannot deviate from those versions entirely as readers seek to tally the subject they encounter within the text with the versions they have already encountered from multiple other sources. Ghostwritten memoirs occupy a different ontological status from either autobiography or novels because of the ways in which they interact with an extratextual reality, and the fact that this interaction is fundamental to their functioning.

Celebrity culture prizes authenticity but the very concept is a contradictory construct. Such discourse is rooted in Enlightenment models of the value of the unique individual and the coherent, essential self, encouraging belief in the possibility of 'gaining access to some essential knowledge'.[136] Media texts claim to offer access to this 'real', essential self through varying means. For example, stars are presented in the confessional mode to construct a relationship of affective intimacy[137] or are 'caught' (or constructed) as 'off-guard, unkempt, unready'[138] to suggest the logic of the exposé. In this regard, the private, or the hidden, is prized as the locus of 'truth'. However, representations of the star's private,

---

[133] Dan Shen, 'Unreliability in Autobiography vs. Fiction,' *Poetics Today* 28.1 (2007), 48.

[134] Hilton, p. 176.

[135] Gérard Genette, *Paratexts: Thresholds of Interpretation* (Cambridge: Cambridge University Press, 1997).

[136] Turner, Bonner, and Marshall, p. 12.

[137] Redmond (2008).

[138] Holmes (2005).

confessed, or unkempt selves are as much images that require construction as their 'on-screen' personas. The idea that any one aspect of a star
identity is more real than another is a logical impossibility.[139] Thus, the
authenticity so prized in the celebrity world functions as a paradox: it
requires effort to appear true to oneself. Authentic identity, then, is a
construct that contradicts the very notion it supposedly represents.[140] It
is a value judgement, externally imposed: its proof residing in the audience
who receives the celebrity self or text and deems it authentic or otherwise.

Yet, in spite of this (often explicitly evident) interference, antagonism
and unattainability, authenticity persists as a vexed yet valuable currency,
retaining its exchange value, however openly it is undermined. Thus, the
negotiation of authenticity is increasingly explicit in celebrity culture's
discussions of artifice and authenticity—both within self-conscious media
texts and within an audience that is increasingly well versed in the
processes of manufacturing fame.[141]

Authenticity, its visual, verbal and textual codes, its high celebrity
exchange value, and its paradoxical impossibility, are fundamental to the
celebrity memoir. Despite their evident status as carefully, slowly honed,
edited and ghostwritten texts, these memoirs claim to offer the self
in its fullest, stressing veracity at every opportunity and using various
methods to construct the appearance of authenticity. These methods
differ from text to text, residing variously in some of the following
textual features: explicit promises of access to 'the real me' (Hilton, Price,
Jameson, Goody, McAllister), the idiosyncratic textual address suggestive of verbal oration (Price, Jameson, Goody, Kardashian, M.I.A., Ezarik,
Sugg), a history of suffering (Anderson, Jameson, Price, Goody, M.I.A.,
Kardashian, McAllister), emotional extremity (Gaga, Jameson, Goody,
Anderson), narrating the 'stripped bare' naked body, locating authenticity in ever greater exposure (Gaga, Price, Anderson, Jameson), and the
narration of lives that are out of control (Gaga, Price, Anderson, Jameson,
Goody, Sugg). Even when these texts purport to engage in postmodern,
self-reflexive play with performed identities, in what I have elsewhere

---

[139] Dyer (1986), p. 2.

[140] Lionel Trilling, *Sincerity and Authenticity* (London: Oxford University Press, 1972),
pp. 5–6.

[141] Joshua Gamson, *Claims to Fame: Celebrity in Contemporary America* (Berkeley:
University of California Press, 1994); Holmes (2005); Su Holmes and Sean Redmond,
'Introduction: Understanding Celebrity Culture,' *Framing Celebrity*, p. 4.

termed 'doing' celebrity[142] (Hilton, Gaga, M.I.A.), they default to the currency of authenticity in one way or another.

CELEBRITY CAMP

This book demonstrates that the counterpoint to celebrity authenticity is the embrace of camp and the celebration of artificiality that comes with it. Certainly, the examples here fervently assert their status as authentic celebrity texts, but this does not preclude the mobilisation of camp: from Katie Price's proud pronouncements of performative self-creation through cosmetic surgery, to Paris Hilton's defensively evasive playfulness and irony, to Lady Gaga's use of reference, quotation and pastiche in her wide-ranging visual output.

There is a clear relationship between the performed subjectivity at the centre of both memoir and celebrity culture and Susan Sontag's definition of camp as 'being as playing a role'.[143] For Sontag, camp is a postmodern sensibility characterised by irony, artifice, exaggeration and unnaturalness (themes that we shall see recur throughout the memoirs analysed here).[144] However, scholars such as Dyer[145] and Jack Babuscio[146] have been keen to assert the specifically queer, survivalist politics of camp. This performative role-playing is, for them, a consequence of existing as a gay man within a hostile, heteropatriarchal society that necessitates an act to 'pass' as 'straight' and thereby inculcates a sensitivity to wider, everyday theatricality. In this context, camp is defined as communicating seriousness through humour, something we shall see in the way 'glamour girl' memoirs attempt to handle histories of abuse.[147] The question of the politics, or lack thereof, in the camp stance has been central to discussion surrounding it. Angela McRobbie argues that 'glamour, glitter and gloss

---

[142] Yelin, 2019.

[143] Susan Sontag, 'Notes on Camp,' *Against Interpretation and Other Essays* (London: Eyre & Spottiswoode, 1967), p. 280.

[144] Ibid.

[145] Richard Dyer, *The Culture of Queers* (London: Routledge, 2002).

[146] Jack Babuscio, 'Camp and Gay Sensibility,' *Camp Grounds: Style and Homosexuality*, ed. by David Bergman (Amherst: University of Massachusetts Press, 1993).

[147] Christopher Isherwood, *The World in the Evening* (London: Methuen, 1954), p. 125.

should not so easily be relegated to the sphere of the insistently apolitical',[148] and, certainly, the glossy performance of feminised aesthetics enacted by women's celebrity memoir interacts with the charges of inauthenticity and artifice that see celebrity memoir commonly relegated to the sphere of inconsequential froth, rather than, as this book contends, sites of intervention with their own politics.

This understanding of femininity as performance is indebted to Butler's theorisation of 'gender trouble', the process by which gender reveals itself to be a socially constructed performance without any essential basis. Drag, for example, 'is not an imitation or a copy of some prior true gender [...] drag enacts the very structure of impersonation by which *any gender* is assumed'.[149] Within this conception, Katie Price's performance of deliberately constructed and artificial femininity could be seen to be a moment of feminine impersonation, or 'gender trouble'. Here, the repetition of heterosexual cultural forms can be the very site of their denaturalisation, bringing 'into relief the utterly constructed status of the so-called heterosexual original'.[150] However, that is not to say that Price's self-reflexivity around her performance of femininity necessarily 'disrupt[s] the categories of the body, sex, gender, and sexuality and occasion their subversive resignification'.[151] Indeed, the performances in this book in turn both strengthen and destabilise existing mores.

CONCLUSION

In the competing assertions of willed, agentic performance and earnest authenticity we see the precarious and contested space afforded to public women. The interrelations of artifice, authenticity and ornament are a specifically feminist issue. Impossibly competing demands are placed upon women. In Tseëlon's terms, a 'duplicity paradox' sees women constructed

---

[148] Angela McRobbie, *Postmodernism and Popular Culture* (London: Routledge, 1994), p. 175.

[149] Judith Butler, 'Imitation and Gender Insubordination,' *Women, Knowledge, and Reality: Explorations in Feminist Philosophy*, ed. by Ann Garry and Marilyn Pearsall (New York and London: Routledge, 1996), p. 378.

[150] Ibid., p. 380.

[151] Butler (1990), p. xii.

as artifice, socially required to 'improve' their appearance and simultaneously criticised for superficiality, inauthenticity and a 'lack of essence'.[152] This leaves woman occupying an 'impossible space'[153] where she is always already failing these competing demands. The contradictory performances of earnest authenticity and willed artifice in these memoirs can be seen as the contortions required to present a successful feminine subjectivity in such a paradoxically impossible space. We see these texts attempting to simultaneously adhere to mutually exclusive, contradictory and impossible female norms rather than being able to wholly accept, subvert or reconcile them.

If readers enjoy and continue to purchase these texts, the author-subject has an opportunity to rebrand, and the ghostwriter gets paid, one might wonder why it matters how much input Pamela Anderson, Katie Price, Jenna Jameson, Paris Hilton, the Kardashians, Jade Goody, Zoella, iJustine, JennxPenn, Lady Gaga, or M.I.A. had in the generation of their published life stories.

Memoir is an intervention that allows a degree of control in a media ecosystem that otherwise proliferates unauthorised exposés about women's lives and their meaning. It is an opportunity for strategic presentation of the public self.[154] They are not solely texts, in and of themselves, but rather part of broader constellations of meanings, both about these stars and about society.[155] However, we need to consider what it means if some of the highest circulating texts about and 'by' women today are not actually written by women, or, if they are written by women, not by the women whose stories are told. The ghostwriter creates a space where women's lives and, in some cases, bodies can be reinscribed with the imposition of external meaning. This doesn't mean that celebrities are necessarily without authorial agency. Indeed, we can never confidently ascertain the presence or absence of agency where celebrity culture is concerned, only seek textual details which invite inference or look at *representations* of agency.

---

[152] Ibid., p. xxxi.

[153] Ibid., p. 34.

[154] Marshall and Barbour.

[155] P. David Marshall, 'Persona Studies: Mapping the Proliferation of the Public Self,' *Journalism* 15.2 (2014), 153–70.

Agency is complex, negotiated, and gendered. Collaborative authorship can take many forms. Even wilfully relinquishing agency in self-authorship is an act that might individually serve a celebrity's interests. And yet, if we smooth over the presence of the ghost as previous reading models have, we miss the ways in which the space of the ghost comes with a risk of reinforcing the fallacy that real women are secondary to generic convention, readerly satisfaction, commercial profit or 'every young boy's fantasy'[156] (as Anderson describes herself).

BIBLIOGRAPHY

Anderson, Pamela. *Star Struck*. London: Simon & Schuster, 2006.
Annandale, David. 'Rabelais Meets Vogue: The Construction of Carnival, Beauty and Grotesque.' *The Performance Identities of Lady Gaga*, ed. by R. J. Gray. Jefferson, NC: McFarland Publishing, 2012.
Arulpragasm, Mathangi "Maya". *M.I.A.* New York: Rizzoli, 2012.
Babuscio, Jack. 'Camp and Gay Sensibility.' *Camp Grounds: Style and Homosexuality*, ed. by David Bergman. Amherst: University of Massachusetts Press, 1993.
Barthes, Roland. *Roland Barthes by Roland Barthes*, trans. Richard Howard. New York: Hill and Wang, 1977.
———. 'The Death of the Author.' *Image/Music/Text*, trans. Stephen Heath. New York: Hill and Wang, 1977: 142–47.
Bell, Emma. 'Bad Girl to Mad Girl: British Female Celebrity, Reality Products, and the Pathologization of Pop-Feminism.' *Genders* 48, 2008. Retrieved on 6 June 2013, from http://www.genders.org/g48/g48_bell.html.
Berger, Richard. *Framing the Subversive: Journalism, Celebrity and the Web*. Paper presented at *The End of Journalism? Technology, Education and Ethics*. University of Bedfordshire, 18 October 2008. Retrieved on 6 June 2013, from http://theendofjournalism.wikidot.com/richardberger.
Berlant, L. *The Female Complaint: The Unfinished Business of Sentimentality in American Culture*. Durham, NC: Duke University Press, 2008.
Bignell, Paul. 'Decline and Fall of the C-List Female Celebrity Memoirs.' *The Independent*, 23 December 2007. http://www.independent.co.uk/arts-entertainment/books/news/decline-and-fallof-the-clist-female-celebrity-memoirs-766946.html.
Booth, Wayne C. *The Company We Keep: An Ethics of Fiction*. Berkeley: University of California Press, 1988.

---

[156]Anderson (2006), p. 34.

Bourdieu, Pierre. *Outline of a Theory of Practice*. Cambridge: Cambridge University Press, 1977.

———. *Distinction: A Social Critique of the Judgement of Taste*. London: Routledge, 1984.

Boyle, Karen. 'Producing Abuse: Selling the Harms of Pornography.' *Women's Studies International Forum*, 34, 2011: 593–602.

Butler, Judith. *Gender Trouble: Feminism and the Subversion of Identity*. London: Routledge, 1990.

———. 'Imitation and Gender Insubordination.' *Women, Knowledge, and Reality: Explorations in Feminist Philosophy*, ed. by Ann Garry and Marilyn Pearsall. New York and London: Routledge, 1996.

———. *Precarious Life: The Powers of Mourning and Violence*. London: Verso, 2004.

Cadwalladr, Carole. 'All Because the Ladies Love Jordan.' *The Observer*, 12 February 2006. http://www.guardian.co.uk/theobserver/2006/feb/12/features.review47.

Carey, John. *The Intellectuals and the Masses: Pride and Prejudice Among the Literary Intelligentsia*. London: Faber,. 1992.

Cohen, Nadia. 'Beep, Beep, Beep … It's Big Brother!' *The Daily Mail*, May 2002. http://www.dailymail.co.uk/tvshowbiz/article-117087/Beep-beep-beep—Big-Brother.html#ixzz2UiGGZpS9.

Couser, G. Thomas. 'Making, Taking, and Faking Lives: The Ethics of Collaborative Life Writing.' *Style*, 32 (2), 1998: 334–51.

———. *Memoir: An Introduction*. Oxford: Oxford University Press, 2012.

Crone, Jack. 'Are We Seeing the Death of the Celebrity Memoir?' *Mail Online*, 20 December 2014. Retrieved on 29 February 2016, from http://www.dailymail.co.uk/news/article-2881571/End-chapter-celebrity-memoirs-Autobiographies-rich-famous-no-longer-sell-says-publishing-house.html#ixzz3icP5MsBk.

Curran, James and Jean Seaton. *Power Without Responsibility: Press, Broadcasting and the Internet in Britain*. London: Routledge, 2010.

Dyer, Richard. *Stars*. London: British Film Institute, 1979.

———. *Heavenly Bodies: Film Stars and Society*. New York: St. Martin's Press, 1986.

———. 'Lana: Four Films of Lana Turner.' *Movie*, 25, 1977–78: 30–54. Reprinted in M. Landy, ed. by *Imitations of Life: A Reader on Film & Television Melodrama*. Detroit, MI: Wayne State University Press, 1991.

———. *The Culture of Queers*. London: Routledge, 2002.

Ede, Lisa, and Andrea A. Lunsford. 'Collaboration and Concepts of Authorship.' *PMLA*, 116 (2), 2001: 354–69.

Edwards, Tim. 'Medusa's Stare: Celebrity, Subjectivity and Gender.' *Celebrity Studies*, 4 (2), 2013: 155–68.

Evans, Adrienne and Susan Riley. 'Immaculate Consumption: Negotiating the Sex Symbol in Postfeminist Celebrity Culture.' *Journal of Gender Studies*, 22 (3), 2013: 268–81.

Evans, Mary. *Missing Persons: The Impossibility of Auto/Biography*. London: Routledge, 1999.

Fairclough, Kirsty. 'Fame Is a Losing Game: Celebrity Gossip Blogging, Bitch Culture, and Post-feminism.' *Genders Online Journal*, 48, 2008.

Faludi, Susan. *Backlash: The Undeclared War Against American Women*. New York: Crown, 1991.

Foucault, Michel. 'What Is an Author?' *Textual Strategies: Perspectives in Post-structuralist Criticism*, ed. by Josue V. Harari. Ithaca: Cornell University Press, 1979: 141–60.

Fox, Pamela. 'Recycled "Trash": Gender and Authenticity in Country Music Autobiography.' *American Quarterly*, 50 (2), 1998: 234–66.

Frey, James. *A Million Little Pieces*. London: John Murray, 2003.

Gaga, Lady and Terry Richardson. *Gaga X Richardson*. London: Hodder and Stoughton, 2011.

Gamson, Joshua. *Claims to Fame: Celebrity in Contemporary America*. Berkeley: University of California Press, 1994.

Genette, Gérard. *Paratexts: Thresholds of Interpretation*. Cambridge: Cambridge University Press, 1997.

Geraghty, Christine. 'Re-examining Stardom: Questions of Texts, Bodies and Performance.' *Stardom and Celebrity: A Reader*. London: Sage, 2007.

Gill, Rosalind. 'Critical Respect: The Difficulties and Dilemmas of Agency and "Choice" for Feminism.' *European Journal of Women's Studies* 14 (1), 2007: 69–80.

———. 'Postfeminist Media Culture: Elements of a Sensibility.' *European Journal of Cultural Studies*, 10 (2), 2007: 147–66.

———. 'Culture and Subjectivity in Neoliberal and Postfeminist Times.' *Subjectivity*, 25, 2008: 432–45.

Gilmore, Leigh. 'American Neoconfessional: Memoir, Self Help and Redemption on Oprah's Couch.' *Biography*, 33 (4), 2010: 657–79.

Goody, Jade. *Jade Fighting to the End*. London: John Blake, 2009.

Gosselin, Abigail. 'Memoirs as Mirrors: Counterstories in Contemporary Memoir.' *Narrative*, 19 (1), 2011: 133–48.

Gough-Yates, Anna. *Understanding Women's Magazines: Publishing, Markets and Readerships*. London: Routledge, 2003.

Gwynne, Joel. *Erotic Memoirs and Postfeminism: The Politics of Pleasure*. Basingstoke: Palgrave Macmillan, 2013.

Hanley, Lynsey. 'Reality Cheque.' *New Stateman*, 16 October 2008. http://www.newstatesman.com/books/2008/10/jade-goody-star-brother-life.

Harris, John. 'Why Celebrity Memoirs Rule Publishing.' *The Guardian*, 13 December 2010. http://www.guardian.co.uk/books/2010/dec/13/celebr ity-memoirs-bestsellers-autobiography-christmas#ixzz2UhtsjwCT.

Hester, Helen. *Beyond Explicit: Pornography and the Displacement of Sex*. Albany: State University of New York Press, 2014.

Hilton, Paris. *Confessions of an Heiress: A Tongue-in-Chic Peek Behind the Pose*. New York: Fireside Books, 2004.

Hollingshead, Ian. 'Is It Curtains for the Celebrity Memoir?' *The Telegraph*, 9 December 2011. http://www.telegraph.co.uk/topics/christmas/8943536/ Is-it-curtains-for-the-celebrity-memoir.html.

Holmes, Su. '"All You've Got to Worry About Is the Task, Having a Cup of Tea, and Doing a Bit of Sunbathing": Approaching Celebrity in *Big Brother*.' *Understanding Reality Television*, ed. by Su Holmes and Deborah Jermyn. London: Routledge, 2004.

———. '"Off-Guard, Unkempt, Unready"? Deconstructing Contemporary Celebrity in Heat Magazine.' *Continuum: Journal of Media & Cultural Studies*, 19 (1), 2005: 21–38.

Holmes, Su and Diane Negra. 'Introduction.' *In the Limelight and Under the Microscope: Forms and Functions of Female Celebrity*, ed. by Su Holmes and Diane Negra. New York: Continuum, 2011.

Holmes, Su and Sean Redmond. 'Introduction: Understanding Celebrity Culture.' *Framing Celebrity: New Directions in Celebrity Culture*, ed. by Su Holmes and Sean Redmond. London and New York: Routledge, 2006.

Isherwood, Christopher. *The World in the Evening*. London: Methuen, 1954.

Jameson, Jenna. *How to Make Love Like a Pornstar: A Cautionary Tale*. New York: HarperCollins 2010.

Kardashian, Kim, Kourtney Kardashian, and Khloe Kardashian. *Kardashian Konfidential*. New York: St. Martin's Press, 2011.

Kavka, Misha. 'Hating Madonna and Loving Tom Ford: Gender, Affect and the 'Extra-Curricular' Celebrity.' *Celebrity Studies*, 5 (1–2), 2014: 59–74.

Lee, Katja. 'Not Just Ghost Stories: Alternate Practices for Reading Coauthored Celebrity Memoirs.' *The Journal of Popular Culture*, 47 (6), 2014: 1256–70.

Lejeune, Philippe. 'The Autobiography of Those Who Do Not Write.' *On Autobiography*, ed. by Paul John Eakin. Minneapolis: University of Minnesota Press, 1989.

Levy, Ariel. *Female Chauvinist Pigs: Women and the Rise of Raunch Culture*. New York; London: Free Press, 2006.

Maatta, Jerry. 'Apocalypse Now and Again: Mapping the Bestselling Classics of the End of the World.' *Hype: Bestsellers and Literary Culture*, ed. by Jon Helgason, Sara Kärrholm, and Ann Steiner. Lund, Sweden: Nordic Academic Press, 2014.

Marshall, P. David. *Celebrity and Power: Fame in Contemporary Culture.* Minneapolis: University of Minnesota Press, 1997.

———. 'Personifying Agency: The Public–Persona–Place–Issue Continuum.' *Celebrity Studies*, 4, 2013: 369–71.

———. 'Persona Studies: Mapping the Proliferation of the Public Self.' *Journalism*, 15 (2), 2014: 153–70.

Marshall, P. David, and Kim Barbour. 'Making Intellectual Room for Persona Studies: A New Consciousness and a Shifted Perspective.' *Persona Studies*, 1 (1), 2015: 1–12.

May, Ernest R. 'Ghost Writing and History.' *The American Scholar*, 22 (4), 1953: 459–65.

McAllister, Jenn. *Really Professional Internet Person.* London: Scholastic, 2015.

McLennan, Rachael. *American Autobiography.* Edinburgh: Edinburgh University Press, 2013.

McNay, Lois. *Foucault and Feminism: Power, Gender and the Self.* Cambridge: Polity, 1992.

McRobbie, Angela. *Postmodernism and Popular Culture.* London: Routledge, 1994.

———. 'Postfeminism and Popular Culture: Bridget Jones and the New Gender Regime.' *Interrogating Posfeminism: Gender and the Politics of Popular Culture.* Durham and London: Duke University Press, 2007.

———. 'Top Girls? Young Women and the Post-feminist Sexual Contract.' *Cultural Studies*, 21, 2007: 718–37.

Moran, Joe. *Star Authors: Literary Celebrity in America.* London: Pluto, 2000.

Muntean, Nick and Anne Helen Petersen. 'Twitter: Strategies of Intrusion and Disclosure in the Age of Technoculture.' *M/C Journal*, 12 (5), 2009.

Patterson, Natasha and Camilla A. Sears. 'Letting Men Off the Hook? Domestic Violence and Postfeminist Celebrity Culture.' *Genders*, 53, 2011.

Price, Katie. *Being Jordan: My Autobiography.* London: John Blake, 2005.

Rak, Julie. *Boom! Manufacturing Memoir for the Popular Market.* Waterloo, ON: Wilfrid Laurier University Press, 2013.

Redmond, Sean. 'Intimate Fame Everywhere.' *Framing Celebrity: New Directions in Celebrity Culture,* ed. by Su Holmes and Sean Redmond. London and New York: Routledge, 2006.

Redmond, Sean. 'Pieces of Me: Celebrity Confessional Carnality.' *Social Semiotics*, 18 (2), 2008: 149–61.

Ringrose, Jessica. *Postfeminist Education: Girls and the Sexual Politics of Schooling.* London and New York, NY: Routledge 2013.

Sanders, Mark A. 'Theorizing the Collaborative Self: The Dynamics of Contour and Content in the Dictated Autobiography.' *New Literary History*, 25 (1994): 445–58.

Searle, Leroy. 'New Criticism.' *The Johns Hopkins Guide to Literary Theory*, 2nd ed., ed. by Michael Groden, Martin Kreiswirth, and Imre Szeman. Baltimore: The Johns Hopkins University Press, 2005.

Shen, Dan. 'Unreliability in Autobiography vs. Fiction.' *Poetics Today*, 28 (1), 2007: 48.

Smith, Sidonie, and Julia Watson. *Reading Autobiography: A Guide for Interpreting Life Narratives*. Minneapolis: University of Minnesota Press, 2001.

Sontag, Susan. 'Notes on Camp.' *Against Interpretation and Other Essays*. London: Eyre & Spottiswoode, 1967.

Spanier, Gideon. 'Celebs Lose Their Sheen for Publishers as Gift-Buyers Spurn Celebrity Biographies.' *The Independent*, 19 December 2014. http://www.independent.co.uk/news/business/news/celebs-lose-their-sheen-for-publishers-as-giftbuyers-spurn-celebrity-biographies-9937012.html.

Spicer, Jakki. 'The Author Is Dead, Long Live the Author: Autobiography and the Fantasy of the Individual.' *Criticism*, 47 (3), 2005: 387–403.

Stuart, Avelie and Ngaire Donaghue. 'Choosing to Conform: The Discursive Complexities of Choice in Relation to Feminine Beauty Practices.' *Feminism & Psychology*, 22 (1), 2012: 98–121.

Sutherland, John. 'Among the Ghosts.' *Spectator*, 11 June 2011. http://www.spectator.co.uk/features/7009933/among-the-ghosts.

Tasker, Yvonne and Diane Negra. *Interrogating Postfeminism: Gender and the Politics of Popular Culture*. Durham, NC: Duke University Press, 2007.

Tiidenberg, K. 'Bringing Sexy Back: Reclaiming the Body Aesthetic via Self-Shooting.' *Cyberpsychology: Journal of Psychosocial Research on Cyberspace*, 8 (1), 2014.

Trilling, Lionel. *Sincerity and Authenticity*. London: Oxford University Press, 1972.

Tseëlon, Efrat. *The Masque of Femininity: The Presentation of Woman in Everyday Life*. London: Sage, 1995.

Turner, Graeme, Frances Bonner, and P. David Marshall. *Fame Games: The Production of Celebrity in Australia*. Cambridge: Cambridge University Press, 2000.

Tyler, Imogen and Bruce Bennett. '"Celebrity Chav": Fame, Femininity and Social Class.' *European Journal of Cultural Studies*, 13 (3), 2010: 375–93.

Williams, Rebecca. 'From Beyond Control to in Control: Investigating Drew Barrymore's Feminist Agency/Authorship.' *Stardom and Celebrity*, 111–126, 2007: 111.

Williamson, Milly. 'Female Celebrities and the Media: The Gendered Denigration of the "Ordinary" Celebrity.' *Celebrity Studies*, 1 (1), 2010: 118.

———. 'Celebrity, Gossip, Privacy, and Scandal.' *The Routledge Companion to Media and Gender*, ed. by Cynthia Carter, Linda Steiner, and Lisa McLaughlin. New York: Routledge, 2014.

Wilson, J. A. 'Star Testing: The Emerging Politics of Celebrity Gossip.' *The Velvet Light Trap*, 65, 2010: 30.

Yagoda, Ben. *Memoir: A History*. New York: Riverhead Books, 2009.

Yelin, Hannah and Jonathan Wise. 'Dave: Now Everyone Has a Mate Called Dave.' *Advertising Works 17: Case Studies from the IPA Effectiveness Awards 2008*, ed. by Neil Dawson. Henley-on-Thames: WARC, 2009.

York, Lorraine. 'Star Turn: The Challenges of Theorizing Celebrity Agency.' *The Journal of Popular Culture*, 46 (6), 2013: 1330–47.

Yunuen Lewis, Caitlin. 'Cool Postfeminism: The Stardom of Sofia Coppola.' *In the Limelight and Under the Microscope*, ed. by Holmes and Negra. New York: Continuum, 2011.

CHAPTER 3

The *Economics of Access*: Constructedness and the Commoditisation of Harm in the Porn-Star Memoirs of Jenna Jameson, Katie Price and Pamela Anderson

INTRODUCTION

This chapter examines the tensions that arise when life writing—an act of *subject*ification—is undertaken by an individual with a professional investment in their own *object*ification (an investment shared by wider society). The conventions of pornography are sufficiently pervasive that they intersect with many cultural fields. Karinne Steffans' memoir, *Confessions of a Video Vixen*, for example, shows the continuum from her career in the sex industry to her career performing in the music videos of some of the most famous Hip Hop stars in Hollywood. Porn star Stormy Daniels' memoir, *Full Disclosure*, intersects with law and politics as it offers an account of the author's relationship with President of America, Donald Trump, and the legal battles which followed the relationship being made public. This chapter focusses on the memoirs of three women who crossed over to mainstream celebrity after becoming famous through hardcore porn films or soft-core porn modelling: Katie Price, Pamela Anderson and Jenna Jameson.

Examining how the celebrity memoir is shaped by the specificities of the celebrity's domain reveals these texts to be acts of persona construction that must simultaneously tally with, extend, and retrospectively justify, their pornographic careers. What the celebrities were originally famous for shapes what their memoirs reveal: pornographic tropes and

© The Author(s) 2020
H. Yelin, *Celebrity Memoir*,
https://doi.org/10.1007/978-3-030-44621-5_3

51

idioms prescribe the preferred language through which they depict their subjectivity. Three themes arise as crucial to understanding how these texts function: the commoditised self, contradictory representations of sexual agency, and a deliberate emphasis upon constructedness as a pervasive formal and thematic concern.

Despite the predominantly female target audience of celebrity autobiography, these women—made famous by male-targeted 'adult' media—have 'authored' some of the most commercially successful and widely read contemporary texts within the genre. Jameson's memoir, *How to Make Love Like a Porn Star* (2004), spent six weeks on *The New York Times* bestseller list.[1] A senior publishing executive, who turned down Price's *Being Jordan* (2004) because he 'believed that the public was only interested in getting stories about the size of pop stars' penises from the tabloids', states that 'the book's success caught the publishing world off guard' and created its own 'new sub-genre'[2] when it reached number one in the Nielsen Bookscan chart,[3] selling over a million copies in its various forms by 2007.[4] This success is arguably attributable to Price's celebrity appeal across a number of audiences, as evidenced in a book-signing tour for *Being Jordan* 'that drew crowds aged from 11 to 70 and, contrary to expectations, almost exclusively female'.[5]

The role of the ghostwriter in the construction of such conflicted representations of the 'empowered' (and eroticised) female subject requires interrogation. These texts offer a case study in the ghosting relationship as charged with complex, gendered power dynamics, with implications for how we understand the genre's dual promises of 'access' and 'authenticity', and what I will term the *economics of access*—where female celebrities are coaxed to reveal their bodies and 'private' thoughts as celebrity currency. In the case of Anderson and Jameson, the ghosts with whom they collaborate are male. It is significant that these texts, sold as 'true' female experiences, are often co-authored by men, existing

---

[1] Edward Wyatt, 'Political but Not Partisan: A Publisher Has It Both Ways,' *The New York Times*, 13 October 2004.

[2] Trevor Dolby, 'Publishing Confessions,' *Prospect Magazine*, 14 January 2007.

[3] Philip Stone, 'Jade Title Reaches Number One,' *The Oxford Editors*, 7 April 2009.

[4] Patrick Barkham, 'I'm Famous, Buy Me,' *The Guardian*, 15 January 2007.

[5] Danuta Kean, 'Celebrity Memoirs: Bookshop Bingo!' *The Independent*, 24 September 2015.

as they do in a space of historical, representational lack—both as women's sexual autobiography and, more specifically, as the voices of women in the sex industry. Examination of the power dynamics of ghosting is especially necessary when these texts narrate (and make palatable) stories of trauma, abuse and sexual violence. It is not my intention to enter into debates around potential causative relationships between a history of abuse and sex work.[6] Rather, I will investigate the power dynamics of a performance of eroticised subjectivity when, despite a majority female audience for these texts,[7] the specular (and at points abusive) sexuality presented within them transmits the male pornographic gaze from the visual to the verbal. What surfaces is a tension between narratives of erotic titillation and accounts of abuse, which implicates readers in a prurient relationship with abuse as entertainment. These texts construct a readerly subject position in which permission is granted to read and enjoy another's suffering without that seeming to be exploitative. At the same time, a thematic and formal emphasis on constructedness interacts with testimonies of trauma survival that make claim to truth status.

Porn Debates and Textual Fantasies

The promise of the 'real', extratextual self and the possibility of access are themes that are intrinsic to the celebrity memoir genre. Questions of the 'real' and of purported 'presence' have, similarly, been central to scholarly debates about pornography and harm. Anti-pornography debates are framed in terms of harm and the potential for force, coercion or damage to the real bodies of the women involved.[8] Erotic content within the written word, meanwhile, has been seen as a harmless space of woman-friendly sexual exploration.[9] The memoirs discussed here bear elements of both critical positions, but do not fit neatly into either category.

---

[6] For this kind of reading, see Boyle (2011).

[7] Cadwalladr; Sager.

[8] See, for example, Catharine A. MacKinnon and Andrea Dworkin, *In Harm's Way: The Pornography Civil Rights Hearings* (Cambridge, MA, and London: Harvard University Press, 1997).

[9] Susanna Paasonen, 'Good Amateurs: Erotica Writing and Notions of Quality,' *Porn.Com: Making Sense of Online Pornography*, ed. by Feona Attwood (New York: Peter Lang, 2010), p. 139.

They feature many narratives of sexual violence and bodily harm. For example, Price narrates her experience of sexual assault in the park as a child; Anderson's protagonist relates having been raped when she was twelve; and Jameson relates a harrowing story of being violently gang-raped and left for dead when in high school. These testimonies sit alongside eroticised tales of idealised past love affairs, and both types of narratives are, together, packaged as an entertaining exploration of the lives of real women. As such, they construct a reading position in which permission is given to consume stories of purported real-world abuse without considering oneself implicated in the commercialisation of harm. Whilst the audiences for both pornography and celebrity memoir are diverse and may contain some overlap, all three women have made a transition from appearing in magazines or films targeting a male audience, for whom they revealed their body, to a range of media texts targeting a female audience, for whom they purport to reveal their innermost thoughts.

In the case of Pamela Anderson, for example, she crossed over to mainstream fame in the American hit TV series *Baywatch* after a career topless modelling for men's magazines such as *Playboy*. In a promotional interview with men's magazine, *Esquire*, at the time of the release of her second memoir, *Star Struck*, she explains:

> You'd think that my fans would be the guys who are too drunk to turn the channel after football. But surprisingly, from all the demographic research that people have done on me, we've found out that I have a huge female following. It's a girl-girl type thing.[10]

Casting the relationship with her audience as one of mutual sexual desire could suggest a model of female spectatorship beyond either masochistic identification with the object of the gaze, or metaphoric 'transvestism' in identification with the objectifying male gaze.[11] However, her use of the terminology of pornography targeting heterosexual men does not exclude the male gaze—far from it. The suggestion of a 'girl-girl' dynamic in the relationship between female sex symbol and female readership, instead, co-opts her new female-targeted ventures as another means to titillate the

---

[10] Sager.

[11] Laura Mulvey, 'Afterthoughts on 'Visual Pleasure and Narrative Cinema' Inspired by King Vidor's *Duel in the Sun*,' *Visual and Other Pleasures* (Bloomington: Indiana University Press, 1989), p. 33.

male readers of *Esquire*. The shift in audiences is part of a transition which expands the female celebrity's fame, lifecycle and breadth of commercial opportunities as they bare themselves, one way or another, from physical exposure to psychic confession.

Scholarly discussion of pornography has tended towards either defensive endorsement or trenchant protest.[12] Porn has stimulated scholarly debate over whether it is a legitimate cultural form and site of resistance, which must be protected from repressive censorship,[13] or whether causative links exist between the symbolic violence of representations of and by the sex industry and the empirical realities of structural inequality.[14] Both sides agree that pornography has proliferated across mainstream culture to exist in many forms that too easily go unexamined. Such mainstreaming is evidenced by the existence and commercial success of the memoirs examined in this chapter: cross-over texts which bring bestselling representations of the sex industry to wide audiences beyond those of pornography, as well as offering content which is sexually explicit in and of itself.

Since Linda Williams' 1989 work, *Hard Core*, the growing field of porn studies has defined itself in contrast to previous anti-porn feminist arguments.[15] However, as Susanna Paasonen observes, pro-porn scholars predominantly write about 'independent, queer, artistic projects that challenge gender norms, porn clichés, and the commodity logic of the porn industry'.[16] A theorisation of pornography based upon its most alternative examples proves less useful when critiquing texts such as those authored by Anderson, Jameson and Price, which, very obviously and deliberately, deal in 'gender norms' and 'commodity logic'. Not only are these features constitutive of the 'mainstream' heterosexual porn industry,

---

[12] Hester.

[13] Feminists Against Censorship, *Pornography and Feminism: The Case Against Censorship*, ed. by Gillian Rodgerson and Elizabeth Wilson (London: Lawrence & Wishart, 1991).

[14] Maddy Coy, Josephine Wakeling, and Maria Garner, 'Selling Sex Sells: Representations of Prostitution and the Sex Industry in Sexualised Popular Culture as Symbolic Violence,' *Women's Studies International Forum* 34 (2011), 441–48.

[15] Linda Williams, *Hard Core: Power, Pleasure, and the "Frenzy of the Visible"* (Berkeley: University of California Press, 1989), pp. 4–5.

[16] Susanna Paasonen, *Carnal Resonance: Affect and Online Pornography* (Cambridge, MA, and London: MIT Press, 2011).

but 'gender norms' and 'commodity logic' underpin both the celebrity and memoir industries as well. These texts, therefore, represent a unique overlapping of genres (pornography, celebrity and autobiography) which all revolve around the gendered manufacture and commoditisation of intimacy.

Helen Hester observes that this protective stance, focussing on pornography's most progressive potential, has led to a newly proscriptive, insufficiently critical body of scholarship and not to the dispassionate nonpartisan approach that was claimed.[17] With this in mind, I approach the memoirs of Anderson, Price and Jameson, not as examples by which to exalt or vilify pornography in general, but as individual texts with their own politics.

Combining the intimate revelations that form the appeal of celebrity coverage, autobiography's promise of self-disclosure of personal truth, and the visual exposure and physical availability of pornography, these texts occupy a unique nexus of promises of 'access'. As such, they cannot be viewed as purely memoir, as celebrity texts, as sexually explicit literature, or sex industry testimony, but rather as a combination in which physical undress and psychic confession reinforce and magnify one another in a dynamic that presupposes access and consent. This nexus of cultural appetites around the concept of psychic and physical access to famous women is an economy running throughout celebrity culture. The visual and physical access promised by pornography literalises the *economics of access* in starkest terms. Linda Williams suggests that claims that pornography 'expressed the power and the pleasure of heterosexual men [is] one of the serious limitations' of feminist scholarship on pornography.[18] In the readings of these memoirs, however, one cannot put aside questions of patriarchal power: agency, 'empowerment', consent, and sexual violence are themes which all three celebrity authors invoke, demanding that such discourses be interrogated.

Whilst these memoirs contain sexually explicit material, and narrate career paths through the sex industry, they should also be treated as written life narratives. As Paasonen argues, 'the tendency to understand porn in terms of the visual is common, yet this ignores the fact that

---

[17] Hester.

[18] Linda Williams, 'Introduction,' *Porn Studies* (Durham: Duke University Press, 2004), p. 7.

the history of pornography has largely been one concerning the written word'.[19] This oversight is present in the emphasis of both public and scholarly debates upon visual pornography. Hester proposes the possibility that 'linguistic porn receives comparatively little negative attention, perhaps due to the fact that the graphic sexual scenarios it depicts do not depend upon the presence of real bodies—bodies that, in the popular imagination, could be vulnerable, or unwilling, or subject to damage'.[20] The memoirs of Anderson, Jameson and Price, however, do narrate stories of harm visited upon the real bodies of their authors. Hester's binary of 'textual fantasies' versus filmed 'use and potential abuse of real bodies'[21] cannot contain these sexually explicit written accounts which narrate the real abuse of real bodies.

SANITIZING SEXUAL TRAUMA: THE COMPETING AGENDAS OF PAMELA ANDERSON'S *STAR*

Anderson's first memoir, *Star*, interweaves a narration of the path into soft-core porn modelling with an account of traumatic sexual history. The book relates the story of a fictionalised celebrity, Star, whose life so closely follows the narrative of its author's that, when Anderson was asked 'What comment do you hear most often from your readers?', she claimed that readers respond to her books for their truth value, answering, 'Thanks for telling the truth'.[22] Even if we take at its strongest the notion that Anderson is not Star, the text must still reflect an attitude, attributed to Anderson as 'author', towards issues that are extremely pertinent to the facts of Anderson's own life. In other words, the approach to pornography and objectification expressed in her book must inform an understanding of the way that Anderson's star image is constructed (which in turn impacts upon her self-presentation in memoir). The peculiar status of the fictionalised memoir that is read for insight into a 'real' extratextual person will be analysed later in this chapter. For now, however, the sexual history presented in Anderson's memoir serves as an example which illustrates how, in these porn memoirs, experiences of coerced sex are

[19] Paasonen (2010), p. 67.

[20] Hester, p. 11.

[21] Ibid., p. 12.

[22] 'Interview with Pamela Anderson,' *Goodreads*, February 2010.

presented in terms which diminish their seriousness. Anderson's memoir draws a parallel between her experience of forced sex and her experience of posing nude for men's magazines. The implicit link between these two experiences (one which could be argued to be reproduced in the production and sale of a memoir) is that she is treated as an object for consumption.

Not only does Anderson's memoir depict a woman with a traumatic sexual history, but she narrates a wider model of sexuality in which consent is absent. Describing an early sexual experience at a party as a teenager the narrator states: 'Bobby got them each a screwdriver from the absentee parents' bar, then he led Star up to the wastrel's room, where he locked the door, downed his drink, pulled out his erection, and pushed Star down onto the bed'.[23] The sex is described in non-consensual terms, and yet the seriousness of such a situation is underplayed, and instead Bobby's masculinity is mocked as 'it was over too quickly for Star to find it objectionable'.[24] The implication that, as long as it is over quickly, non-consensual sex is not objectionable (and can even be humorous) is further normalised when Star's mother glibly replies, 'welcome to dating'—as if non-consensual sex is a universal, even tolerable, inevitability of hetero-sexual relations.[25] Even when consenting, Star's early sexual experiences are defined by negotiation and transaction. When relating the way her first relationship, began, she describes herself as conceding to sex she doesn't want to have and trading it as currency: '"Put that away," she said disgustedly, "I don't want anything to do with your wiener." "Please, just put your hand around it... You can borrow my mountain bike for a week...." "A month," she said at last...And so their sexual adventures began'.[26] This dynamic of stating that she does not want to have sex, but succumbing anyway, is sustained throughout the adult sexual encounters related. Whilst Anderson can be seen to be laughing at the arbitrari-ness of teenage relationships, what is presented as innocent, childish, and somehow wholesome, is a dynamic of masculine power. This dynamic privileges the sexual desires of men and runs throughout both of her autobiographical novels.

[23] Pamela Anderson, *Star* (London: Simon & Schuster, 2004), p. 197.

[24] Ibid.

[25] Ibid.

[26] Ibid., p. 199.

As a retrospective construction with the specific intention of securing a favourable reception amongst potential fans for a continuing celebrity career, Anderson can be presumed to be anticipating the possible judgements of her audience. The placing of benign and recognisable details at the heart of sexual negotiations (in this case a mountain bike) may be an attempt to ease the reader into a world outside their experience with some reassuringly wholesome familiarities. Likewise, depicting oneself as subject to patriarchal structures which deny women sexual agency is an active means of situating oneself within such power structures and negotiating with them. As cross-over texts with an intended audience far beyond that of their original careers in pornography, these memoirs must explain their lives in terms which intended audiences will find acceptable, despite social opprobrium for women who enjoy their pornographic careers (or even sex itself). In this respect, Anderson could be seen to be explaining her later career choices in terms that society understands, appealing to the entrenched moral logic of the 'fallen' or 'damaged' woman that is an established theme in Western literature.[27] This would suggest the ways in which the star author-subject is required to fashion a life story to accord with pre-existing stock narratives and perceived social norms.

The absence of consent defines Star's sexual encounters—some of which are highly eroticised. The book offers a teenage scene in which Star's female friend, Brandi, presses her to try marijuana, then offers her a massage: 'A lot of stuff is amazing after you smoke a jay. Here, lean back; I'll rub your shoulders. You'll see'.[28] This escalates, again without active participation on the part of Star: 'A finger slipped under the leg of the loose-fitting shorts she was still wearing from work. It wasn't unpleasant, but it was unexpected'.[29] Again, Star protests, then capitulates: '"Br... Brandi," Star began, but her objections were overruled. "It's okay, it's perfectly natural," Brandi urged, silencing her with tiny hungry kisses. Star fought and then succumbed, soft lips on soft lips. "It doesn't mean a thing..."' This eroticisation of sex as something that happens to a passive protagonist, who succumbs despite protestations, is a common trope of

---

[27] See for example Daniel Defoe's *Moll Flanders* (London: Harper Collins, [1722] 2010) or Samuel Richardson's *Pamela, or Virtue Rewarded* (Oxford: Oxford University Press, [1740] 2001).

[28] Anderson (2004), p. 28.

[29] Ibid., p. 29.

erotic fiction.[30] What is especially problematic about this scene in *Star* is its uncomfortable parallel with and proximity to a scene of child rape that is described later in the memoir.

At the point of her big break on a nude shoot with *Mann* Magazine (a thinly veiled reference to Anderson's career with *Playboy*), the male photographer's coaxing of her to perform sexual poses triggers a flashback to her childhood: "'Relax Star, it's going to be great,' she heard his voice, felt his breath on her neck, his hands on her. She had only been twelve years old'.[31] The soothing yet insistent words parallel those of Brandi and, just as with their encounter, the situation escalates from an intoxicated massage:

> It started innocently enough. Bringing her a fresh, forbidden, and hence decidedly grown-up rum and Coke, he'd come up behind the chair where she was sitting and rubbed her shoulders. "You're so tense," he'd said, "How about a massage?"[32]

This is the only time non-consensual sex is, albeit indirectly, acknowledged as rape as the text states: 'She thought of the experience with Al as forced, but never rape'. This represents the victim's struggle to make sense of what has happened, the challenge of being taken seriously as a 12-year-old girl, and the difficulty of holding her rapist accountable in a victim-blaming culture which routinely naturalises male desire as aggressive. In the model of sexuality offered in the text, however, this reads as part of a wider paradigm that also naturalises male sexual aggression. The parallels with the way the scene with Brandi is related—the similarities in dialogue, the massage, the intoxication further diminishing agency and the ability to consent—raises the question of the nature of the reading pleasures offered by these texts, with strikingly similar events narrated once as trauma and once as titillation. Such close proximity and parallels raise the question of what erotic or entertainment value either scene confers on the other.

Scholars such as Boyle have argued that the histories of abuse contained within the memoirs of female porn stars demonstrate 'the conditions

---

[30] Janice Radway, *Reading the Romance: Women, Patriarchy, and Popular Literature* (Chapel Hill: University of North Carolina Press, [1984] 2009).

[31] Anderson (2004), p. 174.

[32] Ibid., p. 176.

for her entry into pornography'.[33] Whilst it is beyond the scope of this book to engage in debates about potential causative links between histories of sexual trauma and entry into the sex industry, it is Anderson's memoir that explicitly links the two: 'She never even thought about [the forced sexual encounter with Al] anymore, but then that morning, in the studio with those strangers, her clothes still in the dressing room, her body touched and adjusted, it had come back to her'.[34] This has the potential to offer a moment of resistance through critique of her industry, demonstrating the parallels between work in the sex industry and abuse argued by anti-pornography feminists. However, whilst the narrator makes a connection between being 'adjusted by strangers' for a nude photoshoot and her experience of sexual assault as a child, this link is disavowed as positive self-sexualisation and is simultaneously presented as both the traumatic flashback trigger and the means to triumph over abuse:

> Star felt angry and indignant that a man so many years before could make her feel ashamed of herself at this, her big moment. She arose from where she was sitting and crossed to the mirror. She dried her eyes carefully with a tissue... And then, very deliberately, she took off the robe.[35]

This positions her experience of sexual assault as formative in her attitudes to, and motivations for, her entry into the industry, whilst positivising the latter in a way that disavows gender politics or any sort of institutional critique. The narrator segues between discussion of the photoshoot and the assault, concluding: 'It had been fun and liberating. She could not get back what had been taken from her as a young girl nearly ten years earlier. But she didn't have to give up anything more'.[36] Thus, structural issues of gender are 'reprivatised'[37] as a postfeminist sensibility frames experiences of gendered violence 'in exclusively personal terms in a way that turns the idea of the personal as political on its head'.[38]

---

[33] Boyle, p. 596.
[34] Anderson (2004), p. 176.
[35] Ibid., p. 177.
[36] Ibid., p. 179.
[37] McNay, p. 106.
[38] Gill (2007), p. 153.

Here, we have seen the tension created as narratives of erotic titillation and testimonies from working in the sex industry are placed in close proximity to, and given explicit parallels with, narratives of abuse. Whilst these memoirs are not without potentially resistant moments, which appear to be approaching critique, structural inequities of gender are ultimately disavowed. Beyond the sensibilities of postfeminist media culture, we can see these tensions as intrinsic to the celebrity memoir form. The celebrity's commercial investment is extended and capitalised upon through such photoshoots and necessitate the construction of a reading position from which audiences have permission to continue consuming such images free from concern. Herein lie the competing agendas within a porn-star memoir that attempts to simultaneously fulfil the promise of voyeuristic satisfaction integral to both pornography and autobiography, and the strange position of testimonies of sexual trauma within them. These narratives appear repeatedly, offering a voyeuristic quality of their own, but must ultimately be positivized or, at the very least contained, to put the reader at ease despite their apparent appetite for celebrities 'telling the truth'.[39]

The 'Glamour Girl' Memoir: Narrative Subject/Corporeal Object

In the celebrity memoir, it is unclear where self-making ends and brand-building begins, as celebrity authors occupy dual roles as narrative subject and commoditised object in a marketplace. Foucault argues that confessional practices have evolved into modern-day 'technologies of the self', whereby the modern subject comes into being by means of a process of identity formation through self-surveillance: 'a nearly infinite task of telling'[40] that internalises, and thus replaces, traditional disciplinary power structures. The 'incitement to discourse'[41] can be seen as a foundation of contemporary celebrity culture as stars confess in magazines, TV talk shows and reality products as well as memoirs.[42] Using the name Jordan,

---

[39] *Goodreads* (2010).

[40] Michel Foucault, *The History of Sexuality: Volume 1*, trans. Robert Hurley (New York: Pantheon, 1978), p. 20.

[41] Ibid., p. 17.

[42] Redmond (2008).

British celebrity Katie Price is famous for 'glamour' modelling—a British euphemism for topless modelling in which models are called 'glamour girls', perpetuating the postfeminist 'girling' of adult women. Having, at the time of writing, produced six memoirs and eleven purportedly semi-autobiographical novels to date, Price could be seen to exemplify the celebrity confessional as a 'nearly infinite task' in the *economics of access.* As a confessional means by which identities are constructed and negotiated, memoirs can be considered to be a primary example of technologies of the self. In celebrity memoir, then, self-making and merchandising are one and the same. These texts are profitable objects for sale in themselves and, furthermore, are tools for making their celebrity authors, as commoditised objects, more saleable.

Julia Watson notes the objectification required in autobiography's imperatives of narrative and witnessing[43] and yet, as Margaret McLaren argues, the process of critically examining 'how one came to be as one is' must, at the same time, be viewed as 'a process of subjectification'.[44] This objectified subjectivity is inherent to all (and especially celebrity) memoir. However, the tension in the status of objectified subject is nowhere more evident than in the memoirs of 'glamour models' or 'porn stars' as their professional investment in their status as object of the male gaze demands a performance of eroticised subjectivity. American, hardcore, gonzo porn film star Jenna Jameson, the first real 'cross-over' star to move to mainstream TV and radio presentation, notes, 'you are the product'.[45] Her words are as true of autobiography and of wider celebrity culture as they are of the porn career that she was describing.

In 'glamour' photographs, Price is the object of desire. In her celebrity career in gossip magazines, she is an object of speculation, judgement and ridicule. The narrator of autobiography, however, necessarily performs her subjectivity, interrupting these subject/object positions. However, regardless of how much celebrity authors claim to use memoir to show new or different aspects of their identity, or a 'real' self, the account of the life given in celebrity memoir must, to some degree, correlate with the

[43] Julia Watson, 'Towards and Anti-Metaphysics of Autobiography,' *The Culture of Autobiography: Constructions of Self-representation,* ed. by Robert Folkenflik (Stanford, CA: Stanford University Press, 1993), p. 77.

[44] Margaret A. McLaren, *Feminism, Foucault, and Embodied Subjectivity* (Albany: State University of New York Press, 2002), p. 152.

[45] Jameson, p. 333.

persona that inspired readers to purchase the book. The memoir reader is always 'consciously or half-consciously comparing the textual world with the extratextual reality'.[46] Thus, pornographic conventions dominate her depiction of her subjectivity.

The tensions between the roles of narrative subject and corporeal object are acknowledged as Price's autobiography promises to demonstrate that 'there's more to' her than being 'famous for [her] boobs'.[47] Price claims that the *autobiographical occasion* of her memoir, the rationale or apparent trigger to embark upon the task of writing her life,[48] is the chance to reveal the 'person inside this body'.[49] She suggests her desire is to reclaim control of her identity and redress portrayal in the media as 'a slapper, a tart, a man-eater [and] a freak [who is] addicted to plastic surgery'.[50] Price's rebuttal to the gendered public condemnation she has received is located within the celebrity memoir genre convention of claiming the need to 'reveal the real me' for fans—a promise made in many of the memoirs examined in this book, and one that is foundational to the *economics of access*. With her emphasis on taking back control of the meaning given to her life and shifting attention from her body to her thoughts, this text is presented as an act of self-making, an assertion of agency that locates the author's identity in a subjectivity beyond her role as embodied spectacle.

However, here one can see the contradictions presented by celebrity memoir: to redress her overexposure, Price must 'open up' more completely. To counteract her public image of being a woman 'obsessed with fame [who] will do anything for publicity', she will propel that fame further with a well-publicised book.[51] To avoid being known for taking her clothes off, she must 'reveal' herself in new ways—still operating within an *economics of access*. Her purported goal of counteracting the way in which 'journalists write about [her] as if [she is] a dumb bimbo' situates her as resistant: rebelling against a 'history of woman as an object

---

[46] Shen, p. 48.
[47] Price (2005), p. 1.
[48] Smith and Watson (2001), p. 207.
[49] Price (2005), p. 1.
[50] Ibid.
[51] Ibid.

of speculation and specularization'.[52] And yet, Price is an agent of her own display, and her memoir is an intervention which claims to disrupt her specularity whilst fuelling it further.

The subjectivity of the eroticised woman is a site of contestation. For example, anti-prostitution scholars such as Sheila Jeffreys risk dehumanising 'the prostituted woman' who is paid, in Jeffrey's terms, 'to be a person who is not a person,'[53] and see this erasure of subjectivity as what enables men to ignore the ethical implications of their participation. Similarly, in her enthnographic study of a successful, independent, white British sex worker, Julia O'Connell Davidson concluded that 'whether he is submissive, flattering or abusive, the client's treatment of the prostitute represents a denial of her subjectivity and humanity...the essence of the transaction is that she is an object, not a subject, within it'.[54] This argument, whilst not invalid in its critique of the client's evasion of responsibility, risks denying the woman-as-prostitute any subjectivity or agency, suggesting that the way that women gain subjectivity is by having it conferred upon them by men. Whilst prostitution and 'glamour-girl' celebrity cannot simply be equated, these examples show how eroticised female subjectivity is vulnerable to erasure. Meanwhile, by contrast, postfeminist culture, and third-wave feminism position women's sexual subjectivity as a crucial site of empowerment. As Joel Gwynne observes, 'popular culture's prevailing message that the most successful way to become financially empowered – and therefore liberated – is through the cultivation of an active and hedonistic sexuality'.[55] In their simultaneous occupation of the positions of narrative subject and sexualised corporeal object, the authors of these memoirs both contradict and compound each of these reductive characterisations. These texts do not fit the model offered by Jeffreys and O'Connell Davidson listed above because all first-person autobiographical narration is an act which performs subjectivity, humanity and personhood, regardless of whether the stories narrated are those of the experiences of professional objectification. However, even when these authors espouse postfeminist values of empowerment, they

[52] Sidonie Smith and Julia Watson, *Interfaces: Women, Autobiography, Image, Performance* (Ann Arbor: University of Michigan Press, 2002), p. 5.

[53] Sheila Jeffreys, *The Idea of Prostitution* (North Melbourne: Spinifex, 1997), p. 182.

[54] Julia O'Connell Davidson and Derek Layder, *Methods, Sex, and Madness* (London and New York: Routledge, 1994), p. 189.

[55] Gwynne, p. 10.

do so whilst narrating stories which clearly demonstrate moments of being *out* of control and depicting models of sexuality which, rather than being free, directly or indirectly reveal the constraints upon them. In an interview promoting her memoir, Anderson says jokingly of her writing, 'I don't know if you can call me an artist or not, but I feel like I've created my life day by day. [...] I've made a career out of it somehow'.[56] She thus locates her life writing as a deliberate, agentic process of self-making. And yet she jokes about the tensions in her objectified subject position, saying, 'my breasts have a career. I'm just tagging along'.[57] Whilst these women's memoirs demonstrate an intervention into their objectification, and appear to counteract the erasure of the subjectivity of the eroticised woman, the resulting texts are deeply contradictory and reveal their authors as caught between genres: autobiography and pornography with their respective privileging of mental depth and physical surface.

Ghosting the 'Glamour Girl' Memoir: Between Fact, Fiction, Constructedness and the 'Real'

Thus far, I have established the importance of the twin concepts of the 'real' extratextual bodies, and constructed intimacies, ideas integral to the promises of both autobiography and pornography. Similarly, we have seen how autobiography is a performative act of self-construction. Constructedness is a recurring theme throughout these memoirs. This is not unusual for celebrity narratives in 'reality products'. Reflexivity about the construction of the image is central to much celebrity coverage where 'celebrity-watcher cynicism'[58] is underpinned by a belief that all celebrity narratives are constructed for purposes of marketability. Celebrity autobiographies, especially, gain some of their value in an *economics of access* from their ability to offer a 'behind-the-scenes' perspective by revealing construction processes underpinning the celebrity image and its commodification. Whilst these texts are substantially comprised of testimonies of trauma survival, they consistently emphasise discourses of constructedness, falsity or fabrication, whether in relation to bodies, pleasures or narratives. This raises particular questions of what is at stake in these

---

[56] Sager.

[57] Ibid.

[58] Gamson (1994), p. 149.

representations, what can(not) be uttered and what, once attested to, must be undermined. This demands examination of their various claims to truth status and the ramifications of the (variously known, hidden or presumed) mediating presence of the ghostwriter.

Although Katie Price's *Being Jordan* claims to be a frank and honest autobiographical account, Pamela Anderson's *Star Struck* is presented as fiction, and Jameson's *How to Make Love like a Porn Star* combines modes of telling associated with both fact and fiction, all three texts attempt to offer the same model of reading pleasure constitutive of the *economics of access*: promoting the existence of a 'real' woman behind the image that readers can get closer to through their life stories.

Written in the first-person, addressing the reader directly with the colloquial idiom of the spoken word, Price and her ghostwriter create a sense of unedited and unpolished immediacy. For example, Price addresses her readers in the second person: 'I can almost hear you thinking, She must think a lot of herself'.[59] Whilst this could be a product of an oral, collaborative construction process, the 'you' referring to ghost-writer, the late Rebecca Farnworth, the effect, deliberate or otherwise, is a constructed intimacy through a disarmingly unprocessed aesthetic.[60] Farnworth's name is buried, unmarked in the acknowledgements page along with other employees of the publishing house, John Blake. In accordance with the logic of the *economics of access*, Price claims to offer herself up in unedited, unpolished entirety, appealing, 'I've held nothing back [...] It's all here. My life is in your hands'.[61] Price's model of autobiography thus reveals its investment in the appearance of a sole author capable of narrating an authentic self and in creating a feeling of proximity between narrator and reader.

Whilst Price's memoir strives to make claim to authenticity, and to stress the veracity of an account that will 'set the record straight',[62] Anderson's memoir employs various distancing devices. Although *Star* only bears Anderson's authorial signature, the inside cover credits both her and her ghostwriter, Eric Shaw Quinn, equally, and Quinn was a visible presence on the promotional tour: 'Unlike any ghost writers we

---

[59] Price (2005), p. 7.
[60] Smith and Watson (2002), p. 3.
[61] Price (2005), p. x.
[62] Ibid., p. 69.

can recall, he was sitting next to the celebrity as books were being signed. Ms Anderson, he said, was never interested in keeping his existence a secret'.[63] This may in part be because of the book's status as fictionalised memoir, billed as a *roman-à-clef*.[64] The protagonist, whilst explicitly based on Anderson, is presented as 'Pammy's alter-ego'.[65] She is given a symbolic, but distinct name, Star, and with the ghostwriter, writes herself in the third person. These representational choices grant Anderson licence to embrace the artifice which might be presumed regardless, owing to mistrust of autobiography in general,[66] and celebrity culture in particular.[67]

Despite these acts of disassociation, dustjacket quotes exclaim that 'STAR is more than a novelisation of Pammy's life. It *is* Pammy'.[68] As Lee argues, 'readers are burdened with the knowledge that prior to the text, there exists a celebrity who shares that proper name; and they must practice severe and, perhaps, a little unnatural restraint to prevent themselves from reading that signature in light of the real body signified by that same proper name'.[69] Sufficiently explicit parallels are made to seduce readers into reading Star as Anderson, as they know her through other gossip media. For example, Anderson gained widespread fame playing CJ in *Baywatch* (1991), Star as BeeGee in *Lifeguards*. Where Anderson married Tommy Lee from *Mötley Crüe;* Star marries Jimi Deeds of *Fools Brigade*. Anderson starred in her first feature film as action hero *Barb Wire* (1996) and has a tattoo of barbed wire around her bicep. After landing the role as *Hy Voltz*, Star celebrates with a tattoo of electric cable in the same spot. This wordplay offers an extra level of enjoyment for the engaged Anderson fan, inviting them to feel pleased to have spotted the in-joke, whilst offering permission to read the character Star for insights

---

[63] Joyce Wadler, 'Boldface Names,' *The New York Times*, 10 August 2004.

[64] 'Pamela Anderson Is the Shameless Ploy of the Week,' *Entertainment Weekly*, 16 July 2004.

[65] Anderson (2006), back cover.

[66] Timothy Dow Adams, *Telling Lies in Modern American Autobiography* (Chapel Hill and London: University of North Carolina Press, 1990), p. 3.

[67] Lee, p. 1259.

[68] Anderson (2006), back cover.

[69] Lee, p. 1259.

into the real woman they know from extratextual celebrity media. Thus, whilst they create space for acknowledgement of the performance and fabrication that go into the construction of celebrity identity, Anderson's texts still function according to the *economics of access* and its search for a 'real' woman behind the public image.

In *How to Make Love Like a Porn Star*, Jameson adopts various modes of life writing within a single text, segueing between first-person retro-spective address, interview transcripts, childhood diary pages, graphic novel, 'how to' instruction lists and a great number of old photographs from Jameson's porn career, amongst other artefacts. Nonetheless, the book opens with an introductory page dedicated to claiming the truth status of its contents:

> For years, in private, I wrestled with myself. The truth won. The following, then, is a true story... Only some names and identifying features of individuals have been changed in order to preserve their anonymity and protect their innocence. In addition, some characters are composites, and one movie title has been changed.[70]

And yet, by stressing the truth, Jameson invokes the possibility of lying. The caveats above are sufficiently broad to cover anything from insignificant tweaks to fundamental fabrications. This, however, does little to interrupt the model of reading offered. The memoir is still judged by its ability to offer 'access' to the revealed woman as evidenced by reviews such as *Salon.com*'s claim that 'in this book, Jameson gets you rooting for her ... a real person comes through in its pages'.[71] This is despite the fact that Jameson's memoir offers a further variation in models of identifying the ghostwriter and their role. Unlike Price and Anderson's memoirs' (at least partial) claim to a singular author, the authorial signature states 'Jenna Jameson with Neil Strauss', whilst the back cover of the paperback edition lists his other co-authored celebrity memoirs and his bestselling manuals for male 'pick-up artists' including *The Game* (2005). Alongside his career as a journalist and ghostwriter, Strauss worked in

[70] Jameson.

[71] Charles Taylor, '"How to Make Love Like a Porn Star" by Jenna Jameson,' *Salon.com*, 25 August 2004.

the 'pick-up artist' community, training men at 'bootcamps' in predatory techniques of sexual 'escalation' such as 'negging': a tactic of strategically damaging a woman's self-esteem so that she will concede to having sex. *The Game* offers a 10 step programme to coerce women into sex with chapters such as 'Isolate the Target', 'Extract to a Seduction Location', 'Pump Buying Temperature', and 'Blast Last-Minute Resistance'.[72] In publicity interviews, Strauss has stated that the publisher brought him and Jameson together,[73] so it is impossible to be certain what Jameson knew of her ghostwriter's side-line. However, the choice of such a figure, known for successfully commoditising predatory masculinity, to ghost-write a traumatic personal history as a repeated victim of sexual violence adds additional complexity to the ethical questions raised around who has the *author*ity to interpret the meaning of certain events.

Despite these modal variations, all of these memoirs are presented as authentic personal narratives, trading in the *economics of access* as they enable readers to better know the woman 'behind' the star image. If the ghostwriter is hidden, their presence is presumed (doubting, as we do, the celebrity's literary capabilities). Yet, if the ghostwriter's presence is highlighted, the text is still, nonetheless, judged by whether it succeeds in giving the feeling of access to an essential self of the star-author, thus erasing the known ghost. Contemporary celebrity is consumed with an 'ironic knowingness'.[74] Simultaneously admiring the star, and acknowledging that she is a 'fabricated, performed image', the knowing audience member can 'avoid becoming the sucker' without having to disavow the celebrity-gazing that they enjoy.[75] Thus, despite the visible mediations of ghostwritten memoir, or the assumption of performance that surrounds any life lived on display, the 'glamour girl' memoir presents itself as offering access to the woman behind the image, real or otherwise.

---

[72] Neil Strauss, *The Game: Penetrating the Secret Society of Pick-Up Artists* (New York: HarperCollins, 2005).

[73] Jill Singer, 'So What Do You Do, Neil Strauss?' *MediaBistro.com*, 17 August 2004.

[74] Joshua Gamson, 'The Assembly Line of Greatness: Celebrity in Twentieth Century America,' in *Stardom and Celebrity*, p. 151.

[75] Ibid., p. 152.

The ghostwriters of celebrities have been variously theorised as 'outranked' scribes,[76] as ethnographers studying 'from above,'[77] and as 'harmless imposter[s] in the hallowed halls of autobiography'.[78] As G. Thomas Couser observes, 'ethical dilemmas seem to be inherent to collaborative life-writing in ways that are peculiar to it'.[79] For Couser, the 'liabilities of collaboration' centre around the fair representation of the subject.[80] For Lee, the ethical questions of ghostwriting lie in attribution and concerns of erased labour.[81] I propose a further ethical consideration, independent of the evident perplexities of attribution, labour or fair representation.

In the packaging and sale of stories of abuse as entertainment, these texts encourage the reader to acknowledge mediation and gain comfort that none of it is *really* real, thus enabling guilt-free consumption. These texts construct a subject position for the reader in which it is possible to simultaneously gain pleasure from the knowledge that the person they are reading about exists beyond the text and contradictorily find refuge from being implicated in the commoditisation of harm by reading them as fabrications. The presence of the ghostwriter, along with conventional wisdom about stars as manufactured, fabricated identities, allows readers to consume celebrity memoirs about abuse from a distance. Of course, it is not possible to determine the degree to which these memoirs are 'true' or 'accurate' testimonies of their authors' sexual histories. Autobiographical truth is a vexed question in itself,[82] independent of questions of celebrity agency and manufacture. However, it is important to note that these texts are sold as non-fiction, or at least a blending of fiction with autobiographical fact. When best-selling books[83] are constructed in ways

---

[76] Couser (1998).

[77] Lejeune, p. 199.

[78] Lee, p. 1256.

[79] G. Thomas Couser, *Vulnerable Subjects* (Ithaca: Cornell University Press, 2004), p. 34.

[80] Ibid., p. 55.

[81] Lee.

[82] Spicer, p. 387.

[83] Matthew Miller, 'The (Porn) Player,' *Forbes* magazine, 4 July 2005; Lionel Shriver, 'How Did Glamour Model Jordan Become a Bestselling Author When She Doesn't Even Write?' *Mail Online*, 4 September 2008.

which invite a sceptical reading position towards testimonies of surviving sexual trauma, the credibility of rape victims in the popular imagination is at stake.

Jenna Jameson and Neil Strauss: A Case Study in the Problematics of Ghosting Celebrity Memoir

As porn stars, existing in a mutually reinforcing, connected media web, these authors have an economic investment in sustaining an image of themselves in service of male pleasure. Significantly, so too does Jameson's ghostwriter, Neil Strauss. A man who writes a ten-step bible in how to 'close' with women, one who celebrates 'Cavemanning' ('CAVEMAN— *verb:* to directly and aggressively escalate physical contact, and progress toward sex')[84] brings a particular perspective to co-writing, for example, Jameson's Ten Commandments of Oral Sex. Indeed, such a co-author brings a particular perspective to the decision to include such a list (the advice in which, for example, 'VIII: Honour the Scrotum,' assumes oral sex is only given by women and received by men for male plea-sure).[85] Meagan Tyler argues that sexual self-help literature in general, despite adopting pseudo-feminist language, 'promotes the (active) sexual servicing of men by women' and thus should be understood as 'advocating the sex of prostitution as an ideal for women to follow'.[86] Whilst Tyler is at risk of making conservative assumptions that preclude the possibility of 'topping from the bottom',[87] these memoirs do similarly consistently construct a universe founded upon conservative, heterosexual relations: despite being sold as female-authored narratives of sexual desire, they primarily promote the sexual interests of men and position the sexual role of women as one of sexual service, a feature I shall later discuss in detail.

As a career ghostwriter keen to associate himself with the success of Jameson's book, it is not surprising that in promotional articles Strauss

---

[84] Strauss (2005), p. 440.

[85] Jameson, p. 109.

[86] Meagan Tyler, 'Sex Self-help Books: Hot Secrets for Great Sex or Promoting the Sex of Prostitution?' *Women's Studies International Forum* 31 (2008) 363–72, p. 363.

[87] This phrase from a queer sexual lexicon proposes that penetration is not the sine qua non of sex and dominance and refers to occasions where the ostensible subordinate instigates and directs sexual play.

would emphasise his agency and creative control, for example, describing his role as telling 'the stories the way Jenna would tell them, if she were a writer'.[88] However, comparison between her memoir and his book, *The Game*, reveals telling similarities. Conflating nudity and confession, Jameson's introductory page before the contents asserts 'The following, then, is a true story. It is more naked than I have ever allowed myself to be seen'.[89] Strauss has a near identical page before the contents which claims 'The following is a true story. [...] Naked, vulnerable and disturbingly real'.[90] The use of the same sentence reveals the imprint of, not only Strauss' labour, but, also, his personal stylistic preferences and turn of phrase. Reviewers have commented on the unexpected literary references Jameson makes when describing sex on porn sets, suggesting that 'the Russian literature reference might seem odd' when Jameson states of a porn co-star that 'trying to maintain eye contact with him was like trying to read Dostoyevsky on a roller-coaster'.[91] Meanwhile, Strauss' *The Game* opens with a quote from Dostoyevsky's *Notes from the Underground*. These similarities of idiom and reference support Strauss' claims of creative control.

As Hester contends in her arguments about the displacement of sex in an ever-expanding range of material that is termed 'pornographic', sex and violence occupy the same space of 'incoherent blending of affective responses'[92] and thus both are together utilised here to titillate readers and stimulate prurient interest in the confessions of the celebrity author-subject. Foucault casts confession as a technology of power and a form of subjugation, internalising and superseding disciplinary power structures. However, for Freud, the other important theorist of confession of the twentieth century, confession—the divulgence of traumatic, often sexual, memories—constituted the curative path to psychic liberation.[93]

---

[88] Singer (2004).

[89] Jameson.

[90] Strauss (2005).

[91] Jane Stern and Michael Stern, '"How to Make Love like a Porn Star": Lovers and Other Strangers,' *The New York Times*, 5 September 2004.

[92] Hester, p. 91.

[93] Sigmund Freud, *Three Essays on Sexuality* (trans. James Strachey; London: Hogarth Press, [1905] 1962).

Strauss describes receiving Jameson's testimony as an affecting experience for himself as he witnesses her relive her trauma:

> She ended up sharing things she'd never told anyone before. When we stopped the tape, we were both totally shaken. She couldn't even sleep that night. The interview sessions were very intense. She had to take a lot of cigarette breaks.[94]

This positions the ghostwriting process in the therapeutic tradition in which, in Butler's terms, 'no one has ever worked through an injury without repeating it'.[95] It also acts as paratextual promotional material, promising that hitherto unheard secrets will be revealed—the primary currency for the celebrity memoir and the *economics of access*. In this account, Jameson's affective response to the process is offered as authentication. Boyle argues that the porn industry demonstrates an investment in stories of harm to its female stars: 'That porn can be profoundly damaging to women is now part of the story the industry tells about itself, to itself (and its actual consumers)'.[96] If this is the case, then the traumatic nature of these revelations must be seen as an important part of the promotional appeal. Thus, whilst these memoirs, and the confessional interactions that produce them, are framed within Freudian, therapeutic terms, the Foucauldian accountability to wider structures is also evident. These two modes of confession thus operate together. Confession is here presented, and perhaps indeed experienced, as self-affirming and freely given in the Freudian mould. It is possible that this, again, functions to positivise the confessed traumas and reassure the audiences who consume them. However, as shall be discussed in more detail in the following chapter, the presence of multiple layers of interlocutors, along with generic, gendered and market expectations, make a Foucauldian consideration of the power dynamics at play the more productive model for the confessional practices of the glamour girl memoir as they can here be seen to also be coaxed and coached, if not explicitly coerced.

---

[94] Singer (2004).

[95] Judith Butler, *Excitable Speech: A Politics of the Performative* (New York: Routledge, 1997), p. 102.

[96] Boyle, p. 601.

Just as the gonzo porn director frames the violent action in the films in which Jameson stars, her male ghostwriter claims to control how her testimony of traumatic life events is told:

> The stories in the book were so dark and heavy that I thought it needed a lighter, more fun element. So, I talked to Bernard Chang, one of the artists who works on Batman for DC Comics. He had done some animation for a short I co-directed. So, I gave him the text for those sections, and he drew the comics.[97]

Usually one can only infer the roles of ghost and celebrity author-subject, and, paratextual material such as Strauss' interview should also be read sceptically, operating as it does with a specific promotional agenda. Nevertheless, the fact that he intervenes to transform 'dark and heavy' experiences into 'fun' is telling despite, or perhaps especially because of, its promotional role. The three events that are thus presented as 'lighter' 'fun' are lists of injuries sustained whilst working in strip clubs, relationships with controlling, parasitic men (called 'suitcase pimps'), and a period of being contractually forced to have sex with her ex-husband. The need to make such experiences less 'dark' shows the work of the ghostwriter in this genre as finding ways to offer up authenticated pain whilst making trauma palatable for a paying audience.

NAKEDNESS VS. EXPOSURE: CONSENT AND THE 'SNATCH'

We have seen pornography and autobiography's shared obsession with the 'real', and how the mediating presence of the ghostwriter compounds assumptions about the constructedness of the celebrity life in ways which interact problematically with the truth claims of the testimonies of surviving sexual violence narrated within. A further way in which these memoirs make a thematic feature of constructedness is in the writing of the 'glamour girl' body. Emphasis upon the constructedness of trauma survivors' bodies serves to mitigate potential readerly discomfort in knowing that real bodies must bear the consequences of the experiences related.

Both pornography and autobiography offer documents of embodied experience. In the field of porn studies, Joan Mason-Grant argues against

[97] Singer (2004).

the possibility of separation between 'pornographic meaning-ideas [and] the embodied realm'.[98] From the perspective of autobiography, Sidonie Smith similarly argues for the centrality of materiality: 'the autobiographical subject carries a history of the body with her as she negotiates the autobiographical 'I,'... the history of the body intersects with the deployment of subjectivity'.[99] The centrality of the bodies of Price, Anderson, and Jameson to both their celebrity and their memoirs is clear: the experiences related are inherently embodied and, as we shall see, these texts centre on their author-subjects' bodies as surfaces. Feminist scholarship on the body has been concerned with this apparent duality; debates have surrounded the idea of the female body as surface inscription versus affective embodiment.[100] The 'irreducibility between the subject and object' and the complexity of the relationship between body and self means that embodied female experience cannot be straightforwardly understood either simply as a passive surface on which cultural meanings are inscribed, nor as a natural physical foundation.[101] Rather, 'the self-body relation' must be understood as interrelated and complex.[102]

The examples given in this section demonstrate that these memoirs share a concern with the surface of bodies but less investment in depicting the inherent complexity contained within. Indeed, they work to simplify bodily experience and reduce it to its specularity. A repetitive fixation in the memoirs on (what the memoirs call) 'fake' breasts and waxed pubic hair carries the imprint of the visual codes of pornography. They evoke the visual images for which the celebrity is famous and so compensate for the dominance of text in her memoir. This can be seen in the colour photographs of the (naked body of the) celebrity author-subject which feature prominently on the covers and throughout these texts.

---

[98] Joan Mason-Grant, *Pornography Embodied: From Speech to Sexual Practice* (Lanham, MD and Oxford: Rowman & Littlefield, 2004), p. 14.

[99] Sidonie Smith, *Subjectivity, Identity and the Body: Women's Autobiographical Practices in the Twentieth Century* (Bloomington: Indiana University Press, 1993), p. 23.

[100] Shelley Budgeon, 'Theorizing Subjectivity and Feminine Embodiment: Feminist Approaches and Debates,' *Handbook of Children and Youth Studies*, 30 January 2015, pp. 243–56; Shelley Budgeon, 'Identity as an Embodied Event,' *Body & Society* 9.1 (London, Thousand Oaks, and New Delhi: Sage, 2003), 35–55.

[101] Budgeon (2003), p. 35.

[102] Budgeon (2015), p. 243.

The star images of Anderson, Jameson and Price are closely associated with their naked bodies. As Ruth Barcan argues, nudity has become a powerful shorthand signifying different meanings in different contexts. For example, both sex and honesty.[103] In *Star Struck*, honesty takes the form of 'naked sincerity'.[104] When Jameson promises in her memoir's opening pages, 'It is more naked than I have ever allowed myself to be seen' next to a photograph of her removing her underwear, she conjoins the discourses of physical and emotional exposure in the symbol of her naked body. The revelation of personal secrets is positioned as a continuation of sexualised striptease: one which goes further than Jameson's day job as 'porn star', but which, nonetheless, exists on the same continuum. Celebrity memoir (along with much gossip media) is the commodification of access to personal stories endowed with the appearance of something private being shared. The 'glamour girl' memoir locates this dynamic within the literalising commodity logic of pornography, showing the overlapping appeals in an *economics of access* on the basis of both exposed bodies and selves.

The combined effect of the frequent release of new memoirs and repeated celebrity appearances across an assemblage of women's magazines, social media and TV chat shows is that female celebrities appear to be in a perpetual state of 'revealing all'. In *Being Jordan*, Price says, 'it's time to talk about my biggest assets, the ones that have put me in the papers more than anything else: my boobs'.[105] The glamour girl genre creates parameters for the types of discourse though which she narrates herself as she depicts her naked body as her primary commodity to be carefully managed and traded as the key to fortune and success.

Even after a transition from media targeting men to media targeting women, their naked bodies are still integral to their brand. In the *economics of access*, female celebrities may transition between audiences as long as they bare themselves one way or another. Anderson's protagonist spends most of the novel naked: 'it was stranger for the pair to be dressed in each other's company than nude'.[106] Whenever Star's experience of her body is narrated, it is in terms of arousal: 'the feeling of her own skin was awesome, not to mention the sensation of her hand touching her naked

---

[103] Ruth Barcan, *Nudity: A Cultural Anatomy* (Oxford: Berg, 2004).

[104] Anderson (2006), p. 81.

[105] Price (2005), p. 89.

[106] Anderson (2006), p. 63.

breasts'.[107] Emphasis on the 'naturalness' of her naked state, and on her constant arousal, works to naturalise the objectification of the character, Star.

Adam Knee observes the 'fundamentally voyeuristic' impulses whereby celebrity nudes 'render *all* stars as porn stars' offering the bare body 'as a crucial site of authenticity'.[108] Accordingly, in the accounts offered of these authors' public images, nudity and exposure are confused: 'She felt so naked,' describes *Star Struck*... 'It wasn't just that she didn't have any clothes on. She felt vulnerable—raw and exposed'.[109] As with Jameson's confessional 'striptease' which begins in her dayjob, for Anderson's protagonist, posing naked is banal and workaday, rendering nudity something other than the absence of clothes. A career in the *economics of access* depends on both nakedness and exposure. This leaves the unwillingly overexposed star in what Ruth Barcan calls the 'odd predicament as a victim torn between moral distress and economic gain',[110] where those two pillars of her agency, nakedness and exposure, are conditioned through the lens of vulnerability.

In a world of perpetual performance, the last shred of privacy becomes the essence of the self: 'What's left to hide?' Star is asked. "Me,' she said simply. 'The part I save for myself'.[111] The hunt for the last shred of privacy feeds a whole media economy of unauthorised exposés. Paparazzi lie (often literally) ready to pounce upon a glimpse of crotch during an unguarded exit from a taxi; magazines, newspapers and gossip blogs circulate these images with their (often unfavourable) added commentary judging their unruly bodies and appetites[112]; and adult websites reveal the rest in 'leaked' sex tapes.[113] Knee observes that all other criteria can fall by the wayside 'as long as there is a seemingly unauthorised glimmer

---

[107] Ibid., p. 36.

[108] Adam Knee, 'Celebrity Skins: The Illicit Textuality of the Celebrity Nude Magazine' *Framing Celebrity*, pp. 162, 168, 169.

[109] Anderson (2006), p. 4.

[110] Barcan (2004), p. 247.

[111] Anderson (2006) p. 50.

[112] 'Katie Flashes The Photogs A Smile Her Panties!' *Perezhilton.com*, 11 February 2011.

[113] 'Pamela Anderson and Tommy Lee Sex Tape,' 1995.

of skin'.[114] The production of images of these women's bodies strad-dles consent and violation where the last shred of privacy becomes highly prized prey.

Celebrity memoir offers an opportunity to speak back to this ecosystem. Presenting her own celebrity selfhood as a commodity, her protagonist says of a paparazzi photographer:

> He has [...] pictures of me walking the dog, on the set, having lunch with friends, on dates, kissing, holding my mother's hand. He even has pictures of me sleeping. It's like he's stealing my life. Not the part that we all give to the world, but the part I keep for me.[115]

In this construction, Star's image is her selfhood, her private life the part with the highest exchange value, and like any other currency or commodity of great value, it can be stolen. This chimes with industry lingo, as journalists and photographers refer to shots taken without consent—usually as a celebrity leaves the building—as 'snatches', an exceptionally gendered term uncomfortably combining theft and a slang reference to women's genitals (regardless of which part of the woman's body is the subject of the photograph).[116]

WRITING THE 'GLAMOUR GIRL' BODY: 'WELL HELLO! I ADMIT THAT I'M FAKE'

Intervention into the *economics of access* is still participation in it. Although celebrity memoirs provide an opportunity to respond to the assemblage of images circulated in the media against these women's will, the representations within the memoirs closely correlate with the paparazzi images of their authors seen on both men's and women's maga-zines. Breasts, specifically *'fake'* breasts, are presented as the *real* stars of the glamour girl memoir, and are endowed with agency beyond that of their owners, narrated with humour and an emphasis on empowered 'choice' which smooth over the fact that 'accounts of the porn industry— however celebratory they may be—are frequently littered with the debris

---

[114] Knee, p. 169.

[115] Anderson (2006), p. 50.

[116] Scott Douglas, 'Baffled Tony Marsh Gets a View from the Other End of the Lens,' 12 March 2008.

of other women's lives'.[117] At the same time, this approach veils the structures which demand specific bodily norms.

Price informs her readers that 'bigger is definitely better when it comes to breasts'[118] and wants to live in L.A. because there 'boob jobs are just a part of life'.[119] Her own breast enlargement made her 'even more famous and brought [...] even more work. The silicone-enhanced Jordan has been in constant demand'.[120] Price presents herself as a good postfeminist, neoliberal subject conducting the necessary labour of transformative 'beauty work'[121]: making money from her body through continuous work on her body.[122] Further, by building a celebrity persona closely associated with cosmetic surgery and frequently *having work done*,[123] Price secures work and income. By writing memoirs offering a commentary on, or 'story behind', these procedures, she is able to maximise this body work to its fullest commercial potential.

The idea of physical appearance as literal currency is not new. As Naomi Wolf argues, histories of bourgeois marriage markets have taught women to understand their own beauty as part of the economy. Thus, as a society we have become perfectly 'accustomed to having beauty evaluated as wealth'.[124] More recently, rapid expansion of a lucrative medical sector has worked to valorise cosmetic surgery as positive self-perfection. Diane Negra observes 'promotional rhetoric that (re)assures female clients that they are demonstrating agency and self-management when they avail themselves of such services rather than capitulating to regressive (sometimes misogynistic) appearance norms'.[125] These narratives of beauty work as agency, self-making and currency are

[117] Boyle, p. 599.

[118] Price (2005), p. 97.

[119] Ibid., p. 194.

[120] Ibid., p. 97.

[121] Evans and Riley, p. 276.

[122] Ibid., p. 268.

[123] Olivia Foster, 'From a 32C to a 32G, and Back Again! How 16 YEARS of Cosmetic Surgery Gave Katie Price the Most Famous Boobs in the Country,' *Daily Mail*, 8 December 2014.

[124] Naomi Wolf, *The Beauty Myth: How Images of Beauty Are Used Against Women* (New York: Anchor Books, 1992), p. 20.

[125] Diane Negra, *What a Girl Wants? Fantasizing the Reclamation of Self in Postfeminism* (London and New York: Routledge, 2009), p. 121.

accepted as givens and further literalised in the 'glamour girl' memoir universe.

Of Price's trip to the Playboy mansion, she says, 'I had been nervous that Hugh's bunnies might not like me. But I needn't have worried. [...] They were totally fascinated by my boobs'.[126] Social success takes the form of having fascinating boobs, large ones leading to the greatest endorsement: 'They [...] couldn't get over how big they were, and how natural looking. I took it as a real compliment: they've seen enough of these things to be real connoisseurs!'[127] In their power to determine where a woman lives, the success of her career and how she relates to both men and other women, *Being Jordan* portrays breasts, specifically big, 'fake' breasts, as central to women's existence. Breasts are work, capital, conversation, curios—anything *but* sexual. What is presented as a discourse of sex is, rather, a matter of work—performed by and upon the body.

This emphasis is matched in Anderson's *Star Struck*. In its opening sentence, we are introduced to the protagonist's breasts before we meet the woman herself, literally putting breasts first and foremost in the story of her life:

> Why do my nipples hurt? was Star's first thought as she woke from a strangely deep sleep, her hands gliding along her naked body to the tender nipples that had awakened her. She winced as she made contact, realizing only belatedly that she was naked.[128]

Star is characterised primarily by her breasts. Indeed, they are given agency enough to wake her from a strangely deep sleep. Like Price, breasts are similarly credited with agency over Star's destiny as her friend charts their centrality to her career trajectory: 'They got you the job at Mother's. They got you the standing ovation at the Dolphin's game. They got you the job with Zax. And they got you on the cover of *Mann* magazine'.[129] Throughout the memoir, the character treats her breasts, and the arousal

---

[126] Price (2005), p. 207.

[127] Ibid.

[128] Anderson (2006), p. 1.

[129] Anderson (2004), pp. 314–15.

they cause her, as a continual reference point to the action. A woman's breasts are a separate entity with their own life story to tell.

In the perfect synthesis of three hallmarks of postfeminism—emphasis on consumer choice, self-sexualisation and self-improvement through work on the body—Anderson's protagonist marvels at what she perceives as the control afforded her by the cosmetic surgery: 'Nipple placement. I can decide'.[130] Even thirty years ago, Kathryn Morgan was arguing that the rhetoric of empowered 'choice' surrounding cosmetic surgery emerges as thinly veiled 'necessity'.[131] This negotiation between individual agency and obedience to social norms typifies the 'contradictions of the rhetoric of choice that the postfeminist woman grapples with: what looks like individual empowerment, agency and self-determination can also signal conformity and docility'.[132] The tension between power and powerlessness is especially pertinent to this passage of *Star* because, whilst the text heavily emphasises Star's power and freedom to choose, the breast augmentation occurs at the request of the Editor of Playboy magazine (here renamed *Mann magazine*), and at the expense of a wealthy former boyfriend.

Jameson humorously recalls the time that she 'bought two cakes (one for each implant) [and] threw a birthday party for my boobs'.[133] Disembodied breasts with a life of their own are presented to the reader as the true stars in the glamour girl memoir genre. It is hard to imagine celebrities throwing parties for their large, natural breasts, suggesting that the celebration itself is a function of their constructedness. These authors speak with knowing humour about the artificiality of their appearance, ascribing positive value to the fake aesthetic: 'Natural beauty takes at least two hours in front of a mirror', says Anderson,[134] subverting cultural discourses in which constructed beauty is 'de-valued for being

---

[130] Ibid., p. 314.

[131] Kathryn Pauly Morgan, 'Women and the Knife,' *Hypatia* 6.3 (1991), 25–53, p. 26 (emphasis in original).

[132] Stéphanie Genz and Benjamin A. Brabon, *Postfeminism: Cultural Texts and Theories* (Edinburgh: Edinburgh University Press), p. 151.

[133] Jameson, p. 170.

[134] Sager (2004).

made visible', and thereby revealing the necessity for effort.[135] Price, meanwhile, credits Anderson for inspiration: 'I like the "fake" look: big hair, big make-up, big boobs. Pamela Anderson has the perfect figure as far as I'm concerned',[136] admitting that her persona involves a degree of impersonation of a prior referent.

Butler argues that 'gender is a persistent impersonation that passes for the real and destabilises distinctions between natural and artificial'.[137] Price often refers to her modelling persona, Jordan, with the use of a second name, as a performance: 'up until my appearance on *I'm a Celebrity* the public only really knew me as Jordan and probably thought that was the only role I could play'.[138] Butler argues that becoming gendered is a process of interpreting cultural norms constituted of both choices and restrictions: 'the choice to assume a certain kind of body, to live and wear one's body a certain way, implies a world of already established corporeal styles' in which the natural body is increasingly suspect.[139] Cosmetic surgery is central to the Jordan persona, and Price's open embrace of this upturns traditional discourses in the gossip media where female stars are 'outed' for attempting to conceal the 'work' done on their bodies. In her (potentially ironically titled?) fourth memoir, *You Only Live Once*, she exclaims, 'Journalists write that I'm so fake. Well hello! I *admit* that I'm fake'.[140]

Here, Price can be seen to be embracing artifice in a camp performance of exaggerated femininity, demonstrating the incongruity, theatricality and humour that Esther Newton's foundational ethnography of drag queens identifies as the qualities of gender impersonation.[141] Unlike the drag queens in Newton's sample, Price performs femininity as a cisgender woman, and yet such theatrical exaggeration can nonetheless be understood to be 'performing the social character of "women" (that is, the signs

---

[135] Bev Skeggs, *Class, Self, Culture* (London: Routledge, 2003), p. 101.

[136] Price (2005), p. 91.

[137] Butler (1990), p. x.

[138] Katie Price, *A Whole New World* (London: Century, 2006), pp. 40–41.

[139] Judith Butler, 'Sex and Gender in Simone de Beauvoir's Second Sex,' *Yale French Studies* 72 (1986), 35–49, p. 40.

[140] Katie Price, *You Only Live Once* (London: Century, 2010), p. 20.

[141] Esther Newton, *Mother Camp: Female Impersonators in America* (Chicago: University of Chicago Press, 1972), p. 107.

and symbols of a socially defined ... category) by artificially creating the image of glamorous women'.[142] Bruce LaBruce calls this 'a performative femininity by females filtered through drag queens'.[143]

On the one hand, this openness about the 'fakeness' of her body can be seen as transgressing traditional patriarchal feminine codes of middle-class respectability which, as Bev Skeggs argues, valorise the appearance of 'natural' beauty.[144] For Skeggs, the politics of respectability are always at play in the confessional or autobiographical acts of working-class women, as she explains: 'Different techniques of telling enable the attribution of the "self" to different groups; for the working-class, it always had to be a way of displaying respectability'.[145] Price's overt rejection of discourses of propriety, and absence of reticence about purchasing beauty through multiple cosmetic surgeries, could be seen to be a rebellion against the politics of respectability at play in celebrity culture. Tracing the historical discursive construction of respectability, Skeggs observes, 'respectability entailed moral rectitude, economic continence and self-sufficiency; in short, a distillation of evangelical disciplines. [...] In any definition of respectability, sexuality lurks beneath the inscription. For instance, prostitution, as the constitutive limit to propriety'.[146] Price's celebrity revels in a space beyond this limit, performing a plastic, worked-for, constructed femininity that acts as a constant referent to her career origins in soft-core porn modelling. This, alongside the sexual 'confessions' that make up much of the 'glamour girl' memoir, transgresses the respectability politics of gendered celebrity. As Smith and Watson argue, women's sexual autobiography 'exploits and flaunts norms of gendered modesty about self-disclosure, testing the limits of decorum that women artists confront'.[147]

---

[142] Rosemary J. Coombe, 'Author/Izing the Celebrity: Publicity Rights, Postmodern Politics, and Unauthorized Genders,' *Cardozo Arts and Entertainment Law Journal* 10 (1992), 365–95, p. 380.

[143] Bruce LaBruce, 'Notes on Camp/Anti-Camp,' *Nat.Brut.*

[144] Skeggs (2003), p. 101.

[145] Ibid., p. 123.

[146] Ibid., p. 38.

[147] Smith and Watson (2002), p. 4.

And yet, whilst in this regard these memoirs could be argued to be a mode of resistance to these norms, they work equally hard to rein-scribe them. Indeed, in the assemblage of cross-promotion, there is a clear commercial logic to the packaging and sale of the sexual confessions of porn stars alongside a narration of the appearance of their synec-dochal 'bigger,' 'better' breasts.[148] If self-making and brand-building overlap in celebrity memoir, this emphasis can be seen as reinforcing the link between the memoirs and the extratextual identities of their porn star author-subjects. Foucault argues that, within a regime of 'power-knowledge-pleasure', offering up a sexual confession imbues one with the 'speaker's benefit'; 'the mere fact that one is speaking about it has the appearance of deliberate transgression'.[149] This appearance of trans-gression is integral to the appeal of celebrity memoir in the *economics of access* and the types of stories people may expect when purchasing a memoir. Skeggs argues that 'a residue of value remains, one that makes those at the constitutive limit potentially much more exciting than those valued through [...] respectability'.[150] Thus, whilst Price, Anderson, and Jameson's memoirs may appear to be resisting the gendered politics of respectability in their preoccupations with narrating the female body, this aspect is ultimately a norm of its own, in service of commercial appeal. If these texts offer a 'confession of the flesh'[151] it is of the appearance, over the experience, of their bodies.

'Simplified and Made Visible': Public Privates and the Performance of Extreme Femininity

The genre of celebrity memoir and the *economics of access* demand that celebrities reveal personal information in an act of 'making a private history public'.[152] In a move which both eroticises and literalises privacy, these women have responded to that demand by narrating their 'pri-vates'. Historically, pre-Enlightenment ideas of 'assessing the status of the soul or the meaning of public achievement' have been integral to

---

[148] Price (2005), p. 97.
[149] Foucault (1978), p. 6.
[150] Skeggs (2003), p. 39.
[151] Foucault, p. 6.
[152] McLennan, p. 7.

the development of the autobiography genre and presumptions about what autobiography is *for*.[153] The prominence of 'fake' breasts and waxed pubices in this space subverts such generic expectations and/or communicates that these atomised body parts are deemed sufficiently integral to these authors' identity to feature heavily in their life story. These memoirs consistently assert that pubic hair must be removed or, at the very least, discouraged. For Price 'it's either all off, or there's a minimal landing strip. [She is] in the all-off camp in case you were wondering'.[154] Anderson's protagonist explains, 'I don't really have any... Just naturally, and I don't encourage what's there'.[155] Jameson even has her own line of branded intimate hair removal products.[156] Through waxing, the object of desire is to be laid bare, arguably the role of memoir, also.

Relating a scene from her time staying at Hugh Hefner's *Playboy* mansion, Price browses a corridor of pictures of former 'playmates' with pubic hair, like an archaeologist perusing a peculiar relic of a bygone era: 'In the seventies a full bush was all the rage'.[157] Anderson's protagonist states that the publisher of her nude images, 'has a thing about pussy hair. It's his little kink—I guess he misses the seventies'.[158] Whilst not made explicit, there is a specific subtext invoked; as they recoil from the seventies as a phase of backward sexual etiquette, they distance themselves from second-wave feminism and, with it, from a model of womanhood that is complex, demanding and seeks parity with men.

One of the more obvious significations of body hair is that of a marker of sexual maturity. The rejection of this corresponds with the wider postfeminist trend in which adult women are 'made safe by being represented as fundamentally still a girl'.[159] These memoirs designate pubic hair as anathema to femininity and position their authors as more innately feminine (and thus desirable) than other women—even in farcical extremes:

[153] Smith and Watson (2001), p. 2.

[154] Price (2005), p. 192.

[155] Anderson (2006), p. 94.

[156] 'Jenna Jameson Hair Hot Trimmer Shaver,' *Amazon.com*.

[157] Price (2005), p. 192.

[158] Anderson (2006), p. 94.

[159] Yvonne Tasker and Diane Negra, 'In Focus: Postfeminism and Contemporary Media Studies,' *Cinema Journal* 44.2 (2005), 107–10, p. 109.

> They brought in this little old man who specialised in making fake beards and mustaches, and I had to lie on a table like I was at the doctor's office while this poor little man crawled between my legs and glued crepe hair onto me.[160]

The extremity of Anderson's protagonist's innate desirability is underlined by the absurd lengths gone to so that she can be like other women. It is not simply a straightforward investment in the signification of pre-pubescence that mandates the treatment of public hair with disgust. Breasts, after all, are a marker of sexual maturity and their centrality to these texts cannot be overstated. Unlike breasts, an increase in post-puberty body hair is a secondary sexual characteristic that is also shared by men. Thus, the two-part emphasis upon the presence of breasts and the absence of pubic hair constructs femininity in binary opposition to male bodies.[161] With their cosmetically enhanced breasts and their inability to grow pubic hair, this binary logic is mobilised for a performance of feminine identity at its most extreme.

Diane Negra argues pubic hair waxing is 'one of a number of female beauty and exercise trends that originated in pornography' which 'reflects a misogynist belief that female genitalia are excessively complex and need to be simplified and made visible for the comfort and pleasure of a male sex partner'.[162] Even through the written word, these authors' sexuality remains purely specular rather than tactile. As a result, in the 'glamour girl' memoir, female sexuality is safely 'kept within the realm of male visual pleasure'[163] as the authors describe at length the appearance, not their experience, of their genitals. This containment within the parameters set by careers in glamour modelling creates a confusion between telling secrets and revealing bodies. Invested in preserving images of themselves as highly desirable, these texts portray women as a hyper-feminine, heterosexual male fantasy for other women to read. Under these

---

[160] Anderson (2006), p. 95.

[161] Jane Kenway and Elizabeth Bullen, 'Consuming Skin: Dermographies of Female Subjection and Abjection,' *Critical Pedagogies of Consumption: Living and Learning in the Shadow of the "Shopocalypse,"* ed. by Jennifer A. Sandlin and Peter McLaren (New York: Routledge, 2010), pp. 157–68.

[162] Negra (2009), p. 119.

[163] Margaret Schwartz, 'The Horror of Something to See: Celebrity "Vaginas" as Prostheses,' in *In the Limelight*, p. 228.

contradictory investments, memoir, the medium of subjectivity, becomes a tool to reinforce the author-subject's role as object. The performative extremity of femininity that is depicted operates in service of a wider sensibility of fabrication. The claim in these memoirs is that the bodies narrated within them are 'just naturally' suited to the visual conventions of, and therefore a career within, soft-core pornography: hyperbolically, comically, synthetically feminine in the extreme. This works to rationalise, simplify and smooth over the more harrowing aspects of the conflicting accounts of these (at times, very difficult) careers. Bodies that appear but seemingly do not feel are narrated alongside the accounts of sexual violence upon those bodies, as if such a testimony of physical and sexual trauma must be mitigated to ameliorate potential readerly discomfort. To borrow Negra's explanation of the pubic wax, the, often traumatic, embodied experiences of the author-subjects must be 'simplified and made visible for the comfort and pleasure of' the reader.[164]

SERVICE AND HYPERBOLE: THE CONTRADICTIONS OF 'EMPOWERED' FEMALE SEXUALITY

The sheer fact that these memoirs offer accounts of women's sexual desires is significant, existing as they do in a context of historical representational lack.[165] However, they are accounts of female sexuality which primarily place their protagonists in service to male pleasure. This accords with feminist arguments that feminine sexualities have been constructed in subordination to dominant, predatory male sexualities which 'remain a celebrated theme and a commercially successful formula' in contemporary culture.[166] These texts present their author-subjects' sexual subjectivity as the crucial site of their empowerment, building upon their existing star images from the world of porn. Ros Gill argues that the commodification of sexual empowerment has been ultimately enabling for sexist

---

[164] Negra (2009), p. 119.

[165] See Gwynne, p. 6; Butler (1990) p. 14; Simone De Beauvoir ([1949] 2011).

[166] Lynne Jamieson, *Intimacies: Personal Relationships in Modern Societies* (Cambridge: Polity Press, 1988), p. 133.

objectification: 'Empowerment is everywhere [...] emptied of [its] polit-ical force'.[167] The postfeminist sensibility of these memoirs is not least in evidence in their rhetoric of 'empowerment'.

These texts engage directly with questions of personal power. For example, Jameson celebrates the fact that she 'was finally learning to take control of people instead of being so passive'.[168] Price stresses the fact that she is 'strong and independent'.[169] Indeed, she considers herself to be 'much too independent' saying, 'I could never do what someone tells me'.[170] The advice, delivered with gravitas, from the deathbed of Ander-son's protagonist's mother is that 'it's your choice who you are'.[171] Star's husband is surprised by her 'lack of intimidation'[172] when he shouts at her.

At the same time, it is an account of empowerment that is contradic-tory and defined within pre-existing parameters of female subservience. Jameson is 'taking control' by pretending to be sexually interested in men to persuade them to pay for erotic dances. Price is 'too independent' to be one of Hugh Hefner's subservient 'bunny girls'. The fate that Star would have chosen for herself had she not been robbed of the choice would have been to die with her husband to show her devotion. These conceptions of 'empowerment' are certainly, to use Gill's terms, 'emptied' of any femi-nist or political force and, rather, aggressively assert the primacy of men and male pleasure.

Scholarly discussions of female sexual agency range from those who argue for reading self-sexualisation as its own autonomous, authentic and therefore agentic act,[173] to those who argue that sexual agency can only

---

[167] Ibid., p. 743.

[168] Jameson, p. 48.

[169] Ibid., p. 2.

[170] Price (2005), p. 211.

[171] Anderson (2006), p. 212.

[172] Ibid., p. 69.

[173] Linda Duits and Liesbet Van Zoonen, 'Headscarves and Porno-Chic: Disciplining Girls' Bodies in the European Multicultural Society,' *European Journal of Women's Studies* 13.2 (2006), 103–17.

be understood in its relation to structural inequalities and wider coer-
cive contexts.[174] Exemplifying McRobbie's 'postfeminist sexual contract'
where new freedoms are seemingly afforded to women, but kept within
the sexual arena,[175] these memoirs assert that sex is a route to empowerment and agency: 'having sex,' states Katie Price, 'made me feel like I had
power over him'.[176] These memoirs embrace the eroticisation of power.
Rather than a pleasure to be experienced, sex is a tool to be utilised. Price
punishes men for treating her badly by providing sexual gratification:

> I was planning to take my revenge. I was going to shag his brains out one
> last time, make him realise what he was missing. [...] I made sure the sex
> was passionate, intense and totally satisfying – for him at least. [...] I felt
> like a slag but I wanted to torture him. Finally I was free.[177]

Whilst Price relates this anecdote confident that she has used sex to reverse
any power imbalance and that ex-boyfriend, Dane Bowers, is the victim
of the situation, it is questionable whether he is really the injured party
and will be chastened by the experience. Not only does this depiction
construct sex through adversarial power relations, it paradoxically asserts
an increase in Price's power at the very moment that pleasure is one-
sidedly for male benefit and she is shamed for participation.

Star Struck adopts a hyperbolic investment in male pleasure which
is seen as a matter of women's labour. Jimi Deeds is Star's rock star
husband based on Anderson's then real-life husband, Tommy Lee. When
Jimi isn't 'pushing her head down' in the car,[178] Star is 'grin[ning], slipping under the table and taking him in her mouth'[179] during breakfast.
The 'grin' communicates enthusiasm and, as Gwynne argues of postfeminist memoirs of non-famous women, 'the reader is expected to perceive
this as empowering simply because the authors/narrators claim to enjoy

---

[174] Sumi Madhok, *Rethinking Agency: Gender, Development and Rights in North West
India* (New York and London: Routledge, 2010).

[175] Angela McRobbie (2007), p. 718.

[176] Price (2005), p. 28.

[177] Anderson (2004), p. 272.

[178] Ibid., p. 84.

[179] Ibid., p. 66.

these experiences'.[180] Fellatio is a source of pride: 'Star had developed some oral talent over the years'[181] especially with 'big cock she had really honed her skills'.[182] This emphasis on male pleasure as a result of female 'talent' and 'skill' promotes the idea that, for women, sex is work and male pleasure is a form of labour to take pride in. The hyperbolic celebration of male pleasure, symbolised in the enthusiastically performed labour of fellatio, is epitomised in a hot-tub scene which promotes the act as such an achievement that it is worth making the ultimate sacrifice for: 'She took him into her mouth, her head under the water. [...] She almost drowned, but what a way to go'.[183]

Despite the promotion of male pleasure as a site of active female labour, these texts are invested in conservative gender roles of female passivity and male dominance. These authors narrate sex as something done *to* them by men, rather than something people do together. Price says of dating Ralf Schumacher, 'I lay next to him, burning with desire, but I didn't feel able to initiate things myself'.[184] Price describes her sex-life with another partner without any active participation on her part: 'I'd let him have sex with me'.[185] When Star instigates sex, she is slipping under the table and onto her knees in an act of service. By contrast Jimi's agency and power is represented as being tied up in his status as agent of penetration, 'driving himself inside her'.[186] Passages describing the couple's intercourse repeatedly emphasise Jimi's physical power and dominance: he 'drove himself into her with all his force'.[187] As the word is repeated, sex and force become inextricably linked: he 'drove himself mercilessly into her again and again with such force'.[188] *Star Struck* thus presents passionate expression of male sexuality as inherently violent. These scenes demonstrate a model of female sexuality in which a dual fantasy of activity and passivity together serve male pleasure and dominance.

[180] Gwynne, p. 118.

[181] Anderson (2006), p. 84.

[182] Ibid., p. 85.

[183] Ibid., p. 18.

[184] Price (2005), p. 114.

[185] Ibid., p. 28.

[186] Anderson (2006), p. 62.

[187] Ibid., p. 121.

[188] Ibid., p. 92.

In contrast to the skilled labour of fellatio, female sexual gratification is effortlessly instantaneous: 'Star shrieked. The orgasm was instantaneous, swift and fierce. Jimi merely brushed against that most sensitive spot and she went off like a gunshot'.[189] Reinforcing the pornographic paradigm of male convenience, and Star's role as naturalised sex object, her body immediately and intensely rewards Jimi's least efforts at pleasing her: 'As his fingers explored, it just kept happening [...] too numerous to count'[190] In this way, the writing of Star's experience of sex reinforces her status as 'every young boy's fantasy'[191] (to her female audience). In contrast to the skilled labour of fellatio, female sexual gratification is achieved immediately and with ease. For Star, having sex was 'like orgasms came by the gallon and she was drinking too fast'.[192]

Williams defines hardcore pornography as the 'representation of living, moving bodies engaged in explicit, usually unfaked, sexual acts'.[193] However, the impossibility of such promises of access to the 'real' leads to a reciprocal obsession with the fake:

> The woman's ability to fake the orgasm that the man can never fake (at least according to certain standards of evidence) seems to be at the root of all the genre's attempts to solicit what it can never be sure of: the out-of-control confession of pleasure, a hard-core "frenzy of the visible".[194]

In this reading, the absence of external evidence creates the problem of an 'invisible place' for pornography's codes of 'proof'; an invisibility for which pornography must compensate through other means.[195] The testimonies of female porn stars therefore insistently affirm their own sexual satisfaction with emphatic overstatement. Anderson's contradictory account of sex as both physical labour for male pleasure and hyperbolically easy for her own echoes that of porn star Kami Andrews who blogged about her experience on set: 'I ended up doing 2 scenes yesterday [...] In

---

[189] Ibid., p. 40.
[190] Ibid.
[191] Ibid., p. 34.
[192] Ibid., p. 40.
[193] Williams (1989), p. 30.
[194] Ibid., p. 50.
[195] Ibid., pp. 49 and 147.

the first scene my ass tore and there was a fair amount of blood, It was not my best scene by far! The second scene went way smoother and I came a zillion times'.[196] As Boyle argues, despite the first-hand accounts of women in the porn industry playing an important role in debates around pornography and violence, hyperbolic discourses of female arousal locate harm as a result of female sexual failure and thus ultimately serve the interests of the porn industry.[197] The assertion of extreme pleasure and ease in Anderson's ambivalent account, like her insistence that her body hair naturally grows according to the pornographic fashions of the day, both work to sell her as ideally suited to the role of 'glamour girl' and sells glamour modelling as a lifestyle, whilst smoothing over the experiences of harm and exploitation encountered along this career path. Thus, again we see the 'glamour girl' memoir's thematic and formal investments in explicit constructedness functioning in service of permission to read the purported sexual and physical harm of real bodies as light-hearted entertainment.

Whilst it is not surprising that mainstream texts should reproduce the dominant ideas in society, it is significant that they speak for self-authored female sexual desire, performing, as Gwynne posits, a 'reclamation of the first-person sexual,'[198] in an area lacking representation. Gwynne views women's erotic memoir as a genre offering the possibility of 'achieving representational parity in public narratives of sexual expression'[199] in a culture which otherwise eclipses female desire because the 'vocabulary of sex is much more concerned with describing what happens to a man's body during sexual arousal than a woman's'.[200]

It is this representational lack which makes it so significant that some of the most widely read texts authored by women, and the best-selling accounts of the sex-lives of women contained within them, are not necessarily (or at least not solely) authored by women. Whilst, as I have argued, it is problematic and disempowering to automatically conclude that the

[196] Boyle, p. 600.

[197] Ibid.

[198] Gwynne, p. 6.

[199] Ibid.

[200] Diane Richardson, 'Constructing Lesbian Identities' *Feminism and Sexuality: A Reader*, ed. by Stevi Jackson and Sue Scott (Edinburgh: Edinburgh University Press, 1996), p. 279.

presence of a ghostwriter negates the agency of the celebrity author-subject as the popular imagination presumes, it is nonetheless impossible to determine conclusively the extent to which each party controls the resulting life story and its meaning. The result is a narration of a female desire that is sold as true, self-authored confessional whilst presenting female desire as existing to serve male pleasure. This model of sexuality is offered in the historic convention of the instructional guide,[201] and yet if advice from such a guide were followed, the beneficiaries of this model are not the female readers.

Thus, the glamour girl memoir reveals its investment in the porno-graphic field from which its author-subjects originate. In the universe presented, sex, for women, is work: sex is the means and male pleasure is the end. As with the performance of extreme feminine physicality, and the presence of the (sometimes male) ghostwriter, hyperbolic accounts of female pleasure that comes 'by the gallon' feed an undercurrent of constructedness, which, work to undermine the truth claims of these rare accounts of female sexual autobiography. I seek to avoid the bina-rising tendency to cast the author—in either uncomplicatedly liberatory or pessimistically castigatory terms. Rather, I seek to trace the, some-times contradictory, ways in which these texts depict the sexual agency of their authors, both overtly and implicitly. These texts suggest both agentic interjections, for example, redressing criticisms of undeserved fame, and a persistent wider paradigm of male activity and aggression and female passivity and service. What powerfully emerges is the investment these stars have in asserting their individual sexual agency, in ways that aren't seen in the memoirs from celebrities from other fields—for example, claiming that they gain power over men primarily through having sex with them or offering inventories of the economic proceeds of their role in the sex industry. This reflects the cultural anxieties that surround ques-tions of female sexual agency, especially that of women in the sex industry. Thus, in their repeated (if at points shaky) assertions of power, we see the burden of reassurance that is at stake in the life writing of the female porn-star celebrity in particular.

---

[201] Benjamin Franklin, *The Autobiography of Benjamin Franklin* (New York: Dover, 1996 [written between 1771–1790]), p. 1.

Negotiating Cultural Value and Creative Agency

More successfully, these memoirs represent their author-subjects as agentic through their depiction of careers that have required creative input, business acumen and professionalism. In so doing, they run counter to understandings of glamour modelling and of wider female celebrity, in the popular imagination, which associates female celebrities with easy-won rewards that bypass hard work or talent.[202] Perhaps in response to such assumptions, Price's autobiography offers frequent statements which emphasise the labour which goes into her career: 'what I do is called glamour modelling, which makes me laugh because if people knew what went on at a shoot they wouldn't think it was glamorous at all'.[203] As Dyer has established, claims such as Price's, 'I've worked for everything I've got,'[204] are paradigmatic to the star archetype established at least as long ago as classic Hollywood, as reassurances of hard work potentially neutralise audience envy at the unequal distribution of wealth.[205] In this way, memoir offers an opportunity to intervene into the discourses that surround a celebrity. Moreover, I would argue that the emphasis upon the labour of modelling is a riposte to punitive discourses of gendered cultural value[206]—discourses which hinge upon the concept of underserved fame and see Price, for example, categorised as an 'attention seeking'[207] 'fame whore'.[208]

As Holmes notes: 'Jordan is often invoked as the epitome of the worthless nature of contemporary fame'.[209] Memoir offers the appeal of the

[202] Kim Allen, 'Girls Imagining Careers in the Limelight: Social Class, Gender and Fantasies of "Success,"' *In the Limelight*, p. 157.

[203] Price (2005), p. 59.

[204] Ibid., p. 8.

[205] Dyer (1979), p. 7

[206] Geraghty, p. 99; Allen, p. 157.

[207] Owen Tonks, 'Jodie Marsh Predicts Katie Price's Fall from Showbiz as She Slams Her Attention Seeking Ways,' *The Mirror*, 26 March 2013.

[208] 'Katie Price Reveals Her Struggle to Conceive a Child with Alex Reid,' *Perezhilton.com*, 25 October 2010.

[209] Su Holmes, '"Starring... Dyer?" Re-visiting Star Studies and Contemporary Celebrity Culture'. *Westminster Papers in Communication and Culture* 2.2 (2005), 6–21, p. 13.

invitation '"behind-the-scenes" of fame production'[210] by revealing the work that goes into the finished image for an *economics of access*. Moreover, as a medium it offers glamour models a means to legitimise careers which have been stigmatised by hierarchies of value that doubly devalue both the sex industry and female celebrity more generally.

The similarities between the ways in which the three memoirs depict their author-subjects' work are significant. Jameson's memoir features a comic strip called 'Jenna Jameson's Stripper Dancer Injuries 101'[211] and even includes example business contracts for porn actresses.[212] Such inclusions are outside the norms of both autobiography and celebrity memoir and do not appear in any of the reality or pop-star memoirs that are discussed later in this book. Here they serve to emphasise Jameson's physical labour and business savvy in a professionalised industry. When Price discusses 'creating [her] own poses,'[213] she asserts, 'I know what works and what will sell',[214] and inducts her readers into the 'tools of the trade,'[215] she similarly presents herself as a professionalised expert rather than a celebrity.[216] Anderson's memoir describes the peculiar graft that goes into glamour modelling:

'A,E,I,O,U,' she said laughing.
'What the fuck?' Jimi asked, amused but confused.
'It's what they had me say when they were taking the gatefold shots of me for *Mann*. [...] I'm lying there, wrenching my spine, dislocating a shoulder, with a beard glued to my coochie, going, 'AEIOU'.[217]

This description offers the same combination of discomfort, absurdity and make believe as the now famous passage where Price explains the effort that goes into 'being Jordan':

[210] Ibid., p. 16.
[211] Jameson, p. 64.
[212] Ibid., p. 353.
[213] Price (2005), p. 58.
[214] Ibid.
[215] Ibid., p. 57
[216] Ibid.
[217] Anderson (2006), p. 95.

I'm too busy concentrating on the job, on looking good, on breathing in just enough to keep my stomach flat, but not so much that I'll show off too many ribs. I'm worrying about my hair being in place. And of course I'm perfecting my Jordan stare. While I'm looking at the camera I try and imagine I'm gazing into the distance at a sunset – for some reason that seems to give me the perfect challenging, come-and-get-it-if-you-dare look in my eyes. And I'm very proud of my pout, which I achieve by pretending I'm blowing bubbles very gently.[218]

These passages demonstrate an ironic, self-parodic humour that delights in the gap between the polished erotic image and the (decidedly un-erotic) labour that goes into producing it. Crucially, these descriptions of their work disassociate them from the image of the mute, inert clotheshorse or porn-star-as-victim and position them as active performers, instrumental to the production of the images that make them famous. They are represented in these examples as the agents of a career that they have worked for, deserving of the resultant rewards and successes, resisting their characterisation as passive objects.

CONCLUSION

These memoirs are an act of self-making in which the authors seek to assert who they are and reclaim control of their identity, the process of subjectification that memoir necessitates taking them beyond their traditionally conceived roles as object. This can be seen as a corrective to prevalent attitudes that 'dehumanise sex workers – that, for example, deny them the right to speak for themselves'.[219] Not only have sex workers' voices historically been silenced, but, there has been a representational lack in terms of the first-person accounts of sexual pleasure of *all* women.[220] It is in this context that these best-selling memoirs are sold as women's first-hand experience of sexual pleasure and of working in the sex industry. However, the reality of both the production and consumption

---

[218] Price (2005), p. 59.

[219] Leslie Ann Jeffrey and Gayle MacDonald, *Sex Workers in the Maritimes Talk Back* (Vancouver: UBC Press, 2006), p. 64.

[220] Gwynne, p. 6.

of these texts is far more complex. As established in Chapter 2, authenticity is a vexed yet valuable currency for both autobiography and celebrity culture.

There is much at stake in the truth value of accounts of survival of abuse. In this context, it is significant that these texts make a thematic, and in places formal, feature of constructedness. Firstly, the scepticism that attends celebrity culture—the expectation of marketing mediations—and its exacerbation in the figure of the ghostwriter enables the reading of texts of abuse survival with a stance of 'ironic knowingness' and an avoidance of being duped,[221] rather than one of sincere concern. Secondly, where feminist debates about pornography have centred around the potential for harm to real bodies, and autobiography is historically understood as an account of embodied experience, these memoirs focus upon harm in a different way. The severity of the harm visited upon the bodies of their author-subjects is mitigated by presenting the defining characteristic of those bodies as their 'augmented' 'fakeness' and function primarily as surface spectacle. Lastly, the accounts of female sexuality pivot between humorously hyperbolic ecstasy and absolute passivity in ways that do more to uphold the performative tropes of mainstream pornography than to claim truth status. The interweaving of this emphasis upon constructedness with narratives of surviving sexual and physical abuse raises questions of survivor credibility in extremely problematic ways, whilst the creation of proximity and parallel between accounts of sexual abuse and accounts of sexual pleasure that are (both eroticised and) defined as erotic both implicates and absolves readers in the consumption of narratives of harm as (erotic) entertainment.

Whilst, as demonstrated in the previous chapter, these texts are culturally disparaged along highly gendered lines, they are not without their moments of resistance. In highlighting their active and creative labour, celebrity author-subjects write against the cultural hierarchies that would deny them the status of creative agent because of their careers. Their accounts of the harm encountered in their careers approaches (if stopping short of) industry critique. They speak back to the *economics of access* of a media culture which disregards their consent when hunting to (over)expose them. Their psychic and physical revelations deliberately contravene a patriarchal politics of respectability that valorise feminine

---

[221] Gamson, p. 149.

restraint. And yet, despite a stated autobiographical occasion of the reclamation of their public identities, these texts perpetuate the tropes of their
authors' erstwhile representation, for example, the specularisation of their
own sexuality, and the preservation of 'every young boy's fantasy' of them
as sexually servile.[222]
The appearance of transgression is a form of currency in the celebrity
memoir, however, all three texts are bookended with very similar contem-
plations upon the redemptive power of motherhood: 'I'm done with
movies', states Jameson's epilogue, in the same paragraph as her hopes for
the future of her porn movie production company. 'My mind is elsewhere,
and soon my body will be too: I picked up an ovulation predictor kit from
the doctor's office yesterday'.[223] Anderson's protagonist announces her
pregnancy in the final pages, closing with her embracing her pregnant
stomach.[224] Meanwhile, Price's prologue opens with her baby kicking
and the book closes with her meeting the baby's soon-to-be father, Peter
Andre. This shows the normative pressures upon female sexuality that
such an account must negotiate despite, or because of, their investment
in the breaking of taboos around the sex lives of highly visible women.

BIBLIOGRAPHY

Allen, Kim. 'Girls Imagining Careers in the Limelight: Social Class, Gender and
    Fantasies of "Success".' *In the Limelight and Under the Microscope*, ed. by
    Holmes and Negra. New York: Continuum, 2011, pp. 149–173.
Anderson, Pamela. *Star*. London: Simon & Schuster, 2004.
———. *Star Struck*. London: Simon & Schuster, 2006.
Anderson, Pamela and Tommy Lee. 'Pamela Anderson and Tommy Lee Sex
    Tape.' 1995. www.pornhub.com/view_video.php?viewkey=467533263.
Barcan, Ruth. *Nudity: A Cultural Anatomy*. Oxford: Berg, 2004.
Barkham, Patrick. 'I'm Famous, Buy Me.' *The Guardian*, 15 January
    2007. http://www.theguardian.com/books/2007/jan/15/biography.patric
    kbarkham.
Benjamin Franklin. *The Autobiography of Benjamin Franklin*. New York: Dover,
    1996 [written between 1771–1790], p. 1.

---

[222] Anderson (2006), p. 34.

[223] Jameson, p. 577.

[224] Anderson (2006), pp. 296–97.

Boyle, Karen. 'Producing Abuse: Selling the Harms of Pornography.' *Women's Studies International Forum*, 34, 2011: 593–602.

Budgeon, Shelley. 'Identity as an Embodied Event.' *Body & Society*. London, Thousand Oaks and New Delhi: Sage, 2003, 9 (1): 35–55.

———. 'Theorizing Subjectivity and Feminine Embodiment: Feminist Approaches and Debates.' *Handbook of Children and Youth Studies*, 30 January 2015: 243–56.

Butler, Judith. 'Sex and Gender in Simone de Beauvoir's Second Sex.' *Yale French Studies*, 72 (1986).

———. *Gender Trouble. Feminism and the Subversion of Identity*. London: Routledge, 1990.

———. *Excitable Speech: A Politics of the Performative*. London: Routledge, 1997.

Cadwalladr, Carole. 'All Because the Ladies Love Jordan.' *The Observer*, 12 February 2006. http://www.guardian.co.uk/theobserver/2006/feb/12/features.review47.

Coombe, Rosemary J. 'Author/Izing the Celebrity: Publicity Rights, Postmodern Politics, and Unauthorized Genders.' *Cardozo Arts and Entertainment Law Journal*, 10, 1992: 365–95.

Couser, G. Thomas. 'Making, Taking, and Faking Lives: The Ethics of Collaborative Life Writing.' *Style*, 32 (2), 1998: 334–51.

———. *Vulnerable Subjects*. Ithaca: Cornell University Press, 2004.

Coy, Maddy, Josephine Wakeling, and Maria Garner. 'Selling Sex Sells: Representations of Prostitution and the Sex Industry in Sexualised Popular Culture as Symbolic Violence.' *Women's Studies International Forum*, 34, 2011: 441–48.

de Beauvoir, Simone. *The Second Sex*, trans. H. M. Parshley. London: Penguin Books, 1997.

Defoe, Daniel. *Moll Flanders*. London: Harper Collins, [1722] 2010.

Dolby, Trevor. 'Publishing Confessions.' *Prospect Magazine*, 14 January 2007. http://www.prospectmagazine.co.uk/arts-and-books/publishingconfessions.

Douglas, Scott. 'Baffled Tony Marsh Gets a View from the Other End of the Lens.' 12 March 2008. https://scottdouglas.wordpress.com/tag/paparazzi/.

Dow Adams, Timothy. *Telling Lies in Modern American Autobiography*. Chapel Hill and London: University of North Carolina Press, 1990.

Duits, Linda and Van Zoonen, Liesbet. 'Headscarves and Porno-Chic: Disciplining Girls' Bodies in the European Multicultural Society.' *European Journal of Women's Studies*, 13 (2), 2006: 103–17.

Dyer, Richard. *Stars*. London: British Film Institute, 1979.

Evans, Adrienne and Susan Riley. 'Immaculate Consumption: Negotiating the Sex Symbol in Postfeminist Celebrity Culture.' *Journal of Gender Studies*, 22 (3), 2013: 268–81.

Feminists Against Censorship. *Pornography and Feminism: The Case Against Censorship*, ed. by Gillian Rodgerson and Elizabeth Wilson. London: Lawrence & Wishart, 1991.

Foster, Olivia. 'From a 32C to a 32G, and Back Again! How 16 YEARS of Cosmetic Surgery Gave Katie Price the Most Famous Boobs in the Country.' *Daily Mail*, 8 December 2014.

Foucault, Michel. *The History of Sexuality: Volume 1*, trans. Robert Hurley. New York: Pantheon, 1978.

Freud, Sigmund. *Three Essays on Sexuality*, trans. James Strachey. London: Hogarth Press, [1905] 1962.

Gamson, Joshua. *Claims to Fame: Celebrity in Contemporary America*. Berkeley: University of California Press, 1994.

———. 'The Assembly Line of Greatness: Celebrity in Twentieth Century America.' *Stardom and Celebrity: A Reader*, ed. by Su Holmes and Sean Redmond. London: Sage, 2007: 141–55.

Genz, Stéphanie and Benjamin A. Brabon. *Postfeminism: Cultural Texts and Theories*. Edinburgh: Edinburgh University Press.

Geraghty, Christine. 'Re-examining Stardom: Questions of Texts, Bodies and Performance.' *Stardom and Celebrity: A Reader*. London: Sage, 2007.

Gill, Rosalind. 'Postfeminist Media Culture: Elements of a Sensibility.' *European Journal of Cultural Studies*, 10 (2), 2007: 147–66.

Goodreads. 'Interview with Pamela Anderson.' February 2010. http://www.goo dreads.com/interviews/show/484.Pamela_Anderson.

Gwynne, Joel. *Erotic Memoirs and Postfeminism: The Politics of Pleasure*. Basingstoke: Palgrave Macmillan, 2013.

Hester, Helen. *Beyond Explicit: Pornography and the Displacement of Sex*. Albany: State University of New York Press, 2014.

Hilton, Perez. 'Katie Price Reveals Her Struggle To Conceive A Child With Alex Reid.' *Perezhilton.com*, 25 October, 2010. http://perezhilton.com/2010-10-25-katie-price-reveals-her-struggle-to-conceive-a-child-with-alex-reid.

———. 'Katie Flashes The Photogs A Smile Her Panties!' *Perezhilton.com*, 11 February 2011. http://perezhilton.com/2011-02-11-katie-price-wardrobe-malfunction-london-panties-shot.

Holmes, Su. '"Starring... Dyer?" Re-visiting Star Studies and Contemporary Celebrity Culture.' *Westminster Papers in Communication and Culture*, 2 (2), 2005: 6–21.

Jameson, Jenna. *How to Make Love Like a Pornstar: A Cautionary Tale*. New York: Harper Collins, 2010.

Jamieson, Lynne. *Intimacies: Personal Relationships in Modern Societies*. Cambridge: Polity Press, 1988.

Jeffrey, Leslie Ann and Gayle MacDonald. *Sex Workers in the Maritimes Talk Back*. Vancouver: UBC Press, 2006.

Jeffreys, Sheila. *The Idea of Prostitution*. North Melbourne: Spinifex, 1997.

'Jenna Jameson Hair Hot Trimmer Shaver,' *Amazon.com*, http://www.amazon.com/Jenna-Jameson-Hair-Trimmer-Shaver/dp/B00041MB2U.

Kean, Danuta. 'Celebrity Memoirs: Bookshop Bingo!' *The Independent*, 24 September 2015.

Kenway, Jane and Elizabeth Bullen. 'Consuming Skin: Dermographies of Female Subjection and Abjection.' *Critical Pedagogies of Consumption: Living and Learning in the Shadow of the "Shopocalypse,"* ed. by Jennifer A. Sandlin and Peter McLaren. New York: Routledge, 2010: 157–68.

Knee, Adam. 'Celebrity Skins: The Illicit Textuality of the Celebrity Nude Magazine.' *Framing Celebrity*, ed. by Holmes and Redmond. London: Routledge, 2006, 161–77.

LaBruce, Bruce. 'Notes on Camp/Anti-Camp.' *Nat.Brut*, http://www.natbrut.com/essay-notes-on-campanti-camp-by-bruce-labruce.html.

Lee, Katja. 'Not Just Ghost Stories: Alternate Practices for Reading Coauthored Celebrity Memoirs.' *The Journal of Popular Culture*, 47 (6), 2014: 1256–70.

Lejeune, Philippe. 'The Autobiography of Those Who Do Not Write.' *On Autobiography*, ed. by Paul John Eakin. Minneapolis: University of Minnesota Press, 1989.

MacKinnon, Catharine A., and Andrea Dworkin. *In Harm's Way: The Pornography Civil Rights Hearings*. Cambridge, MA and London: Harvard University Press, 1997.

Madhok, Sumi. *Rethinking Agency: Gender, Development and Rights in North West India*. New York and London: Routledge, 2010.

Mason-Grant, Joan. *Pornography Embodied: From Speech to Sexual Practice*. Lanham, MD and Oxford: Rowman & Littlefield, 2004.

McLaren, Margaret A. *Feminism, Foucault, and Embodied Subjectivity*. Albany: State University of New York Press, 2002.

McLennan, Rachael. *American Autobiography*. Edinburgh: Edinburgh University Press, 2013.

McNay, Lois. *Foucault and Feminism: Power, Gender and the Self*. Cambridge: Polity, 1992.

McRobbie, Angela. 'Top Girls? Young Women and the Post-Feminist Sexual Contract.' *Cultural Studies*, 21, 2007: 718–37.

Miller, Matthew. 'The (Porn) Player.' *Forbes* magazine, 4 July 2005. http://www.forbes.com/free_forbes/2005/0704/124.html.

Mulvey, Laura. 'Afterthoughts on 'Visual Pleasure and Narrative Cinema' Inspired by King Vidor's *Duel in the Sun*.' *Visual and Other Pleasures*. Bloomington: Indiana University Press, 1989.

Negra, Diane. *What a Girl Wants? Fantasizing the Reclamation of Self in Postfeminism*. London and New York: Routledge, 2009.

Newton, Esther. *Mother Camp: Female Impersonators in America*. Chicago: University of Chicago Press, 1972.

O'Connell Davidson, Julia and Derek Layder. *Methods, Sex, and Madness*. London and New York: Routledge, 1994.

Paasonen, Susanna. 'Good Amateurs: Erotica Writing and Notions of Quality.' *Porn.Com: Making Sense of Online Pornography*, ed. by Feona Attwood. New York: Peter Lang, 2010.

———. *Carnal Resonance: Affect and Online Pornography*. Cambridge, MA and London: MIT Press, 2011.

'Pamela Anderson Is the Shameless Ploy of the Week.' *Entertainment Weekly*, 16 July 2004.

Pauly Morgan, Kathryn. 'Women and the Knife.' *Hypatia*, 6 (3), 1991: 25–53.

Price, Katie. *Being Jordan: My Autobiography*. London, John Blake, 2005.

———. *A Whole New World*. London: Century, 2006.

———. *You Only Live Once*. London: Century, 2010.

Radway, Janice A. *Reading the Romance: Women, Patriarchy and Popular Literature*. Chapel Hill: University of North Carolina Press, 1991.

Redmond, Sean. 'Pieces of Me: Celebrity Confessional Carnality.' *Social Semiotics*, 18 (2), 2008: 149–61.

Richardson, Samuel. *Pamela, or Virtue Rewarded*. Oxford: Oxford University Press, [1740] 2001.

Sager, Mike. 'What I've Learned: Pamela Anderson.' *Esquire Magazine*, 31 December 2004. http://web.archive.org/web/20121217055346/http://www.esquire.com/features/ESQ0105-WIL_Anderson.

Schwartz, Margaret. 'The Horror of Something to See: Celebrity "Vaginas" as Prostheses.' *In the Limelight and Under the Microscope*, ed. by Holmes and Negra. New York: Continuum, 2011, pp. 224–241.

Shen, Dan. 'Unreliability in Autobiography vs. Fiction.' *Poetics Today* 28 (1), 2007: 43–87.

Shriver, Lionel. 'How Did Glamour Model Jordan Become a Bestselling Author When She Doesn't Even Write?' *Mail Online*, 4 September 2008. http://www.dailymail.co.uk/femail/article-1052243/How-did-glamour-model-Jordan-best-selling-author-doesnt-write.html#ixzz42EBvHip4.

Singer, Jill. 'So What Do You Do, Neil Strauss?' *MediaBistro.com*, 17 August 2004. http://www.mediabistro.com/So-What-Do-You-Do-Neil-Strauss-a2441.html.

Skeggs, Bev. *Class, Self, Culture*. London: Routledge, 2003.

Smith, Sidonie. *Subjectivity, Identity and the Body: Women's Autobiographical Practices in the Twentieth Century*. Bloomington: Indiana University Press, 1993.

Smith, Sidonie and Julia Watson. *Reading Autobiography: A Guide for Interpreting Life Narratives*. Minneapolis: University of Minnesota Press, 2001.

————. *Interfaces: Women, Autobiography, Image, Performance.* Ann Arbor: University of Michigan Press, 2002.

Spicer, Jakki. 'The Author Is Dead, Long Live the Author: Autobiography and the Fantasy of the Individual.' *Criticism*, 47 (3), 2005: 387–403.

Stern, Jane and Michael Stern. '"How to Make Love like a Porn Star": Lovers and Other Strangers.' *The New York Times*, 5 September 2004. http://www.nytimes.com/2004/09/05/books/review/05STERNL.html?_r=0.

Stone, Philip. 'Jade Title Reaches Number One.' *The Oxford Editors*, 7 April 2009. http://www.theoxfordeditors.co.uk/?p=216.

Strauss, Neil. *The Game: Penetrating the Secret Society of Pick-Up Artists.* New York: HarperCollins, 2005.

Tasker, Yvonne and Diane Negra. 'In Focus: Postfeminism and Contemporary Media Studies.' *Cinema Journal*, 44 (2), 2005: 107–10.

Taylor, Charles. '"How to Make Love Like a Porn Star" by Jenna Jameson.' *Salon.com*, 25 August 2004. http://www.salon.com/2004/08/25/jenna_6/.

Tonks, Owen. 'Jodie Marsh Predicts Katie Price's Fall from Showbiz as She Slams Her Attention Seeking Ways.' *The Mirror*, 26 March 2013. http://www.mirror.co.uk/3am/celebrity-news/jodie-marsh-predicts-katie-prices-1786469.

Tyler, Meagan. 'Sex Self-help Books: Hot Secrets for Great Sex or Promoting the Sex of Prostitution?' *Women's Studies International Forum*, 31 (5), 2008: 363–72.

Wadler, Joyce. 'Boldface Names.' *The New York Times*, 10 August 2004. http://www.nytimes.com/2004/08/10/nyregion/boldface-names-582794.html.

Watson, Julia. 'Towards and Anti-Metaphysics of Autobiography.' *The Culture of Autobiography: Constructions of Self-Representation*, ed. by Robert Folkenflik. Stanford, CA: Stanford University Press, 1993.

Williams, Linda. *Hard Core: Power, Pleasure, and the "Frenzy of the Visible".* Berkeley: University of California Press, 1989.

————. *Porn Studies.* Durham and London: Duke University Press, 2004.

Wolf, Naomi. *The Beauty Myth: How Images of Beauty Are Used Against Women.* New York: Anchor Books, 1992.

Wyatt, Edward. 'Political but Not Partisan: A Publisher Has It Both Ways.' *The New York Times*, 13 October 2004. http://www.nytimes.com/2004/10/13/books/13bbox.html?_r=0.

Žižek, Slavoj. *The Plague of Fantasies.* London: Verso, 2008.

CHAPTER 4

'White Trash' and the Celebrity-as-Assemblage: Class, Race and Authority in the Reality TV Star Memoirs of Jade Goody, Paris Hilton and the Kardashians

INTRODUCTION

Whilst celebrity culture and its supporting gossip media have been viewed as a 'low' field with tabloid sensibilities, its value system is punitively middle class, policing the appropriateness of its players and shaming those who fall short. Although memoirs offer an intervention into the assemblage of narratives that surround them, the game is rigged because they are inevitably in conversation with normative ideas of a woman's moral, sexual virtue. Whilst a memoir is an act of agentic self-representation, it implicitly contains its surrounding strands of criticism and normativity in its responses to them. These responses frequently take the form of attempts to align the celebrity subject with dominant ideas of middle-class femininity, such as restraint, cleanliness or motherliness.

This chapter uses reality TV stars, Jade Goody and Paris Hilton as examples, but not because either can be seen as representative of female celebrity—indeed many academics have argued for the particularity of

© The Author(s) 2020
H. Yelin, *Celebrity Memoir*,
https://doi.org/10.1007/978-3-030-44621-5_4

their celebrity.[1] Rather, a productive interplay between their polar class positions enables a reading of the ways in which access to certain capitals inflects the celebrity's status as subject of her own life story. British reality TV star Jade Goody provides a stark illustration of some of the dynamics at play between ghostwriter and subject and the ways in which agency in self-representation is multiple, negotiated and inflected through different capitals each brings to the exchange. Paris Hilton offers a rich example for comparison as her antithetical class position enables a reading of the ways in which a celebrity subject with an excess in certain capitals is granted certain freedoms. In Hilton's case, one such freedom is from the obligation of full disclosure, as evidenced by her camp play. However, resistance to disclosure is ultimately undermined by the fact that celebrity memoirs exist within an assemblage of interconnected media webs, in which narratives about the celebrity circulate beyond their control. This means that the ellipses in the memoir left by denial can be filled in from alternative sources.

In the latter half of this chapter, I interrogate the construction of the figure of the 'white trash' celebrity, as demonstrated through Goody and Hilton. Looking at online responses to Hilton and Goody, and the alternative discourses they contribute to the narratives that surround these women and their memoirs, reveals that, despite their apparently polar class origins, they are understood through similar discursive frameworks which are gendered, raced and classed. Reality stars the Kardashian's (*Keeping up with the Kardashians*) Armenian ethnicity and Sam Faiers' (*The Only Way is Essex*) tanning practices are brought into this analysis of celebrity whiteness as a category that remains unmarked until certain feminine ideals are transgressed. The nature of reality TV, and its imperative to live a life of exposure and display, provides a basis for the gendered classing of its female stars as 'trash', a status deriving from the failure to demonstrate 'acceptably' feminine restraint rather than from socioeconomic status.

---

[1] See Holmes (2004); Beverley Skeggs and Helen Wood, 'The Labour of Transformation and Circuits of Value "Around" Reality TV,' *Continuum* 22.4 (2008), 559–72; Thomas Fahy, 'One Night in Paris Hilton: Wealth, Celebrity, and the Politics of Humiliation,' *Pop-Porn: Pornography in American Culture*, ed. by Ann C. Hall and Mardia J. Bishop (Westport, CT: Praeger, 2007), 75–98.

GOODY AND HILTON: AN UNLIKELY PAIR OF CELEBRITY CLASS ANOMALIES

'I felt like utter shit. As I lay on my bed I even started hitting myself, somehow trying to take the pain away'.[2]
Jade: Fighting to the End, Jade Goody

'Possibly the best thing about being an heiress is that you don't necessarily have to work. Everyone else must work, though, so it immediately sets you apart'.[3]
Confessions of an Heiress, Paris Hilton

Existing work in celebrity studies has convincingly drawn links between class and gender in the role of judgement in celebrity discourses. Skeggs and Wood argue that reality TV upholds the middle-class 'subject of value' over the undesirable working-class participant, inviting audiences to make moral judgements based upon how successfully its stars perform the 'labour of femininity'.[4] Similarly, Allen and Mendick's investigation into the centrality of class and gender to distinctions between 'proper and improper celebrity' reveals discursive frameworks in which 'it is the female working-class celebrity in particular that is constructed as abject other'.[5] Whilst developed in relation to sexuality, Butler's theorisation of the abject can be productively applied to these classed practices of exclusion, which require the production of a category of abject beings who are 'not yet "subjects", but who form the constitutive outside to the domain of the subject'.[6] Here, the abject Other serves to define those social positions and spaces that are regarded as uninhabitable and to mark those

---

[2] Goody (2009), p. 13.

[3] Hilton, p. 100.

[4] Skeggs and Wood, pp. 560, 564.

[5] Kim Allen and Heather Mendick, 'Young People's Uses of Celebrity: Class, Gender and "Improper" Celebrity,' *Discourse: Studies in the Cultural Politics of Education* 34.1 (2013) 77–93, p. 79.

[6] Judith Butler, *Bodies that Matter* (London: Routledge, 1993), p. 3.

'whose living under the sign of the "unlivable" is required to circumscribe the domain of the abject'.[7] Tyler and Bennett theorise celebrity culture as functioning as a 'class pantomime' in which gendered social hierarchies are cemented in the collectively censured figure of the (usually female) 'celebrity chav'.[8] Thus, reality TV and celebrity discourses have been established as class-based, exclusionary practices, reinforcing dominant social hierarchies through the delegitimisation of certain practices, bodies and selves.

Such a discursive paradigm is typified by Jade Goody.[9] This is why bringing Paris Hilton's antithetically privileged celebrity background as point of comparison offers such a productive contrast: the middle-class discourses of value, impropriety and undesirability remain, suggesting that the hegemony of middle-class values operates in both directions, both 'downward', towards the working-class, and 'upward', towards the wealthy elite.

Whilst what can broadly be called reality TV was the vehicle by which both women entered mainstream public consciousness, their positions within their breakthrough shows are a direct inversion of one another. Paris Hilton, as an heiress and socialite, is held up as an extraordinary individual who, in 2003 American TV show, *The Simple Life*, clashes with 'ordinary' life.[10] Hilton and fellow socialite Nicole Richie give up the privileges of their L.A. lifestyle and travel around America attempting to undertake demanding, poorly-paid labour in a humorous, carnivalesque—and, crucially temporary—inversion of their class status.[11] By contrast, Goody appeared in 2002s *Big Brother UK* as a member of the public and thus a representative of 'ordinariness' who was thrust into an extraordinary situation. Having made the transition to serial celebrity reality contestant, Goody made an ill-fated return to *Celebrity Big Brother* in 2007 from which she was evicted for the racist bullying of Indian co-star Shilpa Shetty.[12] Attempting rehabilitation, she then

[7] Ibid., p. 3.

[8] Tyler and Bennett, p. 376.

[9] See Skeggs and Wood; Allen and Mendick; Tyler and Bennett.

[10] *The Simple Life*, 2003–2007. TV, 20th Century Fox.

[11] Mikhail Bakhtin, *Rabelais and His World* (Bloomington: Indiana University Press, 1965).

[12] *Celebrity Big Brother*, 2007. TV, Endemol. Series 5.

participated in its Indian franchise *Bigg Boss*, but was diagnosed mid-filming with the cervical cancer which subsequently caused her death in 2009.[13] 20 years later, in August 2019, a three-part Channel 4 documentary hailed Goody *The Reality Star Who Changed Britain*, pitching her life story as illustrative of 'a wider story of class, politics and cultural change'.[14]

A further reason for pairing these two stars together is the sexual inflexion that structures the origins of both star stories. In her first visit to the *Big Brother* house, filming caught a sexual encounter between Goody and fellow contestant PJ, which was announced in tabloid newspaper, *The People*, with the exclamatory headline 'JADE: YES I DID GIVE PJ THE BJ!'[15] In 2003, the same year that *The Simple Life* first aired, a sex tape of Hilton and then-boyfriend Rick Salomon was leaked, resulting in numerous court cases which unsuccessfully sought to control the distribution of the video. Thus, both reality stars' early fame in part originates from sex on screen.

Ordinariness and specialness are not neutral, descriptive terms, but rather are constructed and value-laden to privilege certain things over others. What is described as ordinary is disparaged for its quotidian mundanity, but also has the normative power to present something as naturalised. In the celebrity marketplace, ordinariness can be traded to make a star likably accessible, specialness to inspire aspiration. Dyer argues that both ordinariness and specialness must combine in a star image to balance envy and aspiration.[16] Like Goody, Hilton is an outlier in celebrity class identities and far from representative of celebrity in general. Rather than reconciling contradictions through a balance of representational elements as Dyer suggests, each appears to sit at opposite extremes of a spectrum. Discourses of class have been theorised as central to central to the conception of 'ordinariness' in reality television. The presence of so-called, ordinary members of the public has been considered by some

[13] *Bigg Boss*, 2008. TV, Endemol. Series 2.

[14] *Jade: The Reality Star Who Changed Britain*, 2019, Channel 4.

[15] James Desborough, 'JADE: YES I DID GIVE PJ THE BJ!' *The People*, 28 July 2002, p. 4.

[16] Dyer (1979), p. 7.

to be a sign of the democratisation of fame.[17] However, a model of fame based upon 'exposure rather than "talent"' merely constructs a myth of social mobility, which instead mobilises thinly veiled, highly gendered class prejudice.[18] We shall see Goody illustrate these paradigms; however, Hilton's contrasting class identity complicates these models, throwing questions of gendered exposure into sharp relief.

The contrast between Goody's memoir and Hilton's is stark. From its title, *Confessions of an Heiress*, to its chapters 'How to be an Heiress' and 'My Jet-set Life', and its photographs of mother and daughter on the catwalk in the height of 80s luxury fashion, Hilton's memoir is first and foremost about being born rich.[19] In this regard, Hilton's star identity is characterised most strongly by inherited wealth. Thus, as Thomas Fahy argues, Hilton 'fails to embody the typical promise of modern-day celebrity—that anyone can achieve the same. If celebrity is a function of birth, it is as exclusive as we've always feared, and supremely undemocratic'.[20] Contradictorily, her memoir simultaneously displays her privilege and undertakes an extraordinary denial of socioeconomic reality, issuing advice to her readers to channel their 'inner heiress' because 'being an heiress is really all in your head'[21]; and to 'choose who you're born to' because 'lineage can be a state of mind'.[22] Whilst these statements seem to play to the cultural narratives of 'a country so steeped in the myth of classlessness',[23] the very existence of Hilton, who has claimed to be 'American royalty',[24] refutes this myth.

Goody's memoir informs readers that she is the daughter of a man 'found overdosed in the toilet of a Kentucky Fried Chicken restaurant

---

[17] Anita Biressi and Heather Nunn, *Reality TV: Realism and Revelation* (London: Wallflower Press 2005), p. 147.

[18] Williamson (2010), p. 199.

[19] Hilton.

[20] Fahy.

[21] Hilton, pp. 5–6.

[22] Ibid., p. 10.

[23] Annalee Newitz and Matt Wray 'Introduction,' *White Trash: Race and Class in America*, ed. by Newitz and Wray (New York: Routledge, 1997), p. 1.

[24] Nancy Jo Sales, "Hip-Hop Debs," *Vanity Fair* (September 2000), p. 378 cited in Fahy.

– which must go down as one of the classiest exists in history'.[25] Where celebrity memoir convention sees its authors heavily emphasising their difficult beginnings, Goody uses sarcastic paralipsis to reject her background for not being 'the classiest', whilst emphasising how far she has come. Offset against this scene, her memoir instructs readers that reality TV can be the catalyst for triumphing over such adversity: 'I had to find an escape...when I saw the advert for *Big Brother* it felt like I'd been offered a lifeline'.[26] Goody paints a picture of deprivation, desperation and shame.

Typically of the genre, both women claim that their memoirs offer up their 'true' selves, as distinct from their public identity. 'A lot of people have the wrong idea about me', opens Hilton's memoir, 'So I've finally decided to give you a sneak peek into my very hyped life – so you can know the real me'.[27] Where Goody offers up inglorious revelations that she 'never dared tell' before, in an earnest tone that implies shame and distress,[28] Hilton makes no such earnest promise and offers no such shameful detail. She is playful and titillating, offering only a 'sneak peek' that suggests her private self is hers to share at will.[29] The subtitle of her 'Confessions' is 'A tongue-in-chic peek behind the pose'. This tells her readers three things: she is not being serious; this is not the full story; and none of it was 'real' in the first place. The promises of a glimpse of 'the real me' and of revelations one has 'never dared tell' both appeal to the same desire in the audience to cross the line between a public and private self. However, these contrasting stances suggest a power differential between the two women in relation to their status as subjects of their memoirs. The stakes, of course, are higher for Goody, who views celebrity as her 'lifeline' and depends upon remaining in the celebrity spotlight as her sole source of income. In comparison, Hilton has a celebrity career which merely supplements her inherited wealth. Each book's title reflects these differing positions: *Jade: Fighting to the End*, a title strongly suggestive of struggle and adversity, and Hilton's *Confessions of an Heiress*, with its promise of tales of wealth and luxury.

---

[25] Goody (2009), p. xxxvii.

[26] Goody (2009), p. 14.

[27] Hilton, p. 4.

[28] Goody (2009), p. xxxv.

[29] Ibid., p. 4.

GOODY AND HER GHOST: NEGOTIATED
AGENCY IN THE CELEBRITY ASSEMBLAGE

As established in Chapter 2, Couser's understanding of ghostwriting as a one-directional hierarchy—in which the celebrity subject can always be assumed to outrank the writer—is too simplistic for the texts discussed here.[30] Returning to the example of Jade Goody and Lucie Cave, the ghostwriter of three out of Goody's four memoirs, their extreme difference in cultural capital and educational privilege confounds assumptions that Cave is merely an exploited scribe doing Goody's bidding.[31] Goody's agency in the process of her self-representation is therefore not straightforward but involves complexities which I shall discuss below.

When Cave opens Goody's memoir with a pre-prologue from her point of view as ghostwriter she forecloses possible interpretations of Goody's life by directing readers as to how the text should be read. Cave instructs that the text should 'serve as an inspirational reminder that success can be built on hard work, persistence and inner strength',[32] firmly locating the meaning of Goody's life in the convention of the autobiography genre fixated upon 'meaning of public achievement',[33] whilst reinforcing the success myth Dyer identifies as so integral to celebrity narratives.[34] Cave makes a claim to the validity and authority of the text as a continuation of a privileged literary form. Yet, at the same time, by imposing external meaning upon Goody's life, she interrupts the validity and authority of the celebrity subject.

Goody's memoir emphasises its ghostwriter's presence more openly than is conventional for the celebrity memoir genre. Katie Price and British pop-star and TV personality Tulisa, for example, both bury the name of their ghostwriters in the acknowledgements pages with nothing

---

[30] Couser (1998).

[31] Now the Editorial Director of Bauer Media, the company which owns UK celebrity gossip magazines, *heat* and *Grazia*, Cave is a university educated journalist and broadcaster. Goody, a working-class woman repeatedly excluded from her state secondary school, became famous, and publicly mocked, for her malapropisms, confusion and lack of education.

[32] Goody (2009), p. vii.

[33] Smith and Watson (2001), p. 2.

[34] Dyer (1979), p. 42.

to mark out their role from any other employee of the publishing house.[35] By contrast, a prologue to Goody's memoir by Cave offers twenty-three pages in Cave's own voice. Despite the promise of the genre to reveal the real woman behind the image, the book displays the mechanisms by which Goody's identity is mediated, a feature avoided elsewhere to protect the appearance of authenticity, and the authority and validity that come with it. This is perhaps because, as a reality TV star rather than actress or pop-star she exists in a genre characterised by 'the heightened awareness of the very *process of representation*', a genre where 'the acquisition of fame can simply be about being "mediated"'.[36] Cave attempts to mitigate this visible mediation by repeatedly stressing the verity of 'her' Jade. As the first page relates:

Jade brought me on board as her ghost writer to help her pen an honest account of her colourful life. [She] was more open, honest and candid than any celebrity I'd ever met (and probably ever will again) […] Unique […], big-hearted and extremely vulnerable, Jade wore her heart firmly on her sleeve in a way no-one else, especially those in the public eye, would dare.[37]

This is the alternative source of authenticity for Goody, stemming from an emotional excess, which is itself a failure to live within the boundaries of social acceptability.

The final example of Cave's greater control over the representation of the life of Goody in this text is that it was published after her death. Criticised by the publishing industry as a hasty, cynical move to capitalise upon renewed affection for the star, the book is a republishing of 2008 memoir *Catch a Falling Star*, with a brief closing section taken from her 2009 cancer diary, *Forever in my Heart*.[38] The only new content, therefore, is that provided by Cave, from her own point of view as ghostwriter and, according to *The Times*, without the permission of Goody's family.[39] 20 years after her death, Cave remains the public authority on Goody's

[35] Tulisa Contostavlos, *Honest: My Story So Far* (London: Headline, 2012).

[36] Holmes (2004), p. 128.

[37] Goody (2009), p. vii.

[38] Patrick Foster, 'Media Scrum Continues After Jade Goody's Death, with Rehashed Book and a Film Plan,' *The Times*, 24 March 2009.

[39] Ibid.

life and its meaning in TV documentaries such as *Jade: The Reality Star Who Changed Britain*.[40]

The presence of fame-industry apparatus such as the interventions of management, branding, and public relations teams are an open secret that creates complex webs of mediation rendering both the memoirs and the star images of their author-subjects assemblages. This further complicates any claims of unrestricted expression of subjectivity, traditionally an inherent promise of the memoir genre. Goody's memoir describes her former manager, John Noel, making decisions about her career on her behalf, without the full ramifications being explained to her. Goody recounts 'being trapped into saying yes' to appearing on *Celebrity Big Brother* in 2007 after he responded 'Don't be a fucking idiot!' when she tried to say no.[41] She retrospectively states, 'I didn't realise then how much of an involvement John actually had with Endemol'.[42] Goody suggests that her autonomy over how she is represented is compromised, claiming that she has been manipulated, or even forced, by those with commercial interests in her high profile. Of course, depicting oneself as lacking agency can be an agentic act. Nonetheless, the management team must be added alongside the ghostwriter as a strand in the assemblage of a celebrity's mediation.

This depiction of relations between Goody, her management and production company, Endemol, invites a consideration of how the wider industrial machinery of celebrity contributes to the web of reciprocal influences and stakes that collectively produce the life story. Celebrity memoirs are texts that operate in a particular marketplace. They are exercises in the branding of the celebrity as a desirable 'product' to ensure their enduring profitability for both the individual celebrity and the industries that support them. They are commercial ventures in themselves, with reportedly huge advances paid in anticipation of correspondingly large sales volumes and resultant profits for their multiple, powerful stakeholders, who can be added to the list of interested parties with a claim on the way that the life of the star is presented.[43] The existing celebrity brand

---

[40] Channel 4, 2019.

[41] Goody (2009), p. 74.

[42] Ibid.

[43] Mandy Morrow, 'Celebrity Book Deals: The Latest, Highest-Paid Advances,' *The Richest*, 3 August 2014.

and its commercial stakeholders are thus threads in this assemblage with which the life story must interact. Significant upfront outlay creates a risk-averse industrial environment that favours bankable formulas which create confidence that past successes can be replicated. Thus, what has worked previously will affect what type of life story the publisher is willing to back, making previous successes elements of the assemblage to which the presentation of the life must respond.

As a commodity in a marketplace, the celebrity memoir must stimulate, anticipate and, to some degree, satisfy consumer desires. Only to *some* degree, as Goody, for example, published five autobiographical texts in three years, which suggests a strategic withholding of information to ensure future publications. To stimulate readers' desires, these texts must promise to enclose contents worth the exchange value of, roughly, £7.99. Ghostwriter to Katie Price, Virginia Blackburn, suggests that a certain type of personal revelation is key to selling celebrity memoirs. Speaking of the disappointing sales of Peter Kaye's second memoir, retailed at £20, she told *The Observer*: 'People aren't mugs; for that kind of money, they want 400 pages and at least one juicy revelation'.[44] Blackburn describes readers as consumers seeking value for money. In this market, driven by the *economics of access*, value takes the form of access to, at the very least, the personal, ideally the juicily scandalous or shameful. Anticipation of readers' desires, then, is another force that inevitably shapes both the form and content of the life presented.

HILTON AND HER GHOST: 'IT'S ALL ABOUT TAKING CHARGE AND BRANDING YOURSELF'

Like Goody's memoir, Hilton's *Confessions of an Heiress* emphasises its ghostwriter more prominently than is usual for the memoir genre, having a cover bearing the authorial signature 'Paris Hilton with Merle Ginsberg'. Like Goody, rather than defend appearances of authenticity, Hilton claims to be revealing her 'real' self whilst displaying the mechanics of her mediation. Contradictorily, these women play no scripted part above and beyond *playing* themselves, but the process of mediation is part of their identity. In the context of a reality TV fame that offers

---

[44]Virginia Blackburn, 'Katie Price's Life? It's a Price Worth Paying,' *The Guardian*, 17 January 2010.

multiple sites of conflicting 'real' selves, the instability of binaries of identity—on/off-screen; performance/self—is evident.[45] The visibility of ghostwriters suggests that these women are not invested in having their audience believe in their ability to author a book unaided. This is a view perpetuated within their memoirs with Goody stating, for example, 'As always, I was clueless'[46] and Hilton making statements such as 'I may not know how to do brain surgery (who wants to? Guys don't want girls to know that stuff)'.[47] In this way, they collude with criticisms of their intellect that have accompanied their reception.

When it comes to Hilton's agency in self-presentation, her memoir explicitly claims her own careful orchestration and control. Her image is referred to as something for her to construct: 'It's all about taking charge and branding yourself'.[48] She advises her readers: 'Learn how to pose. [...] Always know your best angle – for your body and your face – and work it. Study your own pictures and you'll figure it out'.[49] This suggests that manufacture can be gotten away with as long as the celebrity can claim it is within her own control. This is presented as Hilton's 'work': the study of her image to craft the ideal presentation of the self. The fruits of this labour are to be seen throughout the book's many photographs. The memoir invites the reader to infer signs of Hilton's hand in her representation. However, even here, agency must be negotiated between ghostwriter and subject.

Looking at Merle Ginsberg's career history, it is possible that she was chosen (whether by Hilton or her management) not only for her writing ability. As a television personality in her own right and, at the time of Hilton's memoir's release, the Senior Writer for the *Hollywood Reporter*, a magazine that is influential both with consumers and within the entertainment industry, Ginsberg has influence in the web of celebrity gossip as well as a platform to aid the promotion of the book once published. Hilton's memoir relates her hopes to embark on acting and singing careers. In these and Hilton's other aspirations for her celebrity career, Ginsberg would likely be a prominent and valuable contact. To what extent Ginsberg has subsequently helped Hilton is

[45] Holmes (2005b).
[46] Goody (2009), p. 49.
[47] Hilton, p. 130.
[48] Ibid., p. 100.
[49] Ibid., p. 11.

difficult to ascertain. However, under Ginsberg's tenure, *The Hollywood Reporter*'s editorial line on Hilton has been favourable, giving her ensuing second album and career as an Electronic Dance Music DJ frequent, and solely positive coverage.[50] One can only infer to what degree Hilton truly is 'taking charge and branding [her]self,' nonetheless, a memoir is a carefully crafted product, whether orchestrated by Hilton or by those who surround her.[51]

Whilst non-disclosure contracts mean that the ghost is paid for their discretion as well as their writing, there is a risk in choosing a vocal, public figure with a platform for celebrity commentary as a 'ghost'. The traditional conception of the ghostwriter is that their job is to render themselves invisible in the process to allow the reader the feeling of unmediated access to the subject of the book.[52] By choosing someone highly visible, this dynamic is impossible. When a celebrity career depends upon the continued interest and favour of the gossip press, a prominent entertainment writer and presenter may be a savvy choice for a ghost. It does, however, mean that the ghost brings different capitals to the exchange: influence and useful connections. It is another example in which the celebrity far outranks the ghostwriter in economic capital, and, once again but for different reasons, the ghostwriter is far from being simply a lackey scribe, but is rather a strategic alliance.

GOODY AS AUTOBIOGRAPHICAL SUBJECT: SHAME, CONFESSION AND AUTHORITY

In accordance with Blackburn's expectations of 'juicy revelations', Goody's memoir promises ignominious, hitherto untold secrets. The memoir fulfils the genre convention of 'warts and all' anecdotes that Gilmore theorizes as the 'neoconfessional'.[53] This narrative trend in memoirs under neoliberalism sees a boom in 'endless versions of down

---

[50] Billboard Staff, 'Paris Hilton Signs with Cash Money; Second Album to Feature Lil Wayne,' *The Hollywood Reporter*, 2 May 2013; 'Paris Hilton on Her Global Tour and Drug Use in the EDM Scene,' *The Hollywood Reporter*, 8 October 2013; Matt Medved, 'Paris Hilton Reveals Las Vegas Residency, Defends DJ Career,' *The Hollywood Reporter*, 31 March 2015.

[51] Hilton, p. 100.

[52] See Couser (1998).

[53] Gilmore (2010).

and outers who make good', which displace life narratives that could invite structural critique of the causes of inequality.[54] Instead, critical energies are recruited to the task of judgement of the individual.[55] Seemingly committed to revealing how unlovely they are in reality, many contemporary female celebrities use their memoirs to reveal that behind the public image, their lives are a mess. Goody exclaims, 'to have to admit to my friends that Mum was a drug addict! They would think she was dirty'.[56] Thus, she duly shares her shame and narrates the lowest points in her life:

> I felt like utter shit. As I lay on my bed I even started hitting myself, somehow trying to take the pain away... I bashed my head repeatedly against the wall as hard as I could, I pulled my hair out of my head until my scalp was red raw.[57]

Goody acknowledges the possibility of not revealing the whole truth, explaining that she was able to choose to hold back information in her previous memoir: 'this was what I was being forced to talk about. Something I'd never admitted...I'd glossed over it in my last book – I'd been too frightened to tell a living soul'.[58] However, for reasons she does not explain, she claims not to have that option now (thus shoring up the commercial value of this particular memoir): 'You might think I'm a wuss, but tears are streaming down my cheeks just knowing I have to talk about my mum in this way in the pages of this book'.[59] The suggestion is that her commitment to 'telling all' to her readers is so great that she is willing to upset both herself and her mother to do so. The demonstration of the pain it causes her is another means by which she attempts to authenticate the verity of her book. Moreover, the suggestion that she has no other option relinquishes agency and thereby responsibility.

Readers are instructed that they can rely upon the representation of Goody contained within this book to be truthful because Goody was

---

[54] Ibid., p. 657.
[55] Ibid., pp. 657–58.
[56] Goody (2009), p. 9.
[57] Ibid., p. 13.
[58] Ibid., p. xxxvi.
[59] Ibid., p. xxxviii.

innately, uniquely, perhaps pathologically, incapable of anything other than excessive candid outpourings—something Goody describes as the 'floodgates opening'.[60] Whilst this may be framed as a form of authenticity, it is a form that actively denies the authority that usually attends authenticity, dovetailing perfectly with the criticisms of a lack of both intelligence and restraint that beleaguered Goody's public reception.

Goody frames her revelations in the language of therapy, casting her memoir as part of a wider confessional process of 'address[ing] stuff'.[61] As Rachel E. Dubrofsky argues, the reality TV genre is characterised by the hallmarks of the therapeutic mode, combining self-reflexivity, self-disclosure under surveillance and an emphasis on talk and confession.[62] Indeed, Goody cites the process of going through therapy as the catalyst that has freed her to publish these confessional 'secrets'. The power dynamics of confession are theorised by Foucault thus:

> The confession is a ritual of discourse [...] that unfolds within a power relationship, for one does not confess without the presence (or virtual presence) of a partner who is not simply the interlocutor but the authority who requires the confession, prescribes and appreciates it, and intervenes in order to judge, punish, forgive, and reconcile.[63]

Having become famous through reality TV with its confessional tropes that invite the judgement of its viewers, Goody's (already polarised) star image later became a national hate figure after charges of racism during her 2007 *Celebrity Big Brother* appearance. A breakdown followed, which led Goody to the Priory where she received therapy requiring her to talk about her upbringing and her mother's drug addictions. Her memoir is positioned as a seamless continuation of this process, transferring the authority of the therapist to the ghostwriter, who will present her case to readers. In this regard, the public is the authority ultimately asked to judge and forgive her.

[60] Ibid., p. xxxv.

[61] Goody (2009), p. xxxv.

[62] Rachel E. Dubrofsky, 'Fallen Women in Reality TV: A Pornography of Emotion,' *Feminist Media Studies* 9.3 (2009), 353–68.

[63] Foucault (1978), pp. 61–62.

MEMOIR AS AGENCY, CELEBRITY AS ASSEMBLAGE

My intention is not to cast Goody's memoir as merely the artificial product of the industrial machine of celebrity manufacture, nor Goody herself as its unwitting puppet. Indeed, Goody's memoir presents an opportunity for her to make an intervention in her public image. Regardless of however much the seemingly unrestrained outpourings contained within her memoir may be imbued with the emotional authenticity of what Dyer called 'an untrammelled flow,'[64] and Goody herself described as 'the floodgates opening',[65] she does have the choice of which anecdotes to share with her ghostwriter. As well as omission, one has the option to be disingenuous. Both of these are forms of agency, but impossible to identify with certainty in a text. For example, the exchange cited earlier between Goody and her former manager John Noel, where Noel calls her a 'fucking idiot' for not wanting to return to *Celebrity Big Brother* precedes her account of the racism that ended her run of popularity. By claiming a lack of autonomy from her management, she distances herself from poor decisions that, along with her racism, brought about her unpopularity. The representation of Goody as 'coaxed' to participate in certain celebrity or life-storying acts could itself be read as a mechanism by which she resists, negotiates and manages those who may be 'coaxing' her.[66]

Another means by which these memoirs are interpreted as being a source of power for their subjects is the sheer volume in which they sell. However, any model of influence based on mass communication and sheer scale fails to account for the nature of the relationship between subject and audience. Interest in a star does not necessarily translate as admiration, but rather may offer audiences the pleasure of collective censure. As Imogen Tyler and Bruce Bennet observe, Goody could be giving audiences the opportunity to affirm their comparative superiority through 'community-forming attachment to a "bad object"'.[67]

At points in her career, Goody very clearly provided a function, not just as 'bad object', but as a symbol of all society's ills. In the days after her funeral, the British right-wing press described Goody as 'poster girl' of the

---

[64] Dyer (1979), p. 138.

[65] Goody (2009), p. xxxv.

[66] Smith and Watson (2001), p. 51.

[67] Tyler and Bennett, p. 377.

curious contemporary cult of 'talentless celebrity'[68] and as representing 'all that is wretched about Britain today'.[69] Similarly, a left-of-centre think tank stated 'she symbolises the problem', 'our education system let her down'.[70] This suggests that another important element in the *celebrity-as-assemblage*, circling with the others, is the mediation of the symbolic function that the life provides to society. This presentation of woman as symbol is both an interpretation of the life and an imposition upon it and plays as much to stock convention as Cave's imposition of success myths or generic tropes. It is one of the multiplicity of narratives that converge around and create versions of Goody's public life. In this context, she is neither a manipulated pawn, nor a sovereign at the apex of society. Rather, her agency in self-representation is negotiated between aspects of her mediation and takes many forms, for example, presenting oneself as wholly lacking agency as a direct claim *to* agency.

Cultural products and producers exist within hierarchical and relational cultural fields, spaces 'of positions and position-takings' in which social status is negotiated.[71] One is neither a slave to structuring conditions, nor free of them as the cultural field 'is a field of forces, but it is also a field of struggles'.[72] These negotiations are clearly illustrated in Goody's memoir. In this particular overlapping set of subfields that constitute the working-class, female, reality TV celebrity, the space of possible positions she can adopt are structured in terms of emotion over intellect, confession and shame. Women in particular must always negotiate social expectations around how they should present themselves, expectations which are so deeply rooted in ancient cultural traditions that they come to shape a woman's self-perception.[73] Thus, whilst the memoir provides a privileged space for negotiation, the subjectivity depicted within is heavily coaxed and structured, dependent as it is upon its negotiations of central

[68] Obituary: 'Jade Goody,' *The Telegraph*, 22 March 2009.

[69] Anita Singh, '"Jade Goody Represented Wretched Britain", Says Sir Michael Parkinson,' *The Telegraph*, 7 April 2009.

[70] Nick Morrison, 'What Can Schools Learn from Jade Goody?' *Times Educational Supplement*, 17 April 2009.

[71] Pierre Bourdieu, *The Field of Cultural Production: Essays on Art and Literature* (Cambridge: Polity, 1993), p. 30.

[72] Ibid.

[73] Tseëlon, p. 1.

cultural values and upon the expression of a self-image that has already been formed under significant pressure.

Where all autobiography seeks an inaccessible first-hand experience, mediated by memory, the lives of the subjects of ghostwritten celebrity memoir must be accessed through additional strands of a web of interference. They offer the opportunity to intervene in a public image that often otherwise lies beyond the celebrity's grasp. However, the ghostwriter's editing, surrounding industries, literary convention, the star's symbolic function and—in Goody's case, a deficit in certain capitals—undermine authority and circumscribe the ways in which that agency can be manifested. These texts resist authoritative interpretation, leaving the critical reader to work by inference and rendering the genre, like many of its subjects, a bad object.

HILTON AS AUTOBIOGRAPHICAL SUBJECT: ELLIPTIC DENIAL, CAMP PLAY AND SUPPLEMENTARY EXTRATEXTUAL WORLDS

'We were like a couple of cute blond Eloises running around the Plaza, except it was the Waldorf Towers, and it wasn't fiction'.[74]

Confessions of an Heiress, Paris Hilton

The above quote comes from Paris Hilton's description of her childhood with her sister, Nicky. The reference is to *Eloise*, a series of children's books written in the 1950s by Kay Thompson about a six-year-old girl who lives in the Plaza Hotel in New York. The message is that Hilton has lived a lifestyle of which her readers can only dream, so fabulous that it is hard to distinguish from fiction. Hilton makes clear that she is 'special': 'we knew we were special and different'.[75] As the quote shows, one thing that will distinguish one from 'ordinary' people is being born rich—something which again suggests the class discourses inherent in such constructions. Indeed, Hilton looks with disdain upon the ordinary, advising, 'You never want to be normal. Anyone can be normal. How

---

[74] Hilton, p. 20.
[75] Ibid., p. 20.

boring. I'm yawning'.[76] Further marking out her exceptionality, Hilton holds herself up, not just as special compared with her ordinary readers, but even compared with other heiresses: 'Not every heiress is famous. Or fun. There are a lot of boring heiresses out there'.[77] Not only is she an heiress, she is a fun, famous, celebrity-heiress and, as such, doubly special. This sits outside of the aforementioned theorisations of reality television, developed in relation to British reality TV stars.

In this regard, Hilton's implied audience is constructed as ordinary relative to her and assumed not have experienced anything like the rich, famous life she describes. 'Possibly the best thing about being an heiress,' she states, 'is that you don't necessarily have to work. Everyone else must work, though, so it immediately sets you apart'.[78] She issues advice to readers, explicitly offering her memoir as an instructional guide, complete with 'dos and don'ts', for those who wish to emulate her. It includes, for example, a list entitled 'My Instructions on How to be an Heiress', the ironic humour of stating the impossible only serving to reinforce the fact that the distance is untraversable.[79]

Hilton offers the *autobiographical occasion* of her wish to 'correct' misconceptions about her that result because 'newspapers and magazines write that [she is] privileged, and that all [she does is] party'.[80] However, far from counteracting this characterisation, the memoir and the many photographs within it deliberately emphasize these very aspects of her persona. It is a whole book *about* privilege, which she explicitly acknowledges is a function of her birth: 'Heiresses are born with privileges'.[81] Another chapter is dedicated to parties, listing favourites and party secrets, explicitly stating, 'my life is a party'.[82] Therefore, whilst she acknowledges her detractors and their charges that she is a privileged party-girl, this is evidently not an idea that she wishes to counter, but an aspect of her image which her memoir exists to emphasise and perpetuate. That is

[76] Ibid., p. 11.
[77] Ibid., p. 5.
[78] Ibid., p. 100.
[79] Ibid., p. 10.
[80] Ibid., p. 4.
[81] Ibid., p. 6.
[82] Ibid., p. 82.

not to say that Hilton's wealth fails to insulate her from certain celebrity pitfalls.

Hilton and Goody's different class positions are explicitly narrated in their memoirs and their relative agency is manifested through a different relationship with confession and shame. Where Goody prostrates herself, sharing stories of her pain for the reader's judgement and forgiveness, Hilton's *Confessions*, despite its title, confesses little. If Goody's memoir puts the readers into the position of the confessed-to interlocutor and authority, Hilton's memoir refuses. Indeed, accompanying merchandise for Hilton's *Confessions* comes in the form of a journal titled, *Your Heiress Diary: Confess it all to me*, retaining the position of confessed-to authority. The reader searching for 'at least one juicy revelation'[83] for their $22 may be disappointed by the limited nature of Hilton's 'confessions', for example: 'Here's one of my major secrets revealed: I have curly hair. I get it blown straight all the time, so no one has to know'.[84] Statements such as, 'Yes, I admit I've taken the subway in New York'[85] pale next to Goody's abjection. The hyperbolic tone with which she presents these 'major secrets'[86] suggests an awareness of the expectations of the genre and a refusal to play by those terms. Despite the fact that she claims, 'At this point, I'm not afraid of controversy',[87] this book firmly avoids making reference to any controversial content.

Past disgraces only appear in the text elliptically, as she explains: 'I have pretty much grown up in public and I've done some pretty immature things along the way [...] Everything tends to get written about, so people don't forget as easily. I learned this lesson the hard way'.[88] Unlike Goody, Hilton does not appear to be required to justify her actions. Misdemeanours are alluded to but not named. The assumption may be that readers already know these stories from outside of the text. So comprehensive has the coverage been from the tabloids, gossip blogs and glossy magazines that, when it comes to events like her sex tape or jail time for drink-driving, these stories need not be repeated in her memoir.

---

[83] Blackburn.

[84] Hilton, p. 44.

[85] Ibid., p. 93.

[86] Ibid., p. 44.

[87] Ibid., p. 103.

[88] Ibid., p. 176.

A memoir is one element that contributes to a celebrity assemblage that is, ultimately, intertextual. Although developed with reference to film, Barbara Klinger's concepts of intertextual circulation highlight the ways in which a text is surrounded by promotional materials, which do not cohere to a singular reading, but rather accentuate competing aspects in the hope of widening a text's appeal to multiple audiences: 'The intertextual situation of a text is then characterised by a semiotic "spanning" from exterior sites that bear on the text with significatory pressure'.[89] Here, the 'text' is Hilton's celebrity persona, so overexposed through multiple media outlets that her memoir cannot be read as a discreet, self-contained text. Rather, it is supplemented by a repository of stories and impressions that circulate within her star image, accumulated through newspapers, magazines, websites, television and radio programmes where Hilton appears or is discussed. As Holmes and Redmond observe, tabloid news media 'would now seem strangely empty without celebrity disclosures'.[90] This increased visibility of celebrity stories in mainstream news means that even the most disinterested consumers of popular culture and 'news' at the time are likely to have had some awareness of certain stories about Hilton.

Given that a memoir is fan merchandise, a product whose readership pays to know more about its author-subject, it is not unlikely that readers come to the book with a thorough working knowledge of Hilton's previous scandals. Thus, *Confessions of an Heiress* cannot be separated from its position as, for example, the autobiography of a woman made famous for incidents including a leaked sex tape and jail time for driving under the influence, despite these incidents never being mentioned in its pages. Hilton claims that the reason for her writing this memoir is that, 'a lot of people have the wrong idea about' her, indirectly raising the spectre of sexual shame in the form of the 'right' and 'wrong' kind of woman.[91] Whether or not Hilton views the sex tape *1 Night in Paris* as contributing to this 'wrong idea', there is an intertextual association between her own star image and the sexual exposure and humiliation encapsulated in the video's existence. In a media environment where much celebrity coverage

---

[89] Barbara Klinger, 'Digressions at the Cinema: Reception and Mass Culture,' *Cinema Journal* 28.4 (1989), 3–19, cited in Holmes (2004), pp. 121–22.

[90] Su Holmes and Sean Redmond, 'Fame Damage: Introduction,' *Framing Celebrity*, p. 289.

[91] Hilton, p. 4.

takes the form of seemingly 'unapproved' exposés, control of the nature of the discussion about them lies beyond a celebrity's reach. By contrast, the celebrity memoir offers the possibility of an intervention where the identity presented can be carefully controlled. This version of the star's identity, however, can only be consumed in combination with the rest of a star's media image. Understanding the *celebrity-as-assemblage* reveals the ways in which the media web that a celebrity is part of undermines the capacity of memoir to impose the star's preferred reading upon their life.

That the reading Hilton offers is 'a tongue-in-chic peek behind the pose', suggests a playful pleasure in the artificial that casts Hilton as a knowing, humorous and resistant subject.[92] Statements signal to readers that the version Hilton presents within these pages is a construction: 'Create your own image. [...] Always act like you're on camera'.[93] As noted previously, the promise of access to an unrestrained subjectivity is intrinsic to the appeal of the celebrity memoir genre. Where construct-edness was functioning in the memoirs of Chapter 3 as an ameliorative reassurance around traumatic stories, Hilton's emphasis upon her own fabrication is altogether more playful. Not only does she flout generic convention, but she also retracts the promise to her readers that we 'can know the real' Hilton.[94] Where the confessional tropes of Goody's memoirs are an extension of the genre of reality television she worked in, the same could be said for Hilton: she is able to produce a memoir that continues her brand of surface, gloss, and cheeky artifice (and there-fore escapes the compulsion to narrate the 'real' or confess) because her reality television show launched her in that mode. Hilton's memoir taunts, 'You can't always believe what you read, right?'[95] She is referring to her tabloid press coverage as an element of her assemblage, but such a comment in the opening page of her *Confessions* reads as a self-reflexive refusal to be pinned down. The memoir seeks to upset expectations both about what Hilton should share, and also, what she should seek to hide: 'Tell everyone you're wearing hair extensions even if you aren't, because

[92] Ibid., frontispiece.
[93] Ibid., p. 6.
[94] Ibid., p. 4.
[95] Ibid.

they don't expect you to tell them'.[96] In this way, Hilton personifies what Kavka identifies as reality TV's undermining of 'discursive distinctions between reality and fiction, private and public identities, authenticity and performance'.[97] Hilton's flamboyance emphasises the performative aspect to 'being Paris Hilton'. In this way, Hilton could be seen to be embracing the 'love of the unnatural: of artifice and exaggeration' that defines Sontag's conception of camp.[98]

Hilton posits self-reflexive theories on the function of celebrity in society and the role she plays within it:

> I'm a fantasy to a lot of people. They *want* to think that I have more fun than they do, have fewer problems, wake up looking great, go to sleep looking great, can buy and eat anything in the world I want, and get any hot guy I want. They think I'm "Paris Barbie." (I take that as a compliment).[99]

In this highlighting of what people *want* to believe, the implication is that this fantasy does not match reality. However, her memoir firmly stays within this Paris Barbie character as it goes on to relate precisely that she has huge amounts of fun, no problems, buys and eats whatever she wants and has a lot of 'hot guys'. Hilton's memoir articulates then plays out the fantasy narrative, illustrated with photographs of Hilton styled with the glitzy, excessive femininity of a Barbie doll, which are even printed on Barbie-esque pink pages. Hilton pre-emptively punctures the narrative she is about to tell with a smirking irony that highlights the fact this is Paris Hilton, 'the pose'. Sontag's observation is that to 'perceive camp in objects and persons is to understand Being-as-Playing-a-Role'.[100] Hilton is positioned as performing a role of fantasy excess that is knowingly comic, anticipating and disarming potential criticism of her artificiality or privilege. Dyer argues that camp is 'a weapon against mystique [...] it

---

[96] Ibid., p. 14.
[97] Misha Kavka, *Reality TV* (Edinburgh: Edinburgh Press, 2012), p. 77.
[98] Sontag (1967), p. 275.
[99] Hilton, p. 8.
[100] Sontag (1967), p. 280.

demystifies by playing up the artifice'.[101] Here Hilton's memoir acknowledges audience expectations that '"manipulation" is fairly widespread',[102]
using the transparent, self-aware, revelling artificiality of camp as a weapon
against criticisms of artifice.

Another characteristic shared between Hilton's memoir and Sontag's
conception of camp is its 'playful, anti-serious' nature.[103] 'Rule Number
Two' of 'How to be an Heiress' is:

> An heiress should never be too serious [...] If you make fun of your-
> self first, no one gets the urge to do it behind your back. You've taken
> all the power away from them – AND made them laugh. It's a double
> whammy.[104]

This refusal of seriousness and insistence upon fun is a form of camp play
that is presented as aiding her in a power struggle with adversaries who
would seek to humiliate her. Rather than be defeated by press mockery,
by campily refusing seriousness herself, Hilton is positioned as being able
to give them permission to laugh:

> While the stuff printed about me over the last few years is amusing and
> makes me laugh, I've finally decided to let the world know: Okay, *I get
> it*. Everyone can have fun with my image because *I* like to have fun with
> it too. [...] While I like my lifestyle, I don't take it – or my media image
> – all *that* seriously.[105]

Hilton's playful, camp pose insulates her in various ways. She is insulated
from press mockery by permitting their laughter; furthermore, she is freed
from accountability for what she says within the memoir. For example,
Hilton's memoir states, 'Some people might say I'm a hypocrite because
I eat burgers but don't wear fur. My response to that is: Heiresses don't
need to be consistent'.[106] At every opportunity, readers are assured that
Hilton means little of what she says, leaving critics with little basis to hold

[101] Dyer (2002), p. 52.
[102] Dyer (1979), p. 110.
[103] Sontag (1967), p. 288.
[104] Hilton, p. 9.
[105] Ibid., p. 4.
[106] Ibid., p. 60.

her to her words. Dyer argues that 'by living out a high camp life-style [one develops] serenity and a sense of being-at-one-with-yourself'.[107] In her camp heiress performance, Hilton is positioned as above having to worry about charges such as hypocrisy. Therefore, when Hilton makes patently offensive comments such as 'being an heiress is all in your head', she is insulated, having already undermined her own position.[108]

As the problematic aspects of Hilton's star image are smoothed over as humorous fun, readers are perhaps similarly released from the obligations of a sincere stance. Hilton's ironic posture contravenes celebrity memoir genre convention. It is, however, reflective of contemporary reality TV discourses. Faye Woods argues that British structured reality TV show *The Only Way is Essex's*

> celebration of excess tilts toward caricature, yet they seek to defuse their problematic representations by employing a knowing tonal address [to] flatter a British youth audience well versed in the constructed nature of reality TV. It offers a sceptical viewing position and knowing address that allows viewers to be detached yet simultaneously invested.[109]

Similarly, Holmes argues that British celebrity gossip magazine *heat* is a 'text in which the commercial machinery of celebrity represents *part* of the narrative itself and—duly the province of irony and 'knowingness'— *heat* describes itself as "brimming with tongue-in-cheek humour."'[110] As Hilton exposes her constructedness, both she and her reader are exonerated from their part in it.

This may free audiences who might otherwise feel shame attached to consuming such a book. Hilton's publisher has acknowledged that the primary target audience for Hilton's memoir was teenage girls. However, Hilton's best-seller success has hinged upon her ability to cross-over to other audiences. The diversity of book-signing attendees surprised Fireside editor Trish Todd: 'We thought it was mostly going to be teenage girls [...] but it was moms with strollers, it was little old ladies, it was

---

[107] Dyer (2002), p. 49.

[108] Hilton, pp. 5–6.

[109] Faye Woods, 'Classed Femininity, Performativity, and Camp in British Structured Reality Programming,' *Television New Media* (2012).

[110] Holmes (2005a).

gay guys, it was businessmen in suits—it was everyone'.[111] Hilton can sell a princess fantasy, replete with childish pink pages and sparkly tiaras, to adults, because both are at a safe ironic distance. This business logic also makes sense of Hilton's collaborative construction. Not only does the ghostwriter collaborate on the writing of her life, as Paris Hilton Incorporated, profitable brand, many people's labour combines to produce her everyday public life. Again, what might elsewhere be hidden due to appearances of cynical inauthenticity is here explicitly revelled in: 'How can you brand yourself if you're in somebody else's label?'[112] 'Your face is your trademark'[113]; 'Secrets are assets, so are rich friends'.[114] This language of business is presented as knowing wit; a sign that Hilton knows what is really going on. That this is an exercise in elevating her 'social net worth'[115] is made palatable by the fact that the sale of the 'real' Hilton is so explicitly undermined that both Hilton and readers are permitted to be in on the joke.

Hilton's elliptical, evasive play, alluding to what is already in the public domain whilst refusing to satisfy audiences' appetites for her to narrate her shame, is presented as a deliberate, defensive strategy:

> If the media plays with you, well, play with them. I went on *Saturday Night Live* soon after my name was in the headlines for something I wasn't proud of […] the script had [presenter, Jimmy Fallon] asking me, 'Is it hard to get a room in the Paris Hilton? Is it roomy?' and he wanted to cut it. But I wouldn't let him. No way. That was the funniest line. And I got the upper hand with the media the moment he said it on national TV. That's when it all clicked and things started to change. People knew I could laugh at myself.[116]

[111] Fahy.
[112] Hilton, p. 39.
[113] Ibid., p. 48.
[114] Ibid., p. 90.
[115] Ibid.
[116] Ibid., p. 14.

This is the closest her memoir comes to showing any kind of vulnerability. It is presented as a personal triumph and successful power-play. She may have successfully positioned herself as in on the joke, invulnerable and untouched by society's mockery, however, this does not alter the fact that it is a sexist joke at her expense.[117] Just as Dyer highlights the pitfalls of camp as 'the self-mockery of self-protection',[118] Hilton's agency is compromised when she is forced to collude in her mockery in order to be accepted. Ultimately, Hilton's repeated dictums to 'MAKE FUN OF YOURSELF'[119] serve to reinforce that there is little place in the public eye for celebrity women who take themselves seriously. Hilton's memoir does show a different status from Goody in relation to her audience and, as a result, does not have to fulfil potential audience appetites for her shame. However, this does not mean that such appetites do not exist, or that they are not potentially satisfied by the text, whether Hilton willingly participates or not.

TALENTLESS 'WHITE TRASH' CELEBRITY: UNDESERVING RICH OR POOR

As celebrities and their memoirs are surrounded, and given meaning, by assemblages of contradictory narratives, the resulting connected landscape provides a forum for alternative discourses about a star to flourish. Celebrity memoirs, as supposedly 'official' narratives, therefore, can only be understood in relation to the celebrity's wider construction by tabloid news, cultural commentators, and fan (and anti-fan) user-generated websites. This reveals the ways in which celebrity memoir is constructed in negotiation with extratexts, implicitly containing surrounding normative criticisms in their responses to them.

Both women are subject to the class (and racial) slur 'white trash', suggesting that their class identities render them vulnerable to ridicule. However, as established, their socioeconomic backgrounds are diametrically opposed. Goody is held to epitomise what Holmes calls the

---

[117] The joke hinges upon a pun conflating the hotel chain that is the source of her inherited wealth and her body, the implication that it is equally easy to pay for access to either, making a link between her perceived promiscuity and the size of her vagina.

[118] Dyer (2002), p. 50.

[119] Hilton, p. 15.

'celebritisation' of the 'ordinary' person,[120] whilst Rojek summarises Goody's persona thus: 'Brash, vulgar, overweight, physically plain and self-opinionated, Jade featured in media coverage as, not to mince words, a representative of white, working-class trash'.[121] Goody embodies the type of stardom bemoaned by Daniel Boorstin for a lack of 'greatness, worthy endeavours or talent'[122] and has often been foregrounded as emblematic of the apparently 'regrettable' nature of reality TV fame. Indeed, this conservative appraisal remains influential, characterising much of the popular critique of celebrity culture fifty years after it was first published. The problematic assumption here is that only certain talents are of worth and that there is a consensus on what counts as worthy. A talent for placing oneself at the centre of a media furore, for example, providing an audience with opportunities to laugh at one's expense, or earning a net worth of millions of pounds, are deemed to be inauthentic talents and denied cultural value. This, however, poses no problem for Goody's celebrity. Indeed, an apparent absence of talent both defines and authenticates her stardom. Her own publicist, the late Max Clifford, whom Goody described as a 'father figure',[123] and who might be expected to emphasise her talent to legitimate her claim to the spotlight, said after her death, 'Jade would be the first to tell you she had no talent. She was just herself'.[124] In both popular and academic debate, reality TV celebrity is often constructed as antithetical to 'traditional' stardom—however vaguely this is often defined. Returning to the construction of the success myth, Dyer identifies how this embodies the discourses of ordinariness, lucky breaks, specialness and hard work.[125] Yet reality TV shows like *Big Brother* remove hard work, talent and specialness from the equation. Even the lucky break element is diluted through the visibility and openness of the application process for participation. Holmes argues that in the absence of a discernible talent, the work discourse in

---

[120] Holmes (2004), p. 114.

[121] Chris Rojeck, *Fame Attack: The Inflation of Fame and Its Consequences* (London: Bloomsbury, 2012), p. 29.

[122] Daniel Boorstin, *The Image* (London: Penguin, 1963), p. 11.

[123] Goody (2009), p. 22.

[124] 'Jade Goody, "Had No Talent—And She Knew It" Says Max Clifford,' *The Mirror*, 6 May 2009.

[125] Dyer (1979), p. 42.

the success myth is 'replaced by an ever more fervent negotiation of the "real" self'.[126] Clifford's description of his ward as talentless but 'just herself', clearly fits this model of fame. Over fifty years after Boorstin, to be famous for talentlessness is to be famously unworthy, or famous for not deserving one's fame.

In the opening pages of her memoir, Goody explicitly and self-consciously deals with questions of class, stating: 'I was actually a chav before they were given a name'.[127] Chav, a term of contempt used to depict the British white, working-class as tasteless, excessive, dangerous and immoral, grew in popular usage in the early part of the twenty-first century, to the point that right-wing, British newspaper the *Daily Mail* reported 2004 to be 'The Year of the Chav'[128] due to its inclusion in an annual of newly popular idioms.[129] The *Daily Mail's* description of 'a word coined to describe the spread of the ill-mannered underclass - a rival to the American trailer trash - which loves shellsuits, bling-bling jewellery and designer wear',[130] highlights the confluence of fear, blame and judge-ment that surround the word, along with anxieties about the poor having access to more than they 'deserve'. Whilst Goody's classing (of herself) as a 'chav' derives in part from aesthetic and cultural markers of taste and class, the conception of her as talentlessly famous speaks directly to the anxieties of undeserved rewards that the word 'chav' represents.

Tyler and Bennett argue that British celebrity is a class pantomime in which the celebrity chav is the butt of the joke; a Foucaultian theatre of punishment that polices the threats posed by social mobility.[131] Rather than inspiring aspiration or identification, the celebrity chav offers her audience the pleasure of collective censure. She defines what the audi-ence are glad *not* to be and gives them the opportunity to affirm their comparative superiority through 'community-forming attachment to a "bad object"'.[132] Whilst it is perfectly possible that readers may turn to

---

[126] Holmes and Jermyn, 'Introduction,' *Understanding Reality Television*, p. 22.

[127] Goody (2009), p. 2.

[128] 'The Year of the Chav,' *The Daily Mail*, 19 October 2004.

[129] Susie Dent, *Larpers and Shroomers: The Language Report* (Oxford: Oxford University Press, 2004).

[130] 'The Year of the Chav,' *The Daily Mail*.

[131] Tyler and Bennett, p. 380.

[132] Ibid., p. 377.

memoirs as a guilty pleasure, read from a knowing, ironic distance,[133] these texts are predominantly published as fan merchandise and as such can expect to receive a more admiring, sympathetic audience than the wider celebrity gossip media. However, despite this, Tyler and Bennett's point is borne out in Goody's autobiography. Whilst it is difficult to draw firm conclusions about the subject's *self*-awareness in a text produced through a ghostwriter, Goody's memoir suggests that she knows she is a 'bad object'. Of dining at Claridges, a place she describes as 'soooo posh!', Goody suspects that upon recognising her, other diners 'must secretly have thought, Bloody hell, we come in here to get away from the likes of her!'[134] This suggests an awareness of the fact that her bad object status is based upon her class origins and the opportunities her fame and subsequent wealth afford her to exceed the boundaries that her British audience is taught ought to circumscribed.

Celebritisation as Class Drag

Contradictorily, Goody is presented as proudly, unchangingly working-class *and* as having progressed beyond shameful origins. Writing about Goody, Tyler and Bennett claim that what is 'both comic and poignant is [her] conviction that it is possible to escape rigid class origins through highly visible careers in entertainment'.[135] Goody's autobiography invokes this concept directly in an example which highlights the regulatory workings of class and femininity. Describing her mother's participation on the TV programme *Extreme Makeover*, she states:

> She had a nose job, a neck lift, an eyelift, a boob job, her teeth done, her tattoos removed...waving like royalty... I've never seen my mum behaving in such a ladylike manner...She kept saying, 'This is fabulous!' It was all, 'Oh, thanks for the drink, it's fabulous. My teeth are fabulous, my boobs are fabulous! I said, 'Fabulous'? Piss off! Just because you've had your face tweaked doesn't mean you have to change the way you talk... It felt so wonderful that she could put her past behind her and be a new person.[136]

[133] Gamson (2007).

[134] Goody (2009), p. 36.

[135] Tyler and Bennett, p. 389.

[136] Goody (2009), pp. 65–66.

Here, Goody undermines her mother's attempts at what Bev Skeggs identifies as 'doing femininity',[137] casting her mother's performance as 'an unconvincing and inadvertently parodic attempt to pass'[138] in a class drag act in which 'she had never been allowed to' succeed.[139] At the same time, Goody endorses the postfeminist belief in 'consumption as a strategy...for the production of the self'.[140] Goody reveals, however, that this is ultimately a temporary and therefore failed process of self-making: 'Of course this wasn't to last. Mum was soon back to her old loudmouth, lairy ways and couldn't have appeared less of a lady if she tried'.[141] Loudness is coded as a particularly unfeminine form of unrestraint—a discourse that valorises an image of deferential middle-class femininity. Goody's desire that, in Skeggs' terms, 'working-classness can be overcome and eradicated'[142] and disappointment in her mother's failure to 'pass' is repeated when she sees her mother in the *Celebrity Big Brother* house: 'Her behaviour, her language, her manners were appalling. But she was my mum'.[143] Goody speaks from the point of view of someone who has undertaken the same process through which she is now watching her mother flounder: 'I knew how people would view her on the outside, because they'd viewed me in the same way when I'd first gone in there in 2002. And I'd behaved like a right ignorant idiot'.[144] Repenting for her previous behaviour, Goody speaks as if occupying a comparative position of safety: as if she had successfully made the transition to acceptable, middle-class femininity, and could view her working-classness retrospectively, its markers having, but for her mother's humiliations, been shed, permitting her to 'pass'.

[137] Bev Skeggs, 'The Toilet Paper: Femininity, Class and Misrecognition,' *Women's Studies International Forum* 24.2–4 (2001), 297.

[138] Tyler and Bennett, p. 381.

[139] Su Holmes, 'Jade's Back and This Time She's Famous: Narratives of Celebrity in the Celebrity Big Brother "Race" Row.' *Entertainment and Sports Law Journal* 7.1 (2009), 22.

[140] Tasker and Negra (2007), p. 2.

[141] Goody (2009), p. 66.

[142] Skeggs (2001), p. 298.

[143] Goody (2009), p. 81.

[144] Ibid., p. 82.

'White Trash' Celebrity as Lack of Self-Control

Returning to Goody's 2007 racism controversy in more detail, she was accused of the racist bullying of fellow *Celebrity Big Brother* contestant and Bollywood film star, Shilpa Shetty. Media uproar ensued, with Goody ejected from the public's affections and branded as repugnant 'white trash'. This particular incident, and the reactions to Goody that followed, have been a cultural reference point for many celebrity studies scholars.[145] For Holmes, this pivotal moment in Goody's career trajectory reveals the way in which discourses of fame and celebrity are mobilized as disciplinary forces as whatever gains she had 'won' were gleefully stripped from her and any 'passing' possibilities were publicly retracted.[146] For Biressi and Nunn, the apologetic media tour which followed the Goody/Shetty 'race row' offers an exemplary case of celebrity as an 'contract of on-going public intimacy' that demands the performance of emotional labour (ideas which I shall build upon further in the ensuing chapter on YouTubers).[147]

By contrast to Goody, Shilpa was praised for dealing with Goody's insults with grace, decorum and civility—words which are themselves inherently classed. Bourdieu describes 'the refusal to surrender to nature, which is the mark of dominant groups – who start with *self*-control – [as] the basis of the aesthetic disposition'.[148] The division between imperturbable Shetty and intemperate Goody falls along these lines of classed self-control. As polar identities were constructed for Goody and Shetty by the media, reference was made to each woman's physical attractiveness. For example, Stuart Jeffries' article in the *Guardian* titled 'Beauty and the beastliness' describes the *Big Brother* house as 'divided between ugly, thick white Britain and one imperturbably dignified Indian woman'.[149]

---

[145] Radha S. Hegde, 'Of Race, Classy Victims and National Mythologies: Distracting Reality on Celebrity Big Brother,' *Feminist Media Studies* 7.4 (2007), 457–60; Lieve Gies, 'Pigs, Dogs, Cows, and Commerce in Celebrity Big Brother 2007,' *Feminist Media Studies* 7.4 (2007), 462.

[146] Holmes, 'Narratives of Celebrity in the Celebrity Big Brother 'Race' Row,' *Entertainment and Sports Law Journal* 7.1 (2009).

[147] Heather Nunn and Anita Biressi, '"A Trust Betrayed": Celebrity and the work of Emotion,' *Celebrity Studies* 1.1 (2010), 49–64.

[148] Bourdieu (1984), p. 40.

[149] Stuart Jeffries, 'Beauty and the Beastliness: A Tale of Declining British Values,' *The Guardian*, 19 January 2007.

In the contrasting of an 'ugly' woman's crass vulgarity against a 'beautiful' woman's elegant propriety, narratives of 'proper' femininity become enmeshed with those of race and class. Shetty conducts herself with comparative ease. Bourdieu argues, that ease represents

> the visible assertion of freedom from the constraints which dominate ordinary people, the most indisputable affirmation of capital as the capacity to satisfy the demands of biological nature or of the authority which entitles one to ignore them.[150]

Goody's autobiography attempts to frame the argument that was at the centre of the allegations in terms of class, rather than race:

> We were fighting because we were from different classes and different values in life...I have a chip on my shoulder about that. I don't want anyone to think that they're better than me, just because they have more money or a more educated upbringing. I felt like, to her, I was common. And, to me, she was a posh, up-herself princess.[151]

Goody claims that what she objected to in Shetty, was not her race, but her privilege and condescension. She attempts to explain away her racism as an accidental, if unfortunate, product of her working-class background. 'It's not in me to be racial about anyone', Goody claims.[152] This disconnects the exchange from the realities of racism as a systemic problem with far-reaching consequences, misrecognising structural inequalities as depoliticised individual pathologies.[153] Stuart Jeffries responds to Goody's media apologies with a personal attack on her poor grasp of grammar and her undeserved wealth: 'the word you want, Jade, is not racial, but racist: do spend some of that estimated £8m you have earned on a remedial education rather than boob jobs and liposuction'.[154] Goody's racist bullying provided the commentariat with their own opportunity for self-righteous bullying of her on the grounds of class and femininity revealing that, alongside racism, class hate and sexism remain

[150] Bourdieu (1984), p. 255.
[151] Goody (2009), p. 91.
[152] Ibid.
[153] Hegde.
[154] Jeffries.

socially acceptable forms of bigotry in contemporary Britain. Audiences welcomed the opportunity to perform their abhorrence of racism, without necessarily interrogating the ways in which they, too, are implicated in and benefit from racist structures.

When Goody steers the conversation away from the politics of race to those of class, she uses her autobiography to attempt to justify actions that made her a national hate figure, or, as Lieve Gies suggests, 'Jade's own media savvy has been to convert the humiliations which she suffered [...] into a highly bankable asset'.[155] Goody's memoir reframes the debate in terms of class rather than, or as well as, race, and attempts to claim that, in a hierarchy of oppression, to be a privileged woman of colour is a preferable, more acceptably feminine, position to occupy than to be white, working class. During this time, fellow *Celebrity Big Brother* contestant Jermaine Jackson allegedly called Goody 'white trash'.[156] John Hartigan argues that 'in a political moment when derogatory labels and innuendoes for ethnic groups are being rigorously policed in social and institutional exchanges, 'white trash' still flies with little self-conscious hesitancy'.[157] Of course, in the era of Trump and Brexit, many forms of culturally sanctioned racism undeniably persist.[158]

'White trash' itself is a slur in which race and class combine. Whilst used interchangeably with the aforementioned term 'chav' in reference to Goody, the term has specific historical resonances. Matt Wray and Annalee Newitz trace the concept back to the US Eugenics Research Office who, between 1880 and 1920, attempted to demonstrate scientifically that rural poor whites were 'genetically defective' by 'locating relatives who were either incarcerated or institutionalised and then tracing their genealogy back to a "defective" source' (definitions of 'defectiveness' often proving to be euphemisms for Black).[159] The rural poor entered the public imagination as 'poor, dirty, drunken, criminally

---

[155] Gies, p. 462.

[156] 'Jermaine in Frame: New Big Bro Race Row,' *The Daily Star*, 3 February 2007.

[157] John Hartigan, 'Unpopular Culture: The Case of "White Trash",' *Cultural Studies* 11.2 (1997), 317.

[158] Hannah Yelin and Laura Clancy, 'Doing Impact Work While Female: Hate Tweets, 'Hot Potatoes' and Having "Enough of Experts",' *European Journal of Cultural Studies*, forthcoming.

[159] Newitz and Wray, p. 2.

minded, and sexually perverse people'.[160] This was used to call an end to welfare and other forms of giving to the poor and introduce involuntary sterilisation and incarceration. One hopes eugenics has been fully discredited as a scientific practice, but, as a system of thought it dangerously persists. As Wray and Newitz argue, 'the stereotypes of rural poor whites as incestuous and sexually promiscuous, violent, alcoholic, lazy, and stupid remain with us to this day'.[161] 'White' is racialised, serving as an invisible norm: white bodies are 'unmarked, normative bodies and social selves, the standard against which all others are judged (and found wanting)'.[162] 'Trash' is classed as the dregs, dirt or refuse of society. Wray and Newitz observe that 'the white trash stereotype serves as a useful way of blaming the poor for being poor'.[163] In this respect, the American term functions in the same way as the British 'chav', as an explanation for cultural and class differences that blames the poor not only for their own situation, but for a nation's ills.

WHITENESS AS AN UNMARKED CATEGORY: COMPARING HILTON AND THE KARDASHIANS

When Hilton and Goody transgress (and in so doing highlight the existence of) celebrity's codes of idealised white femininity, they reveal a whiteness which retains the privilege of an unmarked category until such celebrities fall short of its ideals of purity and restraint and are thus deemed 'white trash'. The unmarked status of whiteness is seen most clearly through comparison with celebrities of colour who are understood primarily through their ethnic or racial identity. Consider Hilton in relation to her celebrity peers, the Kardashians, whose memoir constantly references, explains and even apologises for, their Armenian ethnic identity. Hilton's memoir never once mentions her white racial identity.

In terms of socioeconomic background, Kim Kardashian and Paris Hilton have extremely similar profiles. Both attended prestigious, independent school, The Buckley School in California and live in Beverly Hills as the offspring of wealthy, high-profile parents. Indeed, Kardashian

[160] Ibid.
[161] Ibid.
[162] Ibid., p. 3.
[163] Ibid., p. 1.

describes Hilton as a friend and mentor in cultivating and coping with fame: 'she said "whatever you do, just smile. And don't say anything under your breath because now they have video cameras too"'.[164]

As Redmond observes, 'The symbolism of whiteness is also found in the everyday world, in the wedding dress, the doctor's uniform and in the 'signs' of health and hygiene, for example, establishing whiteness as index-ical, or rather iconic, of purity'.[165] In the collective memoir, *Kardashian Konfidential*, we see the three Kardashian sisters negotiating their public identity in relation to ethnicity, hygiene and purity, in a way that Hilton is not at any point required to do.[166] They describe a beauty regime that must deal with the perceived 'problems' associated with their Arme-nian heritage. Hilton's memoir similarly makes frequent references to her beauty regimen. Not one of them is presented as a necessity because of her race. *Kardashian Konfidential* contains a chapter titled 'So Armenian', expressing pride in their Armenian heritage. However, the women simul-taneously present it as the source of undesirable physical attributes which need to be erased: Khloë, for example, explains that she would never leave home without face powder because 'I'm an Armenian and I get oily!'[167]

Another example states, '[We] are all dark, and we're hairy, like most Armenians'.[168] The reference to hairiness, which in this context is delineated as a negative attribute—incompatible with acceptable femi-ninity—renders the statement an apology for their ethnic make-up and explains away what they consider to be unsightly flaws. In their anal-ysis of the reality TV series *Keeping Up with the Kardashians*, Maria Pramaggiore and Diane Negra observe that 'the women overtly signal aspirations toward a convincing whiteness through, for example, multiple series mentions of the importance of hair removal'.[169] This emphasis extends, in this memoir, to an entire chapter entitled 'Wax Work', a phrase highlighting the labour behind what is presented as important and

[164] Kardashian, Kardashian, and Kardashian, p. 100.

[165] Redmond (2006), p. 266.

[166] It is worth noting that, whilst this analysis takes in only the identities performed in the 2011 collective Kardashian memoir, the racialisation of Kim Kardashian in particular has evolved since its the publication, as she has embraced and appropriated signifiers of Black identity such as cornrow hairstyles.

[167] Kardashian, Kardashian, and Kardashian, p. 10.

[168] Ibid., p. 21.

[169] Diane Negra and Maria Pramaggiore, 'Keeping Up with the Aspirations: Commercial Family Values and the Kardashian Brand,' *Reality Gendervision: Sexuality & Gender on*

necessary maintenance: 'waxing leaves everything cleaner', 'at the age of eleven, we were getting waxed', 'your bikini, I believe, should always be waxed'.[170] These statements accompany large colour photographs of the women in their bikinis evidencing the presence of abundant, curly, brown Armenian hair visible only in acceptably feminine places. They equate hair with both Armenianness and dirt, narrating their ethnic identity through displays of both pride and shame. Hilton's memoir, by contrast, never accounts for, explains, apologises for or even acknowledges the fact that she is white. According to her memoir, Hilton has no racial identity: her hegemonic whiteness is not held to be a racial signifier.

In contrast to the claims of Hilton's memoir, however, her popular reception as 'white trash' shows that she disrupts 'the social decorums that have supported the hegemonic, unmarked status of whiteness as a normative identity',[171] undermining the capitals that her whiteness and wealth otherwise confer. Transgressions of cultural appropriateness appear to be most harshly chastised when the boundaries crossed are those set by middle-class ideals of femininity. As Tasker and Negra argue, 'post-feminism is white and middle-class by default'[172] and presents women's lives as defined by 'choice' whilst simultaneously privileging traditional, passive gender roles as the choice above all others. Building upon the work of Bourdieu, Skeggs charts the association of femininity with the habitus of the upper classes: 'ease, restraint, calm, and luxurious decoration. It was a category of pure, white, heterosexuality, later translated into the ideal for middleclass women'.[173] Femininity is inherently classed and defined in opposition to working-class women and women of colour who are 'coded as the sexual and deviant other'.[174]

We have seen in the previous examples how Goody's 'brash', 'ugly', 'ignorant' persona, not only finds her condemned as 'white trash', but also presents a failure of femininity. Having been coded as the shameful, debased other—deficient in femininity and class—her memoir attempts to offer readers a *mea culpa*, not only for her racism, but for who she is. Ultimately, her memoir is an act of repentance, expressing shame at her

Transatlantic Reality Television, ed. by Brenda R. Weber (London: Duke University Press, 2014), p. 86.

[170] Kardashian, Kardashian, and Kardashian, pp. 36–37.

[171] Hartigan, p. 317.

[172] Tasker and Negra (2007), p. 2.

[173] Skeggs (2001), p. 297.

[174] Ibid.

origins, her past behaviour, and the woman she was when she entered the limelight. Society's judgement of her as unacceptable 'white trash' creates the framing conditions within which she must write her life story and shape it accordingly.

Despite having been born at the opposite end of the class spectrum from Goody, Hilton receives the same class slur. Where Goody is considered to be 'representative of [...] white, working-class trash', the user-generated website *Urban Dictionary* claims that Paris Hilton personifies the term. Under the entry for 'white trash' comes the definition: 'anyone who goes by the name Paris Hilton, wants to be Paris Hilton, knows Paris Hilton, or has spent one night in Paris'.[175] Regardless of the difference in their socioeconomic backgrounds, both Goody and Hilton are subject to the class and racial discourses that combine to judge them to be what Shelley Cobb describes as 'women who do not display the cultural tastes appropriate to the privileges of whiteness'.[176] Coming from the world of old money, Hilton represents the most exclusive enclave of white privilege. Her inherited wealth affords her the means to acquire the accoutrements, habits and cultural knowledge of the elite and yet she epitomises 'white trash' celebrity. Whether born rich or poor, neither woman has the symbolic nor cultural capital to save them from ridicule and degradation once they are in the public eye.[177] On the user-generated, online forum *Listology*, under the heading 'Paris Hilton: Rich White Trash,' she is described as a 'no-talent-daddy's-money-what's-a-Walmart-bottle-blonde... Dumb. As. Dirt.' and asks 'What's she famous for again? I can think of very few examples of people making a career out of their mind-numbing stupidity'.[178] The poster's vitriol comes from the view that Hilton lacks the right type of talent to deserve fame and that her inherited wealth renders her out of touch with 'normal' people. To be dumb and famous is an insult to the audience. To be dumb and rewarded with riches is even more so. Their careers in reality television leave both Hilton and Goody vulnerable to the charge of talentless stupidity without the shield of a socially approved 'talent' to hide behind. The bottle blonde

---

[175] 'White trash,' posted by 'Your Mom,' *Urban Dictionary*.

[176] Shelley Cobb, 'Mother of the Year Kathy Hilton, Lynne Spears, Dina Lohan and Bad Celebrity Motherhood,' *Genders* 48 (2008).

[177] Bourdieu (1984).

[178] melladior@ho, 'Paris Hilton: Rich White Trash,' *Listology*.

reference is a charge of inauthenticity, as if the injustice of Hilton's fame
and riches would be mitigated were it springing from a natural beauty.

'White Trash' as Failure
of Femininity and Wilful Self-Display

Skeggs builds upon the work of Bourdieu to argue that appearance classes
femininity through its function as a marker of respectability. Naturalness, and with it associations of ease, are rewarded with a greater cultural
value than constructed beauty, which is 'de-valued for being made visible'
thereby revealing the necessity for effort.[179] As well as both receiving the
slur 'white trash', Goody and Hilton share conventions of appearance,
actively embracing an ostentatiously 'fake' look. Nails, hair extensions,
breasts or manifold other treatments are mentioned in their memoirs,
with the fake tan the symbol above all others of the 'trashy' beauty
regime. Through characteristically polarised lenses of brashly wealthy
versus abject, Hilton advises, 'always have a tan. It looks like you've
been in an exotic (i.e. expensive) place',[180] whilst Goody describes that
one of the first things she did to recover from a miscarriage was spend
'twenty minutes on a sunbed'.[181] Star of reality show *The Only Way is
Essex*, Sam Faiers, dedicates a chapter of her autobiography to the topic
of fake tanning and explains why 'being tanned is like a religion'[182]:
'We like a glamorous, big, full-on look that catches people's attention,
and we are not afraid to look like we have made a lot of effort'.[183]
These augmentations are presented as the consumerist trappings of a
wealthy celebrity lifestyle. However, this 'fake' aesthetic is another means
by which these women are judged to be 'trashy'. Whilst it may be an
expensive look to produce, with its over-the-top excess, it is a look interpreted by society as 'cheap': a term which, when applied to a woman,
has derogative, slut-shaming overtones. Hilton herself attempts to police
the line between 'classy' and 'trashy' for her readers: 'There's a big difference between being fun and provocative and being totally over-the-top

[179] Skeggs (2003), p. 101.
[180] Hilton, p. 13.
[181] Goody (2009), p. 186.
[182] Sam Faiers, *Living Life the Essex Way* (London: Simon and Schuster, 2012), p. 23.
[183] Ibid., p. 21.

and gross'.[184] With the 'white trash' slur, however, Hilton has been judged to have transgressed her own standards. Both women describe their revealing outfits, heteronormatively placing the authority to approve, and the right to judge, with their male partners. Goody states of a birthday outfit, 'I thought I looked great, Jack [her partner] thought I looked like a slut'.[185] Hilton advises readers to, 'show off your navel and belly', wear jeans 'really, really low-waisted', and 'dress supersexy when you don't have a boyfriend, or if you want to make your boyfriend jealous'.[186] As their sexuality is conflated with the visibility of their bodies, the accusation of aesthetic trashiness is born of these women's specularity, having made a display of themselves.

'Making a spectacle out of oneself', argues Mary J. Russo in her book on the female grotesque, can be seen to be 'a specifically feminine danger. The danger was of an exposure. Men, I learned later in life, "exposed themselves," but that operation was quite deliberate and circumscribed. For a woman, making a spectacle of herself had more to do with a kind of inadvertency and loss of boundaries'.[187] The charge of trashiness, and the invocation of the grotesque in the discourses of inadvertency and inappropriateness that surround these women, is in part founded upon the failure of boundaries represented in Hilton and Goody's exposure. Further, Goody's sentimental discourse is also grotesque in these terms: as already discussed, her memoir describes 'the floodgates opening'[188] in a seemingly unrestrained outpouring of personal secrets—suggesting a flouting of the boundaries of decorous speech. However, unlike the inadvertency Russo describes, Faiers relates the 'efforts' made to 'catch people's attention,' suggesting that what further provokes censure in the 'big, full-on look', epitomised by the fake tan, is the deliberate willingness it suggests to be looked at. Or even, a willingness to be seen to make an effort to encourage others to look. Acceptable middle-class femininity has always been decorative and specular. The supposedly unseemly difference in this instance is the invitation to an admiring audience, which one ought to be

[184] Hilton, p. 8.

[185] Goody (2009), p. 46.

[186] Hilton, pp. 52–53.

[187] Mary J. Russo, The Female *Grotesque: Risk, Excess and Modernity* (London and New York: Routledge, 1994), p. 53.

[188] Goody (2009), p. xxxv.

able to attract with ease. Despite their antithetical socioeconomic origins, both women's star identities share many characteristics: they are classed as 'white trash', criticised for occupying our screens without the necessary talent to deserve the attention, and characterised by a supposedly 'trashy' aesthetic. The common ground here is the gendered charge of failing to conduct themselves with the modesty and humility that supposedly befit their being female. If an upper-class habitus and restrained femininity are inextricable, these women are classed together as trashy for their lack of feminine restraint.

In this regard, both women use their memoirs to present themselves as more acceptably 'feminine' than their public reception has classed them. Goody's memoir casts her as a homemaking, ideal mother writing 'a precious record for her two beloved sons'[189] and emphasises the importance she puts on manners and cleanliness. Hilton distances herself from women who 'need to talk about every tight T-shirt they buy, every carbohydrate they eat, every insecurity they have, every single thing a guy says to them'[190] or 'go around spilling [their] guts'.[191] However, their careers as the subjects of reality products, including these very memoirs, require them to live in public. As reality stars they are characterised by a kind of performative excess, an inability to stay demurely out of the spotlight as a 'classy' woman should.

Where the vilification of Goody has been theorised as a 'grotesque representation of the undeserving poor,'[192] Hilton is conversely represented as the undeserving rich, lacking 'the supposedly innate cultural tastes and decorum that wealthy white people should have'.[193] Therefore, the white trash slur derives less from either woman's class status than from their 'inhabiting a transgressive femininity' that renders them vulgar and grotesque. They stimulate cultural anxiety over 'the availability of individual success within capitalism to "inappropriate" members' of society.[194] The female reality star is impelled to share all and thus cannot

---

189 Ibid., p. vii.
190 Hilton, p. 9.
191 Ibid., p. 7.
192 Tyler and Bennett, p. 380.
193 Cobb, p. 6.
194 Ibid., p. 25.

simultaneously occupy both the restrained feminine and a life of display. Whether it is aesthetic trashiness or an undeserved spotlight, the diametrically opposed class backgrounds of these two women show that the charge of trashiness is—above all else—about the sullied virtue of a woman who lives in public and the hegemony of middle-class ideals.

CONCLUSION

This chapter has introduced the *celebrity-as-assemblage* and shown how these books and the star images of their subjects interact with, redress, seek to reconcile, and implicitly contain a multiplicity of overlapping, interconnecting, and often competing narratives. By accounting for the collaborative construction of these texts and finding a space for the ghostwriter in our understanding of them, this chapter provides an approach for the way in which the industrial conditions of celebrity render all star images collaborative constructions.

The overlapping cultural fields in which these celebrities and their status are located, fields of gendered celebrity culture and of reality TV stars in particular, offer the arena in which they can manoeuvre, bringing their habitus and capitals into negotiation with the rules of the field.[195] In this cultural field, acceptable femininity is policed in terms of restraint, and sexual morality is always at stake in female exposure. Exposure is both the means and the end in reality TV celebrity. It is both the requisite condition of participation and the cause of censure and ridicule, especially for women. Restraint, exposure, and sexual morality can therefore be seen to be irreconcilable co-existent pressures.

As the 'official' narratives produced in celebrity memoir react to their media environment, they can be seen to be always in interaction with the multiplicity of coverage, judgements and readings that circulate around the celebrity. The digital structures of celebrity gossip media provide a forum for alternative discourses about a celebrity that can compete with, if not supplant, the 'official story'. As celebrities are judged according to how successfully they perform certain norms, celebrity memoirs can be seen to be attempting to align the celebrity subject with dominant ideas of white, middle-class femininity. A particular brand of celebrity femininity is thus constructed through the negotiation between the subject

---

[195] Bourdieu (1993).

and her audience as 'official' memoir and 'alternative' discourses overlap with, react to, and incorporate one another. In the reception of their images, Jade Goody and Paris Hilton are always already defined in relation to their status as emblems of either the undeserving rich or the undeserving poor. Publicly derided as not having proven their worth according to socially sanctioned ideas of what constitutes talent or worthy fame, these women's images are constructed in relation to their past humiliation such that they are always partially defined by it. These celebrities do not solely seek to disavow their public humiliations. Indeed, the recirculation of these humiliations can work in their commercial interests. However, whilst they may at points embrace and celebrate their unruly femininities, their categorization as 'white trash' shows that society does not. A sexualised inflexion writes trashiness upon the overexposed female celebrity body, and exposes the limits and parameters of this negotiated agency. Agency in self-representation takes many shifting, multi-directional, interconnected forms. However, it is a 'finite multiplicity'[196] in which neither woman can shed her origins.

The conventions of both reality TV and contemporary memoir demand the subject's exposure as they reveal (ideally shameful) secrets, or are caught in candid moments of humiliation. Individual subjects must negotiate this demand for their exposure. The strategies available to each depend on the capitals they bring to the exchanges between a subject, their ghost, and their audience. By analysing two stars who represent antithetical extremes along the class spectrum, this chapter shows that strategies for negotiating shame and confession vary greatly from star to star, revealing different power dynamics in relation to the status of autobiographical subject. And yet, in the memoirs of female celebrities, even if evasively, shame and confession must always be negotiated. Goody's relative deficit in social status forces her to participate in her abjection as she repents the shame of her class background, giving the reader the authority to judge and forgive. In contrast, Hilton's corresponding surfeit insulates her from the genre's demands for confession, mobilising ellipsis and camp play in the performance of 'tongue in chic' persona. At either end of the class spectrum, as heiress and 'chav', neither is perceived to have 'earned' her fame and lifestyle in ways which are particularly gendered. Memoirs represent an intervention into the web of media narratives that surround

---

[196] Dyer (1979), p. 3.

these women, but it is an intervention that attempts to make these women more palatable to the dominant norms that reject them, affording them agency enough to participate in their own humiliation

BIBLIOGRAPHY

Allen, Kim and Heather Mendick. 'Young People's Uses of Celebrity: Class, Gender and 'Improper' Celebrity,' *Discourse: Studies in the Cultural Politics of Education*, 34 (1), 2013: 77–93.

Bakhtin, Mikhail. *Rabelais and His World*. Bloomington: Indiana University Press, 1965.

Bigg Boss, 2008. TV, Endemol. Series 2.

Billboard Staff. 'Paris Hilton Signs with Cash Money; Second Album to Feature Lil Wayne.' *The Hollywood Reporter*, 2 May 2013. http://www.hollywoodrep orter.com/earshot/paris-hilton-signs-cash-money-532750.

Biressi, Anita and Heather Nunn. *Reality TV: Realism and Revelation*. London: Wallflower Press, 2005.

Blackburn, Virginia. 'Katie Price's Life? It's a Price Worth Paying.' *The Guardian*, 17 January 2010. http://www.guardian.co.uk/commentisfree/2010/jan/17/jordan-celebrity-memoir.

Boorstin, Daniel. *The Image*. London: Penguin, 1963.

Bourdieu, Pierre. *Distinction: A Social Critique of the Judgement of Taste*. London: Routledge, 1984.

———. *The Field of Cultural Production: Essays on Art and Literature*. Cambridge: Polity, 1993.

Butler, Judith. *Bodies That Matter: On the Discursive Limits of Sex*. London: Routledge, 1993.

Celebrity Big Brother, 2007. TV, Endemol. Series 5.

Cobb, Shelley. 'Mother of the Year: Kathy Hilton, Lynne Spears, Dina Lohan and Bad Celebrity Motherhood.' *Genders*, 48, 2008. http://www.genders.org/g48/g48_cobb.html.

Contostavlos, Tulisa. *Honest: My Story So Far*. London: Headline, 2012.

Couser, G. Thomas. 'Making, Taking, and Faking Lives: The Ethics of Collaborative Life Writing.' *Style* 32 (2) 1998: 334–51.

Dent, Susie. *Larpers and Shroomers: The Language Report*. Oxford: Oxford University Press, 2004.

Desborough, James. 'JADE: YES I DID GIVE PJ THE BJ!' *The People*, 28 July 2002.

Dubrofsky, Rachel E. 'Fallen Women in Reality TV: A Pornography of Emotion.' *Feminist Media Studies*, 9 (3), 2009: 353–68.

Dyer, Richard. *Stars*. London: British Film Institute, 1979.

———. *The Culture of Queers*. London: Routledge, 2002.

Fahy, Thomas. 'One Night in Paris Hilton: Wealth, Celebrity, and the Politics of Humiliation.' *Pop-Porn: Pornography in American Culture*, ed. by Ann C. Hall and Mardia J. Bishop. Westport, CT: Praeger, 2007: 75–98. http://www.georgesclaudeguilbert.com/fahy.pdf.

Faiers, Sam. *Living Life the Essex Way*. London: Simon and Schuster, 2012.

Foster, Patrick. 'Media Scrum Continues After Jade Goody's Death, with Rehashed Book and a Film Plan.' *The Times*, 24 March 2009.

Foucault, Michel. *The History of Sexuality: Volume 1*, trans. Robert Hurley. New York: Pantheon, 1978.

Gamson, Joshua. 'The Assembly Line of Greatness: Celebrity in Twentieth Century America.' *Stardom and Celebrity: A Reader*, ed. by Su Holmes and Sean Redmond. London: Sage, 2007: 141–55.

Gies, Lieve. 'Pigs, Dogs, Cows, and Commerce in Celebrity Big Brother 2007.' *Feminist Media Studies*, 7 (4), 2007.

Gilmore, Leigh. 'American Neoconfessional: Memoir, Self Help and Redemption on Oprah's Couch.' *Biography*, 33 (4), 2010: 657–79.

Goody, Jade. *Jade Fighting to the End*. London: John Blake, 2009.

Hartigan, John. 'Unpopular Culture: The Case of "White Trash".' *Cultural Studies*, 11 (2), 1997: 316–43.

Hegde, Radha S. 'Of Race, Classy Victims and National Mythologies: Distracting reality on Celebrity Big Brother.' *Feminist Media Studies*, 7 (4), 2007: 455–69.

Hilton, Paris. *Confessions of an Heiress: A Tongue-in-Chic Peek Behind the Pose*. New York: Fireside Books, 2004.

Holmes, Su. '"All You've Got to Worry About is the Task, Having a Cup of Tea, and Doing a Bit of Sunbathing": Approaching Celebrity in *Big Brother*.' *Understanding Reality Television*, ed. by Su Holmes and Deborah Jermyn. London: Routledge, 2004.

———. '"Off-guard, Unkempt, Unready"? Deconstructing Contemporary Celebrity in Heat Magazine.' *Continuum: Journal of Media & Cultural Studies*, 19 (1), 2005a: 21–38.

———. '"Starring... Dyer?" Re-visiting Star Studies and Contemporary Celebrity Culture.' *Westminster Papers in Communication and Culture*, 2 (2), 2005b: 6–21.

———. 'Jade's Back, and This Time She's Famous: Narratives of Celebrity in the Celebrity Big Brother Race Row.' *Entertainment and Sports Law Journal*, 7 (1), 2009.

Holmes, Su and Deborah Jermyn, eds. *Understanding 'Reality' Television*. London: Routledge, 2004.

Holmes, Su, and Sean Redmond, 'Introduction: Understanding Celebrity Culture.' *Framing Celebrity: New Directions in Celebrity Culture*, ed. by Su Holmes and Sean Redmond. London, New York: Routledge, 2006.

Jade: The Reality Star Who Changed Britain, 2019. Blast! Films, Channel 4.

Jeffries, Stuart. 'Beauty and the Beastliness: A Tale of Declining British Values.' *The Guardian*, 19 January 2007. http://www.guardian.co.uk/media/2007/jan/19/broadcasting.comment.

Kardashian, Kim, Kourtney Kardashian, and Khloe Kardashian. *Kardashian Konfidential*. New York: St Martin's Press, 2011.

Kavka, Misha. *Reality TV*. Edinburgh: Edinburgh Press, 2012.

Klinger, Barbara. 'Digressions at the Cinema: Reception and Mass Culture.' *Cinema Journal*, 28 (4), 1989: 3–19.

Listology, melladior@ho, 'Paris Hilton: Rich White Trash.' http://www.listology.com/story/paris-hilton-rich-white-trash.

Medved, Matt. 'Paris Hilton Reveals Las Vegas Residency, Defends DJ Career.' *The Hollywood Reporter*, 31 March 2015. http://www.hollywoodreporter.com/news/paris-hilton-reveals-las-vegas-785656.

Morrison, Nick. 'What Can Schools Learn from Jade Goody?' *Times Educational Supplement*, 17 April 2009. http://www.tes.co.uk/article.aspx?storycode=6011978.

Morrow, Mandy. 'Celebrity Book Deals: The Latest, Highest-Paid Advances.' *The Richest*, 3 August 2014. http://www.therichest.com/expensive-lifestyle/money/celebrity-book-deals-the-latest-highest-paid-advances/.

Negra, Diane and Maria Pramaggiore. 'Keeping Up with the Aspirations: Commercial Family Values and the Kardashian Brand.' *Reality Gendervision: Sexuality & Gender on Transatlantic Reality Television*, ed. by Brenda R. Weber. London: Duke University Press 2014.

Newitz, Annalee and Matt Wray, eds. *White Trash: Race and Class in America*. London and New York: Routledge, 1997.

Nunn, Heather and Anita Biressi. '"A Trust Betrayed": Celebrity and the Work of Emotion.' *Celebrity Studies*, 1 (1), 2010: 49–64.

Obituary: 'Jade Goody.' *The Telegraph*, 22 March 2009. http://www.telegraph.co.uk/news/obituaries/5031343/Jade-Goody.html.

Redmond, Sean. 'The Whiteness of Stars: Looking at Kate Winslet's Unruly White Body.' *Stardom and Celebrity: A Reader*, ed. by Su Holmes and Sean Redmond. London: Sage, 2006.

Rojeck, Chris. *Fame Attack: The Inflation of Fame and Its Consequences*. London: Bloomsbury, 2012.

Russo, Mary J. *The Female Grotesque: Risk, Excess and Modernity*. London and New York: Routledge, 1994.

Sales, Nancy Jo. "Hip-Hop Debs," *Vanity Fair*, September 2000. Cited in Fahy, 'One Night in Paris Hilton': 75–98.

Singh, Anita. '"Jade Goody Represented Wretched Britain", says Sir Michael Parkinson.' *The Telegraph*, 7 April 2009. http://www.telegraph.co.uk/news/

celebritynews/jade-goody/5114664/Jade-Goody-represented-wretched-Bri
tain-says-Sir-Michael-Parkinson.html.
Skeggs, Bev. 'The Toilet Paper: Femininity, Class and Misrecognition.' *Women's
Studies International Forum*, 24 (2–4), 2001.
———. *Class, Self, Culture.* London: Routledge, 2003.
Skeggs, Beverley and Helen Wood. 'The Labour of Transformation and Circuits
of Value 'Around' Reality TV.' *Continuum*, 22 (4), 2008: 559–72.
Smith, Sidonie and Julia Watson. *Reading Autobiography: A Guide for Inter-
preting Life Narratives.* Minneapolis: University of Minnesota Press, 2001.
Sontag, Susan. 'Notes on Camp.' *Against Interpretation and Other Essays.*
London: Eyre & Spottiswoode, 1967.
Tasker, Yvonne and Diane Negra. *Interrogating Postfeminism: Gender and the
Politics of Popular Culture.* Durham, NC: Duke University Press, 2007.
The Daily Mail. 'The Year of the Chav,' 19 October 2004. https://www.dailym
ail.co.uk/news/article-322501/The-year-Chav.html.
The Daily Star. 'Jermaine in Frame: New Big Bro Race Row,' 3 February 2007.
http://www.dailystar.co.uk/posts/view/12423.
The Mirror. 'Jade Goody "Had No Talent—And She Knew It" says Max
Clifford,' 6 May 2009. https://www.mirror.co.uk/3am/celebrity-news/jade-
goody-had-no-talent-392393.
The Simple Life, 2003–2007. TV, 20th Century Fox.
THR Staff. 'Paris Hilton on Her Global Tour and Drug Use in the EDM Scene.'
The Hollywood Reporter, 8 October 2013. http://www.hollywoodreporter.
com/video/paris-hilton-her-global-tour-645126.
Tseëlon, Efrat. *The Masque of Femininity: The Presentation of Woman in Everyday
Life.* London: Sage, 1995.
Tyler, Imogen and Bruce Bennett. '"Celebrity Chav': Fame, Femininity and
Social Class." *European Journal of Cultural Studies*, 13 (3), 2010: 375–93.
Urban Dictionary. 'White Trash,' posted by 'Your Mom.' http://www.urband
ictionary.com/define.php?term=white%20trash.
Williamson, Milly. 'Female Celebrities and the Media: The Gendered Denigration
of the 'Ordinary' Celebrity.' *Celebrity Studies*, 1 (1), 2010.
Woods, Faye. 'Classed Femininity, Performativity, and Camp in British Structured
Reality Programming.' *Television New Media*, 6 November 2012.
Yelin, Hannah and Laura Clancy. 'Doing Impact Work While Female: Hate
Tweets, "Hot Potatoes" and Having "Enough of Experts."' *European Journal
of Women's Studies*, March 3, 2020.

CHAPTER 5

The *Gendered Authenticity Contract*: Exposure Without Insulation in the YouTuber Memoirs of Zoella, iJustine and JennxPenn

INTRODUCTION: THE DEATH OF THE GHOSTWRITER

Ghostwriting receives much scorn, and yet the presence of the ghostwriter is often tolerated or expected (in part due to the low expectations placed upon celebrities' literary capabilities). However, one example where the reception of a book has been vehemently intolerant of ghostwriting is YouTube celebrity Zoe (Zoella) Sugg's 2014 semi-autobiographical novel, *Girl Online*. *Girl Online* is significant in that it triggered a national debate about the ethics of ghostwriting. The tone of press responses to the 'controversy', and the fact that it was considered a controversy at all, offers an opportunity to consider what is at stake in cultural anxieties about both ghostwriters and young, female, YouTube celebrities.

As is customary, Sugg worked with a ghostwriter to produce her book. As is common, Sugg thanks those 'at Penguin for helping [her] put together [her] first novel, especially Amy Alward and Siobhan Curham who were with [her] every step of the way'.[1] Whilst the word ghostwriter is not mentioned, this is a more explicit thanks than is often given. This chapter will examine *Girl Online* alongside the memoirs of YouTube celebrities Justine Ezarik and Jenn McAllister. Each of the books takes a different approach to acknowledging their ghost. None of them feature a second name on the cover but Ezarik's inner title page states, 'Justine

---

[1] Zoe Sugg, *Girl Online* (London: Penguin, 2015), p. 345.

© The Author(s) 2020
H. Yelin, *Celebrity Memoir*,
https://doi.org/10.1007/978-3-030-44621-5_5

153

Ezarik with C.L. Hargrave'.[2] McAllister writes, 'thank you to my co-writer, Nora Kletter, for providing countless cost-free therapy sessions', joking about the overlapping roles of the ghost as confessional inter-locutor that were discussed in the previous chapter. One way or another, all three stars visibly credit their ghosts, and more so than is often the case in the wider genre. However, Sugg was vehemently attacked in the nation's press for what was felt to constitute a dishonest failure to explicitly state that she had not written the book alone. Journalist Lucy Hunter Johnston, for example, wrote a scathing lamentation that in Sugg's use of a ghostwriter 'integrity appears to have been sacrificed in favour of financial gain'.[3]

Siobhan Curham's ghostwriting role became apparent through her website representing her work as a writer. Curham allegedly uploaded and subsequently deleted a blog post complaining that an unnamed publisher was giving her an insufficient six weeks to complete a project that was 80,000 words long: dates and numbers which her readers connected to the publication of *Girl Online*.[4] This speculation and negative attention led to public statements from Sugg, who stated on her blog, 'For the doubters out there, of course I was going to have help from Penguin's editorial team in telling my story, which I talked about from the begin-ning', and from Penguin, who issued a statement to *The Sunday Times*: 'To be factually accurate, you would need to say Zoe Sugg did not write the book *Girl Online* on her own'.[5] So why, when the circumstances of the ghostwriting relationship seem so unextraordinary compared to genre norms, is this the ghosting arrangement that kicked off a national contro-versy? How did Siobhan Curham become a more controversial figure than predatory Neil Strauss who I discussed in the chapter on 'glamour girls', or alleged sex offender Terry Richardson who will be discussed in the chapter on pop-stars? Why is Sugg, of all these stars, specifically felt to have broken what I will call an *authenticity contract*—a gendered expec-tation of access to celebrity selfhood that, if unmet, leaves fans feeling angry or duped.

---

[2] Justine Ezarik, *I, Justine* (New York: Keywords Press, 2015), title page.

[3] Lucy Hunter Johnston, 'Yes, Using a Ghostwriter Matters When Your Whole Brand Is Built on Being Authentic,' *The Independent*, 8 December 2014.

[4] Ibid.

[5] Katie Glass, 'Zoella's Bestseller: The Plot Thickens,' *The Times*, 7 December 2014.

The fact that YouTube celebrity hinges upon the appearance of being unmediated and therefore 'authentic'[6] is certainly a factor in the censure of Sugg's undisclosed working relationship with Curham, as seen in *The Independent* headline: 'Zoella. Yes, using a ghostwriter matters when your whole brand is built on being authentic'.[7] However, other ghostwritten YouTube celebrity memoirs did not kick off similar national controversies. Like Pamela Anderson's *Star*, Sugg's *Girl Online* is presented as fiction but with sufficient parallels between the protagonist and the celebrity author to invite readers to read one as the other. It follows a teenage blogger, Penny, who, like Sugg, lives in Brighton, and whose blog unexpectedly goes viral amassing huge numbers of followers. Like Sugg, the central character is close to her brother, is a keen photographer and blogs about suffering from anxiety and panic attacks. The story hinges around the protagonist revealing her romantic relationship with a celebrity in a blog post, just as Sugg did with her fellow YouTube celebrity boyfriend, Alfie Deyes.[8] The scenes described emulate the aesthetic signature style of the videos Sugg shoots in her own bedroom as Penny describes a bedroom adorned with cosy scented candles and fairy lights, wears animal onesies and lists favourite products like moisturiser and bath bombs. Not only are these the kinds of products Sugg shows and reviews in her videos, one can also buy Zoella branded versions of them in her own beauty and homeware ranges.

Despite these explicit and deliberate parallels, as a semi-autobiographical novel next to two traditional first-person memoirs, Sugg's book makes the least claim to direct autobiographical intimacy of the books that will be examined in this chapter. However, it was met with the highest expectation of delivering authentic access to its star author. It is possible that, had it been a traditional memoir, Curham's involvement would have passed unnoticed. This would suggest that the

---

[6] Andrew Tolson, 'A New Authenticity? Communicative Practices on YouTube,' *Critical Discourse Studies* 7.4 (2010), 277–89; Daniel Smith, '"Charlie Is so 'English'-Like": Nationality and the Branded Celebrity Person in the Age of YouTube,' *Celebrity Studies* 5.3 (2014), 256–74; Sarah Banet-Weiser, 'Branding the Post-Feminist Self: Girls' Video Production and YouTube,' *Mediated Girlhoods: New Explorations in Girls' Media Culture*, ed. by Mary Celeste Kearney (New York: Peter Lang, 2011).

[7] Hunter Johnston.

[8] 'Zalfie,' *Zoella.co.uk*, 11 August 2013.

attempt to claim the cultural value of the status of *novelist* is what rankles, reinforcing the degraded status of celebrity memoir as a cultural form.

One possibility is that it is an opportunity to denigrate a young, female celebrity for her lack of intellectual capacity. My discussions of reality TV memoir made clear the association between celebrity and perceptions of talentlessness, but YouTube celebrity in particular has a generational element to the scorn, being a recent phenomenon, and one that appeals primarily to young people, and is therefore misunderstood and dismissed by an older generation who make up the commentariat.[9] 'If the words "digital ambassador" mean nothing to you, "vlogger" will mean even less', says Zoe Williams in a *Guardian* article titled, 'Zoe Sugg: the vlogger blamed for declining teenage literacy'.[10] As young people with sizable fame and commercial success, who have monetised their niche with minimal mainstream cross-over, YouTubers are particularly at risk of indignation and anxiety about undeserved rewards bestowed on those who are supposedly famous 'for nothing' by those who begrudge a phenomenon they do not understand. Certainly, these discourses run through the attacks upon Sugg, but they do not account for why Sugg inspired this ire when other financially successful YouTubers escaped it.

Curham and Sugg were hauled through the press as if they had committed a great deception, breaking 'the implicit promise that Zoella makes to her followers'.[11] One might assume that having so much of Sugg's life since 2009 documented in blog posts and YouTube videos would aid a ghostwriter in capturing her voice. However, *Girl Online* offers some of the more heavy-handed ghostwriting out there—with many moments that read like they are written by someone with a writerly interest in story formulation. The two romantic protagonists discuss their first meeting as their 'inciting incident'[12] and even use the literary critical term as a nickname. I certainly do not wish to play to popular assumptions about the intellectual labours of young, female celebrities and imply that Sugg is unequal to reading literary theory; it is perfectly possible that

---

[9] Ruth Deller and Kathryn Murphy, '"Zoella Hasn't Really Written a Book, She's Written a Cheque": Mainstream Media Representations of YouTube Celebrities,' *European Journal of Cultural Studies* (July 2019).

[10] Zoe Williams, 'Zoe Sugg: The Vlogger Blamed for Declining Teenage Literacy,' *The Guardian*, 24 February 2017.

[11] Hunter Johnston.

[12] Sugg, pp. 178, 181.

the presence of such novel-writing jargon is evidence of Sugg as first-time author having recently brushed up on her narrative theory. Either way, it sounds more like terminology drawn upon by someone with a preoccupation with writing, seeing the events in somewhat clinical terms for their position in a narrative formula, rather than communicating the emotional immediacy and messiness that suggest the *drawn from life* quality associated with personal memory. Likewise, when the narrator declares the opportunity to go to New York to be a 'Glass Slipper Moment'[13] she self-reflexively draws attention to the many parallels between her own story and the Cinderella fairy tale, in terms that again suggest this preoccupation with the formal components of fiction more strongly than they suggest personal experience.

Penguin and Sugg needed to solve their toxic PR situation if they were to capitalise on *Girl Online's* commercial success with follow-up titles, and their solution was to kill off the figure of the ghostwriter. When book two was announced, Sugg declared that she was going to write this one herself, with only weekly meetings with an editor to guide her—meetings which would be documented on her YouTube channel. In a field which demands constant new ideas for content, there is ingenuity in parlaying past criticism into a new, themed content stream, doubly so when it has an ongoing promotional value, increasing her audience's investment in the forthcoming book. Conceptually, two interesting things are happening here. Firstly, we see YouTube offered as surveillance for her fans, furnishing them with reassuring 'proof' that Sugg is not breaking her *authenticity contract*. Secondly, we see Sugg defining what *counts* as ghosting.

In one video, Sugg explains, 'for book one I did have an editorial consultant who helped me get it all down, but this time it's just me and Amy'.[14] She states this as if Curham was the problem, and swapping Curham for Amy Alward, in house employee of Penguin, is a de facto solution to the problem of the ghost when Alward is similarly offering editorial consultation. In another video, Sugg and Alward describe the work of an editor, carefully setting out the terms of acceptable contribution that do not compromise Sugg's authorship, whilst managing her

---

[13] Ibid., p. 91.

[14] Zoe Sugg, 'Book Meeting, Date Night & Found the Missing Wallet,' 24 April 2015.

audience's perception about what constitutes a normal level of intervention. Even here, Sugg uses the collective first-person plural point of view, occluding the division of labour: 'we even changed quite big things in it, we've gone through and been like "this doesn't work"'.[15] Alward explains 'for a lot of people who don't understand what an editor does', that her role is to 'read people's books, go through them, and help make them the best books they can be, and suggest changes, make suggestions and then work on it together'.[16] They work to normalise the presence of the editor as someone who always helps with the writing process and makes changes to a book: 'every author that's been published has an editor, someone who's read the book and loves it as much as they do and works with them to make it the best it can be'.[17] They discuss the roles of the editor, copy editor and proofreader, all of whom will be contributing to Sugg's book.[18] By the expanded understanding of ghosting that this book works towards, each of these interventions is a ghost of sorts, but for the purposes of Sugg's marketing strategy for book two it is critical that there is no one in the process called a ghostwriter. This semantic sleight of hand seems to have worked, and broadsheet reviews deemed book two, *Girl Online: On Tour*, to be 'more authentic' according to the logic of autobiographical access, despite 'the hand of the editor there throughout': 'Elements of Sugg's own experiences, her chirpy way of speaking and her genuine interest in mental health (both Sugg and her lead character suffer from panic attacks) shine through with greater authenticity here'.[19] Whilst the nature of the work involved is similar—contributing, in Alward's words, ideas for structure, characters and plot—these interventions are acceptable from an editor where they would not be from a ghostwriter.

Crucially, Alward is in the direct employ of Penguin, so offers no risk of a badly veiled complaint on a personal blog, and will use these YouTube videos of their meetings to carefully state and restate the marketing strategy and party line that underscore Sugg's uncomplicated authorship.

---

[15] Zoe Sugg, 'Finishing Book Two & Louise's Launch,' 21 July 2015.

[16] Ibid.

[17] Ibid.

[18] Ibid.

[19] Charlotte Runcie, 'Girl Online on Tour by Zoe Sugg, Review: "More Authentic",' *The Telegraph*, 20 October 2015.

She offers examples of her own involvement—to 'smooth it all out and fine tune' the book—but always carefully, perhaps excessively and unnaturally, emphasises that the writing is Sugg's: 'I was reading everything that *Zoe wrote* last night and going through and it was so good [...] the final line *you wrote* last night' [emphasis added].[20] Another video, called 'Writing With A Pug' shows a minute and a half of dialogue-free, time-lapse footage of Sugg writing at her laptop (whilst being interrupted by a pet pug). In a field where videos are usually short and extremely full to keep the attention of an audience used to videos that are short and extremely full, even with the on-brand, cute and whimsical presence of the pug, this comparatively long and boring cut constitutes a huge amount of emphasis upon the act of writing. She reiterates, 'basically every single day I'm doing a bit of writing'.[21] As well as asserting her labour, she affirms her creative control: 'I have so much power over what could happen'.[22] What looks like the kind of breezy, spontaneous peek into her day that is a staple of YouTuber content is a careful demonstration of the ways in which she is involved in the production of her book, and normalises the writing help she is getting as legitimate intervention, crucially not from someone who calls themselves a ghostwriter. 'People are so invested', Sugg remarks of the book's audience to her YouTube audience.[23] Of course, these audiences are largely one and the same. The people she talks about in her videos are the people she is talking to. Under the guise of offering transparency, she undertakes an exercise in marketing, carefully managing perceptions of her labour and involvement so that her readers do not reject her again, and more importantly, so that they buy book two.

The case of Sugg's ghostwriting 'scandal' sets up many of the specificities of YouTube celebrity examined in this chapter. The example of Sugg's backlash shows the *gendered authenticity contract* I will argue exists as a benchmark for access to the female star and which causes anger when the star falls short. This example highlights cultural expectations that YouTubers in particular are lone workers, architecting their fame unaided, and the tension between this understanding of the lone worker and the wider industrial machinery of fame production that success brings them into

[20] Zoe Sugg, 'Finishing Book Two.'

[21] Zoe Sugg, 'Writing with a Pug, Meetings & Doggy Box,' 15 May 2015.

[22] Zoe Sugg, 'Finishing Book Two.'

[23] Ibid.

contact with. It shows that, whilst YouTubers may make and upload their own videos, it does not necessarily follow that they have full control of their narratives or are any less embroiled in constellations of 'ghost'-like intermediaries than the celebrities discussed in previous chapters.

THEORISING YOUTUBE CELEBRITY

Scholars have theorised the particularities of YouTube fame, often centring upon questions of whether the platform challenges 'traditional' means of producing and representing celebrity. YouTube is understood to have 'forged a celebrity culture of its own'[24] with 'its own regime of entrepreneurialism'.[25] It shares Facebook's 'Like Economy', the practice of clicking a thumbs-up 'like' to 'boost' certain content.[26] In this context, 'self-branding', combining the democratising potential of digital self-representation with the neoliberal mandate of individualised commercial maximisation, is central to YouTube celebrity.[27] Successful YouTube celebrification depends upon viewers' 'positive responses not only to video content, but even more so to the YouTubers' ability to combine "natural" self-promotion with digital technologies of intimacy'.[28] Such technologies enable us 'to love, hate, or feel strongly about someone [we have] never talked to'.[29] In this economy, confessions are shared 'in exchange for quantifiable signifiers of popularity'.[30] The performance of 'authenticity' on YouTube has preoccupied scholars of the platform. Many

[24] Smith, p. 256.

[25] Michael Lovelock, '"Is Every YouTuber Going to Make a Coming Out Video Eventually?": Youtube Celebrity Video Bloggers and Lesbian and Gay Identity,' *Celebrity Studies* 8.1 (2017), 87–103.

[26] Carolin Gerlitz and Anne Helmond, 'The Like Economy: Social Buttons and the Data-Intensive Web,' *New Media and Society* 15.8 (2013), 1348–65.

[27] Banet-Weiser (2011).

[28] Rachel Berryman and Misha Kavka, 'I Guess a Lot of People See Me as a Big Sister or a Friend': The Role of Intimacy in the Celebrification of Beauty Vloggers,' *Journal of Gender Studies* 26.3 (2017), 307–20, p. 309.

[29] Misha Kavka, *Reality Television, Affect and Intimacy* (Basingstoke: Palgrave Macmillan, 2008), p. 24.

[30] Lovelock.

have unpacked the signifiers that construct the appearance of authenticity, for example leaving in malapropisms and mistakes,[31] 'calibrated amateurism',[32] direct address and dialogue[33] or crying.[34]

Others have focussed upon the appearance of lone-working structures that suggest a lack of celebrity industry intermediaries.[35] YouTube celebrity, as Anne Jerslev argues,

> comprises a sense of self-government. Because of the widespread conception of YouTube as a bottom-up social media platform [...] this idea of autonomy, therefore, underpins their trustworthiness and authenticity.[36]

This question of autonomy has been central to the study of online or 'micro' celebrity since Theresa Senft observed that the fame of 'camgirls' was built upon connection and responsiveness, offered the unedited 'real' self, and utilised opportunities created by an engaged audience, rather than traditional entertainment industry structures.[37] This fusing of industrial and amateur results in YouTube's 'double function' as the site offers both a 'topdown' platform for the distribution of popular culture and a 'bottom-up' platform for vernacular creativity.[38]

Sugg is one of the UK's most successful vloggers. Since she began her blog and subsequent YouTube channel in 2009, aged 19, her following has grown to over 12 million subscribers. In 2014, her loosely autobiographical novel, *Girl Online*, sold nearly 80,000 copies in its first week, breaking records to make her the fastest-selling debut author,

---

[31] Anne Jerslev, 'In the Time of the Microcelebrity: Celebrification and the YouTuber Zoella,' *International Journal of Communication* 10 (2016), 5233–51.

[32] Crystal Abidin, '#familygoals: Family Influencers, Calibrated Amateurism, and Justifying Young Digital Labor,' *Social Media + Society* 3.2 (2017), 1–15.

[33] Tolson.

[34] Rachel Berryman and Misha Kavka, 'Crying on YouTube: Vlogs, Self-Exposure and the Productivity of Negative Affect,' *Convergence* 24 (2017), 85–98.

[35] Alice Marwick, *Status Update: Celebrity, Publicity and Branding in the Social Media Age* (New Haven, CT: Yale University Press, 2013); Jerslev (2010).

[36] Jerslev, p. 5240.

[37] Theresa Senft, *Camgirls: Celebrity and Community in the Age of Social Networks* (New York, NY: Peter Lang Publishing, 2008).

[38] Jean Burgess and Joshua Green, *YouTube: Online Video and Participatory Culture* (Cambridge: Polity, 2009), p. 6.

beating previous best-sellers such as J.K. Rowling, Dan Brown and E.L. James.[39] Scholarly interest in Sugg has focussed on her various methods of constructing intimate, or sympathetic, relationships with her audience. Sugg's affective labour has also been understood by scholars as a way of building audience relationships and claiming authenticity through the sharing of negative emotions and struggles with anxiety.[40] Jerslev argues that Sugg is exemplary of the intimacy of YouTube celebrity, creating 'a sense of closeness to her huge following [through] performances of continuity, authenticity, and connectedness'.[41] This intimacy, Berryman and Kavka argue, is directed towards Sugg's 'big sister persona' and, moreover, towards the products she sells and/or endorses in a process which synthesises commodification with femininity and (gendered) intimacy.

In Berryman and Kavka's argument, *Girl Online* is considered as an example of Sugg extending her personal brand across different media and merchandise. Alison Lutton similarly examines *Girl Online* through the lens of 'field migration', demonstrating the legitimising authenticity work that must be undergone when attempting to traverse cultural fields from Internet to literary fame.[42] Deller and Murphy show through press responses to *Girl Online* that YouTubers are routinely met with suspicion that results in the policing of cultural boundaries and are 'presented as fraudulent, inauthentic, opportunist and talentless, making money from doing nothing'.[43] For Jerslev, the launch of *Girl Online* was significant in the disruption it presented to the usual model of instantaneity that characterises YouTube celebrity. For example, at strictly ticketed book-signings photographs were prohibited. As a result, 'the gap between herself and her followers widened—not only offline but also online—in space and in

---

[39] Anita Singh, 'Zoella Breaks Record for First Week Book Sales,' *The Telegraph*, 2 December 2014.

[40] Sophie Bishop, '#YouTuberAnxiety: Anxiety as Emotional Labour and Masquerade in Beauty Vlogs,' *Youth Mediations and Affective Relations*, ed. by S. Driver and N. Coulter (London: Palgrave Macmillan, 2018); Berryman and Kavka (2017).

[41] Jerslev, p. 5240.

[42] Alison Lutton, 'YouTubers-Turned-Authors and the Problematic Practice of Authenticity,' *Celebrity Studies* (2019), 1–16.

[43] Deller and Murphy.

time'.[44] This exemplifies the inconsistencies between different media in the production of celebrity.

Justine Ezarik, known as iJustine, is an American YouTube celebrity who started posting in 2006, the earliest of the stars examined here. Her personal brand is that of the tech-savvy early adopter, featuring content such as queuing for the first release of new Apple products, reviewing gadgets, and reporting from product launches, as well as comic and 'prank' videos. Her following grew after a 2006 YouTube video about her 300-page iPhone bill went 'viral', and in 2007, she began 'lifecasting', wearing a wireless webcam to live broadcast her life, purportedly 24/7.

Ezarik's lifecasting has been theorised by Sarah Banet-Weiser as the 'quintessential example of the self-brand [...] where the self is a product, promoted and sold by individual entrepreneurs'.[45] With its panoptic, technologically enabled surveillance, Ezarik's commodification of her day-to-day life is, for Banet-Weiser, produced through a 'self-policing and self-absorbed gaze' that is fundamentally postfeminist in its centring of Ezarik's visible female body.[46] We shall see the continuation of this postfeminist sensibility into her memoir. Moreover, I shall theorise this in relation to the ways in which the nature of YouTube celebrity, its *economics of access* without insulation coaxes acceptance of, and even collusion with, online misogyny.

YouTuber, Jenn McAllister, started posting comedy and prank videos under the moniker JennxPenn in 2009 age 12, and is the youngest of the celebrities examined in this book. Whilst academic interest in Internet, and particularly YouTube, celebrity has rapidly grown, and despite McAllister's phenomenal success (with 3.5 million subscribers and 324 million views,[47] 1.9m Twitter followers, and an estimated $5million net worth[48]), JennxPenn has yet to attract the kind of scholarly attention Zoella and iJustine have received. This may be because the scale, platforms and audiences of what is sometimes called 'microcelebrity' are a

[44] Jerslev, p. 5245.

[45] Sarah Banet-Weiser, *AuthenticTM: The Politics of Ambivalence in a Brand Culture* (New York: New York University Press, 2012), p. 76.

[46] Ibid., pp. 77–78.

[47] 'JennxPenn,' *socialblade.com*, 29 August 2019.

[48] 'Jen McAllister Net Worth and Earnings 2018,' *ecelebritymirror.com*, 12 July 2018.

complex interrelation of niche community and the potential for immense breadth.[49] This is perhaps why, as McAllister suggests, 'YouTubers were often referred to (well, really are still referred to) as the most famous people you've never heard of'.[50] Certainly, this trope is recycled by journalists in headlines such as 'The most famous girl you've never heard of' and 'Who is Zoella? The YouTube star is probably the most famous person you've never heard of'.[51]

'Broadcast Yourself': The Multiplicity of YouTube Celebrity as Unruly, Networked, Collaborative Autobiography

In 2018, investment bank Morgan Stanley valued YouTube at $160 billion.[52] Its strapline, 'Broadcast Yourself', pitches the platform as a space of self-representation—making and sharing YouTube videos are in themselves autobiographical acts. With its formal conventions of first-person direct address to the audience, diary-style regular entries, and intimate, confessional subject matter, the style, content and appeal of YouTube videos share much in common with autobiography. Likewise, as an act of self-commodification, offering access to a mediated, branded self as a merchandising vehicle,[53] YouTube celebrity and celebrity memoir operate according to related commercial principles. In her 2015 print memoir, *Really Professional Internet Person*, McAllister emphasises and

[49] Crystal Abidin, *Internet Celebrity: Understanding Fame Online* (Emerald Publishing, 2018), p. 15.

[50] McAllister, p. 216.

[51] Sarah Barns, 'Who Is Zoella? The YouTube Star Is Probably the Most Famous Person You've Never Heard of,' *mirror.co.uk*, 18 February, 2015; Anna O'Donoghue, 'The Most Famous Girl You've Never Heard of,' *irishexaminer.com*, 7 August 2014.

[52] Greg Sandoval, 'Morgan Stanley Values YouTube as a $160 Billion Entity,' 18 May 2018.

[53] Senft (2008); Banet-Weiser (2011); Emma Maguire, 'Self-Branding, Hotness, and Girlhood in the Video Blogs of Jenna Marbles,' *Biography* 38.1 (2015); Tobias Raun, 'Capitalizing Intimacy: New Subcultural Forms of Microcelebrity Strategies and Affective Labour on YouTube,' *Convergence* 24.1 (2017), 99–113.

plays with these similarities between YouTube and memoir as autobiographical modes, titling the final chapter 'My Life in Videos'[54] and opening the first chapter with the line,

> Hey, person I can't see, I'm Jenn McAllister. I'm used to talking to people I can't see, because I've been making and posting videos on YouTube for almost 7 years. [...] You probably already know a lot about me. [...] So much of my life is on the internet.[55]

She highlights the similarities in role and address between the authorial 'I' who narrates her memoir and her address to camera when she vlogs, and the relationship between the two forms of autobiographical media as her audience consumes one as a result of their familiarity with another. She shows how online self-representations act both as archive and source material, from which she both constructs a narrative for, and creates a repository of, her heavily recorded life:

> When I was writing this book, I had to scroll back through my Instagram and Twitter, dig into my iPhoto, and even rewatch my vlogs and videos to put the puzzle pieces of my life in the right place.[56]

Digital media open up new means for people to narrate and consume their own and other peoples' lives. Back in 2001, when home Internet access was yet to become the norm, and many of the most prevalent platforms on which we shape and share our life stories had yet to be invented, Smith and Watson called for an understanding of autobiographical self-representation that went 'beyond the literary to consider cultural and media practices'.[57] They use the term *automediality* rather than autobiography to convey self-mediation beyond the written, in ways that could encompass digital forms.[58] More recently, they revisited this concept specifically in relation to the digital expansion of autobiographical modes, observing that the networked, digital life story is inherently 'co-constructed' through connections with family, friends, employers, causes,

---

[54] McAllister, p. 219.

[55] Ibid., p. 10.

[56] Ibid., p. 220.

[57] Smith and Watson, p. 168.

[58] Ibid.

and affiliations in addition to the ways in which 'the materiality of the medium constitutes and textures the subjectivity presented'.[59] There are ghosts, then, in the machines through which we collaboratively compose our digital lives.

Thus, the materiality of YouTube as a platform—its social and creative conventions as well as its technological possibilities—constitutes the autobiographical subjectivities shared there. Social and creative conventions include the tendency to confessional, first-person address, aesthetic choices like the fashion for 'ring' lighting, setting (such as Sugg's tendency to shoot videos sat on her bed) and genre (such as Sugg's beauty and lifestyle videos, McAllister's sketches and prank videos or Ezarik's humour and tech review videos). The technical features which shape the selfhoods that YouTubers are coaxed to perform include algorithms which promote or deprioritise different YouTubers based upon the popularity and frequency of their videos, the counting and display of the number of views and subscribers and the enablement of viewer comments. These are just some of the elements specifically mentioned in the memoirs examined in this chapter, but there will be countless others that influence the construction of subjectivity being shared.

Creative collaboration, the defining feature of the ghostwriting relationship, is heavily emphasised in these authors' accounts of the work of YouTube celebrity. YouTube is a celebrity field where collaborative construction is a named convention of the genre, with creative partnerships and group endeavours discussed as 'collabs'. The authors relate the importance of collabs and use their memoirs to describe many of their own, where they secure effective cross-promotion and new followers by making videos with other known YouTubers for each other's or shared YouTube channels. McAllister offers 'Top 10 Tips For Asking Someone To Collab'[60] and advises that 'doing a collab video with another YouTuber is a great way to grow your channel'.[61] Whilst, making videos with other YouTubers is the main collaborative construction overtly

---

[59] Smith and Watson, 'Virtually Me: A Toolbox about Online Presentation,' *Identity Technologies: Constructing the Self Online*, ed. by Anna Poletti and Julie Rak (Madison, WI: University of Wisconsin Press, 2013), pp. 71, 77.

[60] McAllister, p. 46.

[61] Ibid., p. 45.

discussed in the YouTube celebrity memoir, the philosophy of collaboration is celebrated beyond this. Ezarik's 2015 memoir *I, Justine: An Analog Memoir* emphasises collaborative construction as an important principle, attempting to bring the aesthetics of crowdsourcing, a behaviour native to social media, into the experience of reading her analogue memoir:

> I wanted this to be a collaborative experience. I asked for your input about what anecdotes and inside information you wanted to read; you'll find these stories sprinkled throughout, [...] some of you might even see your questions in the following pages![62]

This is accompanied by a speech bubble with the words 'ASK IJ' in the YouTube brand font and colours. Questions appear with the graphics of a YouTube comment, complete with a small, blank profile photo icon. Online celebrity, existing as it does in constant written dialogue with its audience is necessarily co-written. A 'good' online celebrity is one who responds and listens to these contributions and will be rewarded accordingly by algorithms which push them up the search rankings. This graphic device shows Ezarik attempting to demonstrate a specifically *digital* collaborative openness via printed media which has (the surface appearance of) contrastingly singular authorship and narrative fixity.

Consumers of a celebrity's autobiographical reality products, including printed memoirs, are able to 'speak back' to the celebrity through social media. However, it is not possible to respond at the point of utterance—neither temporally nor spatially; the reading of a memoir occurs at a remove from its production and does not unfold in public. A key difference between written memoir and YouTube as a space for self-representation, then, is the immediacy of communication offered as viewers comment directly onto a YouTuber's page.

Emma Maguire emphasises the difference between print memoir and YouTube automedia in that the YouTube star's audience 'cannot hold a single cohesive version of [her] story in their hands, as readers can with a memoir'.[63] Whilst this is technically true, celebrity memoirs are in reality read as part of an intertextual assemblage, as I have shown.

---

[62] Ezarik, p. 10.

[63] Maguire, p. 74.

They are commonly read from a position of existing familiarity, formed through exposure to a range of media not only self-generated but also external gossip, commentary and exposés. In this context, printed memoir is, more accurately, a doomed attempt to impose a cohesive version of a story onto an ungovernable assemblage with which it is always implicitly and explicitly in dialogue. Understanding YouTube as a form of memoir in this context, with its unruly public dialogue, makes visible this process of ungovernable, inconsistent commentary-as-contribution to a life story that cannot be kept cohesive.

Though perceived to be a 'one man show', YouTubers enter the multiplicity of co-constructed celebrity as they become remediated across different platforms. Ezarik describes the agents and intermediaries that arrived at the point of her viral success:

> I watched in disbelief as my inbox filled with hundreds of emails from literary agents, talent managers, publicists, and reporters and news producers from every major media company in the world. The video - and therefore my face - was splashed across [...] a slew of international outfits from India to Australia.[64]

As her image and story travel across different media and geographical spaces, they evolve beyond the narrative she created in the video she controlled. Thus, despite the predominantly lone-working practice of the YouTube celebrity, the assemblages of their star images are nonetheless co-constructed and propelled by teams of intermediaries.

ANALOGUE MEMOIRS OF DIGITAL SUBJECTIVITY

An endorsement on the back cover of Sugg's *Girl Online* bills the book as a 'coming-of-age tale in the digital age', a characterisation that well describes all three books. The autobiographies of YouTube celebrities offer analogue memoirs of digital subjectivity. Ezarik's *I, Justine*, for example, offers her personal history in parallel with the history of technological developments in the early twenty-first century. The book is as much a memoir of tech, or a chronicle of the Apple brand, as it is of a young celebrity woman, as she tells her story based on where she was and what she was doing during various product launches from the iPhone to

---

[64] Ezarik, p. 4.

Twitter, for example: 'the introduction of the iPod and the rise of social media - were about to have a major impact on my life'.[65] Of her online pseudonym, she states, 'I became ijustine, in honour of the iPod and the iMac'.[66] Not only is her life story intertwined with the history of developing digital technology, but it is also a life that has been lived and narrated on and through these technologies. Of the launch of new social media platforms like Twitter, for example, she relates, 'I didn't just sign up; I more or less started live tweeting my entire life'.[67] For the characters in *Girl Online,* Internet access is life-giving, as they exclaim, 'I can't imagine life without the internet or my phone'[68] and 'you can't take away a teenager's online access; it's like taking away their right to breathe'.[69] Living online shapes the subjectivity of Sugg's protagonist Penny, and her understanding and narrativisation of her life as she experiences it: 'My brain starts doing that thing where it automatically composes a Facebook update: Penny Porter is about to go out to Brooklyn with a super cute New Yorker'.[70]

The lives narrated in this genre of celebrity memoir inextricably intertwine online and offline selves. This is clear in the storylines; all three follow three acts outlining how their protagonists found a passion for expressing themselves online, the moment in which they went 'viral', and how they cope with the vicissitudes of public life online.

Moreover, the semiotics of the Internet are written into the fabric of the books, bringing the experience of digital communication into the experience of reading a paper book. Where Ezarik has the aforementioned 'Ask IJ' YouTube-style illustrations, McAllister employs a colour page design throughout the text which borrows the aesthetics of an Internet browser loaded with a YouTube video page, with play buttons, loading bars, scrolling timers and buttons to minimise the page as if navigating the book with the click of one's mouse.[71] Sugg's novel takes an epistolary form—a genre with long associations with the confessional, as private letters or diary entries reveal secrets through which the plot

[65] Ezarik, p. 45.
[66] Ibid., p. 44.
[67] Ibid., p. 68.
[68] Sugg, p. 233.
[69] Ibid., p. 318.
[70] Ibid., p. 123.
[71] E.g. McAllister, p. 86.

is gradually progressed.[72] In *Girl Online*, action unfolds through blog posts and text messages, updating the epistolary with twenty-first-century technology but retaining the emphasis upon the porous divide between public and private communication. Just as *Girl Online* features graphic design on the page to mark out text messages in speech bubbles suggestive of a smartphone screen and occasional smiley face emojis, Ezarik's *I, Justine* intersperses text with screengrabs of tweets she has both sent and received, and full-colour pictorial emojis—for example emojis of a hatching chick and a smiling poo punctuate her description of growing up raising chickens in rural Pittsburgh.[73] Where for Sugg this graphic element serves to bring to life the predominantly digital communication between teenage protagonists, for Ezarik, the record of the tweets serves as evidence, complete with date marks, supporting the claims made in the text.

The subjectivities of these stars are fundamentally structured by the fact that they built their identities online. Their celebrity personas are erected within digital platforms that inevitably shape how they both share and understand their online identities. Part of the task of a printed, analogue memoir then is to work to emulate the connectivity of their online lives. Their celebrity personas are digital, making any division of online and offline an artificial rupture, when the balance is so heavily tipped towards a life lived, narrativised and shared online. Having rendered the interrelations of self-representations in YouTube and memoir, and the ways the analogue page must work to bring to life the connected, digital self, I shall now examine the cultures of sharing narrated in YouTube celebrity memoirs and the gendered imperatives they reveal.

'As I Started Talking to the Camera More, My Channel Grew': The Gendered Authenticity Contract and the Literalism of YouTube's Economics of Access

In celebrity culture, access and authenticity are intertwined concepts. Offering sufficient access to the private self is a key means of meeting the demands of the appearance of authenticity. Conversely, if expectations of

---

[72] E.g. Samuel Richardson's *Pamela, or Virtue Rewarded* (1740).

[73] Ezarik, pp. 6, 17.

access are insufficiently met, it leads to a rejection of the celebrity as inauthentic. What emerges across the memoirs in this genre is the weight of audience expectation and obligation based on the imperative to share. This mandate, and its gendered demands, I call the *gendered authenticity contract*. The gendering of these expectations can be seen in the demands made in particular upon female celebrities' interiority, 'properly' managed sexuality and performances of femininity. The directness of audience interaction as enabled by the YouTube platform results in continual policing of appropriate exposure and the performance of femininity exposed. Therefore, just as authenticity is a quality that can never be truly ascertained, the demands of the *gendered authenticity contract* operate as a benchmark that can never truly be met.

In previous chapters, I have discussed the *economics of access* as a set of cultural forces that coax stars, often indirectly. These are literalised in YouTube celebrity, owing to the transactional nature of YouTube,[74] and the visibility of those transactions built into the platform. Sharing more gains viewers, especially sharing on more personal topics. The videos of these women sharing are monetised through advertising, every view translating to money that goes directly to the vlogger. 'Traditional' celebrities have always devised personal stories to keep themselves in the spotlight, but the attention garnered often had to be transferred towards the celebrity's other ventures before it was of direct commercial value. As the rewards for sharing via monetised YouTube videos are more direct and immediate, so is the imperative to share.

The YouTubers examined here relate having had to hone their instinct for what will attract views. In line with the *economics of access*, the content that most successfully garners followers and views is the most personal and exposing. McAllister, for example, keenly asserts authenticity as a deliberate goal in her production decisions: 'I never write scripts because [...] I want the video to feel really natural'.[75] Authenticity here is depicted as a product of the refusal to impose order and cohesiveness on her account of her life; it is a feeling, an externally imposed value judgement, paradoxically courted through deliberate effort.[76] Any gap between her on- and off-screen personae is explained as an authentic product of an outpouring

[74] Lovelock.

[75] McAllister, p. 83.

[76] Trilling, pp. 5–6.

of true passion: 'People always ask if the way I am in my videos is the real me. It is - just an excited version of me. [...] I'm that excited version of myself because I genuinely love making videos. When I turn the camera on, that passion just sort of takes over'.[77] McAllister frames her desire to talk directly to viewers in the context of YouTube market forces. What is presented as sincere, serendipitously happens to lead to an increase in followers: 'as I started to gain an audience, I wanted to vlog, because I wanted to talk directly to my viewers. [...] As I started talking to the camera more, my channel grew more popular'.[78] In its adjacency to observations about the currency of YouTube audiences, her stated desire for audience connection cannot be separated from her pursuit of followers, YouTube celebrity success, and direct payment. This offers an explicit rendering of the *economics of access*.

Sugg's protagonist, Penny, similarly keeps circling back to the need to assert and reassert the veracity of her online persona, alongside an awareness of audience desires: 'The fact is I'm totally honest on my blog, totally me - and my readers seem to like me'.[79] As with McAllister's 'passion' which 'takes over', Sugg's book depicts online sharing as a therapeutic act which 'just flows': 'writing the blog post really did help. [...] Just flowed out of me. Once I posted it, I didn't do my usual thing of waiting to see if it got any comments or shares'.[80] Like McAllister's 'passion' and Goody's opening of emotional 'floodgates', this sits within the discourses of authenticity of the 'untrammelled flow'—a force perceived to take over in an outpouring of 'true' emotion.[81] Ignoring audience interaction marks sharing as authentic, rather than an attempt to get attention or renumeration. Nonetheless, Sugg's protagonist has an acute awareness of the *economics of access* around her content and relates audience interaction in terms of cold, hard numbers. After sharing personal details of her anxiety, she observes that her 'followers went up from 200 to just over 1000 in one week'.[82] After writing a blog about her New Year resolution to work on her emotional well-being, she relates 'I refresh the page on

[77] McAllister, p. 85.
[78] Ibid., pp. 81–82.
[79] Sugg, p. 78.
[80] Ibid., p. 23.
[81] Dyer (1979), p. 138.
[82] Sugg, p. 19.

my blog and see that I've already got two comments. [...] I quickly post a reply'.[83] Despite the tensions between authentic emotional outpouring and business logic, the visibility of the *economics of access* of YouTube means that there is no hiding the fact that their performances are a profit-making enterprise. The coexistence of unrestrained emotion and clear-eyed business acumen is a tension that remains unresolved. Sugg's atomised awareness of her success metrics is, by her own standards, inauthentic. It is also the highly professionalised mindset of a corporate agent shrewdly producing monetised content with a good understanding of her market and her product.

What emerges through these repeated, overlapping, yet incomplete assurances is an implicit cultural imperative expecting the celebrity to expose herself in the *economics of access*, and the impossibility of such a benchmark for a sufficiently, authentically revealed self. As discussed, the high cover price of print memoir (in a culture where celebrity subjectivity is shared online for free) requires authors offer something that has not appeared in their other media, no matter how autobiographical and how total those accounts have claimed to be. Of this tension, McAllister asserts, 'even though I post weekly videos of myself on the internet, I've always been a pretty private person'.[84] This is a common claim throughout the memoirs in this category, and one which leaves space for her to assert, 'this book is full of the things you don't know about me'.[85] Ezarik similarly offers an autobiographical occasion that is as essential by business logic as it is incompatible to her online claims that she always gives her audience access to the whole story: 'telling the whole story, for once, is the other reason I decided to write this book'.[86] The contradictions are explicit. Ezarik both declares that she has been 'live tweeting [her] entire life',[87] and also posits, 'I seriously considered titling this book tweets I never sent, just as a reminder that no matter how much access you seemingly have to any one person online, you will never really know his or her whole story'.[88]

[83] Sugg, p. 273.
[84] McAllister, p. 10.
[85] Ibid., p. 11.
[86] Ezarik, p. 12.
[87] Ibid., p. 68.
[88] Ibid., p. 10.

The books relate overlapping accounts of life experiences that have already been filmed and shared online as they were happening. Many chapters of the books are descriptions of their existing online videos, such as Ezarik's 2006 YouTube viral video about her 300-page iPhone bill, and McAllister's descriptions of the videos she's posted of herself playing pranks on her mother. On the rare occasions when an anecdote represents new content, this value is carefully highlighted: 'wait let's back up a minute. Here's what really happened'.[89]

Of course, absolute access is no more possible in printed autobiography than in other automedia forms. Ezarik draws attention to the gaps in her memoir in a manner similar to Hilton's elliptical half-allusions to life events that may have come to readers' attention by other means: 'It's difficult to explain why without telling the whole story, and some things just aren't meant for public consumption. Sorry'.[90] As with Sugg being forced to make a public statement apologising for her use of a ghost-writer, Ezarik's performed contrition suggests an authenticity contract with readers that she ought to be always offering absolute access. As this statement is part of an anecdote with an unspoken subtext of abuse, about a manager who made her feel 'trapped' and uncomfortable,[91] there is an implication that there may be both legal and painful, personal reasons she does not do more than allude to the story behind this anecdote.

Ezarik confesses her inability to meet the demands of an impossible *authenticity contract*: 'Even when I was live streaming, there were times when I said the camera battery had died, just so I could turn the thing off and catch a bit of a break from being iJustine'.[92] She relates that there were certain circumstances where particular control was needed around what should and shouldn't be shared: 'if I was planning on being out late and / or drinking, my backup battery would conveniently "die"'.[93] It is significant, then, that a genre of celebrity based upon live-tweeting and live-streaming life, with purported access all areas, is especially edited in specific contexts: 'Over time I have adjusted my content accordingly: I rarely curse on camera; I don't drink on camera either [...] I don't talk

[89] Ezarik, p. 47.
[90] Ibid., p. 209.
[91] Ibid., pp. 147–48.
[92] Ibid., p. 10.
[93] Ibid., p. 116.

about boyfriends, family drama, work issues, or fights with my friends'.[94] It is no coincidence that these areas of censorship, the spaces where Ezarik has to be especially careful about what to share, are those upon which acceptable femininity hinges.

This is because the *authenticity contract* and the *economics of access* are heavily gendered, exposing female stars to particular risks. YouTube's built-in continuous feedback makes it a site for constant monitoring of, and feedback upon, YouTubers' performances of femininity. It is not surprising that this results in internalised self-policing. Women's modesty is the only solution offered to resolve online harassment: 'If my shorts were "too short", someone was sure to say something crass - without even realising it, I had started wearing pants and long sleeves (rather than shorts and tank tops) when I was on camera'.[95] Whilst it is true that, as Banet-Weiser argues, 'Ezarik positions the feminine body as the crux of her brand',[96] she does so whilst navigating punitive ideas about female modesty.

In the memoirs of young, female YouTube celebrities, then, sharing oneself is a founding principle. It is a mandate with immediate transactional value, literalising the *economics of access*. In a *gendered authenticity contract*, sharing is a prerequisite of appearing to have that authentic quality that this book has shown is a vexed yet valuable celebrity currency. Sharing oneself online is constructed as only coincidentally, serendipitously financially rewarding. It is simultaneously, impossibly, absolute and partial. The spaces alluding to things unsaid reveal the work being done to smooth over the problematic gender politics of a society that presents particular, hostile challenges to highly visible women. The *economics of access* demand these women walk an impossible line, insisting they give as much direct access to their private lives as possible and turning on them if their performance of chaste, restrained femininity is less than perfect. The point at which the YouTuber's otherwise accessible live-streamed life must be hidden, edited or otherwise rendered partial is the point at which the demands of femininity written into the terms of the *gendered authenticity contract* reveal themselves to be set unattainably high. Having established YouTube celebrity's literalisation of the *economics of access*, I shall now

[94] Ibid., p. 208.
[95] Ibid., p. 141.
[96] Banet-Weiser (2012), p. 77.

interrogate the ways in which these memoirs represent celebrity agency (or its lack) within this economy, considering whether the relative absence of wider industry machinery is evidence of freedom in self-authorship or exposure to risk.

'MY FANS BOUGHT ME THESE EGGS': CELEBRITY AGENCY AND YOUTUBE AS THE GIG-ECONOMY CELEBRITY OF MILLENNIAL PRECARITY

Despite the aforementioned intermediaries, the industry machinery of YouTube celebrity is comparatively stripped back, with stars often single-handedly writing, filming and distributing the content that they star in, working from home, outside of the celebrity industrial complex of for example, the TV, movie or music industries, especially in the early stages of their careers. Compared to other celebrity fields, YouTubers perform more of the labour of fame production. However, this does not necessarily lead to a greater level of control and freedom. These memoirs discuss YouTube celebrity in terms of the agency and empowerment it affords, as is common across the memoirs discussed throughout this book. We see the same official, postfeminist account of the young woman empowered by her celebrity towards opportunities, success and a fulfilling lifestyle, and yet, a subtext becomes apparent that casts YouTube celebrity as something of a gruelling treadmill of self-representation, risk and precarity. Where the memoirs of 'glamour girls' reverberate with trauma, and the memoirs of reality TV stars navigate humiliation, anxiety is the emotional state common to the memoirs of YouTube celebrities. This may in part be due to the relentlessness of this celebrity field, which demands that they share new videos of themselves on a strict, regular timetable or lose followers and therefore income.

Whilst both celebrity autobiography and YouTube celebrity automedia create a feeling of access as a form of capital, the assumption (whether true or not) that YouTubers act alone as sole agents of their fame raises particular questions for celebrity agency. The other stars discussed in this book are all working within the various industrial structures that produce celebrity within their fields. I have discussed how the structures of industrial cultural production, which produce both celebrity and memoir, bring accompanying conventions or limitations. However, they also bring various forms of insulation: from financial precarity and from the general public who make up a star's audience. Without this insulation, yet with all the mandate to 'open up' to deliver on a *gendered authenticity contract*, YouTube celebrity exists at the hard edge of the *economics of access*, as a kind of celebrity for the gig economy.

Agency is the central theme of Sugg's novel, *Girl Online*. The narrative centres around a girl discovering for the first time a feeling of control over her life. However, the construction of agency is problematic even before the wider economic backdrop is considered, due to its reliance upon fairy-tale narrative formula and the way it locates the means of self-discovery within the male love interest. Blogger, Penny, refers to herself and her male love interest as 'Cinderella and Prince Charming'[97] and equates feeling like Cinderella with feeling in control: 'This was where my life became like a fairytale. This was where I finally realised that I can actually control what happens to me'.[98] For Sugg's protagonist, the ability to take control of her life is the result of the presence of a male love interest:

> For the first time ever I feel as if my life is my own - that I'm in charge of my own destiny. I'm no longer just reacting to what everyone else does or says. With Noah as my inciting incident, I'm finally writing my own script.[99]

The contradiction of only writing her own script when incited to by a man is a depressingly heteropatriarchal framing of female agency. Nonetheless, it is significant that agency is conceived of in terms of life writing—the ability to write one's own story is to be in charge of one's own destiny. It is of greater significance still that writing one's own script should be the model of agency in a book that is perhaps the most famous recent example in the UK, of a ghostwriting exposé in which the celebrity author-subject's own voice and labour was deemed to be insufficiently present. For Sugg's protagonist, Penny, control or its loss centres around online gossip and information about her life going viral:

[97] Sugg, p. 229.
[98] Ibid., p. 207.
[99] Ibid., p. 181.

I grab my laptop and log onto my blog and delete all of the posts about Noah. Then I change the settings so that no one can post comments. Instantly I feel a tiny bit better, like I've managed to shut the door on the haters.[100]

Whereas Anderson's protagonist's tormentors are the paparazzi and their unsanctioned distribution of images of her life, for Penny it is uncontrollable discussion of her life through online comments. Penny's character progression through these challenges brings to life one of my central arguments, that for women in the public eye, agency over the meaning of one's own life story is in constant negotiation. 'I can control this', she tells herself, before despairing, 'it's all over Facebook. And Twitter. And Tumblr. And-'.[101] Self-narration is depicted as a form of self-making; in taking control of her life story and its circulation Penny is shaping her life as she wants it to be: 'it doesn't matter what anyone says about me online. I know the truth. [...] My life can be anything I want it to be - as long as I remember that it's mine. Not theirs'.[102] When Penny returns to her online profiles after a period of retreat, she asserts that in sharing herself publicly again she restores agency over her life: 'I felt for the first time that my life was my own'.[103] Even in the fictional, fantasy world of schoolgirl blogger Penny, sharing online is fraught with threats to one's agency and wellbeing. Nonetheless, her fairy tale gets a happy ending in which she determines to tell her own life story: 'Tell your side of the story [...] You'll feel way better'.[104]

Sharing one's life offers various forms of agency in the income it generates, the therapeutic qualities of sharing personal experience, and the chance to take some degree of control over one's personal narrative. The autobiographies of McAllister and Ezarik similarly positivise the agency afforded by online celebrity as a way of life, celebrating 'working for myself, broke or not'.[105] At the same time, without the narrative freedoms afforded by the autobiographical novel, Ezarik and

---

[100] Ibid., p. 294.

[101] Ibid., pp. 297–98.

[102] Ibid., p. 308.

[103] Ibid., p. 307.

[104] Ibid., p. 300.

[105] Ezarik, p. 100.

McAllister's memoirs reveal troubling accounts of the labour of YouTube celebrity. They represent particular incursions upon celebrity agency in this field due to the space YouTube celebrity occupies at the hard edge of the *economics of access*. Scholar of employment law, Orly Lobel, argues that gig-economy conditions are often sold with the misleading idea that technological advances which remove intermediary employers enable 'independence, choice, autonomy, and freedom for people to work according to their own terms, time, and desired lifestyle' when in reality 'jobs become something that you constantly-and feverishly-seek with very little regularity or certainty', privacy diminishes, and the labour market becomes increasingly exploitative.[106]

Ezarik makes explicit comment on the spaces for exploitation in mediation and frequently returns to the idea that she is best off working for herself. She worries that she is 'ripe to be taken advantage of [as] some of these so-called managers seemed a little, well, shady'.[107] The management company she ends up signing to, a start-up specialising in YouTube stars, proves to be extremely shady:

> Since I didn't have anywhere else to go, I relocated to L.A. to move in temporarily with one of my brand, new managers. [...] I quickly started to feel trapped, though - I didn't know anyone. I didn't know the city very well. It was just me, by myself, in a big house, sitting around without a whole lot to do. [...] It was slowly dawning on me that perhaps I had made a mistake. [...] It would take a few years before I felt comfortable signing with another management firm.[108]

Thus, these stars are neither insulated by industrial celebrity nor truly free from them. Like Sugg's uplifting fiction, Ezarik's memoir seeks to show its protagonist as a woman in charge of her own destiny through the self-employment opportunities monetised YouTube celebrity offers. Unlike Sugg's uplifting fantasy, Ezarik's account is left with an unsettling subtext of unspoken exploitation of her labour and/or sexuality.

Another example which, deliberately or otherwise, highlights the spaces of potential abuse in the process of mediation invites consideration of the power relations between YouTubers and those who mediate them.

---

[106] Orly Lobel, 'The Gig Economy & the Future of Employment and Labor Law,' *University of San Francisco Law Review* 51 (2017), 53.

[107] Ezarik, p. 134.

[108] Ibid., pp. 147–48.

McAllister explains that, travelling as an underaged minor for DigiTour, a 16-city, travelling stage-show featuring YouTube celebrities, her guardianship is transferred to a male YouTube star: 'Because I was under 18, my mum had to give someone over 21 permission to act as my guardian or I couldn't leave the country. So, for a few days in 2013, Ricky Dillon was my dad'.[109] McAllister relates this as nothing more concerning than a humorous anecdote involving a figure that her audience will likely recognise. Her male co-worker being given legal power over her, able to make decisions on her behalf, puts McAllister in an undermined and vulnerable position demonstrating the patriarchal operating practices of those who supposedly represent her interests at work.

The context of economic insecurity and 'psychic and physical precariousness' under late-stage capitalism, combined with the need to be 'always on' due to the 24-hour connectivity of digital communication, form part of what led commentator Anne Helen Petersen to label the millennial generation (born between 1981 and 1996, like the YouTubers examined here and often, like YouTubers,[110] characterised as decadent and indulged) as 'generation burnout'.[111] This characterisation of burnout and precarity under digitally enabled, gig-economy capitalism aligns with representations of the working lives of YouTubers in these memoirs, which suggest stress, pressure, insecurity and work-induced anxiety. Anxiety and need for emotional catharsis and clarity is offered as the autobiographical occasion both for their online presence and, by proxy, their books about it. Sugg writes: 'my blog seems to have helped me sort things out in my mind'.[112] McAllister likewise casts online sharing as a means to manage panic attacks and help those in her audience who are going through similar: 'When I eventually found out the other people were going through exactly what I was going through (via the internet), it was such a relief. I didn't have to be alone in it'.[113]

[109] McAllister, p. 176.

[110] Deller and Murphy.

[111] Anne Helen-Petersen, 'How Millennials Became the Burnout Generation,' *buzzfeednews.com*, 5 January 2019.

[112] Sugg, p. 73.

[113] McAllister, p. 22.

YouTube celebrities exist in the popular imagination as decadent and cossetted, earning vast amounts of money for nothing.[114] Certainly, through monetised views and sponsorship deals YouTubers can make a lot of money. The need to balance audience envy means emphasising hardship; an affluent background does not aid a narrative of celebrity authenticity (a point I will return to in the next chapter), and all of the celebrity authors examined in this book use their memoirs to show that they work hard to earn their fame.[115] However, there is a sinister subtext to discussions of the labour of YouTube celebrity that goes far beyond these wider trends surrounding celebrity narratives of work.

A shocking number of YouTubers have taken their own lives, including young, female stars Stevie Ryan, Chloe Shaw, Amanda Todd, Nasim Aghdam and Jasmine Sanchez.[116] Whilst it would be inappropriate to draw conclusions about the cause of these tragic deaths, Todd, Aghdam and Sanchez uploaded YouTube videos before they died explaining that the treatment they received on the site was a part of their struggles. In 2018, Aghdam shot and injured three YouTube employees in their California offices before taking her own life. She had posted videos complaining about her treatment by YouTube, which she believed had unfairly 'discriminated' against her through the 'demonetization' of her videos preventing her from making advertising revenue.[117] She complained on her personal website 'There is no equal growth opportunity on *YOUTUBE* […] your channel will grow if they want [it] to!!!!!', and was apparently 'always complaining that YouTube ruined her life' to her family.[118]

In an interview with Guardian journalist Simon Parkin, YouTuber Matt Lees depicts a 'bleak and lonely' life of anxiety, overwork and burnout, imprisoned by algorithmic overlords: 'It's not enough to simply create great things', he says. 'The audience expect consistency. They expect frequency. Without these, it's incredibly easy to slip off the radar and

---

[114] Deller and Murphy.

[115] Dyer (1979).

[116] 'YouTubers Who Died Too Soon,' *ranker.com*.

[117] Adrian Chen, 'Nasim Aghdam, the YouTube Shooting, and the Anxiety of Demonetization,' *The New Yorker*, 6 April 2018.

[118] Ibid.

lose favour with the algorithm that gave you your wings'.[119] Algorithms decide which videos appear on users' home pages, search results, the sidebar of recommended videos and the video that automatically plays next. As a result, algorithms are responsible for more than 70 per cent of all time spent on the site.[120] For Lees, meeting the posting schedule rewarded by algorithms meant working 20-hour days at the expense of his mental and physical health: 'YouTube heavily boosts anything that riles people up. [...] The point at which you're breaking down is the point at which the algorithm loves you the most'.[121] In Lees' description, it is not only the quantity of the work but also its nature, due to the direct access designed into the platform, that makes the cost of YouTube celebrity in particular so high:

> Human brains really aren't designed to be interacting with hundreds of people every day. [...] When you've got thousands of people giving you direct feedback on your work, you really get the sense that something in your mind just snaps.[122]

Lees' account does not represent the fact that the worst online abuse is saved for women and people of colour,[123] and yet it nonetheless highlights the fact that YouTube celebrity exists at the hard edge of the *economics of access*.

Unlike Lees' account, given in a broadsheet newspaper interview, after he spent time out of the spotlight following a public breakdown, the memoirs examined here offer the official story of a fame that their authors wish to continue. It is, therefore, not surprising that their accounts in general work to positivise that career path. However, even when

---

[119] Simon Parkin, 'The YouTube Stars Heading for Burnout: "The Most Fun Job Imaginable Became Deeply Bleak",' *The Guardian*, 8 September 2018.

[120] Kevin Roose, 'The Making of a YouTube Radical,' *The New York Times*, 8 June 2019.

[121] Parkin.

[122] Ibid.

[123] Donald Horton and R. Richard Wohl, 'Mass Communication and Para-Social Interaction: Observations on Intimacy at a Distance,' *Psychiatry* 19.3 (1956), 215–29; Arienne Ferchaud et al. 'Parasocial Attributes and YouTube Personalities: Exploring Content Trends across the Most Subscribed YouTube Channels,' *Computers in Human Behavior* 80 (2018), 88–96.

extolling the career about which they 'don't have any regrets',[124] a subtext unfolds which accounts for the anxious condition of YouTube celebrity, commodified though that anxiety may be[125]:

> The pressure to entertain was enormous, and I was miserable. I was starting to have "technical difficulties" - I turned the camera off and the immediate sense of relief was so cathartic, I'd suddenly be crying. Sleeping, too, became a kind of refuge, a chance for some peace and quiet. I started sleeping in longer and later - I just didn't see the point of waking up early, only to have to come up with some new way to entertain.[126]

Ezarik depicts herself as trapped by the contract she has entered into with her audience, and their expectation of frequent and consistent access to her life. Captive to the labour of maintaining and keeping alive the digital identity she has created, she depicts YouTube and its demand for constant self-mediation as a celebrity hamster wheel, a factory line of the self. McAllister likewise attributes her success to consistency, frequency and her ability to maintain a gruelling and relentless schedule of uploading videos of herself. In a chapter titled 'Finding my Voice', a common celebrity memoir trope of empowerment through self-discovery, McAllister states, 'If you don't post for a few weeks, people may stop coming back to your channel. Trust me, I know it can be challenging to come up with a new idea every week'.[127] A sense of precarity emerges, with YouTube celebrity as the celebrity of the gig economy and its stars ever-conscious that a missed upload will harm their position in the search rankings. This perpetual insecurity is exacerbated by the absence of the insulation of industry machinery should their work abruptly cease. McAllister explains the key difference between the economics of traditional stardom and the direct contract produced by the sole-trading nature of YouTube celebrity:

> My fans are why I have the life I have. I know you always hear actors and musicians say things like "I love you guys, I wouldn't be here without you" to their fans, and I'm not saying that they don't mean it, but it's not necessarily true. Actors get paid by the studio to be in films, and

---

[124] McAllister, p. 143.

[125] Bishop.

[126] Ezarik, p. 141.

[127] McAllister, p. 88.

while their fans have some bearing on the box office, ultimately its studios that keep actors employed. And musicians do make money from tours and record sales, but ultimately all that filters through a record company. In YouTube's case it's literally true. YouTubers have a unique relationship with their fans in that, unlike traditional Media, we really do get to live our lives because our fans watch our videos. My relationship with my fans is not something that I take for granted. Even when I'm doing something as simple as buying eggs at the grocery store, I think, my fans bought me these eggs.[128]

The personal cost of maintaining the relentless schedule of uploads is high. McAllister describes in her memoir how, at the age of 15, she had to give up having boyfriends, hobbies, an offline social life and, eventually, school:

> With school and homework, it was hard to get a video ready to upload during the week. At this point I was working hard on improving the quality of my videos, which meant more time prepping, shooting, and editing. In order to make sure I could always get a video done, I had to cut something else out of my life.[129]

Just as existing outside of the institutional celebrity of Hollywood or the music industry means less financial insulation, as a child working a gruelling schedule, she is not protected by labour laws as she would be as a child star in the television or movie industry. A key feature of the gig economy is the removal of structures of corporate responsibility and liability, and the circumvention of laws in place to protect the vulnerable.[130]

Here, we have seen how these memoirs engage directly with the concept of agency, casting lone-working as empowering, and locating agency in the ability to take control of one's life story. This control is slippery, however, owing to proliferating online commentary and a working culture of insecurity, relentlessness and anxiety. These conditions and the direct financial dependency upon the whims of audiences and algorithms render YouTube celebrity a kind of gig-economy celebrity of millennial precarity. Having

---

[128] Ibid., p. 186.

[129] Ibid., p. 134.

[130] Lobel.

examined the working conditions created by the expectations of digitally enabled access and interaction and the ceaseless 'pressure to entertain', I shall now consider the ramifications of this mandate to be available and interacting with one's audience in a culture of gendered online abuse and trolling.

Trolling Is a Feminist Issue: 'There Were Absolutely Gross and Inappropriate and Lewd Comments, Too - I Mean, This Was the Internet'

There are particular challenges for women in the public eye. Feminist scholars have demonstrated the Internet as a space of proliferating gendered abuse with serious ramifications both online and offline.[131] The memoirs of YouTube celebrities relate the abuse and sexual harassment these women receive. Making visible such crimes is an inherently feminist act.[132] However, in their postfeminist sensibility, these accounts approach but stop short of critique of online misogyny.[133] Simply not reading the comments is not an option, as the economic need to build audience loyalty to maintain one's status as a YouTuber demands interaction with their comments.[134] Instead, the only solution these books present to gendered abuse is 'to grow a thick skin' because 'if you stay positive you can make it through anything'.[135] This internalised, individualised response to the structural, social problem of digital misogyny is in line with Emma A. Jane's findings that women are often blamed for the abuse they receive online.[136] The combination of YouTube's *economics of access* and cultural sexism, which constructs women's sexuality as available for male pleasure, results in a perceived contract which the male audience

---

[131] Banet-Weiser, *Empowered: Popular Feminism and Popular Misogyny* (Durham: Duke University Press, 2018); Debbie Ging and Eugenia Siapera, 'Special Issue on Online Misogyny,' *Feminist Media Studies* 18.4 (2018), 515–24; Amnesty, Toxic Twitter: A Toxic Place for Women, 2018. Emma A. Jane, 'Online Misogyny and Feminist Digilantism,' *Continuum* 30.3 (2016), 284–97.

[132] Yelin and Clancy.

[133] Gill (2007).

[134] Parkin.

[135] McAllister, p. 64.

[136] Jane.

angrily believes has been reneged upon when the sexualised access they feel entitled to is not granted.

In Sugg's fictionalised account of life with an online following, her protagonist experiences online abuse and gendered scrutiny of her appearance. Penny relates the stress of opening Twitter, stating, 'Five more messages telling me that total strangers have mentioned me on Twitter. I click on one and see the word "hate" and quickly click out again'.[137] One such example reads, '@girlonline22 is an ugly dog'.[138] Of the vast quantities of abusive messages she receives, Ezarik describes 'the gut punch of reading so many negative comments about [one]self online'[139]:

> I hadn't quite been ready for the sheer volume of them. [...] I could only scroll, in quiet disbelief, through hundreds of comments describing the many ways in which I was worthless, a moron, and a whore. It was my first real taste of how dark things can get [...] in the public eye.[140]

Ezarik and McAllister describe the psychological cost of having to engage with a constant stream of negative comments. Ezarik states, 'Constantly being judged for what you're doing, for what you're wearing, for how you speak or what you look like, will eventually take a toll'.[141] McAllister similarly describes scrutiny of her appearance as damaging:

> I had to deal with a lot of random online haters. Strangers on the internet started pointing out things about me that I didn't even realise were flaws. [...] People would pick apart literally every detail of my face, which made me super self-conscious.[142]

As well as being subjected to harsh and critical scrutiny of their physical appearance, the authors describe receiving constant lewd and objectifying remarks. Despite this being a form of sexual harassment, it is treated as much less difficult to deal with than critical scrutiny. McAllister shrugs off objectification as too commonplace to be of concern: '"Jenn's boobs" or

---

[137] Sugg, p. 291.

[138] Ibid., p. 289.

[139] Ezarik, p. 83.

[140] Ibid.

[141] Ibid., p. 141.

[142] McAllister, p. 55.

something like that literally became a trending topic on Twitter because so many people were talking about it'.[143] For Ezarik, such harassment is similarly a given in her line of work: 'There were absolutely gross and inappropriate and lewd comments, too - I mean, this was the internet."[144] This normalising statement suggests she expects sexual harassment as part of being a woman online. Examples of sexual harassment are given without comment or any suggestion that it is a particularly negative or problematic phenomenon. For example, of the constant demand to come up with ideas for content, Ezarik states: 'if all else failed, I'd just sit at my desk and field questions and requests [including] take your shirt off'.[145] Without comment, she includes a screengrab from her online feed which shows her viewers commenting on her breasts, the text on which reads as follows:

12:19 Yankeesfan53: boobies?
12:19 Yankeesfan53: watch them rise and fall lol
12:19 Gerard209: she should wear the cam
12:19 Kevin: yes boobies.[146]

The inclusion of these examples approaches, but stops short of, critique of online misogyny. Instead, with her only commentary accompanying examples of online sexual harassment being, 'I mean, this was the internet', the effect is to normalise these interactions as little more than wearying.

It is worth reiterating that the YouTubers examined here benefit from both white privilege and thin privilege. Whilst she similarly glosses over the worst of it, mixed-race, plus-size body positivity YouTuber, Grace Victory, hints at the ways in which online abuse worsens along intersectional axes as she depicts herself as 'an Underdog in the YouTube world' stating, 'I look very different to a lot of my fellow influencers, my choice of taboo subjects definitely hindered me'.[147] She relates 'desperately

---

[143] Ibid., p. 59.
[144] Ezarik, p. 117.
[145] Ibid., p. 116.
[146] Ezarik.
[147] Grace Victory, *No Filter* (London: Hachette, 2017).

toxic' racist and sizeist online abuse, as well as financial discrimination from brands who want to work only with thin, white influencers, compounding both the financial precarity of YouTube celebrity and the vicissitudes of the *gendered authenticity contract* in an *economics of access*.

PARASOCIAL MISOGYNY AND EXPOSURE WITHOUT INSULATION: 'I STOPPED FEELING SAFE IN MY OWN HOME'

In a celebrity field where the appearance of access and intimacy is central to its design, and the imperative to be in contact with audiences is a structuring feature, these YouTubers relate uncomfortably predatory behaviour from their male audiences. McAllister describes receiving 'a 21-page letter that explained how we were going to get married and detailed out some pretty weird plans for our future. [...] This guy was in his 40s'.[148] McAllister was a teenager at the time. These anecdotes about predatory behaviour from male viewers include disturbing examples of stalking and sexual harassment:

> When I got doxxed [...] this little paedophile started calling and leaving really rude and threatening messages for me. My mum never let me listen to them, and to this day she won't tell me what they said, but I was 16 and, apparently, they were pervy enough to get him booked as a sex offender.[149]

Doxxing is the practice of hacking a person's personal data and making it public on the Internet—a crime that perhaps epitomises the dynamics and risks of the *economics of access* at their worst. The exposure of information like addresses and phone numbers puts the victim of doxxing at risk of physical harm. It is a form of online abuse that disproportionately affects women and people of colour with real and alarming offline consequences,[150] in McAllister's case being stalked and sexually harassed over the phone.

---

[148] McAllister, p. 124.

[149] Ibid., p. 125.

[150] Binder, Nellie, p. 55.

Both celebrity in general and YouTube in particular have been theorised as spaces of parasocial relations of one-sided, imagined intimacy.[151] The mandate to respond to audiences means that YouTube transforms 'the parasocial into the potentially social', as hoped for by McAllister's stalker/suitors.[152] Such predatory interactions inflect the one-sided imagined intimacy of parasociality with cultural ideas of male entitlement to women's bodies and sexuality. It is therefore, perhaps, better understood as a parasocial misogyny. This is a key contributing factor to the *gendered authenticity contract*, which men imagine has been broken when their feelings of ownership are not indulged. This is evidenced by the angry backlash McAllister receives from male audiences whenever access to her teenage sexuality is denied:

> As part of a truth-or-dare video, I pranked my mum by telling her that there were naked pictures of me on the Internet, so I titled the video "Naked Pictures Leaked," and I got all these comments from middle-aged men who were really angry that I had lied about naked pictures. [...] The same thing happened when I titled a video "My First Time" [...] a YouTube tag where you talk about the first time you did a bunch of different things (none of which are sex). However, these same guys got mad and posted angry comments and tweets because they wanted to hear about how I lost my virginity.[153]

She shares these experiences as humorous anecdotes. These examples all appear in the memoir as part of a list called 'Top 10 Craziest Things That Have Happened To Me (Besides Getting Doxxed)'. Each item on the list is laid out on an illustrated page in its own miniature browser window, like little email anecdotes with fun headlines such as 'ALMOST GETTING KICKED OUT OF A HOTEL', as if genuine safety concerns like having her address and phone number made public were little more than amusing examples of adolescent fun times. This recalls the efforts of ghostwriter Neil Strauss to make Jenna Jameson's 'dark and heavy' experiences of

---

[151] Horton and Wohl; Arienne Ferchaud et al. 'Parasocial Attributes and YouTube Personalities: Exploring Content Trends across the Most Subscribed YouTube Channels,' *Computers in Human Behavior* 80 (2018), 88–96.

[152] Alice Marwick, 'Instafame: Luxury Selfies in the Attention Economy,' *Public Culture* 27.1 (75) (2015), 137–60.

[153] McAllister, p. 127.

sexual abuse 'lighter [and] more fun'.[154] The worst McAllister has to say about her experiences of online harassment is that they are 'creepy', a word that can elide a wide range of misconduct with a humorous shrug.

Despite the tendency to minimise and shrug off harassment as an unimportant, amusing, everyday norm, the authors' fear for their personal safety casts a shadow of dread over these memoirs that is not seen elsewhere in the celebrity memoir genre as the women relate both the threats they regularly receive from their online audiences, and their concerns that this will spill into real, physical danger. Another ramification of losing the insulation that comes with institutional celebrity is that they have less distance from those who desire direct access. The sense of ongoing personal risk comes through more potently in the memoirs of YouTube celebrities than in other celebrity fields.

Despite her attempts at cheery, empowered positivity, Ezarik's account, at points, relates her powerlessness and the personal risk faced by a woman living in public. Receipt of death threats is presented as something YouTubers must inevitably deal with: 'I should die. I should kill myself.... A rush of increasingly intense, violent, and graphic death threats'.[155] YouTube celebrity puts its stars in direct contact with huge audiences through the exchange of messages: 'I'd definitely come across the occasional weirdo, the kind of creep I would run away from if we ever so much as met in person'.[156] Meeting in person is a genuine risk. Of her home with her co-star, Ezarik states that security was 'a major concern [and that she] would take pains to hide my actual location from the Internet, in particular [her] address'.[157] Although it was never confirmed, she believes that during her live-streaming days someone did break into her apartment, something she continues to fear as people make a sport of revealing her address: 'people realised the influence they could have over my life [...] by figuring out my location and spreading the info across the web'.[158]

[154] Singer (2004).

[155] Ezarik, p. 189.

[156] Ibid., p. 179.

[157] Ibid., p. 111.

[158] Ibid., pp. 140–41.

Even in the fairy-tale, fictional world of *Girl Online*, online harassment causes Sugg's protagonist 'terror' for her physical safety: 'I sit on the edge of my bed, staring at my phone in terror. I picture people all over the world reading about me, posting hate filled messages about me. People I don't know. People who've never even met me. But they know who I am. They know my name. And they know my blog. What if they find out where I live?'[159]

For McAllister, the line between online and offline audience contact does get crossed after her experience of doxxing:

> People started showing up at my house. Now, you guys know I love you, but it's a little invasive to show up to someone's house that you don't really know. [...] The FBI told me I couldn't leave my house through the front door. It pretty much got to the point where I stopped feeling safe in my own home.[160]

Her reassurance to the reader of her love for them shows the line that must be carefully walked when complaining about fan intrusions into her privacy, to fans who have purchased access to her 'private' life in her memoir. The experience of doxxing leaves McAllister unable to feel safe at night, asking herself, 'Is that creaky floorboard the sound of a serial killer opening my front door? Is that rustling the sound of his feet shuffling across my carpet?'[161] In a chapter titled 'Fair Game',[162] Ezarik relates a frightening incident in which she is woken by the police after somebody phoned them with a hoax call saying that she had been murdered. She connects this experience to the culture of online commenting which does not see her as a real person or see that there are real-world consequences to online comments. She relates that abusive commenters post variations of 'I'm just joking', 'I don't *actually* mean I want her to die', 'It's harmless'. By quoting these posts, she implies that she disagrees about the harmlessness. However, her response to these kinds of posts is largely placatory rather than condemnatory:

---

[159] Sugg, pp. 291–92.
[160] McAllister, p. 122.
[161] Ibid., p. 149.
[162] Ezarik, p. 185.

I know that the vast majority of people who make rude or even vaguely threatening statements online do not actually wish harm on the subject of those comments. But it's a slippery slope. And unfortunately, I've seen first-hand what it's like when that line gets crossed.[163]

Whilst Ezarik hints that this 'slippery slope' leads to something bad, she is extremely careful not to blame the commenters themselves. Of course, the *economics of access* determine that she must be conciliatory towards those who have threatened her because these people make up the audience upon whom income depends.

THE BUSINESS AND SAFETY LOGIC OF PACIFYING ABUSERS

This palliative approach to misogyny is seen throughout McAlister's and especially Ezarik's memoirs. Ezarik and McAllister relate their status as lone women in male-dominated fields—tech commentary, and prank and comedy videos, respectively. When talking about a near miss at the MTV Video Music Awards, McAllister states, 'I didn't win (though, for the record, I was up against O2L for Web Star: Comedy. Six boys vs. one girl; I think you get my point)'.[164] She leaves it to her audience to infer that sexism may play a part in her losing. Ezarik similarly describes how, as a gamer, she often finds herself the sole woman in a group:

I was used to being 'one of the guys'. Sometimes it just seemed easier not to draw attention to the fact that I was actually a girl. Using the handle X3, I could play video games without being judged and without feeling guilty whenever I beat my friends with Y chromosomes.[165]

Again, responsibility falls on Ezarik to make the men around her feel better, rather than to challenge any sexist structures that cause the men around her to believe that she should be an inferior player in the first place.

This mollifying of the men around her continues in her memoir as she placates the men who abuse her online. Of the men who made a 'rush of

---

[163] Ibid., p. 193
[164] McAllister, p. 218.
[165] Ezarik, p. 32.

increasingly intense, violent, and graphic death threats' towards her, she conciliatorily states, 'it would be really, really easy - too easy, in fact - to write off comments like these as the work of haters, trolls, or just inherently mean and nasty people, but I think the truth is probably a bit more complicated'.[166] In this way, she justifies or explains away abuse within the gaming community. Like McAllister, Ezarik briefly, but evasively, acknowledges structural misogyny, stating that there are 'widespread concerns about misogyny in the industry' but refusing to comment, instead saying: 'I'll leave the political discussions to other people'.[167] Favouring an anti- or apolitical stance she prefers to align herself with the players of the more controversially violent and misogynistic games: 'my favourite games, including Call of Duty and Grand Theft Auto, are often the most maligned by the mainstream press anyway'.[168] Instead, Ezarik keenly comes to the defence of the community that has rejected and abused her, suggesting it is gamers who have been unfairly slurred with charges of sexism: 'we are seeing the word *gamer* being used as a pejorative all over again; we're right back to suggesting that anyone who likes video games must be a misogynistic, lunkheaded caveman'.[169] She offers a definition of progress focussed primarily on the representational rights of male gamers. Likewise, after the traumatic prank call claiming she had been murdered, Ezarik keenly disassociates herself from the movement to counteract sexism in the gaming community: 'I want to point out that this had nothing to do with gamergate, and it is in no way indicative of the broader gaming culture'.[170] Ezarik gives the final page of her memoir to this effort to appease. She rejects taking a stand, using her final statement to actively refuse to call out online misogynies: 'it would be easy to lash out, to complain about all the ways in which we've been wronged, to point a finger at someone ... but I'd rather be kind'.[171]

This pacifying approach suggests Ezarik must work to avoid alienating one of her core audience groups. Here at the hard edge of the *economics of access*, Ezarik is dependent on the gaming community to

---

[166] Ibid., p. 190.
[167] Ibid., p. 191.
[168] Ibid., p. 192.
[169] Ibid., p. 192.
[170] Ibid., p. 196.
[171] Ibid., p. 225.

continue watching her videos, whether they abuse her or not. These efforts to soothe her audience whenever she mentions the sexism she experiences are likely to be an effort not to inspire further abuse. YouTube celebrity has been understood through the lens of affective emotional labour which forges intimacy.[172] The need to fortify the line between online and offline contact with audiences means that managing the happiness of misogynistic abusers is part of the emotional labour of YouTube celebrity.

Conclusion: The Ghostwriter as Imposter in a Teen Girl's Bedroom

Returning to the 'scandal' surrounding Sugg's ghostwriter and why it was this case and not others that inspired such outrage, it is relevant that, whereas McAllister and Ezarik occupy spaces predominantly populated with male YouTubers, Zoella's brand of beauty and lifestyle vlogging is a highly feminised genre. Sugg has been noted in particular for her cultivation of feeling of sisterly intimacy,[173] often sitting on her bed to film her confessional, first-person, direct addresses. Sugg's videos are by a young girl, for young girls. The discourse around her ghosting 'controversy' highlighted concern about an impressionable 'loyal army' of female fans who were being 'misled' due to their innocence in the face of the industrial production of celebrity: 'teenage girls who worship their idol, and really believe her capable of doing anything'.[174] The presence of a ghost may be seen as particularly threatening here because of a confluence of gendered assumptions about an 'at risk girl'[175] audience supposedly overinvested in parasocial relationships,[176] a *gendered authenticity contract* which sets young, female stars impossible benchmarks for the ways in which they must share themselves, and the nature of this celebrity field which especially seeks to create feelings of intimacy. Together these factors create a space that should be inviolable. If the ghostwriter is an 'imposter

---

[172] Jerslev; Bishop; Berryman and Kavka (2017).

[173] Berryman and Kavka (2017).

[174] Hunter Johnston.

[175] Sarah Projansky 'Mass Magazine Cover Girls: Some Reflections on Postfeminist Girls and Postfeminism's Daughters,' *Interrogating Postfeminism* (2007).

[176] Horton and Wohl; Ferchaud et al.

in the hallowed halls of autobiography',[177] then here the ghostwriter is an imposter in a teen girl's bedroom.

The previously discussed presence of (often male) ghosts in the 'glamour girl' memoir genre is perhaps less of a shock, because the universe they construct is always already permeated by a male gaze we know does not belong to the female, celebrity author-subjects. The previously discussed characterisation of female reality stars in terms of excess through their participation in on-screen sex has a similar effect of locating them as always already sexualised. The teen girl YouTube celebrity, by contrast, works to maintain the appearance of sexlessness, whether through dressing modestly to avoid lewd comments,[178] concealing their romantic and sex lives,[179] or constructing wholesome love stories that climax with a kiss that 'feels like coming home'.[180] Like the predatory men who write to McAllister with their dreams of building a life with her, perhaps part of the perceived problem with the presence of a ghostwriter in Sugg's story is Curham's adulthood. This reveals cultural anxieties around the idea of an unidentified adult secretly in the spaces where teenage girls talk to one another, peer to peer. This is a space we would hope would be inviolable but know is not. The massive, poorly understood phenomenon of YouTube celebrity, and the controversy surrounding Sugg's book and its ghostwriter, both trigger and mirror generational anxieties about who is part of the conversations children are having on the Internet.[181] This reveals cultural concerns that age inappropriate subject matter may be brought into the otherwise innocent peer-to-peer intimacy of teenage girls' conversations. Of course, given the extreme expressions of the commodification of intimacy central to industrial relations of memoir publishing, celebrity culture and YouTube, one could argue that it is adult matters like aggressively capitalist cultures of commercialisation, or the valorisation of exploitative insecure work that are the more corrupting influences.

[177] Lee, p. 1256.

[178] Ezarik.

[179] Ezarik; McAllister.

[180] Sugg, p. 344.

[181] Richard Perloff, 'Social Media Effects on Young Women's Body Image Concerns: Theoretical Perspectives and an Agenda for Research,' *Sex Roles* 71.11–12 (2014), 36–337; Sue Jackson and Tiina Vares, '"Too Many Bad Role Models for Us Girls": Girls, Female Pop Celebrities and "Sexualization",' *Sexualities* (2016).

This chapter has shown how the unruly, networked polyphony of YouTube literalises this book's wider arguments about the inherently collaborative, ungovernable nature of autobiography and the negotiated agency celebrity memoir represents. In Sugg's protagonist's struggle to gain control over the meaning of her own life story, we see the relationship between life writing and agency for women in the public eye. As analogue memoirs of digital subjectivities, these books must work to render the dynamic, collaborative connectivity of the authors' fundamentally digital identities despite their static linear pages. The subjectivities within them are shaped by the cultures of self-representational sharing built into the YouTube platform, with its demands of regular uploads, intimate sharing, and visibly quantified currencies of views, likes and comments. Anxiety emerges in these books as the emotional condition of YouTube celebrity, exacerbated by its function as a factory line of the self. Due to gruelling schedules of content production, these celebrity author-subjects depict a hamster wheel of self-representation.

Where debates around YouTube celebrity have focussed upon whether the platform challenges traditional means of producing and representing celebrity,[182] this chapter has demonstrated that it remains a heavily gendered and disciplinary space for the construction of female celebrity. The financial imperative for YouTube celebrities to respond directly to audience comments places YouTube celebrity at the hard edge of the *economics of access*, without the insulations afforded to celebrities in other fields. Meanwhile, a *gendered authenticity contract* encourages fans to feel a sense of ownership over the stars. Celebrity culture's demands for intimacy and direct access are rendered seemingly more achievable as YouTube celebrities are in constant contact with their viewers. Not only is it frowned upon to neglect to respond to viewer comments but there is also a financial penalty as algorithms only reward those who do interact.

Whilst YouTube celebrity can be lucrative, the directness of the finances of monetised YouTube content and its lone-working structures cast YouTube celebrity as the celebrity of millennial, gig-economy precarity. The removal of intermediaries is celebrated in wider celebrity culture as a sign of greater authenticity in the *economics of access*. As I have shown in previous chapters, the intermediaries of industrial machinery surrounding the production of celebrity and memoir can be limiting through their

---

[182] Smith; Lovelock; Banet Weiser (2011), Kavka and Berryman (2017), Jerslev (2016), Tolson.

imposition of convention. However, intermediaries are a form of insulation. Without this insulation, yet with all of the challenges of sharing oneself according to the impossible demands of the *gendered authenticity contract*, YouTube celebrity takes the logic of the *economics of access* to the extreme. They are placed in contact with a huge amount of gendered, online abuse and harassment but are coaxed to mollify their trolls. If they do not, they risk being penalised by the platforms on which they make their living and exposed to more abuse in online platforms without adequate systems of prevention. The directness of gendered expectations of access ultimately risks spilling over into the threat of physical harm and all three memoirs at points reveal an undercurrent of fear for physical safety as they navigate exposure without insulation.

BIBLIOGRAPHY

'Jen McAllister Net Worth and Earnings 2018.' *ecelebritymirror.com*, 12 July 2018. https://ecelebritymirror.com/youtuber/jean-mcallister-aka-jen nxpenn-net-worth-merch-books-episode/.

'JennxPenn.' *socialblade.com*, 29 August 2019. https://socialblade.com/you tube/user/jennxpenn.

'YouTubers Who Died Too Soon.' *ranker.com*. 13 July 2020, https://www.ran ker.com/list/youtubers-who-died-young/youtuber?page=4.

'Zalfie.' Blog at *zoella.co.uk*. 11 August 2013.

'Zoella.' socialblade.com, 29 August 2019. https://socialblade.com/youtube/user/zoella280390.

Abidin, Crystal. *Internet Celebrity: Understanding Fame Online*. Bingley: Emerald Publishing, 2018.

Amnesty, Toxic Twitter: A Toxic Place for Women, 2018. https://www.amn esty.org/en/latest/research/2018/03/online-violence-against-women-cha pter-1/#topanchor.

Banet-Weiser, Sarah. *AuthenticTM: The Politics of Ambivalence in a Brand Culture*. New York: New York University Press, 2012.

———. 'Branding the Post-Feminist Self: Girls' Video Production and YouTube.' *Mediated Girlhoods: New Explorations in Girls' Media Culture*. New York: Peter Lang, 2011.

———. *Empowered: Popular Feminism and Popular Misogyny*. Durham: Duke University Press, 2018.

Barns, Sarah. 'Who Is Zoella? The YouTube Star Is Probably the Most Famous Person You've Never Heard of.' *mirror.co.uk*, 18 February 2015. https://www.mirror.co.uk/3am/celebrity-news/zoe-sugg---most-famous-3671787.

Berryman, Rachel, and Misha Kavka. 'Crying on YouTube: Vlogs, Self-Exposure and the Productivity of Negative Affect.' *Convergence*, 24, 2017a: 85–98.

———. '"I Guess a Lot of People See Me as a Big Sister or a Friend": The Role of Intimacy in the Celebrification of Beauty Vloggers.' *Journal of Gender Studies*, 26 (3), 2017b: 307–20.

Binder, Nellie. 'From the Message Board to the Front Door: Addressing the Offline Consequences of Race-and Gender-Based Doxxing and Swatting.' *Suffolk University Law Review*, 51, 2018: 55.

Bishop, Sophie. '#YouTuberAnxiety: Anxiety as Emotional Labour and Masquerade in Beauty Vlogs.' *Youth Mediations and Affective Relations*, ed. by S. Driver and N. Coulter. London: Palgrave Macmillan, 2018.

Burgess, Jean, and Joshua Green. *YouTube: Online Video and Participatory Culture*. Cambridge: Polity, 2009.

Chen, Adrian. 'Nasim Aghdam, the YouTube Shooting, and the Anxiety of Demonetization.' *The New Yorker*, 6 April 2018. https://www.newyorker.com/tech/annals-of-technology/nasim-aghdam-the-youtube-shooting-and-the-anxiety-of-demonetization.

Deller, Ruth, and Kathryn Murphy. '"Zoella Hasn't Really Written a Book, She's Written a Cheque": Mainstream Media Representations of YouTube Celebrities.' *European Journal of Cultural Studies*, 23 (1), February 2020: 112–32.

Dyer, Richard. *Stars*. London: British Film Institute, 1979.

Ezarik, Justine. *I, Justine*. New York: Keywords Press, 2015.

Ferchaud, Arienne et al. 'Parasocial Attributes and YouTube Personalities: Exploring Content Trends across the Most Subscribed YouTube Channels.' *Computers in Human Behavior*, 80, 2018: 88–96.

Gerlitz, Carolin, and Anne Helmond. 'The Like Economy: Social Buttons and the Data-Intensive Web.' *New Media and Society*, 15 (8), 2013: 1348–65.

Gill, Rosalind. 'Postfeminist Media Culture: Elements of a Sensibility.' *European Journal of Cultural Studies*, 10 (2), 2007: 147–66.

Ging, Debbie, and Eugenia Siapera. 'Special Issue on Online Misogyny.' *Feminist Media Studies*, 18 (4), 2018: 515–24.

Glass, Katie. 'Zoella's Bestseller: The Plot Thickens.' *The Times*, 7 December 2014. https://www.thetimes.co.uk/article/zoellas-bestseller-the-plot-thickens-6xgwdg5hkc2#commentsStart.

Greg Sandoval. 'Morgan Stanley Values YouTube as a $160 Billion Entity.' *Business Insider*, 18 May 2018. https://www.businessinsider.com/morgan-stanley-values-youtube-160-billion-dollars-2018-5?r=US&IR=T.

Horton, Donald, and R. Richard Wohl. 'Mass Communication and Para-Social Interaction: Observations on Intimacy at a Distance.' *Psychiatry*, 19 (3), 1956: 215–29.

Hunter Johnston, Lucy. 'Yes, Using a Ghostwriter Matters When Your Whole Brand Is Built on Being Authentic.' *The Independent*, 8 December 2014. https://www.independent.co.uk/voices/comment/zoella-theres-nothing-wrong-with-hiring-a-ghost-writer-as-long-as-you-admit-it-9910453.html.

Jackson, Sue, and Tiina Vares. '"Too Many Bad Role Models for Us Girls": Girls, Female Pop Celebrities and "Sexualization".' *Sexualities*, 18 (4), 2015: 480–98.

Jane, Emma A. 'Online Misogyny and Feminist Digilantism.' *Continuum*, 30 (3), 2016: 284–97.

Jerslev, Anne. 'In the Time of the Microcelebrity: Celebrification and the YouTuber Zoella.' *International Journal of Communication*, 10, 2016: 5233–51.

Kavka, Misha. *Reality TV*. Edinburgh: Edinburgh Press, 2012.

Lee, Katja. 'Not Just Ghost Stories: Alternate Practices for Reading Coauthored Celebrity Memoirs.' *The Journal of Popular Culture*, 47 (6), 2014: 1256–70.

Lobel, Orly. 'The Gig Economy & the Future of Employment and Labor Law.' *University of San Francisco Law Review*, 51, 2017: 51–74.

Lovelock, Michael. '"Is Every YouTuber Going to Make a Coming Out Video Eventually?": YouTube Celebrity Video Bloggers and Lesbian and Gay Identity.' *Celebrity Studies*, 8 (1), 2017: 87–103.

Lutton, Alison. 'YouTubers-Turned-Authors and the Problematic Practice of Authenticity.' *Celebrity Studies*, (3), 2019: 380–95.

Maguire, Emma. 'Self-Branding, Hotness, and Girlhood in the Video Blogs of Jenna Marbles.' *Biography*, 38 (1), 2015: 72–86.

Marwick, Alice. 'Instafame: Luxury Selfies in the Attention Economy.' *Public Culture*, 27 (1), (75), 2015: 137–60.

———. *Status Update: Celebrity, Publicity and Branding in the Social Media Age*. New Haven, CT: Yale University Press, 2013.

McAllister, Jenn. *Really Professional Internet Person*. London: Scholastic, 2015.

O'Donoghue, Anna. 'The Most Famous Girl You've Never Heard of.' *irishexaminer.com*, 7 August 2014. https://www.irishexaminer.com/breakingnews/entertainment/the-most-famous-girl-youve-probably-never-heard-of-zoe-sugg-638538.html.

Parkin, Simon. 'The YouTube Stars Heading for Burnout: "The Most Fun Job Imaginable Became Deeply Bleak".' *The Guardian*, 8 September 2018. https://www.theguardian.com/technology/2018/sep/08/YouTube-stars-burnout-fun-bleak-stressed?CMP=Share_iOSApp_Other.

Perloff, Richard. 'Social Media Effects on Young Women's Body Image Concerns: Theoretical Perspectives and an Agenda for Research.' *Sex Roles*, 71 (11–12), 2014: 363–37.

Petersen, Anne Helen. 'How Millenials Became the Burnout Generation.' *buzzfeednews.com*, 5 January 2019. https://www.buzzfeednews.com/article/annehelenpetersen/millennials-burnout-generation-debt-work.

Projansky, Sarah. 'Mass Magazine Cover Girls: Some Reflections on Postfeminist Girls and Postfeminism's Daughters.' *Interrogating Posfeminism: Gender and the Politics of Popular Culture*, ed. by Yvonne Tasker and Diane Negra. Durham, NC: Duke University Press, 2007.

Raun, Tobias. 'Capitalizing Intimacy: New Subcultural Forms of Microcelebrity Strategies and Affective Labour on YouTube.' *Convergence*, 24 (1), 2017: 99–113.

Richardson, Samuel. *Pamela, or Virtue Rewarded*. Oxford: Oxford University Press, [1740] 2001.

Roose, Kevin. 'The Making of a YouTube Radical.' *The New York Times*, 8 June 2019. https://www.nytimes.com/interactive/2019/06/08/technology/youtube-radical.html.

Runcie, Charlotte. 'Girl Online on Tour by Zoe Sugg, Review: "More Authentic".' *The Telegraph*, 20 October 2015. https://www.telegraph.co.uk/books/what-to-read/zoe-sugg-girl-online-on-tour-review/.

Senft, Theresa. *Camgirls: Celebrity and Community in the Age of Social Networks*. New York, NY: Peter Lang, 2008.

Singer, Jill. 'So What Do You Do, Neil Strauss?' *MediaBistro.com*, 17 August 2004. http://www.mediabistro.com/So-What-Do-You-Do-Neil-Strauss-a2441.html.

Singh, Anita. 'Zoella Breaks Record for First Week Book Sales.' *The Telegraph*, 2 December 2014. https://www.telegraph.co.uk/news/celebritynews/11268540/Zoella-breaks-record-for-first-week-book-sales.html.

Smith, Daniel. 'Charlie Is so "English"-Like: Nationality and the Branded Celebrity Person in the Age of YouTube.' *Celebrity Studies*, 5 (3), 2014: 256–74.

Smith, Sidonie, and Julia Watson. *Reading Autobiography: A Guide for Interpreting Life Narratives*. Minneapolis: University of Minnesota Press, 2001.

———. 'Virtually Me: A Toolbox about Online Presentation.' *Identity Technologies: Constructing the Self Online*, ed. by Anna Poletti and Julie Rak. Madison, WI: University of Wisconsin Press, 2013.

Smith, Sidonie. *Subjectivity, Identity and the Body: Women's Autobiographical Practices in the Twentieth Century*. Bloomington: Indiana University Press, 1993.

Sugg, Zoe. 'Book Meeting, Date Night & Found the Missing Wallet.' 24 April 2015. https://www.youtube.com/watch?v=0-m_8d5No5k.

———. 'Finishing Book Two & Louise's Launch.' 21 July 2015. https://www.youtube.com/watch?v=95_xihbNMgw.

———. *Girl Online*. London: Penguin, 2015.

————. 'Writing with a Pug, Meetings & Doggy Box.' 15 May 2015. https://www.youtube.com/watch?v=N2WpZdTVTpU.

Tolson, Andrew. 'A New Authenticity? Communicative Practices on YouTube.' *Critical Discourse Studies*, 7 (4), 2010: 277–89.

Trilling, Lionel. *Sincerity and Authenticity*. London: Oxford University Press, 1972.

Victory, Grace. *No Filter*. London: Hachette, 2017.

Williams, Zoe. 'Zoe Sugg: The Vlogger Blamed for Declining Teenage Literacy.' *The Guardian*, 24 February 2017. https://www.theguardian.com/culture/2017/feb/24/zoe-sugg-zoella-the-vlogger-blamed-for-declining-teenage-literacy.

Yelin, Hannah, and Laura Clancy. 'Doing Impact Work While Female: Hate Tweets, "Hot Potatoes" and Having "Enough of Experts".' *European Journal of Women's Studies*, March 3, 2020.

CHAPTER 6

Accessing Stars Through Autobiographical Images: Resistance, Containment, Consent and Creative Agency in the Pop-Star Visual Memoirs of M.I.A. and Lady Gaga

INTRODUCTION: AUTOBIOGRAPHICAL IMAGES IN AN *ECONOMICS OF ACCESS*

Celebrity is built upon the image: the mediation through which celebrity (and especially female celebrity) is built and circulated is predominately visual. Magazines, films, TV interviews, paparazzi shots, music videos, merchandise, red carpet appearances, social media, YouTube videos and endless press photographs all involve technologies of image construction to trade upon the visual image of the star, and these circulate within an ecosystem dependent upon a regular flow of new images and the audience's recognition of them. To this end, it is common for celebrity memoir to supply images as illustration, verification and further provision of access to the star within their pages. However, it is the written text of memoir that is conventionally presented as the primary content of value with new autobiographical insight to offer about the star. In their promise that fans can purchase a means to better know their celebrity subjects, the visual memoirs of American pop-star Lady Gaga and British-Sri Lankan pop-star M.I.A. serve the same function as the written celebrity memoirs that typify the genre: constructing the star persona and its meaning whilst providing the *appearance* of access to and intimacy with an 'authentic' self. Whilst the means available in a book of images differ to those in a

© The Author(s) 2020
H. Yelin, *Celebrity Memoir*,
https://doi.org/10.1007/978-3-030-44621-5_6

book of written narrative, they ultimately serve the same conceptual and commercial ends.

Gaga and M.I.A. have both achieved widespread mainstream fame (*Time Magazine*, for example, has included both women in their '100 Most Influential People' lists—M.I.A. in 2009 and Lady Gaga in 2010). Additionally, both star images are associated with controversy, counter-cultural music scenes and social causes.[1] Both M.I.A. and Lady Gaga are female pop performers who have combined *avant-garde* or confrontational aspects of their identities with the cheerful, light-heartedness of pop's mass appeal to achieve global success as recording artists. Their association with decentralised subject positions—such as Gaga's performances of gender fluidity or M.I.A.'s alignment with the subaltern dispossessed—suggests that they have carved public careers whose possibilities are not necessarily dominated by pre-existing models of gendered exposure. These two stars and the visual memoirs they have produced provide fruitful examples for comparison—with one another and with the other chapters in this book—in part because they are popularly received as countercultural celebrities counteracting the gender norms identified in previous chapters—a belief that needs to be interrogated. Their autobiographical books promise a different, supposedly more countercultural, type of celebrity: a limit case, I thought, against which to test the theorisations offered thus far.

However, most notable are their points of correlation with the self-representational practices of porn, reality TV, and YouTube stars. These continuities show the endurance of conventions that shape the subjectivities coaxed from female celebrities despite differences in their cultural fields. Whilst these examples demonstrate meaningful differences which show that the memoir genre is not homogenous, they ultimately still trade in the same currencies as the texts in previous chapters: seeking to construct and trade in authenticity which is located either in a claimed history of hardship or the same kind of psychic and physical 'stripping

[1] For examples of Gaga and M.I.A.'s reception as controversial, see Katy Steinmetz, 'Top 10 Controversial Music' Videos,' *Time Magazine*, 6 June 2011; 'Controversial Singer M.I.A. Fighting "Ridiculous" $1.5 Million Fine for Swearing and Making Rude Gesture During Madonna's 2012 Super Bowl Show,' *The Daily Mail*, 20 September 2013; James Lachno, 'Lady Gaga—Top 10 Controversies,' *The Telegraph*, 20 April 2011; 'Lady Gaga's Craziest Stunts and Most Outrageous Controversies,' *Us Weekly*.

bare', emotional extremity and loss of control that underpinned the theorisation of the memoirs in previous chapters. Whilst they do not offer the written confessions that are the norm, a form of confession can be extracted, nonetheless.

By producing visual, rather than written, memoirs Gaga and M.I.A. privilege their distinctive aesthetics. Whilst the promise of celebrity memoir is to reveal the 'real' woman 'behind' the image, these texts present a site for a deeper contemplation of the image itself. Rather than functioning as illustration, accompaniment, verification or supplement to written text, images form the central content of these books and are framed by minimal accompanying written discourse. The fact that M.I.A. and Gaga represent themselves visually rather than verbally cannot be accounted for by different target audiences: all of the stars in this book have, to one degree or another, achieved large-scale, mainstream fame broad enough to be safely considered to overlap.[2] M.I.A.'s anthology and Gaga's photo-memoir appear to be setting themselves up as a postmodern masquerade: a playful bricolage with performed identities which directs attention to the surface in a genre that is usually concerned with finding 'hidden depths'. Rather than written confessional narratives like those of Katie Price and Jade Goody which draw upon nineteenth-century realist modes and an Enlightenment model of a coherent self, M.I.A. and Gaga's texts appear to construct self-conscious performances of 'doing' celebrity.[3] This difference can in part be attributed to the hierarchies of cultural value, which permit female pop-stars with subcultural affiliations a wider range of representational opportunities. As a result, their access to the status of creative agent is less contested.

Lady Gaga, was born Stefani Germanotta. However, Gaga's photo-memoir offers nothing of this backstory. Rather, it takes the form of a visual diary of life on tour, onstage and offstage, in 2010 and 2011. Beyond a one-page introduction in the voice of Gaga, and promotional blurb on the dust jacket, the book is compiled entirely of photographs without any textual framing. Shot by or with controversial fashion photographer Terry Richardson and titled *Gaga x Richardson*,

[2] Nor can this difference be accounted for by their status as pop-stars (and not models, porn-stars, YouTube or reality TV stars like in previous chapters). Pop-stars such as Tegan and Sara, Miley Cyrus, Melanie Brown, Grace Jones, Geri Halliwell and Tulisa Contostavlos all adopt predominantly textual memoir forms.

[3] Yelin (2019).

photographs take in events such as Lollapalooza festival, music awards shows, a Paris fashion show and many dates of her *Monster Ball* tour in what the dust jacket calls a 'year-long global odyssey'.[4]

By contrast, M.I.A.'s work makes much of her family's Sri Lankan origins. Born in the UK, M.I.A. was moved to Sri Lanka as a baby and then on to India due to the Sri Lankan civil war. She returned to London at the age of ten where she stayed until becoming a global star through the success of her first album, *ARULAR*, named after her 'father's code name when he became involved in the Tamil resistance movement'.[5] The book *M.I.A.* by Mathangi 'Maya' Arulpragasam is described by its author as 'a document of the five years of M.I.A. art'[6] and contains over 100 graphic artworks dated between 2002 and 2011. Images are organised by the LPs they were made for: as well as *ARULAR*, there is *KALA*, named after M.I.A.'s mother and ʌ̅ ʌ Υ ʌ (a typographic play on her own name). Each collection of images is prefaced by an autobiographical essay explicitly linking M.I.A.'s life to her music, the artworks made to support it, and the global, political affairs of the time of production. Her music is thus set up as part of an autobiographical expression of the self as commoditised cultural product. The representation of M.I.A.'s ethnicity is central to her creative output. Situated as diasporic cultural production, her work embraces a politics of difference and enacts a politicised, post-colonial identity through both her music and her wider promotional aesthetics. Whilst the book, *M.I.A.*, clearly attempts to stake claim to being an art artefact, much of its contents are made up of marketing collateral such as logos, CD artwork, web design or backdrops from her world tours. Here, marketing is anthologised and presented as both art and autobiography that is in turn used to market her further.

These visual memoirs present an intersection between old and new media. M.I.A.'s images emphasise their digital, recombinant production methods and depict technological evolution in images of computers, discs, music software interfaces and @ signs. Similarly, the rough aesthetic of the photographs of Gaga, with their implied spontaneity, shares much with the proliferating visual autobiographical modes offered by social media sites such as Twitter, Facebook, Flickr, Tumblr and Instagram. These

---

[4] Gaga and Richardson, dust jacket.

[5] Arulpragasam, p. 16.

[6] Ibid., p. 13.

visual memoirs present a juncture between media forms with crudely wrought content designed to document the self and communicate informality, authenticity, and therefore intimacy, whilst their distribution in a large, hardback, glossy, full-bleed colour print, communicate the old media values of the revered art object that grants import to the contents which it anthologises.

This chapter demonstrates the rare moments when traces of power relations between celebrity and ghost can be discerned in the text as well as how these relations shape the meaning of the resultant co-authored memoir. It is true that, as many academics have observed, Gaga has constructed a star persona which has the capacity to trouble the normative cultural boundaries of femininity.[7] However, these non-normative aspects are not what are being captured and canonised in her photographic memoir. Rather, the hand (and gaze) of the 'ghost' that mediates her is visible with his own agenda regarding the role and representation of women. By contrast, the ghosting machinery that collectively produces M.I.A.'s autobiographical text can be traced to pre-existing relationships—employed by her directly—independently of the publishing house or record labels.

This could be what enables M.I.A., uniquely in the sample of memoirs examined in this book, to produce a work which does not linger on the sexuality of its author-subject. Instead, the majority of images in *M.I.A.* are by, rather than of, her. Academic interest in M.I.A. has tended either to focus on her uniqueness as a star who embodies the post-colonial experience of life under atrocity[8] or to interrogate the popular criticism she has received for 'hypocritically' appropriating subaltern experience.[9] These concerns are unarguably at stake in M.I.A.'s star image and in evidence in her memoir. However, these readings neglect her gendered identity and thus the potential she presents for an alternative model of female celebrity

---

[7] J. Jack Halberstam, *Gaga Feminism: Sex, Gender, and the End of Normal* (Boston: Beacon Press), 2012.

[8] See John Hutnyk, 'Poetry After Guantanamo: M.I.A.,' *Social Identities* 18 (5), 555–72; Brian Creech, 'Refugee Status: Tracing the Global Flows of M.I.A.,' *Communication, Culture & Critique* 7 (2014), 267–82.

[9] See Anamik Saha, 'Locating MIA: "Race", Commodification and the Politics of Production,' *European Journal of Cultural Studies* 15 (2012); Candice Haddad, 'Immigration, Authorship, Censorship, and Terrorism: The Politics of M.I.A's US Cross-Over,' *In the Limelight*.

self-representation. Whilst I will argue that M.I.A.'s willed controversy is at times extremely problematic, she evades the *economics of access* demonstrated in previous chapters, refuses to undertake the (sexual) confession that the genre typically demands, and keeps her body out of the frame in favour of her creative and conceptual output. Amongst the sample of memoirs examined throughout this book, M.I.A.'s is unique in that it is not about sex.

VISUAL AUTOBIOGRAPHY, ART SCHOOL FRAMING AND CLAIMS TO CREATIVE AGENCY

As an introduction to the themes and aesthetics of these texts, consider their cover artworks and the identity they each construct. The cover of Gaga's photo-diary presents a combination of the visual codes of the toughness and aggression of Teddy Boy, rebel masculinity and the exaggerated, performed, white femininity of glitter and bombshell blondeness (Fig. 6.1 *Gaga x Richardson*, cover). The image sets up the characteristic confrontational Gaga persona with which her audience will be familiar: leather, plastic, peroxide, studs and sparkles. Her bleached hair, cut to her nape with darker roots visible, presents a femininity which rejects the social value placed on seemingly 'natural' beauty, and one that has (supposedly) not been scrubbed up or perfected to be photographed. She wears a leather jacket with the collar turned up in reference to the punk and rockabilly fashions that have been marked in pop-culture as the sartorial choice of the rebel or outsider. The photograph is cropped to her head and shoulders where the word 'Gaga' is studded across her back, as a Hell's Angel jacket might carry emblems of allegiances. In a combination of toughness and glamorous camp, these studs are wrought in diamanté. Wearing her own name—written in lights—across her back suggests the self-canonisation and performance of fame that have been explicit concerns throughout her career. The cover carries no title. Her status as icon is such that the full-bleed photograph of the back of her head is enough to know that it is her. She needs no further referent. Her eyes hide behind sunglasses, in the classic, black, plastic Wayfarer style that has been the costume of male rock and roll heart-throbs. Her gaze is hidden, denying access to her subjectivity, something she has remarked upon in interviews: 'I don't take off my glasses for many interviews, but I'll take

Fig. 6.1 Cover, *Gaga x Richardson*, 2011

them off for you'.[10] This suggests that eye contact and the connection it implies is a privilege she consciously chooses to admit or deny. With her back to the camera, her performance of indifference literally gives her viewer the shoulder, her head is turned to look off into the distance, her facial expression, what can be seen of it, dispassionate, unsmiling,

---

[10] Ann T. Torrusio, 'The Fame Monster: The Monstrous Construction of Lady Gaga,' *Performance Identities*, p. 161.

bored even. It is a rejection of the viewer's gaze and a performance of her power. And yet, the glaring studio light, bouncing off her shiny leather and gems, and casting her shadow on the bare, white studio backdrop, is harsh, clinical and searching, and signals the closed, confined space of the photographer's studio, where she is up against the wall. This suggests that despite her armour, despite various defences or shields, she has nowhere to hide in the spotlight and may yet be exposed.

M.I.A.'s cover artwork typifies her explicit concerns with post-colonial, post-national subjecthood in a collage of clashing, colourful prints and layers of crudely edited photographs which suggest geographies and concepts that might constitute M.I.A.: palm-trees, globes, patterns which cross fashionable leopard print with military camouflage, abstract silhouettes of machine guns, CDs and money (Fig. 6.2 *M.I.A.*, cover). All are roughly hewn in basic materials such as marker pen, cut-outs, and stencils that imply the authenticity of handmade, small-scale labour. The emphasis is on her role as artist and producer.

M.I.A. herself barely appears and is seen in only a tiny image which is one inch wide. The black-and-white photograph is digitally flattened as if repeatedly photocopied and features M.I.A. dressed as Muammar Gaddafi with leopard print military beret and sunglasses—a man M.I.A. described as her 'style icon [because] he's rock and roll'.[11] Of this controversial impersonation, she states in the book, 'This is like, African Dictator, before Sacha Baron Cohen'.[12] The reference is to Cohen's loosely satirical, slapstick movie, *The Dictator* (2012). M.I.A.'s work makes frequent, controversial, decontextualised reference to military conflict; a strategy Brian Creech praises as the 'intentional unintelligibility that occurs as a part of the processes of translation, appropriation, and estheticization',[13] and which Anamik Saha commends as a tactical, camouflaged politics which 'resists the aversion to politics from mainstream pop audiences, and conversely, prevents her political message from being reduced to a novelty'.[14] Certainly, M.I.A.'s self-styling as a controversial, reviled, once-powerful dictator is a bold representational move not seen amongst other female celebrities. However, Creech and Saha's interpretations may be generous when there is little offered to explain the political insensitivity of appropriating imagery of someone who, just one

[11] Romain Gavras, 'M.I.A.,' *Interview Magazine*, 7 July 2010.

[12] Arulpragasam, p. 112.

[13] Creech, p. 271.

[14] Saha, p. 742.

Fig. 6.2 Cover, *M.I.A.*, 2011

year before her book's publication, was killed by rebels after his violent suppression of a popular uprising. Her concern that she gets credit for having the idea before Cohen, however, typifies her claims to authorial and creative credit. The overall cover image tells much of what is at stake in her star identity: willed controversy, oblique reference to current affairs and global politics, military violence, ethnic identity, globalisation and, like Gaga, a performance of power.

Scholarship on postmodern icons posits the 'post-national', 'nomadic', 'global hybrid' as the subject of postmodernity[15] and collage as its art form.[16] As a text, *M.I.A.* literalises these two aspects of postmodernity. Statements such as, 'I wasn't anywhere, I was everywhere. I was having problems with my us visa, so I recorded in Liberia, Jamaica, Trinidad, and India. I didn't feel like I fit anywhere',[17] position *M.I.A.* as the nomadic post-global subject of postmodernity as well as a global star. Describing the production of the artworks supporting her first album, M.I.A. explains: 'Arular went from jungle to street to wall. It's word-of-mouth, photocopied, black-and-white, neon, lo-fi, printed, scanned, re-filmed, re-photographed, with some tape, staples, a spray can, and some glue'.[18] This deliberate interplay between digital and analogue (re)production provides a perfect example of what John Urry identifies as the 'mechanically, electronically and digitally reproduced' collage of postmodernity.[19] These cut-and-paste aesthetic processes permit an aggregate identity rather than the univocalism of the linear narrative life story; recombinant imagery hybridises nationality, internationality, art, commerce, memoir and marketing.

As discussed, the text-based celebrity memoirs in this book have been considered by both the academy and the media to be 'low',[20] non-literate'[21] literature, sullied by commerce. Whilst their celebrity author-subjects sometimes express pride in having completed a book, they rarely claim any 'higher' purpose than enabling their audience to get to know the 'real' them or 'speaking back' to press misrepresentations. By contrast, the large format, glossy, art texts produced by M.I.A. and Gaga borrow conventions from the fields of more legitimised forms of culture in signifiers of high fashion and fine art, fields associated with creativity and originality. Thus, Gaga and M.I.A. attempt to elevate their

---

[15] John Urry, 'The Global Media and Cosmopolitanism,' 26 April 2001, p. 3, cited in José I. Prieto-Arranz, 'The Semiotics of Performance and Success in Madonna,' *The Journal of Popular Culture* 45.1 (2012), 178.

[16] John Urry and Jonas Larsen, *The Tourist Gaze 3.0* (London: Sage, 2011), pp. 98–99.

[17] Arulpragasam, p. 52.

[18] Arulpragasam, p. 16.

[19] Urry and Larsen, pp. 98–99.

[20] Sutherland.

[21] Cadwalladr.

memoirs (and therefore themselves) up these hierarchies of cultural value. M.I.A.'s description of her text as 'a document of [...] art'[22] signals the comparative seriousness with which the reader is asked to approach her text. The autobiographical occasion, therefore, is presented as the artist's urge to produce. Gaga's book of full-bleed images, its staging, lighting, composition and wardrobe, have the appearance of a fashion house's coffee-table book. Whilst the contents within them trade in the immediacy and presence of seemingly unprocessed image construction, both texts have very high production values, expensively made in terms of print, paper quality and colour saturation. They come only in hard-back and retail at £19.95 and £35, respectively, far above the customary £7.99 cover price of written celebrity memoirs. Thus, the star images of Gaga and M.I.A. privilege the visual, presenting it as the aspect of their identity and creative output that demands serious attention to be fully appreciated.

When the author of *M.I.A.*'s foreword, Steve Loveridge, states, 'I met Maya in 1998 at Central St Martins College of Art and design',[23] he frames M.I.A. first and foremost as an artist. Drawing upon the credibility of art school origins reframes her pop-stardom as a form of performance art: a self-reflexive, postmodern exercise in 'doing' pop-stardom, at the same time as being a bid for success in the music industry.[24] Loveridge elaborates on what these art school credentials mean:

> Saint Martins was the college that everyone wanted to be at in the late '90s. Alexander McQueen, Stella McCartney, and John Galliano are all ex-pupils. [...] The Britpop and Brit art scenes were populated with London art school graduates. Jarvis Cocker and PJ Harvey both had done our degree.[25]

This show of artistic and pop-culture pedigree positions M.I.A. as taking her place alongside important British cultural icons. He conflates 'Britpop and Brit art' conferring the conceptual and creative values of the latter onto the former. M.I.A., the reader is instructed, is not the usual manu-factured pop-star marionette, but an artist of substance and member of

---

[22] Arulpragasam, p. 13.

[23] Arulpragasam, p. 6.

[24] Yelin (2019).

[25] Arulpragasam, p. 6.

the pop-cultural intelligentsia. Association with a credible, cultural clique who have undertaken the same training as her protects M.I.A. from the allegations of undeserved fame seen in previous chapters. When *M.I.A.*'s foreword states, 'the M.I.A. art show became the visual backdrop for M.I.A. the recording artist',[26] her transition from visual artist to pop-star is presented, not as one from the highbrow environment of the gallery to the lowbrow populism of the charts, but as a seamless expansion of conceptual creativity into new forms. With Loveridge claiming, 'Maya had a fully realized aesthetic ready to go', 'she was fully formed from day one', *M.I.A.*'s foreword presents her stage identity as coming from a pre-existing, intrinsic essence of her self, rather than the commercial machinery of the music industry.[27] When M.I.A. states that '*Kala* was the album where I was supposed to get cleaned up, scrubbed up with better producers, and to become an icon that was more palatable to the industry',[28] she does so as a mark of pride. She positions herself as untamable in contrast to the cynical, commercial processes of mainstreaming, offering her resistance to 'scrubbing up' as a mark of authenticity. Elevating her pop career with such statements as 'everything I did as an artist',[29] the presentation of pop-stardom as a continuation of a prior art practice stakes a claim to authenticity and agency over manufacture.

Within *M.I.A.*, within this entire sample of memoirs even, the most significant claim to artistic status and the collapse of hierarchies of cultural value is the inclusion of curator's notes cataloguing what in any other context would be considered promotional materials, according to fine art convention. Each work is listed with the artist's medium and date of production, e.g. 'Print for Arular CD face Spray paint on canvas, 2005', 'M.I.A. logo concepts. Arabic stencils cut from stickers, 2004'.[30] To understand the woman behind the image, this text offers the artworks she has created, presenting a site for a deeper contemplation of the image itself and suggesting it navigates comfortably, and belongs within, the art establishment. This self-representational move clearly seeks to claim cultural value for M.I.A.

---

[26] Ibid., p. 11.
[27] Ibid.
[28] Ibid., p. 52.
[29] Ibid., p. 115.
[30] Ibid., pp. 50–51.

A self-reflexivity suggestive of a conversance with the theoretical critiques of art school is similarly implied within Gaga's star image. Like M.I.A., she also attended art school, at NYU's Tisch School of Arts. In *Rivington Was Ours: Lady Gaga, the Lower East Side and the Prime of Our Lives*, Gaga's former DJ, Brendan Jay Sullivan, describes a friendship founded on a love of being 'up to [their] ankles in theory'.[31] An apocryphal essay purportedly authored by Gaga at art school waxes theoretical about nudity, monstrosity and the human body—themes later explored in her pop persona.[32] Texts such as these interact and combine in Gaga's assemblage with deliberate acts of branding which explicitly and self-referentially intertwine pop music and art to frame her pop-stardom as a critical exercise. For example, Gaga names her third album 'Artpop' and claims it is 'a reverse of Warhol' that puts 'art culture into pop music'.[33] In her concerns with fame, fabrication, surface and mass spectacle, scholars have read Gaga through the lens of Pop Art—specifically that of Andy Warhol.[34] Gaga makes direct reference to Warhol, such as her creation of the character, Candy Warhol, for *The Fame Ball* tour, in an enjambment of the artist and his muse, Candy Darling. Partnerships with respected visual artists and designers such as Terence Koh, Alexander McQueen and Philip Treacy borrow their associations with the creative *avant-garde* to position Gaga's own *oeuvre* as equally credible. In explicitly staking claim to the status of artist, Gaga and M.I.A. run counter to the gendered narratives of celebrity merit, and attempt to distinguish themselves from the narratives of female pop-stardom with its associations of puppetry and manufacture.[35]

---

[31] Brendan Jay Sullivan, *Rivington Was Ours: Lady Gaga, the Lower East Side, and the Prime of Our Lives* (New York: It Books, 2013), p. 19.

[32] Stefani Germanotta, 'Assignment # 4: Reckoning of Evidence' reportedly written 2003 during her freshman year at NYU Tisch, 1 November 2004. Posted in Jordan Carter, 'The Theory Monster,' http://students.brown.edu/College_Hill_Independent/?p=2481.

[33] Fay Strang, 'EXCLUSIVE: '"My Intention Was to Put Art Culture into Pop Music": Lady Gaga Reveals She Aimed to "Reverse Warhol" in New Record,' *Mail Online*, 4 November 2013.

[34] See Lucy O. Brien, Lori Burns, and Marc Lafrance, and Sally Gray and Anusha Rutnam in *Lady Gaga and Popular Music: Performing Gender, Fashion, and Culture*, ed. by Martin Iddon and Melanie L. Marshall (New York: Routledge, 2014).

[35] Geraghty, p. 99.

This distinction is reflected in their rejection of the conventions of female pop-stars' written memoirs, in which stars describe strikingly similar paths into the music industry. In the memoirs of Jessie J. and Victoria Beckham, for example, pop-stardom is the natural progression from a childhood in 'stage school' and the encouragement of a supportive, middle-class family. Gaga's supportive family, economically comfortable upbringing and performing arts background are similar but not made visible. Her characterisation of a performing arts background as the conceptual training of a serious artist contrasts with the image of a finishing school for pop-stars that stage school represents in the popular imagination. Both M.I.A. and Gaga position themselves at odds with middle-class comfort but this is intrinsic to the position they've adopted: art school is classed; artistic purpose is classed; having a cause is classed.

Gaga and M.I.A.'s visual memoirs position them amongst a cultural and artistic elite. As such they claim creative agency, requesting their work be taken seriously despite its embrace of the immediacy, effervescence and mass appeal of pop. Not only is each woman a cultural product, but also each keenly emphasises their role as agent of cultural production. This contradicts gendered division in discourses of star agency, adopting the masculinised position of creative agent and cultural producer.[36] As such, they define themselves in contrast to the feminised passivity of the pop-star as music industry pawn. Spectacle is usually feminised as celebrity culture constructs women as decorative objects to be looked at.[37] However, by creating grand spectacles and using them as a claim to high art, and making explicit connections between their visual identities and their creative agency, these representational moves disrupt the logic of gendered celebrity spectacle. Instead, they could be argued to be undertaking what Smith and Watson have termed 'the artist's engagement with the history of seeing women's bodies'.[38] These books of images are an attempt to occupy the space of the thinking subject and visual artist using their specular, embodied pop-stardom as canvas.

This exercise in pop-stardom as performance art has both women presenting themselves as having a critical stance which understands,

[36] R. L. Rutsky, 'Being Keanu,' *The End of Cinema as We Know It: American Film in the Nineties*, ed. by Jon Lewis (New York: New York University Press, 2001), p. 185; John Berger, *Ways of Seeing* (London: Penguin Books, 1972), p. 47.

[37] Williams (2007), p. 114.

[38] Smith and Watson (2001), p. 7.

accounts for and surpasses traditional pop-stardom through self-reflexivity. It is not simply that they are famous pop-stars, but that each is constructing a performance about being a famous pop-star. Thus, these women are presented as 'doing' pop-stardom rather than, or as well as, being pop-stars.[39] This construction of themselves as deliberately enacting a performance of 'doing' pop-stardom itself constitutes a source of contradictory authenticity: as with the logic of reality television discussed in Chapter 4, openness about the machinery that fabricates the star provides the authenticity of an honest fake.

THE ONTOLOGY OF CELEBRITY MEMOIR AND THE WORKINGS OF IMAGES

Autobiography and photography share a privileged ontological status because of their relationship with a world that exists beyond the page. Just as—despite evidence to the contrary—autobiography is a search for a connection with a reality beyond the page, photography has been understood through its direct links to the actual. Despite asserting the impossibility of untroubled referentiality in autobiographical writing because 'in the field of the subject, there is no referent',[40] Roland Barthes elsewhere expresses belief in the directness of this relationship in photography: 'The photograph is literally an emanation of the referent'.[41] This suggests not only a representational link but indeed a continuous physical link. Barthes writes of the photograph in terms of certainty and trust, casting the photograph as a document that can attest to a truth of what has existed: 'Every photograph is a certificate of presence'.[42] Susan Sontag furthers this idea of physical presence when she states that the photograph is 'something directly stencilled off the real, like a footprint or a death mask'.[43]

---

[39] Yelin (2019).

[40] Roland Barthes, *Roland Barthes by Roland Barthes*, trans. Richard Howard (New York: Hill and Wang, 1977), p. 56.

[41] Roland Barthes, *Camera Lucida: Reflections on Photography*, trans. Richard Howard (New York: Farrar, Straus, and Giroux, 1981), p. 80.

[42] Ibid., p. 87.

[43] Susan Sontag, *On Photography* (New York: Farrar, Straus, and Giroux, 1977), p. 154.

Sontag's reading of the photograph, appearing as if a relic that carries traces of the sitter which we may later worship, is specifically of interest when considering the appeal of books of celebrity images. The materiality of these texts as physical objects compounds this sense of the keepsake that offers physical proximity: 'the force of photographic images comes from their being material realities in their own right, richly informative deposits left in the wake of whatever emitted them'.[44] For the celebrity fan, a sense of intimacy may be achieved through maintaining this belief in the 'deposits', 'emanation' and, ultimately, 'presence' of the sitter contained in the photograph. Digital photography has dematerialised the individual photograph. However, metadata (the information fields that are encoded in digital photographs) creates further certifications in a 'tension between the semiotic inscription of metadata and the inscription understood as the "this was" of the photograph'.[45] Where knowledge about the celebrity's life constitutes a feeling of privileged access within the assemblage of celebrity gossip, belief in a 'certificate of presence' or 'this was' can provide the confidence of documented record amongst the hearsay.

An old photograph of M.I.A.'s father with a group of men, who look like a rebel militia, in a mixture of civilian and partial military dress, some with rifles, is offered as *proof* of her much-questioned family connection to the Tamil Tigers. Photographs of both women's live concerts, with crowds screaming and reaching for their idol, document their status and potency as stars. Photographs of Gaga before and after the infamous appearance wearing what has become known as 'the meat dress' document the labour that went into a team of people dressing her in it, the protective nipple covers required underneath it, the string that held the slabs of beef in place; they verify the company of fellow A-list pop icon Cher during the nervous wait to go on stage, and the backstage hugs from Gaga's mother after a successful appearance. Together they create a narrative around the event, contextualising, giving further dimension to, and offering the 'this was' of a moment that has become an iconic reference point within her career. The remaining documents show us that these things occurred. They reduce the distance because, in the celebrity's

[44] Ibid., p. 180.

[45] Elizabeth Stainforth and David Thom, 'Metadata: Walter Benjamin and Bernard Stiegler,' *Theorising Visual Studies*, ed. by James Elkins (New York: Routledge, 2013), p. 164.

absence, they instead can be touched, held and in the case of these books, bought and owned. 'Photographic images', argues Sontag, 'do not seem to be statements about the world so much as pieces of it, miniatures of reality that anyone can make or acquire'.[46] Such is the logic of the visual celebrity memoir, perhaps of celebrity memoir as a whole, offering a piece, or microcosm, of the star, which anyone can acquire and own.

This illusion of presence and possession is, however, as much a fiction as the self at the centre of the idea of autobiographical truth. André Bazin argues that 'a very faithful drawing may actually tell us more about the model but despite the promptings of our critical intelligence it will never have the irrational power of the photograph to bear away our faith'.[47] In the visual celebrity memoir, we see this irrational power and faith compounded with the belief in the subject's ability to reveal a true self. Writing in 1994, when today's debates about the alteration of celebrities' images with Photoshop were in their infancy, Dow Adams observed that despite decades of discussion about creative techniques enabling photographic forgery 'an inherent belief about the photograph's direct connection to the actual persists'.[48] There are direct parallels between this and the ghostwritten memoir's layers of complex mediation in that each undercuts explicit promises of access, revelation and 'true' selfhood. Thus, 'lifewriting and photography, both by definition and common perception, have a strong felt relationship to the world, a relationship which upon examination seems to disappear'[49] and yet the pull of this relationship, especially in the context of the appetites stimulated by celebrity culture, remains stronger than logic, examination or evidence to the contrary.

The images within Gaga and M.I.A.'s books are supplied to brand, impose meaning upon and commoditise the self through forces of mediation in much the same way as the written memoirs discussed in previous chapters. Indeed, they are offered for that very purpose, as (and in place of) autobiography. They presuppose the same desire for proximity and are similarly searched for access to the real. Within these texts, we see overlapping visual and verbal conventions of autobiography, diary,

---

[46] Sontag (1977), p. 4.

[47] André Bazin, 'The Ontology of the Photographic Image,' *Classic Essays on Photography*, ed. by Trachtenberg, p. 241.

[48] Timothy Dow Adams, 'Introduction: Life Writing and Light Writing; Autobiography and Photography,' *Modern Fiction Studies* 40.3 (1994), 365–66.

[49] Ibid., p. 483.

scrapbook, album, personal snapshot, paparazzi 'snatch', press release, merchandise, pornography, catalogue, art artefact, graphic design and agitprop. Just as all text offers a visual artefact, even in its simplest form of marks on a page, an image is linguistically coded in the process of recognition of what it represents. The difference is that 'the image is the sign that pretends not to be a sign, masquerading as natural immediacy and presence'.[50] It is this claim to 'natural immediacy and presence' that suits the image to the wider masquerade undertaken by celebrity culture in fabricating the sensation of intimacy through revelation. Despite the emptiness of these promises of autobiographical and photographic access and authenticity, I shall now examine how the appearance of access to an authentic subjectivity is, nonetheless, cultivated and performed.

GHOSTED AUTHENTICITY AND ACCESS: CONSENT, BOUNDARIES, AND WHAT IS IN (AND OUT OF) THE FRAME

Just as a ghostwriter mediates the subject of a written celebrity memoir, the photographer mediates the subject of a visual memoir such as Gaga's. In both cases, the process of documentation requires interpretation. Thus, like a ghostwriter, photographer Terry Richardson witnesses and documents Gaga's story in a process which inevitably shapes and contributes to the story. As I have shown, the power dynamics of ghosting sit on a spectrum from the barely acknowledged scribe who ventriloquises their subject to the point of their own disappearance, to the employee of a star's management, who gets the last word after their 'cash cow' subject's death. It is rarely a simple case of one or other extreme. The negotiation between Gaga and Richardson hinges upon similar factors to written memoir: Gaga has chosen, or at the very least agreed, to work with Richardson; Richardson is credited on the cover; he is famous in his own right; Gaga is, ultimately, vastly more famous and is presumably involved in some form of approval process.

There are differences, however, in ghosting dynamics in the case of photography. Like words, photographs can be edited, or cut. It is difficult, however, for them to undergo a fundamental change in subject matter. The moments in which and angles from which Richardson records

---

[50] W. J. T. Mitchell, *Iconology: Image, Text, Ideology* (Chicago: University of Chicago Press, 1986), p. 43.

his subject form the book's source material in a way that cannot be redrafted, unlike memories recalled for a ghost-as-interlocutor. The events recorded (e.g. Gaga's *Monster Ball* tour) cannot easily be repeated. Gaga's contribution occurs in the moment, rather than retrospectively. The 'inevitably partial' and 'imaginative' nature of auto/biography that was discussed in Chapter 2 remains, caused by the (partial and imaginative) acts of Richardson's documentation (plus editorial and design teams), rather than the author-subject's memory.[51] Whereas memory offers subjective, often unverifiable evidence, the 'this was' of the photograph can in contrast (appear to) bear witness with authority.[52] Whilst the subject of written, ghosted memoir may forget, omit or lie to control the account given, the subject of photographic memoir has their ghost present as events occur. Their opportunity for shaping their account, therefore, lies in controlling actual events, negotiating with the ghost as they happen, or withholding approval after the fact. The question of consent and permission in such an example is, therefore, critical.

In *Gaga x Richardson*, Gaga's photographer, Richardson, can be seen to be encroaching on her space as both author and celebrity subject. There are four ways he does this. As I have argued, deliberate mystification of the roles of the ghost and the celebrity author-subject means one can only infer each party's contribution. However, as identified in the case of Neil Strauss and Jenna Jameson in Chapter 3, stylistic preferences, recognisable from a ghosts' solo-authored works, make visible their contribution. Richardson's famous pop-pornographic *oeuvre* has a distinctive style, familiar from campaigns for fashion brands like Tom Ford and Katherine Hamnett, or books and exhibitions such as *Terryworld* and *Kibosh*. Richardson's resultant visibility, even behind the camera, claims the pictures of Gaga as his interpretation. Whilst the pictures document Gaga's creations (shows, persona, poses), Richardson's visibility positions her more as subject than producer of the memoir itself.

In choosing such a famous ghost, Gaga borrows certain values, capital and associations from Richardson's existing reputation. These include edginess, fashion, irony, hipsterism and sexual controversy. Richardson's career has been accompanied by allegations of sexual coercion of young

---

[51] Smith and Watson (2001), p. 6.

[52] Stainforth and Thom, p. 164.

models and many of his works graphically depict his penetration of his female subjects.[53] As Louise Wallenberg describes:

> Models appear in the nude, often with Richardson placing himself next to them, as if saying: "Look, I made them undress." Yet his photos are read as fashion, due to his legacy. [He also produces work] depicting himself engaging in oral, vaginal (and anal?) sex with young women – often 'decapitated' with their faces out of the frame.[54] (Fig. 6.3 Smiling Terry Richardson receiving oral sex from a model in a dustbin)

Richardson's tendency to appear in the shoots he orchestrates, handing the camera to his assistants whilst he steps into the frame is a second way in which he encroaches on Gaga's space as celebrity subject. There are two different scenarios in which this happens: either in images of young, female models performing sex acts upon him or in his portraits of extremely famous subjects, such as Gaga, or then President, Barack Obama (Fig. 6.4 Smiling Terry Richardson with Barack Obama). These documents of 'pally' familiarity with some of the most famous and powerful people on earth is a clear demonstration of Richardson's power and approval within the establishment (a power which helps enable him to ask young models to participate in the former scenario). The relationship between these two types of photographs is explicit in an account by Jamie Peck who modelled for Richardson when she was 19:

> He decided to just get naked. Before I could say "whoa, whoa, whoa!" dude was wearing only his tattoos [...] "Why don't you take some pictures of me?" he asked. Um, sure. So his assistants took pictures of me taking pictures of him. *All the while, he was dropping names like they were hot* [...]. I'm not sure how he maneuvered me over to the couch, but at some point he strongly suggested I touch his terrifying penis [emphasis added].[55]

---

[53] See Jenna Sauers, 'Meet Terry Richardson, The World's Most F—ked Up Fashion Photographer,' *Jezebel.com*, 16 March 2010.

[54] Louise Wallenberg, 'Fashion Photography, Phallocentrism and Feminist Critique,' *Fashion in Popular Culture: Literature, Media and Contemporary Studies*, ed. by Joseph H. Hancock, Toni Johnson-Woods, and Vicki Karaminas (Bristol: Intellect, 2013), p. 146.

[55] Jamie Peck, 'Terry Richardson Is Really Creepy: One Model's Story,' *The Gloss*, 16 March 2010.

Fig. 6.3 Smiling Terry Richardson receiving oral sex from a model in a dustbin, *Kibosh*, 2006

Fig. 6.4 Smiling Terry Richardson with Barack Obama, *Vibe Magazine*, November 2007

Echoes of Peck's account are visible in Gaga's memoir. Richardson appears in the frame in 24 of the photographs in *Gaga X Richardson*, often giving his typical grinning thumbs-up, sometimes approaching her on the bed in a combination of both the aforementioned scenarios, blending (implied) physical intimacy and access to established powerful figures (Fig. 6.5 Smiling Terry Richardson with Gaga as puppet).

Thirdly, the title *Gaga X Richardson* is deliberately ambiguous about who is author and who is subject. It claims to be neither Gaga by Richardson nor vice versa. Rather, various ambiguous possibilities are implied by 'X': partnership, X-ratedness, a kiss, the progeny when the two of them combine, or that they multiply one another and are thus bigger together. Another (perhaps unintended) reading, given his encroachment

Fig. 6.5 Smiling Terry Richardson with Gaga as puppet, *Gaga x Richardson*

on her space as both author and subject and his branding of her with his own renowned style, could be that he is crossing her out.

The fourth, and most significant, way in which Richardson as ghost proves overly visible is the overwhelmingly male gaze that conditions the photographs of Gaga. Gaga's introduction references her unsuccessful protestations to stop him photographing her: 'Oh Terry, get out of here', signalling his control of the camera and of the moment in which the photograph is taken. Despite the power asymmetry in her favour outside of the frame, the camera puts the audience into his heterosexual, male perspective as he lingers over her body as erotic object, decapitates her head, or reduces her to disembodied parts. These worn pornographic tropes of male agent and female spectacle are deployed knowingly and ironically throughout Richardson's work. In response to Richardson's porn pastiche, journalist Alissa Quart developed the term 'Hipster Sexism', which involves 'the objectification of women but in a manner that uses mockery [and] quotation marks'.[56] Quart argues that when perusing '"Uncle Terry's" pictures, we may imagine that we are cool connoisseurs of fun, stagy perversity'.[57] Richardson and Gaga together are positioned as above concern for offence. In McRobbie's terms, feminism is 'taken into account' only to suggest its redundancy.[58] Richardson's work could be understood through McRobbie's reading of media which plays back to its audience a crude appropriation of Laura Mulvey's theory of women as objects of the gaze.[59] Gaga's participation shows that she 'gets the joke', presenting her as fun, sexy and worldly.[60] As discussed, all the celebrity memoirs examined here incorporate photographs, many of which, especially for Price, Jameson and Anderson, conform to these same conventions. However, when photographs form the entire memoir, being constituted through an (ironic or otherwise) objectifying gaze other than her own, reduces her appearance as agent of her own representation.

Both M.I.A.'s and Lady Gaga's texts employ aesthetic tropes to enhance the image's appearance of authenticity and, with it (the illusion of) access. Ruth Barcan argues of homemade (or constructed to look homemade) pornography that 'graininess becomes a virtue, a sign of the authenticity and the brazenness of the image'.[61] These books juxtapose images with low production values with high celebrity subjects to imply an unfinished mediation process, a contrast with official star output and, thus, an 'off-screen' identity or glimpse of a more 'real' self 'behind' the polished celebrity image.[62] This is what Smith and Watson, in their study of women's autobiographical art, describe as a 'disarmingly unprocessed' aesthetic which 'emit[s] an aura of authenticity'; an authenticity which is 'commodified as cultural capital in the age of confession'.[63] The forms of 'graininess' differ between the two texts. However, in both, an 'unprocessed' aesthetic signifies a 'brazenness' and authenticity that ultimately

[56] Alissa Quart, 'The Age of Hipster Sexism,' *New York Magazine*, 30 October 2012.
[57] Ibid.
[58] Tasker and Negra (2007), p. 28.
[59] Ibid., p. 33.
[60] Ibid., pp. 28 and 33.
[61] Barcan (2004), p. 245.
[62] Dyer (1979), p. 22.
[63] Smith and Watson (2001), p. 3.

imply that a form of confession is taking place and that a self is being revealed through a series of images.

The appearance of images that were produced 'off the cuff'—unfinished, unpolished and without the usual refinements, finessing and manipulations of the perfected images of celebrity culture—serves a further goal beyond communicating access to something authentic. These visual effects act as signifiers of countercultural, anti-corporate, 'hipster' values, which, perhaps ironically, are what make them such effective merchandise in the marketing of the celebrity as product. This implication of access to an unprocessed, unmediated star is crucial to their power. If 'the image is the sign that pretends not to be a sign, masquerading as natural immediacy and presence',[64] these images are the adverts that pretend not to be adverts, selling the charade of the immediacy and presence of the star in their carefully perfected imperfection.

The visual memoirs of these women could be seen as an attempt to resist the 'incitement to discourse' previously discussed, but they do offer a form of confession.[65] In his study of celebrity confessionals, Redmond observes of candid celebrity photography 'it is deeply affectively moving' and 'with each photograph, the viewer is presented with a seemingly private, intimate moment'.[66] This form of confession can be seen in *Gaga x Richardson*'s awkward, unsettling angles which highlight rather than conceal imperfection to endow the images with an accidental, unprofessional and therefore supposedly spontaneous quality—a signature aesthetic which runs throughout Richardson's career. Harsh glare from the camera flash illuminates bright, white walls and emphasises flaws, sitting at odds with the smoothed, digitally altered images that form the majority of 'official' celebrity-endorsed photographs. This contrast is especially evident in images which 'catch' (and construct) Gaga as dirty or passed out, with clothes torn or make-up smeared (Fig. 6.6 Gaga passed out; Fig. 6.11 Gaga being carried after collapse; Fig. 6.12 Gaga crying with smeared make-up). It is not that audiences never see celebrities in these compromised or humiliating situations, but rather that these are usually supplied by paparazzi 'snatches'. As discussed, these stolen images usually act as an

[64] Mitchell, p. 43.

[65] Foucault (1978), p. 19.

[66] Sean Redmond, *The Star and Celebrity Confessional* (New York: Routledge, 2013), p. 2.

Fig. 6.6   Gaga passed out, *Gaga x Richardson*

undermining counterpoint supposed to reveal the earthy mess behind the godly perfection. In appropriating these tropes, Richardson borrows their signs and codes of 'realism' and their suggestion of forced exposure, thus playing with the concept of consent (both visually and sexually).

Gaga praises Richardson's working methods in a one-page introduction that, along with dust-jacket blurb, forms the only anchoring text within the book. In it, she proudly attests to the beauty of the mess in these images: 'There is no moment too strange, no angle unflattering, no circumstance relying on blind artifice, and never a time that I feel embarrassed'.[67] She attributes this to her photographer's skill as, 'Terry finds beauty in the most intricate and unassuming of places'.[68] Once again, the question of permissions is crucial. Gaga can argue that '"shame" is an obsolete notion'[69] when regardless of their private, spontaneously captured, strange or unflattering appearance, these images were shot with

[67] Gaga and Richardson, 'Introduction.'
[68] Ibid.
[69] Ibid.

the express intention of producing a book for public consumption, in a process which doubtlessly had a stage of review and Gaga's final approval built-in.

Richardson is presented as her intimate: she writes that 'with Terry the relationship extends beyond the photograph' and observes that 'it is unique to Terry and his subjects that there are *no* limitations. At all'.[70] The ambiguous implication that these images result from intimacies between photographer and subject, beyond the contents of the image, is an entrenched (and gendered) trope within popular culture as a whole[71] and within Richardson's career specifically thanks to women like Jamie Peck coming forward. The ghosting relationship is already one of intimacy, as confidant, or in the case of the ghost-photographer, as a companion present as events occur. The images which confess or construct a relationship beyond the photograph between Gaga and Richardson cast the intrinsic confidence and familiarity of ghosting as a primarily sexual intimacy, further imbuing the text with the appearance of being risqué or transgressive (when in reality this dynamic is possibly the most normative thing about it).

The content of the photographs supports this implication. Gaga's introduction describes, 'the giggling noise he makes at 4:30 in the morning when he's caught me in bed', and many of the images are indeed of Gaga 'caught' in her bed, in her underwear, with the signs that this is a pre- or post-coital moment (Fig. 6.7 Gaga in bed). Of course, this is a commonly deployed photographic genre that features in the memoirs of Anderson, Price and Jameson as discussed in Chapter 3. The sense of the possibility of further intimacies just out of shot adds to the appearance of something private being shared, when these images, whatever their intimate context, were shot as part of a project intended for public display. In this regard, whether or not Richardson has ever been Gaga's sexual partner, as is indirectly implied, he has always been her employee. Promotional blurb on Amazon.com claims that over 100,000 photographs were taken as part of this project before being edited down to the 450 which fill the book. In an official, endorsed book of photographs, billed as a collaboration between two equally contributing artists, the appearance

---

[70] Ibid.

[71] See, for example, '"It Wasn't Rape or Anything" Says David Bailey of His Sexual Conquests,' *The Telegraph*, 22 December 2012; or *Blow Up*, the Metro-Goldwyn-Mayer film inspired by Bailey's life (1966).

Fig. 6.7   Gaga in bed, *Gaga x Richardson*

of Gaga as unexpectedly 'caught' or 'captured' in an intimate, messy or out of control state, is a deliberate play with the familiar celebrity tropes of access and intimacy. As the large-scale circulation of naked celebrity 'selfies' hacked from their mobile phone cloud backup in 2014 shows,[72] it is precisely the appearance of an image that was not intended to be shared which lends it a form of authenticity, and therefore voyeuristic currency compared to the many authorised celebrity images with which it coexists.

   This voyeuristic currency is bound up with the exercise of power, as the pleasure hinges upon an unwitting object of the gaze.[73] The implication that Richardson captures Gaga by surprise further plays with the question of consent to borrow this voyeuristic currency and appearance of authenticity. Despite the overarching evidence of Gaga's participation in, and approval of, the book, individual images show her, at times,

[72] John Naughton, 'Celebgate: It's Not the Internet We Need to Fix but Men's Squalid Behaviour,' *Guardian Online*, 7 September 2014.

[73] Freud ([1905] 1962).

in what appears to be unwitting participation: for example, images of Gaga seemingly asleep or just woken up, or multiple images where the camera has zoomed in on her buttocks, cropping out any other part of her. In one example (Fig. 6.8 Gaga from behind). Gaga, shot from behind, leans out of a car window, another shot shows her at the side of the stage focussing solely on her fishnet covered buttocks that form part of her stage costume. Whether staged or not, the representation of Gaga as 'caught' 'in bed' by Richardson is problematic in the context of Richardson's wider photographic practice and reputation, and the gendered inequities upon which this hinges. Whilst Gaga is never depicted performing a sex act upon or with him, Richardson's more exploitative work is so well known in the assemblage of celebrity media circulation, that whatever the content and whoever the subject, any photograph shot by Richardson is consumed against a backdrop of his wider, deliberately exploitative practice. Her acknowledgement that 'with Terry the relationship extends beyond the photograph', clearly and deliberately draws upon this aspect of Richardson's image.

Fig. 6.8   Gaga from behind, *Gaga x Richardson*

Gaga can disavow shame as an 'obsolete notion' because her star image is built upon deliberate performances of being messy and out of control. Richardson contributes to this performance of extremity, of embracing a 'bad girl' subject position. Unlike stars such as Britney Spears whose early pop career ascribed value to purity, 'Gaga debuted already-defiled'.[74] With lyrics such as those to *Bad Romance* ('I want your ugly, I want your disease') imperfection and impurity have always been integral to Gaga's image. This is performed through the kinds of photographs associated with forced overexposure and humiliation, but which here form Gaga's official narrative. Her book claims to have 'captured the intimate, random, behind-the-scenes moments of Lady Gaga in all aspects of her life'.[75] Amazon promotional text promises 'original, behind-the-scenes photographs', 'one year of her life', 'Lady Gaga as you've never seen her before', 'all access, nothing off limits'.[76] This access-all-areas logic presupposes that authenticity lies in being perceived to be as thoroughly revealed as possible.

The artworks created by M.I.A. realise a disarmingly unprocessed feel through their lo-fi, cut-and-paste aesthetic, that values concept over technical execution and has the cumulative appearance of an art student's scrapbook (Fig. 6.9 *M.I.A.*, AK-47 felt tip illustration to support the album *Kala*). These work to give the appearance of a revealed self, especially in images of material artefacts. M.I.A.'s aged family photographs from Sri Lanka, for example, have a material, archival quality, referring to a time before the creation of the M.I.A. stage persona. A page of M.I.A.'s handwriting entitled 'Page from M.I.A. sketchbook, 2005'[77] is potent because 'we value handwritten manuscripts as "authentic" proofs of historical persons'.[78] Sections of writing authored by M.I.A. use capitals in short sentence fragments suggestive of the patterns of the spoken rather than written word. Her informal use of verbal vernacular has a logic in a genre defined by the promise of access, when we 'view

[74] Jonah Weiner, 'How Smart Is Lady Gaga?' *Slate*, 16 June 2009.

[75] Gaga and Richardson.

[76] 'Lady Gaga X Terry Richardson,' *Amazon.com*.

[77] Arulpragasam, p. 51.

[78] Sonja Neef and José van Dijck, *Sign Here! Handwriting in the Age of New Media* (Amsterdam: Amsterdam University Press, 2006), p. 9.

Fig. 6.9 AK-47 felt tip illustration to support the album *Kala*, *M.I.A.*

verbal meaning as the window into the human mind'.[79] (Whilst never confirmed, this also suggests the previously discussed mode of ghosting where the author-subject dictates to her ghost-as-interlocutor.)

However, the book predominantly claims to offer access to M.I.A.'s subjectivity through her conceptual preoccupations and her creative responses to them. This is offered in the spirit of the celebrity memoir genre: as a means to better know and understand its celebrity subject. However, where other texts discussed here compete to offer more thoroughly exposed representations of their author, *M.I.A.* offers her creative output in place of either physical exposure or psychic confession. This suggests that she hopes to be best understood as a cultural producer, through the images she has produced. The images are about her, but she is not necessarily in them, except as authorial trace.

---

[79] Roland Fletcher, 'The Messages of Material Behaviour: A Preliminary Discussion of Non-Vernacular Meaning,' *The Meanings of Things: Material Culture and Symbolic Expression*, ed. by Ian Hodder (London: Unwin Hyman, 1989), p. 33.

The collaborative authorship of *M.I.A.* conforms to the traditionally conceived ghosting dynamic of celebrity memoir, in which 'the subject outranks the writer'.[80] I have evidenced that the dynamics of ghosting are rarely this simple and can only be inferred. However, M.I.A.'s team of ghosts do indeed appear only as traces of erased and uncredited labour. In describing the production of artwork from the *ARULAR* LP, M.I.A. states:

> The birth of M.I.A. as a concept stems from these stencil paintings [...] when I started in on the art thing. We would pause the video, take a still, then spray it on cardboard.[81]

The 'we' of this collaborative production process is never identified. M.I.A.'s artworks are produced as assemblages both in their use of recombinant mixed media and in being multiply produced as part of a team, but they are attributed to her only. There is no page of thanks or acknowledgements, only a few details along with the copyright and publisher's details. Mathangi Maya Arulpragasam (M.I.A.) owns the copyright to the book and, we are guided to assume, is author of the images, essays, curatorial notes and song lyrics within it. Arulpragasam, along with Tom Manaton, is credited with the Art Direction and Design of the book. Tom Manaton's CV reads as follows:

> Creative Director, MIA, 2009 – Present
> Working as Creative Director to the Artist MIA. Working directly with her to conceptualise and develop creative directions across her entire practice. And to manage and execute this in collaboration with her management, label, external partners and a network of global talent.[82]

That the partnership with Manaton both predates and extends beyond the production of this book demonstrates that, where the ghosts of other celebrities (such as Jameson's ghost, Strauss) have been employees of, and therefore accountable to, the publishing house, M.I.A. has been in a position to choose existing collaborators who are primarily accountable to, and presumably sympathetic towards, her. Like Manaton,

[80] Couser (1998).

[81] Arulpragasam, p. 51.

[82] 'Thomas Manaton,' *LinkedIn.com*.

foreword author, Loveridge, who introduces himself as a friend of M.I.A.'s from art school, can be seen to be an example of M.I.A. choosing collaborators with existing loyalties. There are six different photographers credited with some of the few photos, shot between 2004 and 2010, in which M.I.A. *does* appear in the frame. That there are so many photographers listed suggests that no one photographer in particular has contributed enough to significantly share the authorial space.

Still, there is the question of who performed the role of ghost-as-interlocutor. Aside from the Co-Art Director and the photographers, the only two remaining credits are as follows: Book Production: Aoife Wasser; and Editor: Leah Whisler, whose CVs reveal them to be the only two credited contributors with prior connections to the publisher. Still, it is unclear which of these two job titles accords with the role of ghost, or who it was that received M.I.A.'s oral account and committed it to text in the process traditionally understood as ghosting.

M.I.A.'s invisible team of unacknowledged ghosts in the production of her book, and the artworks within it, are more visible in a lone moment of slippage than in credited contributions. When describing a photograph of a 2008 live performance at New York's Museum of Modern Art with the listing 'Reflective dress handmade by M.I.A.'[83] she states, characteristically claiming creative ownership and originality, 'It glowed. And it was way before Kanye's Glow in the Dark tour, just wanted to say that. My shit was actually glowing *[laughs]*' [emphasis added].[84] Suddenly, out of character with the conventions established throughout the rest of the book, in that one word, '[laughs]', the oral construction of the text reveals itself and brings attention to the presence of a ghost as erased scribe.

This slippage invites one to question how else M.I.A.'s account may have been edited, raising a retrospective question of trust with regard to the previous 113 pages. Occurring as it does out of nowhere, towards the end of the book, this reads more as a proofing error that has the effect of bursting the suspension of disbelief by making visible a transcription process that had until that point remained erased: by drawing attention to the interlocutor where it had been presented as M.I.A.'s direct written

---

[83] Arulpragasam, p. 114.
[84] Ibid.

account, this moment also draws attention to the fact that the interlocutor is normally erased. This brief lapse in the conventions of written style of the rest of the book highlights the fact that the reader never gets to know to whom M.I.A. is speaking. As previously discussed, texts often never reveal to whom the celebrity author-subject speaks, however, in those instances, attention is rarely drawn to this unknown. Ironically, despite the text's verbal vernacular and repeated promise that it is M.I.A.'s account, what looks like a copy-editing anomaly is the moment which suggests most strongly that it *is* M.I.A. who is speaking. This erasure of a team of ghosts in her direct employment accords with and highlights M.I.A.'s wider concern with being seen to claim ownership of her ideas and with her status as agent of cultural production.

In these examples, we see that, in collaboratively authored celebrity memoir, the questions of authenticity, authorship and agency in self-representation, whilst highly suspect and difficult to decipher with any certainty, are inextricably intertwined. Yet authorial and creative agency is nonetheless a thematic concern in the ways in which these books present their star author-subjects. This section has examined these visual memoirs in relation to their privileged yet, ultimately, undermined, onto-logical status in relation to the real. We have seen the resultant methods employed to cultivate signifiers of authenticity and the *appearance* of offering access. To interrogate these ideas further, the following sections focus on each star image in greater depth, interrogating their representa-tion in memoir and whether either star can be seen to employ resistant strategies to evade the gendered demands to share.

POP PERSONA AND M.I.A.'S
PERFORMANCE OF DIFFERENCE

Just as Gaga erases her 'backstory' of normalcy and middle-class privilege, M.I.A. leverages the aspects of her backstory associated with hardship and her diasporic identity to enact a politics of difference,[85] with references to 'what she'd been through' as a result of 'her childhood and Sri Lanka'.[86]

---

[85] S. Hall, 'New Ethnicities,' *Stuart Hall: Critical Dialogues in Cultural Studies*, ed. by D. Morley and K. H. Chen (London: Routledge, 1996), pp. 441–49. Saha, Anamik, 'Locating MIA: 'Race', Commodification and the Politics of Production,' *European Journal of Cultural Studies*, 15 (2012).

[86] Ibid., p. 9.

Positioning oneself in contrast to narratives of privilege is a necessity if a music artist is to claim authenticity. As argued in Chapter 4 in relation to Goody, in the sale of female celebrity selfhood, one must have suffered. Comfort is popularly interpreted as a mark of inauthenticity. M.I.A.'s star image embraces a deliberate, coherent politics of difference and, in the foreword, white, male classmate, Loveridge, describes M.I.A. as challenging existing hierarchies in a music scene whose homogeneity both excludes her, and provokes her disdain:

> Maya's new artwork was all motivated by a sense of resentment towards the London media scene. [...] Being around white, middle-class people doing well with their bands and their fashion labels and their photography projects began to irritate her. [...] Instead of never talking about it, she became outspoken [...] and started to make completely different work about her childhood and Sri Lanka. And people responded to it. They wanted more. [...] And it all came out of the mouth of a beautiful twenty-three-year-old Tamil girl with a great face.[87]

This passage argues for the particular role of autobiography in the creation of M.I.A.'s public identity. 'Instead of never talking about it' implies her life story had until then been unwelcome, and that it becomes a source of outrage, of creative inspiration, and a means of attracting attention for herself and, in a wider sense, directing the attention of those in the West to the political situation in Sri Lanka.

However, rather than simply seeking the moral capital associated with using one's platform as an artist or musician to direct attention to causes as is commonly seen in narratives of celebrity philanthropy,[88] Loveridge's last sentence ('it all came out of the mouth of a beautiful twenty-three-year-old Tamil girl with a great face') lends the passage a cynical, industry-weary tone. M.I.A. is unapologetically presented as exploiting both personal history and sexual capital as brand assets for personal gain. This is presented as a shrewd and knowing means to highlight and sell herself as different from the homogeneity of the music industry. In a statement of cynicism about the use of racial identity in the music industry,

---

[87] Arulpragasam, p. 9.

[88] Katherine M. Bell, 'Raising Africa? Celebrity and the Rhetoric of the White Saviour,' *PORTAL Journal of Multidisciplinary International Studies* 10.1 (2013); Ilan Kapoor, *Celebrity Humanitarianism: The Ideology of Global Charity* (New York: Routledge, 2013).

M.I.A. presents ethnicity as marketing, a part of creating a saleable image. Despite having a stake in difference, embracing that which Others her, *M.I.A.* is not ashamed to cast this difference as capital to be traded along with the normative value Loveridge places upon her youth and beauty. Whilst such use of ethnic markers is not unusual in the music industry, the marketing intentions are usually hidden. Like Lady Gaga's creation of the feeling of subcultural membership for her 'Little Monsters', M.I.A.'s embrace of Otherness has a commercial logic. Unlike, Gaga, M.I.A.'s text acknowledges this fact.

M.I.A.'s visual memoir performs conflicting subject positions, aligning her variously with artists, terrorists, victims of violence, sweatshop labourers and hegemonic imperial powers. Critics have tended to read these inconsistencies as hypocrisies and to debate her authenticity and resultant (lack of) authority to represent the refugee experience.[89] This scrutiny could be seen to be symptomatic of what Stuart Hall describes as the 'burden of representation' facing people of colour in the role of cultural producer—as M.I.A. is required to account for her ethnicity as a minority in a media that lacks diversity.[90] As demonstrated, authenticity is always at stake in celebrity memoir. Celebrity author-subjects are always under scrutiny, even when the source material of their memoir is drawn only from their experience.[91] The assemblage from which M.I.A.'s identity is constructed is sprawling, encompassing not only her own life experience but also the history and politics of Sri Lanka and even what she calls the 'third world'[92] more generally. As a result, M.I.A.'s claims

---

[89] The most famous example of this is Lynn Hirschberg's 2010 interview for the *New York Times* which contrasted M.I.A.'s pronouncements about her politics with undermining contrasting details of her pop-star lifestyle: 'She thrives on conflict, real or imagined. 'I kind of want to be an outsider,' she said, eating a truffle-flavored French fry. 'I don't want to make the same music, sing about the same stuff, talk about the same things. If that makes me a terrorist, then I'm a terrorist' (Hirschberg 2010). M.I.A. accused Hirschberg of quoting her out of context in a public disagreement which culminated in M.I.A. doxxing Hirschberg, putting her private phone number on Twitter. A resulting editor's note appended to the article apologises for the misquote. Lynn Hirschberg, 'MIA's Agitprop Pop,' *New York Times*, 25 May 2010.

[90] Stuart Hall, 'New Ethnicities,' *Stuart Hall: Critical Dialogues in Cultural Studies*, ed. by David Morley and Kuan-Hsing Chen (London: Routledge, 1996), p. 443.

[91] Smith and Watson (2001), p. 6.

[92] Arulpragasam, p. 54.

to authenticity are vulnerable to further criticisms depending on her interpretations of events beyond her own experience.

Take as an example of these critical responses *Guardian* journalist Douglas Haddow, who admonished her video for the single *Born Free* (an allegorical genocide of red-haired people, rendered in graphically violent detail) saying, 'genocide can now be parodied in order to promote a pop record'.[93] This summarises the untenable position of the pop-star who attempts to combine outspoken politics with mainstream success: regardless of whether any provoked scandal might be intended to make a political statement, politics are overshadowed by the fact that PR controversies equate to commercial gain within the industrial complex of music sales. *Village Voice* journalist Simon Reynolds similarly critiqued: 'Don't let MIA's brown skin throw you off: She's got no more real connection with the favela funksters than Prince Harry'.[94] This reveals that at stake in her censure is the question of authenticity and her resultant authority to speak to the refugee experience. Rather than authenticating her agenda, M.I.A.'s racialised identity becomes a means by which to question her authenticity. As Nabeel Zuberi observes, journalists have 'tended to determine her authenticity or lack of it based on signs of middle-class privilege [and] the veracity of her transnational experience as a Sri Lankan refugee'.[95]

M.I.A. depicts its author-subject as caught between contradictory approaches to autobiography. She draws upon her refugee and diasporic experience for authentication at the same time as openly, ironically commoditising it. She simultaneously constructs playfully multiple, postmodern identities whilst paradoxically appealing to the 'Romantic authenticity'[96] of the rock-star based on authority of personal experience.

---

[93] Douglas Haddow, 'The Real Controversy of MIA's Video,' *The Guardian*, 1 May 2010.

[94] Simon Reynolds, 'Piracy Funds What?' *Village Voice*, 15 February 2005.

[95] Nabeel Zuberi, 'Worries in the Dance: Post-Millennial Grooves and Sub-Bass Culture,' *Britpop and the English Music Tradition*, ed. by Andy Bennet and Jon Stratton (Aldershot: Ashgate, 2010), p. 188.

[96] Keir Keightley, 'Reconsidering Rock,' *The Cambridge Companion to Pop and Rock*, ed. by Simon Frith, Will Straw, and John Street (New York: Cambridge University Press, 2001), p. 136.

M.I.A.'s Hybridity and Ambivalence: Invoking and Rejecting Stereotype

Reading against the aforementioned popular criticisms of M.I.A., Saha argues that M.I.A. succeeds in evading 'the dominant Orientalist discourse that exoticises and reifies Asian artists'.[97] In her characterisation of *herself*, M.I.A. has, as Saha argues, evaded 'the persistent stereotypes of Asian youth as doomed in their Otherness: passive, submissive, conformist'.[98] M.I.A. is none of these things and precisely such tropes are pre-empted and punctured by Loveridge, the white, British author of the foreword, whose voice stands in for the anticipated reader's potential assumptions about, M.I.A.'s racialised identity:

> I suppose I had already formed an idea of what her background was in my mind. I figured she was Indian, and so her mum and dad probably had come over in the '60s with the wave of immigration [...] with an entrepreneurial father and a house-proud mother and one of those strict traditional grandmothers who complained all the time and wanted her to have an arranged marriage to someone's idiot son.[99]

This invokes the power of generic conventions to shape the expectations that are brought to a life story, in this case, through the form of racist stock narratives which operate as a lazy shorthand for decoding difference. This pre-emption of assumption asks readers to reject such reductive expectations, ready to receive the account offered by the memoir. In so doing, *M.I.A.* demonstrates how, in a society where whiteness is given the hegemonic default status of an unmarked category, visually encoded difference must be accounted for.

Whilst it is true that the ethnic identity that M.I.A. performs is free from 'passive, submissive, conformist' racialised stereotypes, that does not mean that these stereotypes are not invoked.[100] Sri Lanka and, later in her career, Africa, comprise M.I.A.'s subject matter, but not her audience. M.I.A. is a transnational star, her global headlining tours taking in the United States, Canada, Central and South America, Europe, Australasia

---

[97] Saha, pp. 737–38.

[98] Ibid., p. 738.

[99] Arulpragasam, p. 6.

[100] Saha, p. 738.

and Japan. However, with primarily the 'first-world'[101] as her audience, Sri Lanka appears as an exotic elsewhere, to which she can uniquely draw attention. Whist M.I.A. herself escapes the abjection of the Asian youth stereotype, her representation of the territories that form her causes do not.

M.I.A.'s alignment with a dispossessed or subaltern struggle is, at points, a strained likeness. This is never more so than when she tries to draw this analogy, not on the basis of her origins, but from her present experience as a pop-star. Of the decision whether to produce promotional merchandise, M.I.A. states:

> I was torn. During *Arular* I wouldn't have even thought of doing something like that, but when I went to America in 2005 I felt more part of that. But it was interesting because at this point I didn't have a visa so I actually became like a Chinese factory – I was both things – I was the American entertainer but I was also the factory in India that made shit.[102]

The disavowal of the promotional behaviours that are integral to music industry economics shows M.I.A. navigating between commercialism and credibility, forces presented as being incompatibly at odds. That she abjures merchandise in a book that is essentially merchandise shows the contradictions in her navigation of the conflicting demands of art and commerce. The suggestion, however, that the imperative to produce renders global pop-stardom comparable with sweatshop labour is, at best, a spurious association.

In fact, discussing the power dynamics that exist within a globalised marketplace, M.I.A. aligns herself with America when identifying herself as the party with power. Speaking of the Jamaican dancers in her video for 2007 single, *Boyz*, she states:

> They were all part of the best dance crews in Jamaica from different areas and gangs. This was the power I had, I am signed to Interscope, I'm like, "Hey, this is a big deal guys, it's worth getting together for." They were like, "She's an American rapper so we're all going to do this video".[103]

---

[101] Arulpragasam, p. 52.

[102] Ibid., p. 113.

[103] Ibid.

She is, of course, not American—at least, not in terms of her origins or nationality. However, as discussed, these are determined to be contingent, fluid and hybrid. She is American in terms of her record label, certainly. However, in the described interaction, to be American means to have the greater economic and cultural sway, to have the pull of fame and, ultimately, to be the global power, in contrast to what she calls 'a third world market'.[104] Thus, whilst M.I.A. certainly does align herself, as Saha argues, with disavowed diasporic subaltern experience,[105] she is, simultaneously, positioned as the global power through whose Orientalist gaze an Othered subaltern struggle is viewed.

Homi K. Bhabha's identification of the 'ambivalence' of the subject positions of coloniser and colonised allows for their interrelation as 'interstitial passage between fixed identifications opens up for the possibility of cultural hybridity'.[106] M.I.A.'s adoption of various contradictory subject positions including Sri Lankan refugee and powerful 'American' star within a single autobiographical text, enacts Bhabha's problematisation of the binarism of coloniser/colonised. Hovering between multiple identities, she is 'never entirely on the outside or implacably oppositional. It is a pressure and a presence which acts constantly, if unevenly, along the entire boundary of authorisation'.[107] As we have seen, within her own work and its popular reception, this boundary of authorisation is highly contested.

M.I.A.'s claim, 'I was both things – I was the American entertainer but I was also the factory in India that made shit',[108] leaves her open to charges of hypocrisy and flippancy regarding the real suffering of the victims of global capitalism. In literal terms, clearly, M.I.A. is not a factory worker, and, whilst the exploited labour of artists in the music industry is a productive area for critique, her experiences as a pop-star and those of the Indian factory worker share little overlap—however directly involved she may be in the labour of production of her creative output. On the level of identity, however, this state of being 'both things' performs the double consciousness Bhabha argues characterises the post-colonial subject: 'In

[104] Ibid., p. 54.

[105] Saha, p. 741.

[106] Homi K. Bhabha, *The Location of Culture* (London: Routledge, 1994), p. 5.

[107] Ibid., p. 156.

[108] Arulpragasam, p. 113.

another's country that it also your own, your person divides, and in following the forked path you encounter yourself in a double movement […] once as stranger, and then as friend'.[109]

At points, M.I.A.'s simultaneous occupation of both positions is highly problematic. Typically conflating the personal, the global, the political and a concern with herself as producer, she states:

> [2nd album] *Kala* represents the birth of a computer in my life. It also represents the digitizing of the third-world taste and the cheap, gritty production of third-world goods for first-world consumption. […] I also felt like a one-woman factory because I was actually making this stuff. My slogan was "you like? I make, you pay 20 dollah." "I make you pay"[110]

As seen throughout her memoir, an understanding of what went into the production of her album and its supporting visual artworks is offered as a means to understanding M.I.A.'s experiences. Her concerns with technology are also in evidence, suggesting that readers can trace her personal experiences in the media through which her artworks are produced. She takes steps towards a critique of the inequalities of production and consumption under global capitalism, but stops short at fetishisation and, ultimately, mockery. Making a joke out of the poor English language skills of those in the 'third world' appears to form the entire concept of the *Kala* album artwork, which comprised simply bold typographic posters with malapropisms of famous English sayings such as 'Get Rich Or Die Trying' mistranslated as 'Goat Rich or Die Frying'[111] (Fig. 6.10 *M.I.A.*, poster and t-shirt design to support the album *Kala*). The thinking behind this she describes thus: 'It's about how kids in the third world digest American rap music. It's slightly off because they don't necessarily speak English and so it always sounds a bit wrong'.[112] However affectionate, or however much it is intended to pass comment on the ways in which imperial domination occurs at the level of cultural export as well as economic or military subjugation, this concept ultimately hinges upon a joke made at their expense. When M.I.A. describes taking

---

[109] Bhabha, p. xxv.

[110] Arulpragasam, p. 52.

[111] Arulpragasam, p. 80.

[112] Ibid., p. 113.

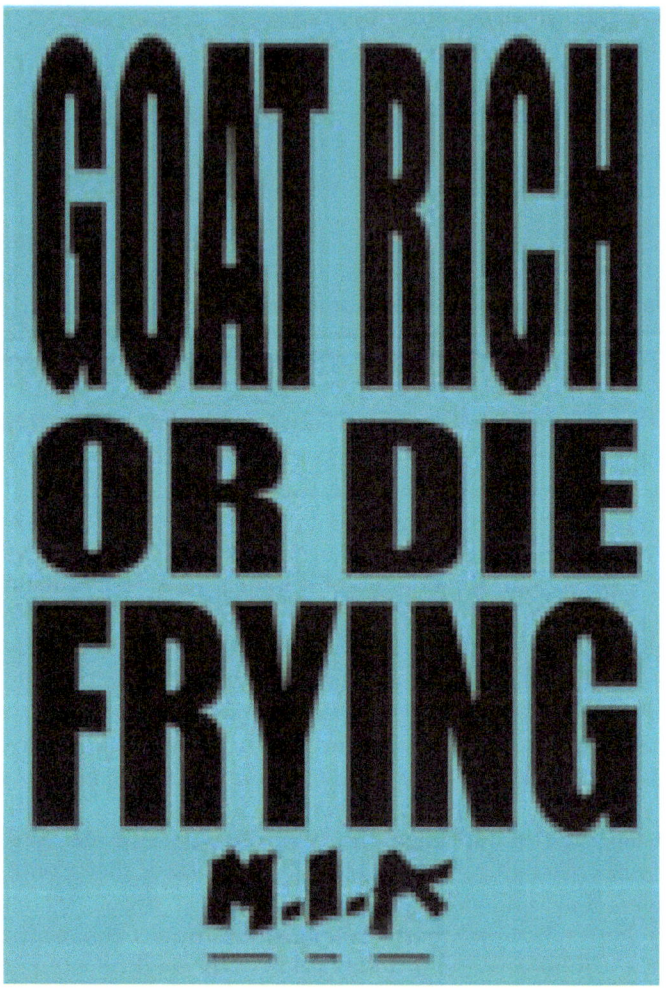

Fig. 6.10   Poster and t-shirt design to support the album *Kala*, *M.I.A.*

album covers and 'making them third world'[113] or speaks of using 'the refugee... aesthetic'[114] to support her single, it is clear that she does fetishise, appropriate and commodify those whose cause she also seeks to support. She finds a space for herself outside of the Orientalist gaze, but constructs an abject Other, whose struggle is reducible to a set of decontextualised, borrowable signs within it.

M.I.A.'s Autobiographical Instrumentalism

Having demonstrated that *M.I.A.* (frequently and problematically) treats difference, struggle and ethnicity as a reducible and exploitable commodity, I will now show that this is consistent with her approach to her own autobiography. Despite the fact that the persona constructed in *M.I.A.* is built upon her Tamil and refugee origin story, a cynicism is displayed towards the role of biography, openly dismissing her back-story as something to be consciously manipulated and reproduced for marketing purposes. In the foreword, Loveridge states:

> I've watched her do so many press interviews about the same story – telling it over and over again. [...] I myself have written it up as a press release to send out to journalists and record reviewers. It's been edited and condensed into a single paragraph, been doubted and defended by music critics and bloggers, become Sunday magazine column inches and a Wikipedia page.[115]

This concisely expresses the currency of life story in celebrity culture in which all the texts discussed in this book are attempting to trade. This describes how celebrity life stories evolve in an *economics of access*, adapting themselves to the imagined appetites of desired audiences. In contrast to genre convention, she makes visible the assemblage of market forces that layer over, intersect with and shape this life story, obscuring the human underneath.

---

[113] Ibid., p. 112.
[114] Ibid., p. 114.
[115] Ibid., p. 6.

Biographical history is integral to the construction of M.I.A.'s star persona. The above quote, however, trivialises the role for biography in stardom, identifying it as a useful commercial asset to be manipulated for exchange in a marketplace fuelled by the desire to know its female stars. In *M.I.A.*, biographical narrative is substituted by M.I.A.'s cultural and commercial product: her work as a visual and vocal artist. This interplay between business and biography creates an identity where difference and the unique selling point are celebrated equally. *M.I.A.*'s foreword reminds us that 'under all the mess of the music, and her outspoken politics, and her family story, and all the Cinderella shit of some little Tamil refugee girl ending up on stage with Madonna at the Super Bowl, is basically a human being',[116] but doesn't claim to be able to offer access to that human being, or anything other than her output. In this depiction, biography is 'mess'; career trajectories are the 'shit' of externally imposed narrative formulae.

As seen in Chapter 4, the use of evasiveness within celebrity memoir is not unique to M.I.A. However, the evasive camp play of Hilton's *Confessions* still operates within the grammar of an invitation to 'know the real' her. The insights into her life may be deliberately shallow, but they are offered within the terms of access: exposure is what is at stake. By contrast, *M.I.A.*'s admission (and devaluation) of strategically deployed autobiography—her model of autobiography as 'column inches and a Wikipedia page'—is undermining to the terms of an *economics of access*. Like Hilton, M.I.A.'s implication is that the life story's details are not needed in her book because these are always already available in the contemporary landscape of multiplying commentary and speculation. Whilst Hilton attempts to navigate the market's demands for intimacy and negotiate shame with a playful, elliptical account, which still ultimately valorises the public/private divide by protecting what is off-limits, *M.I.A.* instead negates the value of the private life. Autobiography, we are told, is for press releases. Autobiography is mere business. A text like *M.I.A.* instead desires to be a space for anthologising an artist's creations, for 'document[ing] art'.

---

116 Ibid., p. 9.

GAGA'S LIBERATORY GOSPEL?

Where M.I.A. undermines what her audience might traditionally seek from her biography, Gaga erases it all together. Gaga was born Stefani Germanotta. Celebrity memoir convention typically offers childhood narrative as an explanation of what drove the woman to become the star and as a means to know her better. However, this identity from before the creation of the Gaga persona is never acknowledged. This accords with the surrounding Gaga rhetoric: the photographs published in this book are of the tour in which she 'hatches' on stage from a giant egg and literally moulds herself with prosthetics, changing the shape of her face and body. Gaga presents herself as a self-determined identity with no prior origin, staging her own birth as a fully formed Lady Gaga. There is a backstage, to which this book purports to grant access-all-areas, but there is no backstory.

The tour in these photographs supported an album called *Born This Way*: a title which could be read as an inconsistent appeal to essentialist immutability, fundamentally at odds with her performance of identity construction.[117] Alternatively, and perhaps more usefully, viewed in the context of Gaga's self-determined self-birthing, *Born this Way* could instead be seen as a denial of born identity in favour of self-manufacture. The refusal of a time before 'Lady Gaga' renders the identity and history of Stefani Germanotta irrelevant to this text, fundamentally contradicting the discourse, not only of memoir, but of wider, confessional celebrity culture, where, as we have seen, a star's trajectory from their origin so often forms the basis of their narrative and its meaning.

Returning to Gaga's flirtations with the themes of Pop Art, Susan Sontag identifies Pop Art as a form that resists knowability by 'using a content so blatant, so "what it is," it [becomes] uninterpretable'.[118] Sontag's *Against Interpretation* describes the defensive 'attempt to have, in the ordinary sense, no content; since there is no content, there can be no interpretation'.[119] Whilst these ideas were developed in relation to the *avant-garde* art of the 1960s, they can be fruitfully applied to the construction of celebrity. In a culture with quenchless appetites for

---

[117] See Suzanna Danuta Walters, 'Born This Way?' *Chronicle*, 5 July 2011 for such a reading.

[118] Sontag, 'Against Interpretation,' *Against Interpretation* (1967), p. 10.

[119] Ibid.

gaining access to, ascribing meaning to, and seeking knowledge of (in Sontag's terms, interpretation of) the 'real' women 'behind' celebrity images, the insistent denial of Gaga's backstory could be seen as a defensive strategy against this hunger for interpretation. Gaga focusses on the surface and insists that there is nothing 'behind' the fakeness, only performed fakeness all the way down. For example, she has used TV appearances to make statements such as 'every minute of my life is performance'.[120] In so doing, Gaga challenges the notion 'that there really is such a thing as the content of the work of art'[121]—or the 'real' woman behind the public spectacle. When Sontag describes an appetite for interpretation which 'excavates, and as it excavates, destroys; it digs "behind" the text, to find a sub-text which is the true one',[122] she could just as well be describing appetites for making the star's private life intelligible, and the harm that can be done in the process.

In this context, the emphasis on the totality of the surface of the image is as much a protection of as it is an erasure of a prior self: 'I wouldn't like people to see me—*me*—in any other way than my music and my stage performances', she asserts.[123] Her emphasis, 'me—*me*', suggests the existence of a private, 'true' self, a rare moment when she breaks from her gospel of total artifice to suggest the possibility of a private self that can be held off-limits: one that is distinct from, and can be kept out of, her performances.

The closest Gaga comes to tying pop persona to real-life history is statements like, 'I didn't fit in in high school and I felt like a freak, so I like to create this atmosphere for my fans where they feel like they have a freak in me to hang out with and they don't feel alone'.[124] This identification with the misfit, emphasis on performing explicitly fabricated and multiple identities, and rejection of a role for historical origin in identity formation, approximate the 'variable construction of identity' beyond the 'socially instituted and maintained norms of intelligibility' without 'invocation of a non-historical "before"' of Butler's *Gender Trouble*.[125]

[120] Lady Gaga, interview with Alison Stephenson, 29 November 2010.

[121] Sontag (1967), p. 5.

[122] Ibid., p. 6.

[123] Alex Cho, 'Lady Gaga, Balls-Out: Recuperating Queer Performativity,' *FlowTV*, 7 August 2009.

[124] On *Ellen*, Ellen DeGeneres's talk show, air date 27 November 2009.

[125] Butler (1990), pp. 5, 13, and 23.

As I have argued, camp artifice is a common counterpoint throughout celebrity construction, always in tension with the celebrity's need to claim authenticity. Gaga's campness has been noted by scholars such as Katrin Horn, who identifies Gaga's '"reducing" [of] identity to clothes, masks and wigs' as a camp strategy.[126] Gaga's campness is more widely acknowledged than other celebrities' and is generally credited as resistant in a way that does not occur in relation to the campness I have identified in Hilton's and Price's star images. This is likely in part a classed product of her associations with an elite art school education that positions her as undertaking a theoretically informed practice of 'doing' celebrity.[127] Further, it is attributable to hierarchies of cultural value that afford less contested status to the pop-star with subcultural affiliations than to the glamour model or reality star. However, Hilton's playful evasion and Price's celebration of artifice are as redolent with the 'irony, aestheticism, theatricality, and humor' that Babuscio designates to be the defining features of camp as any of Gaga's camp gestures.[128] Their camp performances are no less knowing, no less instructive in the performativity at the heart of gender construction and no less negotiations with the discourses that surround and shape their star images.

As someone who openly identifies as bisexual and who writes lyrics about gender-sex-desire fluidity such as those to 'G.U.Y (Girl Under You)',[129] who has welcomed speculation on whether she has intersexed genitals, who campaigns for LGBTQ rights and has a loyal following of drag impersonators, it is unsurprising that much Gaga scholarship has read her image through Butler to find identities which trouble normative conceptions of gender-sex-desire.[130] Teresa Geller, for example, sees Gaga as 'exploding the line between nature and artifice, authenticity and

---

[126] Katrin Horn, 'Follow the Glitter Way: Lady Gaga and Camp,' *Performance Identities*, p. 88.

[127] Yelin.

[128] Babuscio (1993), p. 20.

[129] Lyrics can be found at http://ladygaga.wikia.com/wiki/G.U.Y._(song).

[130] Heather Duerre Humann, '*What a Drag*: Lady Gaga, Jo Calderone, and the Politics of Representation,' *Performance Identities*, p. 74; Amber L. Davisson, *Lady Gaga and the Remaking of Celebrity Culture* (Jefferson, NC: McFarland, 2013), p. 56.

glamour, boy and girl'.[131] Corona is another scholar who states his faith in her subversive and liberatory potential: 'Gaga's hypermodern gospel of liberation hints at the irrelevance of truth or, rather, the creation of one's own truth'.[132] In congruence with these readings, and against celebrity memoir convention, the visual format of Gaga's photo-memoir facilitates the fabrication of multiple identities at a surface level, rather than offering access to a singular, essential autobiographical truth.

As I have shown, the (im)possibility of autobiographical truth-telling is a question that has dominated autobiography scholarship. For Estelle Jelinek, the inevitably partial nature of autobiography enacts a 'conscious shaping of the selected events of one's life into a coherent whole'.[133] Despite the genre's attempts at singular coherence, Susanna Egan concludes that 'neither the person nor the text can reveal any single or final truth'.[134] A text such as Gaga's, which depicts the artifice, multiplicity and performativity of self-making, has the potential to escape the demands of this fiction of coherent and singular meaning and to accord with Corona's interpretation of Gaga's wider star image as emancipatory.

However, despite the fluidity of gender and desire that scholars identify as characterising Gaga's wider star image, and, despite the potential of photo-memoir as a form to allow for multiplicity and explicit artifice, *Gaga x Richardson* is far from being a liberatory memoir. Instead, it presents the violability of the female body, her loss of control, and her fungibility under the male gaze. In contrast to her scholarly and popular reception as an alternative or subversive star, the star image constructed in *Gaga x Richardson* is structured by the same defining themes of bodily spectacle and violation as those in the glamour girl memoir genre interrogated in Chapter 3. As discussed, the introduction page in Gaga's own voice claims that the process of making the text was 'unique' in that there were '*no* limitations'. But rather than expanding the possibilities for female celebrity self-representation, this photo-memoir is a stark

---

[131] Theresa L. Geller, 'Trans/Affect, Monstrous Masculinities, and the Sublime Art of Lady Gaga,' *Gaga and Popular Music: Performing Gender, Fashion, and Culture*, ed. by Iddon and Marshall, p. 209.

[132] Victor P. Corona, 'Gaga Studies,' *Pop Matters*, 24 November 2010.

[133] E. C. Jelinek, *The Tradition of Women's Autobiography: From Antiquity to the Present* (USA: Xlibris, 2003), p. 24.

[134] Susanna Egan, *Mirror Talk: Genres of Life and Death in Autobiography* (Chapel Hill: University of North Carolina Press, 1999), p. 326.

example of how the self-representational possibilities of women in the public eye are limited by gendered conventions of the marketplace in the processes of mediation, according to predetermined paradigms of physical and emotional access.

The Containment of Gaga's Resistant Femininity

A consequence of pop-stars' existence within a web of conflicting discourses is that the gendering of a star's image goes beyond the individual's deliberate, potentially resistant acts. Despite its multiplicity, the contemporary media assemblage ultimately tempers and makes palatable the more resistant aspects of their identities as their performances remain subject to the conservative logic of the market in which 'sex sells', or rather, women's bodies and specularised sexuality are for sale and sell certain models of femininity. As Corona suggests, 'When the image of someone like Gaga becomes so closely associated with spectacle, the question of authenticity inevitably emerges'.[135] However, contrary to Corona's claim that 'the question of authenticity is rendered almost meaningless...given that the star's day-to-day life is thoroughly consumed by the mechanics of performing',[136] Gaga's memoir instead offers gendered displays of emotional lability and corporeal vulnerability in place of the exposing backstory that usually forms the basis of the promise of an account of the authentic self. It is insufficient to claim, as Corona does, that 'Gaga has avoided the authenticity dilemma by affirming that she is the persona she inhabits on stage'.[137] This analysis ignores the gendered nature of the *authenticity contract*: an embrace of the performed, and of explicitly constructed identities, does not excuse the female celebrity from conventional obligations to grant the appearance of access in one form or another to a 'real self'. A celebrity marketplace driven by access and exposure, one which stimulates and promises to satisfy curiosity about how the other half live, constructs an obligation to expose the self that forecloses self-representation. Further, it is a marketplace that thrives on voyeurism;

[135] Victor Corona, 'Memory, Monsters, and Lady Gaga,' *The Journal of Popular Culture* 46 (2011), 733.

[136] Ibid., p. 734.

[137] Ibid.

the images that capture moments not designed for public consumption—
the paparazzi 'snatch', the leaked sex tape and the hacked smartphone
sex selfie—command the highest exchange value. This voyeurism is inextricably tied to the claim of ownership, control, power that are at the
heart of objectification.[138]

Returning to the image of Gaga's denim-clad buttocks and bare upper
thighs, with her head out of shot, we only know that it is Gaga because
the image appears within the context of a book of photographs of her
(Fig. 6.8 Gaga from behind). The dust jacket promises that the photographer 'captured the intimate' and in instances such as these the use of
the word *capture*, so common in photographic discourse, suggests the
word's true definition of 'seize or take forcibly'.[139] In contrast to the
photos in which Gaga presents the crafted identity that is her performance
art, the gaze of these decapitated images suggests a furtive pleasure in
reducing a famous icon to just another anonymous, interchangeable and
violable body in an image whose defining fungibility[140] and reduction to
body parts[141] objectify the star and erase her subjectivity. These images
invoke Mulvey's theorisation of the structurally unequal power dynamics
of looking which cast the 'spectator in direct scopophilic contact with the
female form displayed for his enjoyment'.[142] Margaret Olin problematises the intrinsic negativity of 'gaze' as a term for art criticism, when
she argues that it is always tinged with the connotation of 'the publicly
sanctioned actions of a peeping Tom'.[143] Images such as Lady Gaga's
anonymised but available backside (whilst she, out of shot, may or may
not know the photograph is being taken) use a camera angle that precisely
and deliberately positions the audience as 'peeping Tom'.

[138] Laura Mulvey, 'Visual Pleasure and Narrative Cinema,' *Screen* 16.3 (1975), 13.

[139] "Capture, n." *OED Online*, Oxford University Press, June 2015.

[140] Martha Nussbaum, 'Seven Ways to Treat a Person as a Thing,' *Sex and Social Justice*
(Oxford: Oxford University Press, 1999), p. 257.

[141] Rae Langton, *Sexual Solipsism: Philosophical Essays on Pornography and Objectification*
(Oxford: Oxford University Press, 2009), pp. 228–29.

[142] Mulvey (1975), p. 13.

[143] Margaret Olin, 'Gaze,' *Critical Terms for Art History*, p. 217.

Richardson's use of the camera as an instrument of power in forced intimacy is something he cheerfully admits. Richardson tells *The New York Observer* about persuading girls to pose nude: 'They're like, "I don't want to be naked," So I say, "I'll be naked and you take the pictures. You can have the camera. You can have the phallus"'.[144] He admits that control of the camera is a form of dominance, understanding and exploiting the phallocentrism of the photographer/subject power-dynamic (Fig. 6.3 Smiling Terry Richardson receiving oral sex from a model in a dustbin). This interview, given six years before Peck came out with strikingly similar accounts of Richardson's coercion, is, therefore, not a rebuttal, but a jovial description of working practices. McRobbie's 'taken-into-accountness'[145] is literalised, accounting for unequal power dynamics in Richardson's favour only to joke about them in newsprint. The consequence, in McRobbie's conception, is 'quietude and complicity in the manners of generationally specific notions of cool [that] endorse a new regime of sexual meanings based on female consent'.[146] Richardson's output of sexual representations that presume and demand female consent, operate at the level of both cultural output and of actual abuse. Journalist Sean O'Hagan interviewed Richardson ahead of the publication of the book, *Terryworld*, which includes one photograph in which a model fellates Richardson whilst 'trussed up in a suitcase, just her head - and open mouth – protruding' and another fellates him whilst 'crammed into a dustbin' (Fig. 6.3 Smiling Terry Richardson receiving oral sex from a model in a dustbin).[147]

O'Hagan considers this 'too crude. Too in-your-face'.[148] This criticism operates merely at the level of taste and decency, ignoring gendered power dynamics despite Richardson's openness about his eroticisation of power inequality and non-observance of models' boundaries: 'I'm this powerful guy with his boner, dominating all these girls. In a way, that's the very stuff I'm trying to work out in the work'.[149] In interviews, Richardson

---

[144] Phoebe Eaton, 'Terry Richardson's Dark Room,' *The New York Observer*, 20 September 2004.

[145] Tasker and Negra (2007), p. 28.

[146] Ibid., p. 33.

[147] Sean O'Hagan, 'Good Clean Fun?' *The Observer*, 17 October 2004.

[148] Ibid.

[149] Ibid.

not only shows an awareness of the exploitative dynamics of his work, but suggests that it is the abuse itself that is 'the very stuff' of his 'art'. He has been called 'boundary-nudging talent'[150] in a *New York Magazine* 'puff-piece'. In a career that demonstrably, knowingly utilises material power inequities to document domination by his 'boner', the real boundaries being nudged are those of the penetrability of the female body and the negotiability of consent.

I wish to underline the pertinence of Richardson's abusive practices to a wider understanding of celebrity exposure and authenticity in the *economics of access*. As discussed, Richardson and Gaga are described on the dust jacket as equal creative partners in a 'visual dialogue', and as an established global icon Gaga wields more power than the young, aspiring models who have accused Richardson of sexual assault.[151] However, it is significant that traces of his modus operandi are visible in images of Gaga exhausted, collapsed, drunk or otherwise unable to participate as active posing subject—images with uncomfortable parallels with the allegations against him. However, crucially to the argument in this book, it is precisely these attributes that make it a 'successful' text when judged against the criteria of a culture that presumes fan appetites for access. Richardson's model of uncomfortably creeping boundaries results in a more comprehensive, fully exposed image and, in *Gaga x Richardson*, this sequence constructs a narrative that gradually strips Gaga of her armour.

The book begins with hard images of Gaga, all defensive pose, aggressive leather, pointed talons and red lipstick-warpaint, the Gaga persona that has led to scholarly readings of her as, for example, in Halberstam's terms, 'a celebration of the joining of femininity to artifice, and a refusal of the mushy sentimentalism that has been siphoned into the category of womanhood'[152] (Fig. 6.1 *Gaga x Richardson*, cover). However, it ends with her collapsed post-show, distraught, in tears, unable to walk, and needing to be carried in the arms of her strong, male backing dancer: diminished and returned to normative, sentimental models of weak, white femininity (Fig. 6.11 Gaga being carried after collapse; Fig. 6.12 Gaga crying with smeared make-up). The images in between enact a gradual

---

[150] Benjamin Wallace, 'Is Terry Richardson an Artist or a Predator?' *New York Magazine*, 15 June 2014.

[151] Gaga and Richardson, dust jacket.

[152] Halberstam, p. xiii.

Fig. 6.11   Gaga being carried after collapse, *Gaga x Richardson*

Fig. 6.12   Gaga crying with smeared make up, *Gaga x Richardson*

forcing of access into new areas of privacy and parts of her body (Fig. 6.5 Smiling Terry Richardson with Gaga as puppet; Fig. 6.6 Gaga passed out; Fig. 6.7 Gaga in bed; Fig. 6.8 Gaga from behind). Photographs of emotional extremity and physical vulnerability are offered as a mark of authenticity rooted in the 'direct, intimate fusion of visual and emotional',[153] and in the affective immediacy of an image of intense distress (Fig. 6.11 Gaga being carried after collapse; Fig. 6.12 Gaga crying with smeared make-up). These ultimately accord with the normative femininities that scholars like J. Jack Halberstam argue Gaga otherwise contravenes. Halberstam reads in Gaga 'a symbol for a new kind of feminism' which is 'a monstrous outgrowth of the unstable category of "woman" in feminist theory'.[154] In Halberstam's terms, 'gaga feminism' rejects the 'fixity of roles for males and females'[155] and celebrates 'the withering away of old social models of desire, gender, and sexuality'.[156] *Gaga x Richardson*, however, cannot be read in these terms. Between its pages, it is Gaga's confrontational stance that withers to reaffirm a social order in which femininity equates with physical weakness and emotional instability, and a non-normative figure such as Gaga, stripped of her artifice, can be safely returned to a tamed and untroubling 'category of woman' that exists within celebrity's dominant codes of gendered emotional and physical exposure.

The politics of being looked at are diverse, with a range displayed in *Gaga x Richardson*. The spectrum has the agency in Gaga's pose at one end, as model and hired shooter construct images in partnership: 'a visual dialogue' in which Gaga clearly participates in and relishes her 'to-be-looked-at-ness'.[157] At the other end of the spectrum, the book gradually reveals images which, if their implied content is to be believed, could not have been posed: with Gaga asleep, or unconscious on a kitchen floor, and collapsed after a stage show, photographs which imply she has no agency in their construction (Fig. 6.6 Gaga passed out; Fig. 6.7 Gaga in bed; Fig. 6.8 Gaga from behind; Fig. 6.11 Gaga being carried after collapse; Fig. 6.12 Gaga crying with smeared make-up). Whether or not Gaga is a

---

[153] Benjamin, 'The Work of Art in the Age of Mechanical Reproduction,' *Stardom and Celebrity*, p. 29.

[154] Halberstam, pp. xii–xiii.

[155] Ibid., p. 5.

[156] Ibid., p. 25.

[157] Mulvey (1975), p. 11.

covert participant in staging these scenarios, and, despite the fact that she is a participant in their approval for publication, crucially, it is the image of her violability, not her agency, that her photo-memoir sells.

This process of apparent wearing away at emotional and physical boundaries recalls the pornographic nature of reality products as a whole in which, as Laura Grindstaff argues, 'the money shot' is the moment when the stars break down in tears (Fig. 6.12 Gaga crying with smeared make-up).[158] Images displaying such rawness and abjection can operate as a proxy for the wretchedness of the usual, required celebrity confessional. Mulvey argues that the spectator gains 'control and possession' by 'investigating the woman, demystifying her mystery'[159] and, in the closing images, Richardson's thorough exposure of Gaga's moments of emotional lability and physical weakness renders her, despite her claim to 'high'-cultural legitimacy and confrontational creative agency—'bearer of [his] meaning, not a maker of meaning'.[160] Sontag explained that the 'refusal to leave the work of art alone' reveals it 'has the capacity to make us nervous'.[161] With the hunger to know, 'one tames the work of art. Interpretation makes art manageable, conformable'.[162] Richardson's aggressive interpretation and taming of Gaga reveals the capacity of her resistant, non-normative femininity to make one nervous, and thus reduces her to a femininity that is emotionally labile, physically weak. To borrow Sontag's terms, the thoroughly revealed celebrity woman is 'prey' of both her mediators and audiences, whose 'revenge' is the ever greater, more exposing interpretation, which 'violates art. It makes art into an article for use'.[163]

[158] Laura Grindstaff, *The Money Shot: Trash, Class, and the Making of TV Talk Shows* (Chicago: University of Chicago Press, 2002).

[159] Mulvey (1975), p. 13.

[160] Ibid., p. 7.

[161] Sontag (1967), p. 8.

[162] Ibid.

[163] Ibid., pp. 7 and 10.

CONCLUSION

Whilst Gaga and M.I.A. employ different self-representational forms from the memoirs in previous chapters, the same dynamics of a nego-tiated *economics of access* remain in evidence. They do not offer the written confessions that are the norm, but Gaga's text shows that a form confession can be extracted, nonetheless. It is true that, as many academics have observed, Gaga has constructed a star persona which has the capacity to trouble acceptable femininity and even boundaries of the category 'woman'. However, these non-normative aspects are not what are captured and canonised in her photo-memoir. Rather, the hand (and gaze) of the 'ghost' that mediates her is visible with his own agenda regarding the role and representation of women.

Celebrity exists within, negotiates, and is constituted of a pre-existing field of images. Books such as these are interventions attempting to cement preferred readings of star identities. Gaga's photo-memoir depicts her as living a wild, rebellious, rock and roll lifestyle onstage and offstage, and borrows associations of fashion, ironic hipster cool and bad behaviour from its ghost. M.I.A.'s 'document of art' locates her pop output as part of a deliberate cultural politics of difference, informed by her Tamil and refugee origins. In both books, we see that authenticity is always at stake as a vexed, yet valuable, currency and yet the privileged onto-logical status that photography and memoir share does not stand up to scrutiny. Despite the fact that Gaga's star persona engages in a deliberate performance of self-fabrication and embrace of the 'unnatural', *Gaga x Richardson* proves subject to the logic of conventional gendered celebrity in casting exposure as the locus of authenticity and thus seeking to present her as thoroughly revealed.

M.I.A. can be seen to be following celebrity memoir convention by locating authenticity in a history of hardship and suffering: a posi-tion that means that the question of the legitimacy of her biography has become a source of much debate. *M.I.A.* depicts its star author as caught between contradictory strategies, drawing upon her refugee and diaspora experience for authentication and yet simultaneously commodi-tising it, and admitting and commenting upon this commoditisation. She both constructs playfully multiple, postmodern identities which avoid the Enlightenment model of the centralised, coherent subject and paradoxically appeals to the Romantic authority of personal experience.

In different ways, both M.I.A. and Gaga reject the traditionally crucial role of an origin story in autobiography. Rather than attempting to counter accusations of exploiting her biography for commercial purposes, M.I.A.'s memoir performs them explicitly as part of a wider dismissal of the implication that, in the pop industrial context, her backstory should or even ever could be treated as anything more than marketing. Gaga's origin story is altogether absent from a photo-memoir in which she is seen birthing herself onstage from a giant egg and moulding herself with prostheses. Such undermining of the conventionally fundamental role of the origin story, and with it the dynamics of revelation that form the basis of celebrity memoir, can be read as resistant strategies against interpretation in a culture determined to know them.

The appearance of access to M.I.A.'s subjectivity is offered through a catalogue of her preoccupations and her creative responses to them. This means that in contrast to Gaga, in the majority of her images, M.I.A. is often out of the frame except as authorial trace. Cricually and uniquely, in this way she demonstrates the possibility for alternative models of celebrity self-representation which resist the demands for sexual confession. The ghosting machinery that collectively produces M.I.A.'s autobiographical text can be traced to have existing relationships with her, as subordinate employees, independent from record labels or publishing houses. This suggests a degree of control over the process of mediation. By positioning herself as an artist in the same league as the Brit Art pack, she elevates herself to contradict gendered divisions in discourses of star agency. She adopts the masculinised position of creative agent and cultural producer and defines herself in contrast to the feminised passivity of the pop-star as music industry pawn.

Richardson's visibility as ghost competes for authorial space as his interpretation of Gaga follows a narrative sequence from a famously resistant, misfit, fabricated spectacle, through a conventionally postfeminist self-sexualisation, to the deindividualised, seemingly unwitting object of his gaze. This literalises the dynamics of celebrity revelation where access to the female celebrity's specularised body is offered as a means of gaining insight into the self. The foreclosing of female celebrities' possibilities for self-representation by the logic of forced exposure is most evident where *Gaga x Richardson* concludes: with its collapsed subject offering the authenticity of the emotional 'money shot'. Whilst, as an official memoir, Gaga's permissions have been given, the use of images of her diminished power in her physical and emotional loss of control, regardless of whether they are staged or not, deploy the paparazzi model of unconsenting photographs to hint at a truer image, in a voyeuristic marketplace where violation is held to be ideal dynamic of celebrity exposure. The fact that allegations of sexual force circulate within Richardson's star image, along with his own admissions that a non-observance of his models' boundaries informs his working practice and can be seen in his images, suits him perfectly to the job of constructing the image of authentic celebrity exposure for an *economics of access* which defines 'realness' according to the logic of forced exposure. The history of sexual trauma so thematically integral to 'glamour girl' memoirs is not revealed here but is indirectly invoked in Richardson's star image. For all her presentation of a consciously, aggressively, resistant femininity, that rejects the norms of gendered celebrity, Gaga's photo-memoir structures the performance within its pages according to the gendered attributes of the genre: emotional lability, access to a specularised body, and loss of control. M.I.A. does not prove to be free of the demands of the genre. However, it is significant that by keeping her body out of the frame and placing her artistic output in the space usually reserved for sexual confession, she bucks the convention of access that typifies the celebrity memoir genre, signalling the potential for different models of female, celebrity self-representation.

BIBLIOGRAPHY

Amazon.com. 'Lady Gaga X Terry Richardson.' *Amazon.com*. http://www.amazon.co.uk/Lady-Gaga-X-Terry-Richardson/dp/144474125X.

Arulpragasm, Mathangi. 'Maya.' *M.I.A.* New York: Rizzoli, 2012.

Babuscio, Jack. 'Camp and Gay Sensibility.' *Camp Grounds: Style and Homosexuality*, ed. by David Bergman. Amherst: University of Massachusetts Press, 1993.

Barcan, Ruth. *Nudity: A Cultural Anatomy*. Oxford: Berg, 2004.

Barthes, Roland. *Roland Barthes by Roland Barthes*, trans. Richard Howard. New York: Hill and Wang, 1977.

———. *Camera Lucida: Reflections on Photography*, trans. Richard Howard. New York: Farrar, Straus, and Giroux, 1981.

Bazin. André. 'The Ontology of the Photographic Image.' *Classic Essays on Photography*, ed. by Trachtenberg. New Haven, CT: Leete's Island Books, 1980.

Bell, Katherine M. 'Raising Africa? Celebrity and the Rhetoric of the White Saviour.' *PORTAL Journal of Multidisciplinary International Studies*, 10 (1), 2013.

Benjamin, Walter. 'The Work of Art in the Age of Mechanical Reproduction.' *Stardom and Celebrity*, ed. by Su Holmes and Sean Redmond. London: Sage, 2007.

Bhabha, Homi K. *The Location of Culture*. London: Routledge, 1994.

Blow Up. Film. MGM. London: Michelangelo Antonioni, 1966.

Butler, Judith. *Gender Trouble: Feminism and the Subversion of Identity*. London: Routledge, 1990.

Cadwalladr, Carole. 'All Because the Ladies Love Jordan.' *The Observer*, 12 February 2006. http://www.guardian.co.uk/theobserver/2006/feb/12/features.review47.

Cho, Alex. 'Lady Gaga, Balls-Out: Recuperating Queer Performativity.' *FlowTV*, 7 August 2009. http://flowtv.org/?p=4169.

Corona, Victor. 'Gaga Studies.' *Pop Matters*, 24 November 2010. http://www.popmatters.com/post/133577-gaga-studies/.

———. 'Memory, Monsters, and Lady Gaga.' *The Journal of Popular Culture*, 46, 2011: 1–19.

Couser, G. Thomas. 'Making, Taking, and Faking Lives: The Ethics of Collaborative Life Writing.' *Style*, 32 (2), 1998: 334–51.

Creech, Brian. 'Refugee Status: Tracing the Global Flows of M.I.A.' *Communication, Culture & Critique*, 7, 2014: 267–82.

Danuta Walters, Suzanna. 'Born This Way?' *Chronicle*, 5 July 2011. http://chronicle.com/blogs/brainstorm/born-this-way/37016.

Dow Adams, Timothy. 'Introduction: Life Writing and Light Writing; Autobiography and Photography.' *Modern Fiction Studies*, 40 (3), 1994: 459–92.

Dyer, Richard. *Stars*. London: British Film Institute, 1979.

Eaton, Phoebe. 'Terry Richardson's Dark Room.' *The New York Observer*, 20 September 2004. http://observer.com/2004/09/terry-richardsons-dark-room/.

Egan, Susanna. *Mirror Talk: Genres of Life and Death in Autobiography*. Chapel Hill: University of North Carolina Press, 1999.

Fletcher, Roland. 'The Messages of Material Behaviour: A Preliminary Discussion of Non-Vernacular Meaning.' *The Meanings of Things: Material Culture and Symbolic Expression*, ed. by Ian Hodder. London: Unwin Hyman, 1989.

Foucault, Michel. *The History of Sexuality: Volume 1*, trans. Robert Hurley. New York: Pantheon, 1978.

Freud, Sigmund. *Three Essays on Sexuality*, trans. James Strachey. London: Hogarth Press, [1905] 1962.

Gaga, Lady, and Terry Richardson. *Gaga X Richardson*. London: Hodder and Stoughton, 2011.

Gaga, Lady. 'Interview with Alison Stephenson.' 29 November 2010. http://www.youtube.com/watch?v=eS5tq4F659Q.

Gavras, Romain. 'M.I.A.' *Interview Magazine*, 7 July 2010. http://www.interviewmagazine.com/music/mia/#_.

Geller, Theresa L. 'Trans/Affect, Monstrous Masculinities, and the Sublime Art of Lady Gaga.' *Gaga and Popular Music: Performing Gender, Fashion, and Culture*, ed. by Martin Iddon and Melanie L. Marshall. London: Routledge, 2013.

Geraghty, Christine. 'Re-examining Stardom: Questions of Texts, Bodies and Performance.' *Stardom and Celebrity: A Reader*, ed. by Su Holmes and Sean Redmond. London: Sage, 2007.

Germanotta, Stefani. 'Assignment # 4: Reckoning of Evidence.' Reportedly written 2003 during her freshman year at NYU Tisch. 1 November 2004. Posted in Jordan Carter, 'The Theory Monster', 4 February 2010. http://students.brown.edu/College_Hill_Independent/?p=2481.

Grindstaff, Laura. *The Money Shot: Trash, Class, and the Making of TV Talk Shows*. Chicago: University of Chicago Press, 2002.

Haddad, Candice. 'Immigration, Authorship, Censorship, and Terrorism: The Politics of M.I.A.'s US Crossover.' *In the Limelight and Under the Microscope*, ed. by Su Holmes and Diane Negra. New York: Continuum, 2011.

Haddow, Douglas. 'The Real Controversy of MIA's Video.' *The Guardian*, 1 May 2010. http://www.theguardian.com/commentisfree/2010/may/01/mia-video-real-controversy.

Halberstam, J. Jack. *Gaga Feminism: Sex, Gender, and the End of Normal*. Boston: Beacon Press, 2012.

Hall, Stuart. 'New Ethnicities.' *Stuart Hall: Critical Dialogues in Cultural Studies*, ed. by David Morley and Kuan-Hsing Chen. London: Routledge, 1996.

Hirschberg, Lynn. 'MIA's Agitprop Pop.' *New York Times*, 25 May 2010. www.nytimes.com/2010/05/30/magazine/30mia-t.html.

Horn, Katrin. 'Follow the Glitter Way: Lady Gaga and Camp.' *The Performance Identities of Lady Gaga*, ed. by R. J. Gray. Jefferson, NC: McFarland, 2012.

Humann, Heather Duerre. '*What a Drag*: Lady Gaga, Jo Calderone, and the Politics of Representation.' *The Performance Identities of Lady Gaga*, ed. by R. J. Gray. Jefferson, NC: McFarland, 2012.

Hutnyk, John. 'Poetry After Guantanamo: M.I.A.' *Social Identities*, 18 (5), 2012: 555–72.

Iddon, Martin, and Melanie L. Marshall, eds. *Lady Gaga and Popular Music: Performing Gender, Fashion, and Culture*. New York: Routledge, 2014.

Jelinek, E. C. *The Tradition of Women's Autobiography: From Antiquity to the Present*. Bloomington, USA: Xlibris, 2003.

Kapoor, Ilan. *Celebrity Humanitarianism: The Ideology of Global Charity.* New York: Routledge, 2013.

Keightley, Keir. 'Reconsidering Rock.' *The Cambridge Companion to Pop and Rock*, ed. by Simon Frith, Will Straw, and John Street. New York: Cambridge University Press, 2001.

Lachno, James. 'Lady Gaga—Top 10 Controversies.' *The Telegraph*, 20 April 2011. http://www.telegraph.co.uk/culture/music/rockandpopmusic/8463228/Lady-Gaga-Top-10-Controversies.html.

Langton, Rae. *Sexual Solipsism: Philosophical Essays on Pornography and Objectification.* Oxford: Oxford University Press, 2009.

Manaton, Thomas. 'Thomas Manaton.' *LinkedIn.* Retrieved on 6 December 2013 from https://www.linkedin.com/profile/view?id=188954041&authType=name&authToken=yXgW.

Mitchell, W. J. T. *Iconology: Image, Text, Ideology.* Chicago: University of Chicago Press, 1986.

Mulvey, Laura. 'Visual Pleasure and Narrative Cinema.' *Screen*, 16 (3), 1975: 6–18.

———. 'Afterthoughts on "Visual Pleasure and Narrative Cinema" Inspired by King Vidor's *Duel in the Sun.*' *Visual and Other Pleasures.* Bloomington: Indiana University Press, 1989.

Naughton, John. 'Celebgate: It's Not the Internet We Need to Fix But Men's Squalid Behaviour.' *Guardian Online*, 7 September 2014.

Neef, Sonja, and José van Dijck. *Sign Here! Handwriting in the Age of New Media.* Amsterdam: Amsterdam University Press, 2006.

Nussbaum, Martha. 'Seven Ways to Treat a Person as a Thing.' *Sex and Social Justice.* Oxford: Oxford University Press, 1999.

O'Hagan, Sean. 'Good Clean Fun?' *The Observer*, 17 October 2004. http://www.theguardian.com/film/2004/oct/17/photography.art.

OED Online. 'Capture, n.' Oxford University Press, June 2015. http://www.oed.com/view/Entry/27659?rskey=86l3QA&result=1&isAdvanced=false#eid.

Olin, Margaret. 'Gaze.' *Critical Terms for Art History.* Chicago: University of Chicago Press, 2003.

Peck, Jamie. 'Terry Richardson Is Really Creepy: One Model's Story.' *The Gloss*, 16 March 2010. http://www.thegloss.com/2010/03/16/fashion/terry-richardson-is-really-creepy-one-models-story/2/#ixzz3CjasFCrY.

Quart, Alissa. 'The Age of Hipster Sexism.' *New York Magazine*, 30 October 2012. http://nymag.com/thecut/2012/10/age-of-hipster-sexism.html.

Redmond, Sean. 'Introduction.' *The Star and Celebrity Confessional.* New York: Routledge, 2013.

Reynolds, Simon. 'Piracy Funds What?' *Village Voice*, 15 February 2005.

Rutsky, R. L. 'Being Keanu.' *The End of Cinema as We Know It: American Film in the Nineties*, ed. by Jon Lewis. New York: New York University Press, 2001.

Saha, Anamik. 'Locating MIA: "Race", Commodification and the Politics of Production.' *European Journal of Cultural Studies*, 15, 2012: 736–52.

Sauers, Jenna. 'Meet Terry Richardson, the World's Most F—ked Up Fashion Photographer.' *Jezebel.com*, 16 March 2010. http://jezebel.com/5494634/meet-terry-richardson-the-worlds-most-fked-up-fashion-photographer.

Smith, Sidonie, and Julia Watson. *Reading Autobiography: A Guide for Interpreting Life Narratives*. Minneapolis: University of Minnesota Press, 2001.

Sontag, Susan. 'Against Interpretation.' *Against Interpretation and Other Essays*. London: Eyre & Spottiswoode, 1967.

———. *On Photography*. New York: Farrar, Straus, and Giroux, 1977.

Stainforth, Elizabeth, and David Thom. 'Metadata: Walter Benjamin and Bernard Stiegler.' *Theorising Visual Studies*, ed. by James Elkins. New York: Routledge, 2013.

Steinmetz, Katy. 'Top 10 Controversial Music' Videos.' *Time Magazine*, 6 June 2011. http://entertainment.time.com/2011/06/07/top-10-controversial-music-videos/.

Strang, Fay. 'EXCLUSIVE: "My Intention Was to Put Art Culture into Pop Music": Lady Gaga Reveals She Aimed to "Reverse Warhol" in New Record.' *Mail Online*, 4 November 2013.

Sullivan, Brendan Jay. *Rivington Was Ours: Lady Gaga, the Lower East Side, and the Prime of Our Lives*. New York: It Books, 2013.

Sutherland, John. 'Among the Ghosts.' *Spectator*, 11 June 2011. http://www.spectator.co.uk/features/7009933/among-the-ghosts.

Tasker, Yvonne, and Diane Negra. *Interrogating Postfeminism: Gender and the Politics of Popular Culture*. Durham, NC: Duke University Press, 2007.

The Daily Mail. 'Controversial Singer M.I.A. Fighting "Ridiculous" $1.5 Million Fine for Swearing and Making Rude Gesture During Madonna's 2012 Super Bowl Show.' 20 September 2013. http://www.dailymail.co.uk/tvshowbiz/article-2426878/MIA-fighting-1-5m-fine-controversial-appearance-Madonnas-2012-Super-Bowl-show.html#ixzz3hqQRWnRi.

The Telegraph. '"It Wasn't Rape or Anything" Says David Bailey of His Sexual Conquests.' *The Telegraph*, 22 December 2012. https://www.telegraph.co.uk/culture/9762530/It-wasnt-rape-or-anything-says-David-Bailey-of-his-sexual-conquests.html.

Torrusio, Ann T. 'The Fame Monster: The Monstrous Construction of Lady Gaga.' *The Performance Identities of Lady Gaga*, ed. by R. J. Gray. Jefferson, NC: McFarland, 2012.

Urry, John. 'The Global Media and Cosmopolitanism.' 26 April 2001. Cited in José I. Prieto-Arranz. 'The Semiotics of Performance and Success in Madonna.' *The Journal of Popular Culture*, 45 (1), 2012: 173–96.

Urry, John, and Jonas Larsen. *The Tourist Gaze 3.0.* London: Sage, 2011.

Us Weekly. 'Lady Gaga's Craziest Stunts and Most Outrageous Controversies.' http://www.usmagazine.com/entertainment/pictures/lady-gagas-craziest-stunts-and-most-outrageous-controversies-2014273/36953.

Wallace, Benjamin. 'Is Terry Richardson an Artist or a Predator?' *New York Magazine*, 15 June 2014. http://nymag.com/thecut/2014/06/terry-richardson-interview.html.

Wallenberg, Louise. 'Fashion Photography, Phallocentrism and Feminist Critique.' *Fashion in Popular Culture: Literature, Media and Contemporary Studies*, ed. by Joseph H. Hancock, Toni Johnson-Woods, and Vicki Karaminas. Bristol: Intellect, 2013.

Weiner, Jonah. 'How Smart Is Lady Gaga?' *Slate*, 16 June 2009. http://www.slate.com/articles/arts/music_box/2009/06/how_smart_is_lady_gaga.html.

Williams, Rebecca. 'From Beyond Control to In Control: Investigating Drew Barrymore's Feminist Agency/Authorship.' *Stardom and Celebrity*, ed. by Su Holmes and Sean Redmond. London: Sage, 2007.

Yelin, Hannah. '"I Am the Centre of Fame": Doing Celebrity, Performing Fame and Navigating Cultural Hierarchies in Grace Jones' *I'll Never Write My Memoirs.*' *Celebrity Studies*, 2019: 1–13.

CHAPTER 7

Conclusion: The Gender Politics of Ghostwritten Memoir

At stake in self-representation is the freedom to tell our own stories, to be seen, to exist on record, to not be written out of history. The memoirs of female celebrities tell us much about women's wider status in society. By showing how women in the public eye are coaxed and curtailed by manifold ghostly intermediaries, forces and pressures when giving an account of themselves, celebrity memoirs reveal the burdens circumscribing the ways in which all women exist in the world. For example, we have seen the pressures for famous women to depict themselves in service to male sexuality, to laugh along with jokes at their expense in order to be likeable, to excuse hipster sexism to be the 'cool girl', and to smooth over histories of sexual violence for the comfort of others. It is significant that these best-selling books are sold as women's true experience and so contribute to cultural myths of women's shared subjectivity.

There is no universal female experience. The concept itself is oppressive.[1] What *is* common across these memoirs, however, is evidence of women negotiating their power in a patriarchal society. The opportunity for examining the lives of multiple women, side by side in this way, makes memoir a uniquely valuable access point for recognising patterns across the forces affecting the lives of women in general, and those in the public eye in particular. The overarching picture that emerges offers evidence

[1] Butler (1990); Angela Carter, *The Sadeian Woman: And the Ideology of Pornography* (New York: Pantheon Books, 1978).

© The Author(s) 2020
H. Yelin, *Celebrity Memoir*,
https://doi.org/10.1007/978-3-030-44621-5_7

267

to support the recent findings of feminist scholars that we are living in a cultural context of 'proliferating old and new misogynies'.[2]

The urgency of attending to the power dynamics of ghosting is revealed in starkest terms by the example of Jenna Jameson's testimony of surviving gang rape as a teenager co-written by the poster boy for predatory male sexuality and author of *The Game*, Neil Strauss. That Strauss admitted to intervening to transform Jameson's experiences that he felt were too 'dark and heavy' into something more 'fun' shows the work of the ghost as finding ways to offer up authenticated pain whilst making trauma palatable for an audience wishing to be entertained.

This book has revealed the troubling reading pleasures offered by the memoirs of female celebrities, for example, Anderson's strikingly similar narration of two events once as trauma and once as titillation. This placed a memory of being raped as a 12-year-old girl in parallel with a highly eroticised lesbian seduction scene. The proximity of trauma and titillation raises questions of what erotic or entertainment value each scene confers on the other, and more widely, why female celebrities are required to have suffered.

We have seen that memoir is always in negotiation with cultural appetites for shaming and humiliating women in the public eye, and the sexual inflexion this takes. For example, Hilton's revelation that her only option was to laugh along when confronted on national television with a joke about her sex tape and the size of her vagina: 'Is it hard to get a room in the Paris Hilton? Is it roomy?'[3] Meanwhile, in Ezarik and McAllister's inability to criticise their abusers, we have seen the contortions of self-censorship required when using memoir to narrate one's experiences of the hostilities faced as a woman in the public eye whilst trying not to provoke further backlash.

The foreclosing of female celebrities' possibilities for self-representation by cultures of misogyny was writ large in the images of Lady Gaga, collapsed, exposed, unconscious by a celebrity photographer who faced allegations that he sexually abused his models. The history of sexual trauma, so thematically integral to 'glamour girl' memoirs, is not revealed here, but is indirectly invoked in the ghost's own star image.

---

[2] Banet-Weiser (2018); Kate Manne, *Down Girl: The Logic of Misogyny* (Oxford University Press, 2017).

[3] Hilton, p. 14.

The pressures upon female celebrities' self-representation are evident, as is the fact that these pressures are frequently in service of male power. These examples confound common assumptions that the ghosts of celebrity memoir are merely exploited scribes doing a star's bidding.[4] Agency in ghosted self-representation is complex, and these examples show the urgency of attending to the power dynamics of ghosting and wider celebrity mediation.

There have also been many moments of resistance highlighted throughout this analysis of celebrity memoir. We have seen both the demands of the genre and the strategies put in place in a bid to resist or temper these demands. There was, for example, Anderson speaking back to exploitative media ecosystems of exposure, naming the violations of the paparazzi and how they made her feel. There was Sugg's community building around the shared experience of anxiety. There were many, many examples of authors reframing the labour of celebrity (and femininity, and the adult entertainment industry) to resist their characterisation as passive objects. Many of these resistant strategies deploy camp as a form of self-defence in their playfully elliptical, ironising or fictionalising tactics. For example, Gaga's flirtations with Pop Art performativity evade destructive cultural appetites for intimate knowledge which 'excavate' and 'dig "behind"'.[5] Instead, she directs attention towards surface images and away from conventional ideas of emotional 'depth'. There was Hilton's irreverent dismissal of her confessions as a mere 'pose'[6] and Price's cheerfully defensive 'hello! I *admit* that I'm fake'.[7] And there was M.I.A.'s art anthology, in which the celebrity appears primarily as authorial trace directing the gaze towards her artworks rather than herself.

And yet, whilst resistant strategies are often at play, they are also often thwarted at a textual level. Confessions can be extracted one way or another as stars must feed the demand for the appearance of access (from both autobiography and celebrity culture). Furthermore, these texts exist in assemblages of overlapping narratives that they cannot fully escape. As a result, even the most seemingly non-conforming examples evidence the weight of convention upon them and point to the limits of the field of representational possibilities for highly visible women in contemporary culture.

[4] Couser (1998).

[5] Sontag (1967), p. 6.

[6] Hilton.

[7] Price (2010), p. 20.

Agency and Authorship

Self-representation is a vital form of agency, but it is subject to manifold gendered pressures, many of which are not immediately visible. Providing a platform for stars who need to reclaim the spotlight or 'set the record straight', the celebrity memoir is an intervention of sorts, and thus a source of represented agency. The control afforded to stars is tempered by ghostwriters, the demands of access and authenticity, interactions with extratextual criticism, and the different capitals they bring to these negotiations as a result of the different celebrity fields they occupy. Agency has been a recurring heuristic throughout this book, yet it remains a slippery concept. Agency and authorship in collaborative memoir can take various forms and occur within a negotiation with a range of other forces. Ultimately, they can only be inferred. When it comes to the memoirs of female celebrities (as with wider celebrity culture), we can only speak of the discursive negotiation of agency: not its 'actual' or 'measurable' existence.

Some of these forms of agency can be complex and counter-intuitive. For example, presenting oneself as wholly lacking agency is a direct claim *to* agency. Depicting oneself as subject to patriarchal structures which deny women sexual agency is nonetheless an active means of situating oneself within such power structures and negotiating with them. Further, the lucrative market for such memoirs and their explicitly commercial function complicates the model of victimhood presented within them—profitably selling one's own victimhood is, indeed, a form of agency (in economic terms at least). The celebrity author-subject can also omit or fabricate aspects of her memoir. Both of these are forms of agency, although not without certain risks and impossible to identify with certainty in the text.

As memoir presents an opportunity to reframe the 'work' of celebrity, 'glamour girl' memoirs represent their authors as agents of careers that have required hard labour, professionalised skills, creative input and business acumen. However, the representations of celebrity agency throughout this book have also proven deeply contradictory: for example, the 'glamour girl' memoir uses the rhetoric of empowerment to primarily tell stories of being *out* of control.

Hilton's memoir shows that her extreme privilege affords her a different status in relation to her audience than a star like Goody and, as a result, Hilton does not have to fulfil an appetite for her shame.

However, this does not mean that such appetites do not exist, or that they are not potentially satisfied by the text, whether Hilton willingly participates or not. At points, it appears they are afforded agency enough only to participate in their own humiliation.

The examples in this book reveal the limitations of working within the industrial structures which produce celebrity. By contrast, YouTubers demonstrate that freedom from such structures comes with its own risks. Representations of YouTubers as sole agents of their fame, liberated by working for themselves, compete with accounts of anxious, relentless and insecure working practices. The gig economy promises autonomy whilst increasing labour exploitation and uncertainty. The YouTubers examined here accordingly claim autonomy whilst depicting overwork, burnout and anxiety from trying to please the algorithms that control their success or failure. Such accounts must be taken seriously, firstly, given the shocking number of YouTubers that have taken their own lives, and, secondly, because these sociotechnical forces are shaping our collective futures. The neoliberal embrace of technologically enabled exploitation through insecure labour and diminishing privacy has ramifications across wider society that should concern us all.

As alt-pop-stars, M.I.A. and Gaga start from a point of less contested access to the status of creative agent. Pop-stardom is presented as a continuation of a prior art practice, originating within the endorsed, elite environment of art school, staking a claim to authenticity and agency over manufacture. However, differences between the representations of celebrity agency in the visual memoirs of M.I.A. and Gaga point to the significance of the ghostwriting relationship to the meaning of the text. As she constructs images in partnership with hired photographer Richardson, Gaga claims agency in the model's pose. Other images, however, imply Gaga has no agency in their construction, showing her unconscious or collapsed. Crucially, it is the image of her violability, not her agency, that her photo-memoir sells. By contrast, the unsuccessfully erased ghosting machinery that collectively produces M.I.A.'s autobiographical text reveals traces of existing relationships with subordinate employees, independent from the book's publishing house or her record labels, suggesting control over the process of mediation.

Revealing the Ghosts

It is problematic and disempowering to automatically conclude that the presence of a ghostwriter negates the agency of the celebrity author, as the popular imagination presumes. At the same time, it is nonetheless impossible to determine conclusively the extent to which each party controls the resulting life story and its meaning.

When ghosts reveal themselves, they show that accounting for their presence has implications for understanding the way that meaning is attributed. The range of models for understanding the dynamics of collaborative authorship in this book has been broad: from Merle Ginsberg, Hilton's strategic alliance, to Siobhan Curham who had to be 'killed off' after becoming toxic to Zoella's brand, to M.I.A.'s uncredited team who reveal their erased labour despite it being buried, to Lucie Cave who still gets to ascribe the meaning of Goody's life 20 years after her death. Despite offering vastly different ways of viewing the ghosting relationship, all these examples are too messy to neatly fit into existing models of ghosting offered by existing scholarship, in which the ghost is either an 'outranked' scribe[8] or one who studies 'from above'.[9]

This book begins with the case of Neil Straus—a man who made his fortune from a how-to guide for sexual predation—co-writing the story of surviving sexual violence and admitting to making interventions to make it less 'dark'. This example reveals both the active role of the ghost and the potential coalescence of the ways in which they shape the meaning of the text and their extratextual interests. The book then closes with the example of Terry Richardson, whose high-profile connotations of sexual predation are leveraged to imply a non-consensual, and therefore more authentic, image. This last example is especially instructive in the wider codes of celebrity culture which see the non-consensual image production of the paparazzi 'snatch' as the locus of authenticity.

In each example, consideration of the role of the ghost has implications for how we understand the text. They do not preclude the possibility of celebrity authorial agency. Indeed, many of these examples directly evidence the power of the celebrity to hire, borrow from or benefit from the chosen partnerships. Yet, in every case unpicking the presence of

---

[8] Couser (1998).

[9] Lejeune, p. 199.

the ghost exposes a process of negotiation that complicates how agency, authorship and celebrity meaning-making can be understood.

This book spans examples of great textual diversity and structural complexity, despite the celebrity memoir genre having been disregarded as formulaic, artless or shallow.[10] The entanglements of collaboration, their layers of mediation, their interrelation with extratextual worlds and their intrinsic multiplicity and negotiation create a complexity that is matched by their formal diversity, ranging from traditional first-person retrospective address, to the art anthology, through comic strips, novels, epistolary and photo-memoirs. However, despite these formal differences, a strong set of representational conventions is at play in the memoirs of female celebrities. Below, I shall summarise these conventions in terms of access, authenticity, extratextuality and the celebrity domain.

THE GENDERED AUTHENTICITY CONTRACT AND THE ECONOMICS OF ACCESS

These memoirs exist within a wider *economics of access*, in which female celebrities trade the appearance of access to their commoditised subjectivity and/or exposed bodies. Such access operates as currency, with the appearance of non-consensual access having the highest trade value. A *gendered authenticity contract* holds famous women to an impossible standard of access-as-proof of authentic celebrity selfhood. When this unattainable benchmark inevitably cannot be met—not least because absolute access is a fiction—this provokes an angry backlash and audience accusations of deliberate falsehood.

The promise of access to the 'real' self is often explicit, for example in the texts of Price, Jameson, Hilton and Goody. Even when it is not explicit, for example in the texts of Anderson, M.I.A. and Gaga, it is still implicitly fundamental to the text. These celebrity author-subjects promise to offer up the essential self, whilst simultaneously ironising, fictionalising or taking steps to distance themselves from that promise. The texts frequently claim that authenticity is located in ever greater exposure, in a history of suffering, and in the narration of lives that are out of control. Even when the texts purport to engage in postmodern, self-reflexive play with performed identities—in what I term

---

[10] Harris; Crone.

'doing' celebrity—they default to the currency of authenticity in some form. Whilst authenticity has long been understood as at stake in celebrity image construction, camp artifice offers a counterpoint for understanding celebrity authenticity. It is a strategy deployed in seeming contradiction to the demands of authenticity but one which can offer a means for negotiating the competing simultaneous demands of publicly performed femininity.

The 'glamour girl' memoir particularly illustrates this generic trade in an *economics of access*, demonstrating uniquely heightened overlapping promises of exposure. Memoir, celebrity culture, and pornography, all deal in promises of access, whether to celebrity bodies or minds. The revelation of personal secrets is positioned as a continuation of sexualised striptease—one which goes further than the stars' work in pornography, but which, nonetheless, exists on the same continuum. The 'glamour girl' memoir creates an explicit confusion between telling secrets and revealing bodies. In a move which both eroticises and literalises privacy, these women have responded to the demand for 'making a private history public'[11] by narrating their 'privates'. Outside these texts, non-consensual paparazzi 'snatches' seek to expose these women further. The authors depict memoirs offering an opportunity to 'speak back' to those who 'steal' their commoditised selfhood in this way. The memoir is thus framed as the opportunity to expose oneself on one's own terms. The autobiographical accounts which result, however, still adhere to the same conventions of sexualised exposure. They seek both to tally with the existing star persona, which compelled the reader to purchase, and to compete with a wider landscape of celebrity culture which locates authenticity in the non-consensual.

The memoirs of reality TV stars revealed the gendered censure for *over*exposure and the sexual morality at the heart of it. The failure to deliver upon a *gendered authenticity contract* results in a charge of 'trashiness' that is in part founded upon Hilton and Goody's failure to adhere to social boundaries of feminine restraint. Goody's sentimental discourse is also positioned as grotesque in these terms: her memoir describes the opening of emotional 'floodgates'[12] and offers seemingly unrestrained outpourings of personal secrets, representing an 'over sharing' of physical

---

[11] McLennan, p. 7.

[12] Goody (2009), p. xxxv.

and emotional detail suggesting that she doesn't respect the boundaries of decorous speech. Censure is provoked by the reality TV star's willingness to be seen to be inviting an admiring audience which one ought to be able to attract effortlessly. The conventions of both reality TV and contemporary memoir demand the subject's exposure as they reveal (ideally 'shameful') secrets, or are exposed in 'candid' moments of humiliation.

YouTube celebrity in particular hinges upon the appearance of direct access and an absence of mediation due to perceptions of the YouTuber as a lone worker, making and distributing their own content. This removes the insulation of formal entertainment industry structures, and yet the mandate to 'open up' and deliver feelings of intimacy and access persists, exacerbated by a platform designed around direct dialogue. Charting, as it does, the evolution of the *economics of access* into the age of digital celebrity, this book points to the direction of travel for these currents in wider society as pressures to perform intimacy and access accelerate and intensify in online settings.

The memoirs of alt-pop-stars M.I.A. and Gaga focus on the surface image as a means to resist the demands of a culture which coaxes stars to trade in access to their inner selves. Yet, the dominant codes of gendered celebrity exposure prevail as these books trade in the currencies seen throughout the genre. Rather than being exceptions, they demonstrate the extreme persistence of conventions of access and exposure in female celebrity. They do not offer the written confessions that are present in the wider celebrity memoir, but they offer a form of confession, nonetheless.

In his photos of Gaga, Richardson appropriates the visual tropes of the un-posed paparazzi 'snatch', borrowing both their codes of 'realism' and the suggestion of forced exposure, thus playing with the concept of consent. Imperfection is performed through the kinds of photographs associated with forced overexposure and humiliation, but which here form an official narrative which promises to have 'captured the intimate…in all aspects of her life'.[13] This 'all access, nothing off limits'[14] logic presupposes that authenticity lies in being perceived to be as thoroughly revealed as possible. Richardson's photos enact a gradual forcing of access into new areas of privacy and parts of Gaga's body. This model of uncomfortably creeping boundaries results in a more comprehensive, fully exposed

---

[13] Lady Gaga X Terry Richardson, http://www.ladygagaxterryrichardsonthebook.com/.

[14] 'Lady Gaga X Terry Richardson', *Amazon.com*.

image, and this sequence constructs a narrative that gradually strips Gaga of her defensive artifice. Within this framework, a non-normative figure such as Gaga can be safely returned to a tamed and untroubling 'category of woman' that exists within celebrity's dominant codes of gendered emotional and physical exposure.

In contrast, M.I.A. keeps her body predominantly out of the frame in favour of a focus on her creative and conceptual output. M.I.A. claims to cynically expose the workings of celebrity in an effort to assert the authenticity of the honest fake. Uniquely, the target of her scepticism is manipulated and strategically deployed autobiography as M.I.A. draws attention to the way that the celebrity life evolves in an *economics of access* and adapts itself to the appetites of its desired audience. This model of autobiography as 'column inches and a Wikipedia page'[15] seeks to evade the terms of the genre. Yet, it conducts the very exchange it seeks to undermine, using tropes such as the verbal vernacular and handwriting as if they offer a window to M.I.A.'s subjectivity. The offer of access to M.I.A.'s subjectivity through her art rather than her exposed body shows that demands for exposure can be negotiated. It also demonstrates the potency of the *economics of access* at the heart of gendered celebrity as the appearance of access must still be given.

Such are the strategies available to public women in their self-representation: the politics of production, the importance of what is kept in and left out of the frame, and the struggle to be seen as author of one's own image in a wider context of negotiated exposure. Of course, the idea that access to another person's subjectivity can be offered through a form of mediation, such as the celebrity memoir, is as inherently suspect and paradoxical as celebrity culture's sale of the idea of the 'authentic' self. Access is therefore best understood as a currency: an insistent demand in celebrity culture that—as the examples in this book show—can be negotiated, but that can end up fulfilled one way or another.

---

[15] Arulpragasam, p. 6.

Assemblage, Extratextuality
and the Celebrity Domain

In terms of access, *M.I.A.* functions as a limit case. The specificities of her celebrity field—a pop-star with 'alternative', subcultural caché—create the conditions which enable certain representational freedoms (especially when contrasted with, for example, the 'glamour girl' category and the additional stigmas negotiated within it). Yet M.I.A. is unique in this sample for showing that a sexualised inflection need not frame mediated access to female subjectivity. These texts can only be understood through their extratextual relations, for example the negotiations with the paparazzi 'snatch', negative commentary, and the pre-existing field of both star and ghost. They are always in dialogue with their extratexts, not least in the interaction between the way the life story is told and the field from which its author's fame originated.

The paratextual pornographic persona construction in 'glamour girl' memoirs showed that their accounts are required to tally with, positivise, retrospectively justify, and propel pornographic careers for new audiences. At the same time, they narrate sex, the body, and harm in ways that mitigate concern, and reiterate the visual codes of porn aesthetics in written text.

Reality TV star memoirs interact with and seek to counter the discourses of the 'talentless' overexposure that surround the TV genre and its stars. Reality TV star memoir is always in dialogue with the criticisms, judgements and exposés which circulate around a star in a landscape of networked gossip media as both commentators and (anti)fans contribute to the overlapping meanings that surround the star's life story. Hilton, for example, engages in games of elliptic denial but these gaps are filled in by the assemblage of narratives that circulate around her, showing how the meaning of these texts always resides within their overlap with extratextual worlds.

YouTuber celebrity identities are formed across multiple online platforms which document their lives in constant dialogue with their audiences. This fan feedback represents a potent example of extratextual intrusion. In their analogue memoirs, YouTubers endeavour to transmit digital subjectivities. They bring the dynamic multiplicity of their online identities to life through the aesthetics and co-creational behaviours of the platforms that made them famous. These authors must negotiate algorithms that directly reward interaction with the extratextual world and punish failure to do so. As a result of such directness and primacy of fan interaction, audience comments loom large in YouTuber memoirs, as their authors downplay and normalise the gendered online abuse they receive, for fear of provoking more of it.

The autobiographical output of pop-stars (with some degree of subcultural caché) starts from a point of assumed creativity that grants licence for a wider range of playful self-representation. Both M.I.A. and Gaga responded to this representational scope with texts that focus upon the visual imagery of (and around) their stardom, opening up the working definition of celebrity memoir in this book to include visual forms, and expanding our understanding of ghosting to include agents of mediation such as the creative director or photographer. This showed how the meaning of the account given is shaped not only by the ghost in their conscious acts of interpretation, but also—if they are sufficiently visible—by the extratextual associations that circulate in the ghost's own 'star' image as in the case of Richardson's reported sex offences. M.I.A.'s example revealed risks associated with extratextual meaning-making. She attempts to give meaning to her story, not only from her own life experience, but by drawing upon the history and politics of Sri Lanka and the 'third world'[16] more generally. These external debates are verifiable beyond one's own experience and authority. Thus, stepping beyond one's own life story renders the meaning of that story vulnerable to further criticisms on the grounds of interpretations of external events.

This book provides a framework for understanding memoir in the context of its collaborative authorship and the industrial conditions of construction without dismissing these texts as solely the cynical manufacture of corporate merchandise. Celebrity studies has offered theorisations of the ways in which celebrity texts engage with the competing discourses of privacy and publicity, authenticity and manufacture. Celebrity memoir is an especially valuable case-study for the examination of such themes, being so entirely defined by both visible manipulation and apparent access to essentialised subjectivity. The study of autobiography has offered ways to understand how certain life stories are coaxed according to both pre-existing norms, and the need to be perceived as a reliable narrator despite obvious partiality. Celebrity memoir, with the conspicuousness of its ghostwriters and industrial relations, literalises and makes visible

---

[16] Arulpragasam, p. 54.

these concerns as it seeks to trade in, what I have termed, an *economics of access*. As 'official' celebrity narratives which react to their media environment, modelling the ways in which celebrities are always in interaction with the multiplicity of coverage, judgements and readings that circulate around them, memoir affords a model for understanding the *celebrity-as-assemblage*. By offering an understanding of celebrity memoir—as ghostwritten, as an agentic intervention, as a microcosmic cultural artefact with much to tell us about celebrity culture at large, and as a negotiated terrain which makes its negotiations exceptionally visible on the page—this book has provided new ways to understand the (limits to the) modes of self-representation available to women on a public stage.

BIBLIOGRAPHY

Amazon.com. 'Lady Gaga X Terry Richardson.' *Amazon.com.*
Arulpragasm, Mathangi. 'Maya.' *M.I.A.* New York: Rizzoli, 2012.
Banet-Weiser, Sarah. *Empowered: Popular Feminism and Popular Misogyny.* Durham: Duke University Press, 2018.
Butler, Judith. *Gender Trouble: Feminism and the Subversion of Identity.* London: Routledge, 1990.
Carter, Angela. *The Sadeian Woman: And the Ideology of Pornography.* New York: Pantheon Books, 1978.
Couser, G. Thomas. 'Making, Taking, and Faking Lives: The Ethics of Collaborative Life Writing.' *Style*, 32 (2), 1998: 334–51.
Crone, Jack. 'Are We Seeing the Death of the Celebrity Memoir?' *Mail Online*, 20 December 2014. http://www.dailymail.co.uk/news/article-2881571/End-chapter-celebrity-memoirs-Autobiographies-rich-famous-no-longer-sell-says-publishing-house.html#ixzz3icP5MsBk.
Goody, Jade. *Jade Fighting to the End.* London: John Blake, 2009.
Harris, John. 'Why Celebrity Memoirs Rule Publishing.' *The Guardian*, 13 December 2010. http://www.guardian.co.uk/books/2010/dec/13/celebrity-memoirs-bestsellers-autobiography-christmas#ixzz2UhtsjwCT.
Hilton, Paris. *Confessions of an Heiress: A Tongue-in-Chic Peek Behind the Pose.* New York: Fireside Books, 2004.
Ladygagaxterryrichardsonthebook.com, Lady Gaga X Terry Richardson. http://www.ladygagaxterryrichardsonthebook.com/.
Lejeune, Philippe. 'The Autobiography of Those Who Do Not Write.' *On Autobiography*, ed. by Paul John Eakin. Minneapolis: University of Minnesota Press, 1989.
Manne, Kate. *Down Girl: The Logic of Misogyny.* New York: Oxford University Press, 2017.

McLennan, Rachael. *American Autobiography*. Edinburgh: Edinburgh University Press, 2013.

Price, Katie. *You Only Live Once*. London: Century, 2010.

Sontag, Susan. 'Against Interpretation.' *Against Interpretation and Other Essays*. London: Eyre & Spottiswoode, 1967.

Zuberi, Nabeel. 'Worries in the Dance: Post-Millennial Grooves and Sub-Bass Culture.' *Britpop and the English Music Tradition*, ed. by Andy Bennet and Jon Stratton. Aldershot: Ashgate, 2010.

Bibliography

Primary Sources

Anderson, Pamela. *Star*. London: Simon & Schuster, 2004.
———. *Star Struck*. London: Simon & Schuster, 2006.
Arulpragasm, Mathangi "Maya". *M.I.A*. New York: Rizzoli, 2012.
Brown, Melanie, *Catch a Fire*. London: Headline, 2002.
Beckham, Victoria. *Learning to Fly*. London: Michael Joseph, 2001.
Calloway, Caroline. *Scammer*. Forthcoming. https://carolinecalloway.com/pro
ducts/scammer-pre-order?variant=31554651095086.
Contostavlos, Tulisa. *Honest: My Story So Far*. London: Headline, 2012.
Cyrus, Miley. *Miles to Go*. Bath: Parragon, 2009.
Daniels, Stormy. *Full Disclosur.* London: MacMillan, 2018.
Defoe, Daniel. *Moll Flanders*. London: HarperCollins, [1722] 2010.
Ezarik, Justine. *I, Justine*. New York: Keywords Press, 2015.
Faiers, Sam. *Living Life the Essex Way*. London: Simon and Schuster, 2012.
Franklin, Benjamin. *The Autobiography of Benjamin Franklin*. New York: Dover,
1996 [written between 1771–1790].
Frey, James. *A Million Little Pieces*. London: John Murray, 2003.
Gaga, Lady and Terry Richardson. *Gaga X Richardson*. London: Hodder and
Stoughton, 2011.
Goody, Jade. *Jade Fighting to the End*. London: John Blake, 2009.
Halliwell, Geri. *Just for the Record*. London: Ebury Press, 2003.
Hilton, Paris. *Confessions of an Heiress: A Tongue-in-Chic Peek Behind the Pose*.
New York: Fireside Books, 2004.
J, Jessie. *Nice to Meet You: My Story*. London: Simon and Schuster, 2012.

© The Editor(s) (if applicable) and The Author(s) 2020
H. Yelin, *Celebrity Memoir*,
https://doi.org/10.1007/978-3-030-44621-5

Jameson, Jenna. *How to Make Love Like a Pornstar: A Cautionary Tale*. New York: HarperCollins 2010.

Katona, Kerry. *Too Much, Too Young*. London: Ebury, 2006.

Kardashian, Kim, Kourtney Kardashian, and Khloe Kardashian. *Kardashian Konfidential*. New York: St. Martin's Press, 2011.

McAllister, Jenn. *Really Professional Internet Person*. London: Scholastic, 2015.

Osbourne, Kelly. *Fierce*. London: Virgin, 2010.

Price, Katie. *Being Jordan: My Autobiography*. London, John Blake, 2005.

———. *A Whole New World*. London: Century, 2006.

———. *You Only Live Once*. London: Century, 2010.

Quin, Tegan, and Sara Quin. *High School*. London: Virago, 2019.

Richardson, Samuel. *Pamela, or Virtue Rewarded*. Oxford: Oxford University Press, [1740] 2001.

Steffans, Karrine, *Confessions of a Video Vixen*. New York: HarperCollins, 2009.

Strauss, Neil. *The Game: Penetrating the Secret Society of Pick-Up Artists*. New York: HarperCollins, 2005.

Sugg, Zoe. *Girl Online*. London: Penguin, 2015.

Sullivan, Brendan Jay. *Rivington Was Ours: Lady Gaga, the Lower East Side, and the Prime of our Lives*. New York: It Books 2013.

Trump, Donald. *The Art of the Deal*. New York: Warner Books, 1987.

Victory, Grace. *No Filter*. London: Hachette, 2017.

ACADEMIC SOURCES

Abidin, Crystal. '# familygoals: Family Influencers, Calibrated Amateurism, and Justifying Young Digital Labor.' *Social Media+ Society*, 3 (2), 2017: 1–15.

———. *Internet Celebrity: Understanding Fame Online*. Emerald Publishing, 2018.

Allen, Kim and Heather Mendick. 'Young People's Uses of Celebrity: Class, Gender and "Improper" Celebrity.' *Discourse: Studies in the Cultural Politics of Education*, 34 (1), 2013: 77–93.

Allen, Kim. 'Girls Imagining Careers in the Limelight: Social Class, Gender and Fantasies of "Success."' *In the Limelight and Under the Microscope*, ed. by Holmes and Negra.

Amnesty, Toxic Twitter: A Toxic Place for Women. (2018). https://www.amnesty.org/en/latest/research/2018/03/online-violence-against-women-chapter-1/#topanchor.

Anderson, Linda. *Autobiography*, 2nd ed. London: Routledge, [2001] 2011. Cited in Rachael McLennan, *American Autobiography*. Edinburgh: Edinburgh University Press, 2013.

Andrejevic, Marc. 'Watching Television Without Pity: The Productivity of Online Fans.' *Television & New Media*, 9 (1), 2008: 24–46.

Annandale, David. 'Rabelais Meets Vogue: The Construction of Carnival, Beauty and Grotesque.' *The Performance Identities of Lady Gaga*, ed. by R. J. Gray. Jefferson, NC: McFarland Publishing, 2012.

Attwood, Feona. 'Reading Porn: The Paradigm Shift in Pornography Research.' *Sexualities*, 5 (1), 2002.

———. 'Through the Looking Glass? Sexual Agency and Subjectification Online.' *New Femininities: Postfeminism, Neoliberalism and Subjectivity*, ed. by Rosalind Gill and Christina Scharff. Basingstoke: Palgrave Macmillan, 2011.

Babuscio, Jack. 'Camp and Gay Sensibility.' *Camp Grounds: Style and Homosexuality*, ed. by David Bergman. Amherst: University of Massachusetts Press, 1993.

Bakhtin, Mikhail. *Rabelais and His World*. Bloomington: Indiana University Press, 1965.

Banet-Weiser, Sarah. 'Branding the Post-Feminist Self: Girls' Video Production and YouTube.' *Mediated Girlhoods: New Explorations in Girls' Media Culture*. New York: Peter Lang, 2011.

———. *AuthenticTM: The Politics of Ambivalence in a Brand Culture*. New York: New York University Press, 2012.

———. *Empowered: Popular Feminism and Popular Misogyny*. Durham: Duke University Press, 2018.

Barcan, Ruth. *Nudity: A Cultural Anatomy*. Oxford: Berg, 2004.

Barry, Kathleen. *The Prostitution of Sexuality: The Global Exploitation of Women*. New York: New York University Press, 1995.

Barthes, Roland. *Roland Barthes by Roland Barthes*, trans. Richard Howard. New York: Hill and Wang, 1977.

———. 'The Death of the Author.' *Image/Music/Text*, trans. Stephen Heath. New York: Hill and Wang, 1977, 142–47.

———. *Camera Lucida: Reflections on Photography*, trans. Richard Howard. New York: Farrar, Straus, and Giroux, 1981.

———. *Mythologies*, trans. Annette Lavers. London: Vintage, 1993.

Bazin. André, 'The Ontology of the Photographic Image.' *Classic Essays on Photography*, ed. by Trachtenberg. New Haven, CN: Leete's Island Books, 1980.

Bell, Emma. 'Bad Girl to Mad Girl: British Female Celebrity, Reality Products, and the Pathologization of Pop-Feminism.' *Genders*, 48, 2008. http://www.genders.org/g48/g48_bell.html.

Bell, Katherine M. 'Raising Africa? Celebrity and the Rhetoric of the White Saviour.' *PORTAL Journal of Multidisciplinary International Studies*, 10 (1), 2013.

Benjamin, Walter. 'The Work of Art in the Age of Mechanical Reproduction.' *Stardom and Celebrity*, ed. by Holmes and Redmond. Los Angeles: Sage.

Berger, John. *Ways of Seeing*. London: Penguin Books, 1972.
Berger, Richard. *Framing the Subversive: Journalism, Celebrity and the Web*. Paper presented at *The End of Journalism? Technology, Education and Ethics*, University of Bedfordshire, 18 October 2008. http://theendofjournalism.wikidot.com/richardberger.
Berlant, L. *The Female Complaint: The Unfinished Business of Sentimentality in American Culture*. Durham, N.C.: Duke University Press, 2008.
Berryman, Rachel and Misha Kavka. 'Crying on YouTube: Vlogs, Self-Exposure and the Productivity of Negative Affect.' *Convergence*, 24, 2017a: 85–98.
———. 'I Guess A Lot of People See Me as a Big Sister or a Friend: The Role of Intimacy in the Celebrification of Beauty Vloggers.' *Journal of Gender Studies*, 26 (3), 2017b: 307–20.
Bhabha, Homi K. *The Location of Culture*. London: Routledge 1994.
Binder, Nellie. 'From the Message Board to the Front Door: Addressing the Offline Consequences of Race-and Gender-Based Doxxing and Swatting.' *Suffolk University Law Review*, 51, 2018: 55.
Biressi, Anita and Heather Nunn. *Reality TV: Realism and Revelation*. London: Wallflower Press, 2005.
Bishop, Sophie. '#YouTuberAnxiety: Anxiety as Emotional Labour and Masquerade in Beauty Vlogs.' *Youth Mediations and Affective Relations*, ed. by S. Driver, N. Coulter. London: Palgrave Macmillan, 2018.
Boorstin, Daniel. *The Image*. London: Penguin, 1963.
Booth, Wayne C. *The Rhetoric of Fiction*, 2nd ed. Chicago: University of Chicago Press, 1983.
———. *The Company We Keep: An Ethics of Fiction*. Berkeley: University of California Press, 1988.
Bose, Nandana. 'Big Brother's Frankenstein: The Media Construction of Jade Goody as an "Abject-Other."' *Feminist Media Studies*, 7 (4), 2007: 455–69.
Bourdieu, Pierre. *Outline of a Theory of Practice*. Cambridge: Cambridge University Press, 1977.
———. *Distinction: A Social Critique of the Judgement of Taste*. London: Routledge, 1984.
———. *The Field of Cultural Production: Essays on Art and Literature*. Cambridge: Polity, 1993.
Boyle, Karen. 'Producing Abuse: Selling the Harms of Pornography.' *Women's Studies International Forum*, 34, 2011: 593–602.
Brandt, Deborah. '"Who's the President?": Ghostwriting and Shifting Values in Literacy.' *College English*, 69 (6), 2007: 549–71.
Braudy, Leo. *The Frenzy of Renown: Fame and Its History*. New York: Vintage, 1997.
Budgeon, Shelley. 'Identity as an Embodied Event.' *Body & Society*, 9 (1), 2003: 35–55.

————. 'Theorizing Subjectivity and Feminine Embodiment: Feminist Approaches and Debates.' *Handbook of Children and Youth Studies*, 30 January 2015: 243–56.

Burgess, Jean and Joshua Green. *YouTube: Online Video and Participatory Culture*. Cambridge: Polity, 2009.

Butler, Judith and Sara Salih. *The Judith Butler Reader*. Oxford: Blackwell, 2004.

Butler, Judith. 'Sex and Gender in Simone de Beauvoir's Second Sex.' *Yale French Studies*, 72, 1986: 35–50.

————. *Gender Trouble. Feminism and the Subversion of Identity*. London: Routledge, 1990.

————. *Bodies that Matter. On the Discursive Limits of Sex*. London: Routledge, 1993.

————. 'Imitation and Gender Insubordination.' *Women, Knowledge, and Reality: Explorations in Feminist Philosophy*, edited by Ann Garry, Marilyn Pearsall, New York and London: Routledge, 1996.

————. *Excitable Speech: A Politics of the Performative*. London: Routledge, 1997.

————. *Precarious Life: The Powers of Mourning and Violence*. London: Verso, 2004.

Carey, John. *The Intellectuals and the Masses: Pride and Prejudice Among the Literary Intelligentsia*. London: Faber. 1992.

Carter, Angela. *The Sadeian Woman: And the Ideology of Pornography*. New York: Pantheon Books, 1978.

Childers, Sara M., Jeong-eun Rhee, and Stephanie L. Daza. 'Promiscuous Use of Feminist Methodologies: The Dirty Theory and Messy Practice of Educational Research Beyond Gender.' *International Journal of Qualitative Studies in Education*, 26 (5), 2013: 507–23.

Cho, Alex. 'Lady Gaga, Balls-Out: Recuperating Queer Performativity.' *FlowTV*, 7 August 2009. http://flowtv.org/?p=4169.

Cobb, Shelley. 'Mother of the Year Kathy Hilton, Lynne Spears, Dina Lohan and Bad Celebrity Motherhood.' *Genders*, 48, 2008. http://www.genders.org/g48/g48_cobb.html.

Coombe, Rosemary J. 'Author/Izing the Celebrity: Publicity Rights, Postmodern Politics, and Unauthorized Genders.' *10 Cardozo Arts and Entertainment Law Journal* (1992): 365–95.

Corona, Victor. 'Making, Taking, and Faking Lives: The Ethics of Collaborative Life Writing.' *Style*, 32 (2), 1998: 334–51.

————. *Vulnerable Subjects*. Ithaca: Cornell University Press, 2004.

————. 'Gaga Studies.' *Pop Matters*, 24 November 2010. http://www.popmatters.com/post/133577-gaga-studies/.

————. 'Memory, Monsters, and Lady Gaga.' *The Journal of Popular Culture*, 46, 2011: 725–44.

Couser, G. Thomas. *Memoir: An Introduction*. Oxford: Oxford University Press, 2012.

Coy, Maddy, and Miranda A. H. Horvath. 'Lads Mags, Young Men's Attitudes Towards Women and Acceptance of Myths about Sexual Aggression.' *Feminism & Psychology*, 21 (1), 2011: 144–50. http://eprints.mdx.ac.uk/6595/1/Horvath-lads_mags.pdf.

Coy, Maddy, Josephine Wakeling, and Maria Garner. 'Selling Sex Sells: Representations of Prostitution and the Sex Industry in Sexualised Popular Culture as Symbolic Violence.' *Women's Studies International Forum*, 34, 2011: 441–48.

Creech, Brian. 'Refugee Status: Tracing the Global Flows of M.I.A.' *Communication, Culture & Critique*, 7, 2014: 267–82.

Cuklanz, Lisa M., and Sujata Moorti. 'Television's "New" Feminism: Prime-Time Representations of Women and Victimization.' *Critical Studies in Media Communication*, 23 (4), 2006: 302–21.

Curran, James and Jean Seaton. *Power Without Responsibility: Press, Broadcasting and the Internet in Britain*. London: Routledge, 2010.

Danuta Walters, Suzanna. 'Born This Way?' *Chronicle*, 5 July 2011. http://chronicle.com/blogs/brainstorm/born-this-way/37016.

Davisson, Amber L. *Lady Gaga and the Remaking of Celebrity Culture*. Jefferson, NC: McFarland, 2013.

de Beauvoir, Simone. *The Second Sex*, trans. H. M. Parshley. London: Penguin Books, 1997.

de Cordova, Richard. *Picture—Personalities: The Emergence of the Star System in America*. Chicago: University of Illinois Press, [2001] 1990.

Deller, Ruth, and Kathryn Murphy, '"Zoella Hasn't Really Written a Book, She's Written a Cheque": Mainstream Media Representations of YouTube Celebrities.' *European Journal of Cultural Studies*, 23 (1), 2020: 112–32.

Dow Adams, Timothy. *Telling Lies in Modern American Autobiography*. Chapel Hill and London: University of North Carolina Press, 1990.

———. 'Introduction: Life Writing and Light Writing; Autobiography and Photography.' *Modern Fiction Studies*, 40 (3) 1994: 459–92.

Dubrofsky, Rachel E. 'Fallen Women in Reality TV: A Pornography of Emotion.' *Feminist Media Studies*, 9 (3), 2009: 353–68.

Duits, Linda, and Van Zoonen, Liesbet. 'Headscarves and Porno-Chic: Disciplining Girls' Bodies in the European Multicultural Society.' *European Journal of Women's Studies*, 13 (2), 2006: 103–17.

Dyer, Richard. 'Lana: Four Films of Lana Turner.' *Movie*, 25, 1977–78: 30–54. Reprinted in M. Landy, ed. *Imitations of Life: A Reader on Film & Television Melodrama*. Michigan: Wayne State University Press, 1991.

———. *Stars*. London: British Film Institute, 1979.

———. *Heavenly Bodies: Film Stars and Society*. New York: St. Martin's Press, 1986.

———. 'A Star Is Born and the Construction of Authenticity.' *Stardom: Industry of Desire*, ed. by C. Gledhill. London: Routledge, 1991.

———. *The Culture of Queers*. London: Routledge, 2002.

Eakin, Paul John. *Fictions in Autobiography: Studies in the Art of Self-Invention*. Princeton: Princeton, 1988.

Ede, Lisa and Andrea A. Lunsford. 'Collaboration and Concepts of Authorship.' *PMLA*, 116 (2), 2001: 354–69.

Edwards, Tim. 'Medusa's Stare: Celebrity, Subjectivity and Gender.' *Celebrity Studies*, 4 (2) 2013: 155–68.

Egan, Susanna. *Mirror Talk: Genres of Life and Death in Autobiography*. Chapel Hill: University of North Carolina Press 1999.

Elkins, James. *The Object Stares Back: On the Nature of Seeing*. New York: Simon and Schuster, 1996.

Evans, Adrienne, and Susan Riley. 'Immaculate Consumption: Negotiating the Sex Symbol in Postfeminist Celebrity Culture.' *Journal of Gender Studies*, 22 (3) 2013: 268–81.

Evans, Mary. *Missing Persons: The Impossibility of Auto/Biography*. London: Routledge, 1999.

Fahy, Thomas. 'One Night in Paris Hilton: Wealth, Celebrity, and the Politics of Humiliation.' *Pop-Porn: Pornography in American Culture*, ed. by Ann C. Hall and Mardia J. Bishop. Westport, CT: Praeger, 2007: 75–98. http://www.georgesclaudeguilbert.com/fahy.pdf.

Fairclough, Kirsty. 'Fame Is a Losing Game Celebrity Gossip Blogging, Bitch Culture, and Post-feminism.' *Genders Online Journal*, 48, 2008. http://www.genders.org/g48/g48_fairclough.html.

Faludi, Susan. *Backlash: The Undeclared War Against American Women*. New York: Crown, 1991.

Feminists Against Censorship. *Pornography and Feminism: The Case Against Censorship*, ed. by Gillian Rodgerson and Elizabeth Wilson. London: Lawrence & Wishart, 1991.

Ferchaud, Arienne et al. 'Parasocial Attributes and YouTube personalities: Exploring Content Trends Across the Most Subscribed YouTube Channels.' *Computers in Human Behavior*, 80, 2018: 88–96.

Fletcher, Roland. 'The Messages of Material Behaviour: A Preliminary Discussion of Non-Vernacular Meaning.' *The Meanings of Things: Material Culture and Symbolic Expression*, ed. by Ian Hodder. London: Unwin Hyman, 1989.

Foucault, Michel. *The History of Sexuality: Volume 1*, trans. Robert Hurley. New York: Pantheon, 1978.

———. 'What Is an Author?' *Textual Strategies: Perspectives in Poststructuralist Criticism*, ed. by Josue V. Harari. Ithaca: Cornell University press, 1979: 141–60.

Fox, Pamela. 'Recycled "Trash": Gender and Authenticity in Country Music Autobiography.' *American Quarterly*, 50 (2), 1998: 234–66.

Freud, Sigmund. *Three Essays on Sexuality*, trans. James Strachey. London: Hogarth Press [1905] 1962.

Frith, Hannah, Jayne Raisborough, and Orly Klein. 'Making Death "Good": Instructional Tales for Dying in Newspaper Accounts of Jade Goody's Death.' *Sociology of Health & Illness*, 35 (3), 2013: 419–33.

Gamson, Joshua. *Claims to Fame: Celebrity in Contemporary America*. Berkeley: University of California Press, 1994.

———. 'The Assembly Line of Greatness: Celebrity in Twentieth Century America.' *Stardom and Celebrity: A Reader*, ed. by Su Holmes and Sean Redmond. London: Sage, 2007: 141–55.

Genette, Gérard. *Paratexts: Thresholds of Interpretation*. Cambridge: Cambridge University Press, 1997.

Genz, Stéphanie, and Benjamin A. Brabon. *Postfeminism: Cultural Texts and Theories*. Edinburgh: Edinburgh University Press.

Geraghty, Christine. 'Re-examining Stardom: Questions of Texts, Bodies and Performance.' *Stardom and Celebrity: A Reader*. London: Sage, 2007.

Gerlitz, Carolin and Anne Helmond. 'The Like Economy: Social Buttons and the Data-Intensive Web.' *New Media and Society*, 15 (8), 2013: 1348–65.

Gies, Lieve. 'Pigs, Dogs, Cows, and Commerce in Celebrity Big Brother 2007.' *Feminist Media Studies*, 7 (4), 2007.

Gill, Rosalind. 'Postfeminist Media Culture: Elements of a Sensibility.' *European Journal of Cultural Studies*, 10 (2), 2007a: 147–66.

———. 'Critical Respect: The Difficulties and Dilemmas of Agency and "Choice" for Feminism.' *European Journal of Women's Studies*, 14 (1), 2007b: 69–80.

———. 'Culture and Subjectivity in Neoliberal and Postfeminist Times.' *Subjectivity*, 25, 2008: 432–45.

———. 'Media, Empowerment and the "Sexualization of Culture" Debates.' *Sex Roles*, 66, 2012: 736–45.

Gilmore, Leigh. 'American Neoconfessional: Memoir, Self Help and Redemption on Oprah's Couch.' *Biography*, 33 (4), 2010, 657–79.

Ging, Debbie, and Eugenia Siapera. 'Special Issue on Online Misogyny.' *Feminist Media Studies*, 18 (4), 2018: 515–24.

Gosselin, Abigail. 'Memoirs as Mirrors: Counterstories in Contemporary Memoir.' *Narrative*, 19 (1), 2011: 133–48.

Gough-Yates, Anna. *Understanding Women's Magazines: Publishing, Markets and Readerships*. London: Routledge, 2003.

Gray, R. J., ed. *The Performance Identities of Lady Gaga*. Jefferson, NC: McFarland Publishing, 2012.

Grindstaff, Laura. *The Money Shot: Trash, Class, and the Making of TV Talk Shows*. Chicago: University of Chicago Press, 2002.

Gwynne, Joel. *Erotic Memoirs and Postfeminism: The Politics of Pleasure.* Basingstoke: Palgrave Macmillan, 2013.

Haddad, Candice. 'Immigration, Authorship, Censorship, and Terrorism: The Politics of M.I.A's US Cross-over.' *In the Limelight and Under the Microscope,* ed. by Holmes and Negra. New York: Continuum, 2011.

Halberstam, J. Jack. *Gaga Feminism: Sex, Gender, and the End of Normal.* Boston: Beacon Press, 2012.

Hall, Stuart. 'New Ethnicities.' *Stuart Hall: Critical Dialogues in Cultural Studies,* ed. by David Morley and Kuan-Hsing Chen. London: Routledge, 1996.

Hartigan, John. 'Unpopular Culture: The Case of "White Trash."' *Cultural Studies,* 11 (2), 1997: 316–43.

Harvey, Laura, and Gill, Rosalind. 'Spicing It Up: Sexual Entrepreneurs and *The Sex Inspectors.*' *New Femininities: Postfeminism, Neoliberalism and Subjectivity,* ed. by Rosalind Gill and Christina Scharff. Basingstoke: Palgrave Macmillan, 2011.

Hegde, Radha S. 'Of Race, Classy Victims and National Mythologies: Distracting Reality on Celebrity Big Brother.' *Feminist Media Studies,* 7 (4), 2007: 455–69.

Hester, Helen. *Beyond Explicit: Pornography and the Displacement of Sex.* Albany: State University of New York Press, 2014.

Holmes, Su. '"All You've Got to Worry About Is the Task, Having a Cup of Tea, and Doing a Bit of Sunbathing": Approaching Celebrity in *Big Brother.*' *Understanding Reality Television,* ed. by Su Holmes and Deborah Jermyn. London: Routledge, 2004.

———. 'Off-guard, Unkempt, Unready'? Deconstructing Contemporary Celebrity in Heat Magazine.' *Continuum: Journal of Media & Cultural Studies,* 19 (1), 2005a: 21–38.

———. '"Starring… Dyer?" Re-visiting Star Studies and Contemporary Celebrity Culture.' *Westminster Papers in Communication and Culture,* 2 (2), 2005b: 6–21.

———. 'It's a Jungle Out There! Playing the Game of Fame in Celebrity Reality TV.' *Framing Celebrity: New Directions in Celebrity Culture,* ed. by Su Holmes and Sean Redmond. London: Routledge, 2006: 45–65.

———. 'Jade's Back, and This Time She's Famous: Narratives of Celebrity in the Celebrity Big Brother Race Row.' *Entertainment and Sports Law Journal,* 7 (1), 2009: 22.

Holmes, Su and Deborah Jermyn, eds. *Understanding 'Reality' Television.* London: Routledge, 2004.

Holmes, Su and Diane Negra, eds. *In the Limelight and Under the Microscope: Forms and Functions of Female Celebrity.* New York: Continuum, 2011.

Holmes, Su and Sean Redmond, eds. *Framing Celebrity: New Directions in Celebrity Culture*. London, New York: Routledge, 2006.

———. *Stardom and Celebrity: A Reader*. London: Sage, 2007.

Horn, Katrin. 'Follow the Glitter Way: Lady Gaga and Camp.' *The Performance Identities of Lady Gaga*, ed. by R. J. Gray. Jefferson, NC: McFarland, 2012.

Horton, Donald, and R. Richard Wohl, 'Mass Communication and Para-social Interaction: Observations on Intimacy at a Distance.' *Psychiatry* 19.3 (1956) 215 – 29.

Humann, Heather Duerre. '*What a Drag:* Lady Gaga, Jo Calderone, and the Politics of Representation.' *The Performance Identities of Lady Gaga*, ed. by R. J. Gray. Jefferson, NC: McFarland, 2012.

Hutnyk, John. 'Poetry After Guantanamo: M.I.A.' *Social Identities*, 18 (5): 555–72.

Isherwood, Christopher. *The World in the Evening*. London, Methuen, 1954.

Jackson, Sue, and Tiina Vares. '"Too Many Bad Role Models for Us Girls": Girls, Female Pop Celebrities and "Sexualization."' *Sexualities*, 2016. https://doi.org/10.1177/1363460714550905.

Jameson, Stacy M. 'Televisual Senses: The Embodied Pleasures of Food Advertising.' *The Journal of Popular Culture*, 48, 2015: 6.

Jamieson, Lynne. *Intimacies: Personal Relationships in Modern Societies*. Cambridge: Polity Press, 1988.

Jane, Emma A. 'Online Misogyny and Feminist Digilantism.' *Continuum*, 30 (3), 2016: 284–97.

Jeffrey, Leslie Ann, and Gayle MacDonald. *Sex Workers in the Maritimes Talk Back*. Vancouver: UBC Press, 2006.

Jeffreys, Sheila. *The Idea of Prostitution*. North Melbourne: Spinifex, 1997.

Jelinek, E. C. *The Tradition of Women's Autobiography: From Antiquity to the Present*. USA: Xlibris, 2003.

Jermyn, Deborah. 'Still Something Else Besides a Mother? Negotiating Celebrity Motherhood in Sarah Jessica Parker's Star Story.' *Social Semiotics*, 18 (2), 2008: 163–76.

———. '"Get a Life, Ladies. Your Old One Is Not Coming Back": Ageing, Ageism and the Lifespan of Female Celebrity.' *Celebrity Studies*, 3 (1), 2012: 1–12.

Jerslev, Anne. 'In the Time of the Microcelebrity: Celebrification and the YouTuber Zoella.' *International Journal of Communication*, 10, 2016: 5233–51.

Kapoor, Ilan. *Celebrity Humanitarianism: The Ideology of Global Charity*. New York: Routledge, 2013.

Kavka, Misha, and Amy West. 'Jade the Obscure: Celebrity Death and the Mediatised Maiden.' *Celebrity Studies*, 1 (2), 2010: 216–30.

Kavka, Misha. *Reality Television, Affect and Intimacy*. Basingstoke: Palgrave Macmillan, 2008.
———. *Reality TV*. Edinburgh: Edinburgh Press, 2012.
———. 'Hating Madonna and Loving Tom Ford: Gender, Affect and the "Extra-curricular" Celebrity.' *Celebrity Studies*, 5 (1–2), 2014: 59–74.
Keightley, Keir. 'Reconsidering Rock.' *The Cambridge Companion to Pop and Rock*, ed. by Simon Frith, Will Straw, and John Street. New York: Cambridge University Press, 2001.
Kenway, Jane, and Elizabeth Bullen. 'Consuming Skin: Dermographies of Female Subjection and Abjection.' *Critical Pedagogies of Consumption: Living and Learning in the Shadow of the "Shopocalypse,"* ed. by Jennifer A. Sandlin and Peter McLaren. New York: Routledge, 2010: 157–68.
Klinger, Barbara. 'Digressions at the Cinema: Reception and Mass Culture.' *Cinema Journal*, 28 (4), 1989: 3–19.
Knee, Adam. 'Celebrity Skins: The Illicit Textuality of the Celebrity Nude Magazine.' *Framing Celebrity*, ed. by Holmes and Redmond: 161–77.
LaBruce, Bruce. 'Notes on Camp/Anti-Camp.' *Nat.Brut.* http://www.natbrut.com/essay-notes-on-campanti-camp-by-bruce-labruce.html.
Landes, Xavier, and Morten Nielsen, 'Racial Dodging in the Porn Industry: A Case with No Silver Bullet.' *Porn Studies*, 5 (2), 2018: 115–30.
Langton, Rae. *Sexual Solipsism: Philosophical Essays on Pornography and Objectification*. Oxford: Oxford University Press 2009.
Lee, Katja. 'Not Just Ghost Stories: Alternate Practices For Reading Coauthored Celebrity Memoirs.' *The Journal of Popular Culture*, 47 (6), 2014: 1256–70.
Lejeune, Philippe. 'The Autobiography of Those Who Do Not Write.' *On Autobiography*, ed. by Paul John Eakin. Minneapolis: University of Minnesota Press, 1989.
Levy, Ariel. *Female Chauvinist Pigs: Women and the Rise of Raunch Culture*. New York; London: Free Press, 2006.
Lobel, Orly. 'The Gig Economy & the Future of Employment and Labor Law.' *University of San Francisco Law Review*, 51, 2017: 51.
Lovelock, Michael. '"Is Every YouTuber Going to Make a Coming Out Video Eventually?": YouTube Celebrity Video Bloggers and Lesbian and Gay Identity.' *Celebrity Studies*, 8 (1), 2017: 87–103.
Lutton, Alison. 'YouTubers-Turned-Authors and the Problematic Practice of Authenticity.' *Celebrity Studie*, 10 (3): 380–95.
Maatta, Jerry. 'Apocalypse Now and Again: Mapping the Bestselling Classics of the End of the World.' *Hype: Bestsellers and Literary Culture*, ed. by Jon Helgason, Sara Kärrholm and Ann Steiner. Lund, Sweden: Nordic Academic Press, 2014.

MacKinnon, Catharine A., and Andrea Dworkin. *In Harm's Way: The Pornography Civil Rights Hearings*. Cambridge, MA; London: Harvard University Press, 1997.

Madhok, Sumi. *Rethinking Agency: Gender, Development and Rights in North West India*. New York and London: Routledge, 2010.

Maguire, Emma. 'Self-Branding, Hotness, and Girlhood in the Video Blogs of Jenna Marbles.' *Biography*, 38 (1), 2015: 72–86.

Manne, Kate. *Down Girl: The Logic of Misogyny*. Oxford: Oxford University Press, 2017.

Marshall, P. David. *Celebrity and Power: Fame in Contemporary Culture*. Minneapolis: University of Minnesota Press, 1997.

———. 'New Media—New Self: The Changing Power of Celebrity.' *The Celebrity Culture Reader*, ed. by P. D. Marshall. New York, NY: Routledge (2006): 634–45.

———. 'Personifying Agency: The Public–Persona–Place–Issue Continuum.' *Celebrity Studies*, 4, 2013: 369–71.

———. 'Persona Studies: Mapping the Proliferation of the Public Self.' *Journalism*, 15 (2), 2014: 153–70.

Marshall, P. David, and Kim Barbour. 'Making Intellectual Room for Persona Studies: A New Consciousness and a Shifted Perspective.' *Persona Studies*, 1 (1), 2015: 1–12.

Marwick, Alice. *Status Update: Celebrity, Publicity and Branding in the Social Media Age*. New Haven, CT: Yale University Press, 2013.

———. 'Instafame: Luxury Selfies in the Attention Economy.' *Public Culture*, 27 (1/75), 2015: 137–60.

Mason-Grant, Joan. *Pornography Embodied: From Speech to Sexual Practice*. Lanham, MD and Oxford: Rowman & Littlefield, 2004.

May, Ernest R. 'Ghost Writing and History.' *The American Scholar*, 22 (4), 1953: 459–65.

McLaren, Margaret A. *Feminism, Foucault, and Embodied Subjectivity*. Albany: State University of New York Press, 2002.

McLennan, Rachael. *American Autobiography*. Edinburgh: Edinburgh University Press, 2013.

McNay, Lois. *Foucault and Feminism: Power, Gender and the Self*. Cambridge: Polity, 1992.

McRobbie, Angela. *Postmodernism and Popular Culture*. London: Routledge, 1994.

———. 'Postfeminism and Popular Culture: Bridget Jones and the New Gender Regime.' *Interrogating Postfeminism: Gender and the Politics of Popular Culture*. Durham and London: Duke University Press, 2007a.

———. 'Top Girls? Young Women and the Post-feminist Sexual Contract.' *Cultural Studies*, 21, 2007b: 718–37.

Miller, Toby. 'Why Coldplay Sucks.' *Celebrity Studies*, 4 (3), 2013: 372–76.

Mitchell, W.J.T. *Iconology: Image, Text, Ideology*. Chicago: University of Chicago Press 1986.

Moran, Joe. *Star Authors: Literary Celebrity in America*. London: Pluto, 2000.

Mulvey, Laura. 'Visual Pleasure and Narrative Cinema.' *Screen*, 16 (3): 1975.

———. 'Afterthoughts on "Visual Pleasure and Narrative Cinema" Inspired by King Vidor's *Duel in the Sun*.' *Visual and Other Pleasures*. Bloomington: Indiana University Press, 1989.

Muntean, Nick, and Anne Helen Petersen. 'Celebrity Twitter: Strategies of Intrusion and Disclosure in the Age of Technoculture.' *M/C Journal*, 12 (5), 2009. http://journal.media-culture.org.au/index.php/mcjournal/article/view/194.

Neef, Sonja, and José van Dijck. *Sign Here!: Handwriting in the Age of New Media*. Amsterdam: Amsterdam University Press, 2006.

Negra, Diane and Maria Pramaggiore. 'Keeping Up with the Aspirations: Commercial Family Values and the Kardashian Brand.' *Reality Gendervision: Sexuality & Gender on Transatlantic Reality Television*, ed. by Brenda R. Weber. London: Duke University Press 2014.

Negra, Diane and Su Holmes, eds. 'GOING CHEAP? Female Celebrity in Reality, Tabloid and Scandal Genres.' *Genders*, 48, 2008.

Negra, Diane. *What a Girl Wants?: Fantasizing the Reclamation of Self in Postfeminism*. London; New York: Routledge, 2009.

Newitz, Annalee and Matt Wray, eds. *White Trash: Race and Class in America*. London and New York: Routledge, 1997.

Newton, Esther. *Mother Camp: Female Impersonators in America*. Chicago: University of Chicago Press, 1972.

Nunn, Heather and Anita Biressi. '"A Trust Betrayed": Celebrity and the Work of Emotion.' *Celebrity Studies*, 1 (1), 2010: 49–64.

Nussbaum, Martha. 'Seven Ways to Treat a Person as a Thing.' *Sex and Social Justice*. Oxford: Oxford University Press 1999.

Iddon, Martin and Melanie L. Marshall eds. *Lady Gaga and Popular Music: Performing Gender, Fashion, and Culture*. New York: Routledge, 2014.

O'Connell Davidson, Julia, and Derek Layder. *Methods, Sex, and Madness*. London, New York: Routledge, 1994.

Olin, Margaret. 'Gaze.' *Critical Terms for Art History*. Chicago: University of Chicago Press, 2003.

Olney, James. 'Autobiography and the Cultural Moment: A Thematic, Historical, and Bibliographical Introduction.' *Autobiography: Essays Theoretical and Critical*, ed. by James Olney. Princeton Guildford: Princeton University Press, [1980] 2014.

Orbe, Mark. 'Representations of Race in Reality TV: Watch and Discuss.' *Critical Studies in Media Communication*, 25 (4), 2008: 345–52.

Paasonen, Susanna. 'Good Amateurs: Erotica Writing and Notions of Quality.' *Porn.Com: Making Sense of Online Pornography*, ed. by Feona Attwood. New York: Peter Lang, 2010.

———. *Carnal Resonance: Affect and Online Pornography*. Cambridge, MA; London: MIT Press, 2011.

Patterson, Natasha, and Camilla A. Sears. 'Letting Men off the Hook? Domestic Violence and Postfeminist Celebrity Culture.' *Genders*, 53, 2011.

Pauly Morgan, Kathryn. 'Women and the Knife.' *Hypatia*, 6 (3), 1991: 25–53.

Perloff, Richard. 'Social Media Effects on Young Women's Body Image Concerns: Theoretical Perspectives and an Agenda for Research.' *Sex Roles*, 71 (11–12), 2014: 363–37.

Perrino, Sabina. 'Recontextualizing Racialized Stories on YouTube.' *Narrative Inquiry*, 27 (2), 2017: 261–85.

Projansky, Sarah. 'Mass Magazine Cover Girls: Some Reflections on Postfeminist Girls and Postfeminism's Daughters.' *Interrogating Postfeminism: Gender and the Politics of Popular Culture*, ed. by Tasker and Negra. Durham, N.C.: Duke University Press, 2007.

Radway, Janice A. *Reading the Romance: Women, Patriarchy and Popular Literature*. Chapel Hill: University of North Carolina Press, 1991.

Raisborough, Jayne, Hannah Frith, and Orly Klein. 'Media and Class-Making: What Lessons Are Learnt When a Celebrity Chav Dies?' *Sociology*, 47 (2), April 2013: 251–66.

Rak, Julie. 'Are Memoirs Autobiography? A Consideration of Genre and Public Identity.' *Genre*, 37 (3–4), 2004: 483–504.

———. *Boom!: Manufacturing Memoir for the Popular Market*. Waterloo, Ontario: Wilfrid Laurier University Press, 2013.

Raun, Tobias. 'Capitalizing Intimacy: New Subcultural forms of Microcelebrity Strategies and Affective Labour on YouTube.' *Convergence*, 24 (1), 2017: 99–113.

Redmond, Sean. 'The Whiteness of Stars: Looking at Kate Winslet's Unruly White Body.' *Stardom and Celebrity: A Reader*, ed. by Su Holmes and Sean Redmond. London: Sage 2006a.

———. 'Intimate Fame Everywhere.' *Framing Celebrity: New Directions in Celebrity Culture*, ed. by Su Holmes and Sean Redmond. London and New York: Routledge, 2006b.

———. 'Pieces of Me: Celebrity Confessional Carnality.' *Social Semiotics*, 18 (2), 2008: 149–61.

———. 'Introduction.' *The Star and Celebrity Confessional*. New York: Routledge, 2013.

Richardson, Diane. 'Constructing Lesbian Identities.' *Feminism and Sexuality: A Reader*, ed. by Stevi Jackson and Sue Scott. Edinburgh: Edinburgh University Press, 1996.

Ringrose, Jessica. *Postfeminist Education: Girls and the Sexual Politics of Schooling*. London; New York, NY: Routledge, 2013.

Rodgerson, Gillian, and Elizabeth Wilson, eds. *Pornography and Feminism: The Case Against Censorship*. London: Lawrence & Wishart, 1991.

Rojeck, Chris. *Fame Attack: The Inflation of Fame and Its Consequences*. London: Bloomsbury, 2012.

Rowe. Kathleen. *The Unruly Woman: Gender and the Genres of Laughter*. Austin: University of Texas Press, 1995.

Russo, Mary J. *The Female Grotesque: Risk, Excess and Modernity*. London and New York: Routledge, 1994.

Rutsky, R. L. 'Being Keanu.' *The End of Cinema as We Know It: American Film in the Nineties*, ed. by Jon Lewis. New York: New York University Press, 2001.

Saha, Anamik. 'Locating MIA: "Race", Commodification and the Politics of Production.' *European Journal of Cultural Studies*, 15, 2012: 736–52.

Sanders, Mark A. 'Theorizing the Collaborative Self: The Dynamics of Contour and Content in the Dictated Autobiography.' *New Literary History*, 25 (1994): 445–58.

Schwartz, Margaret. 'The Horror of Something to See: Celebrity "Vaginas" as Prostheses.' *In the Limelight and Under the Microscope*, ed. by Holmes and Negra.

Searle, Leroy. 'New Criticism.' *The Johns Hopkins Guide to Literary Theory*, 2nd ed, ed. by Michael Groden, Martin Kreiswirth, and Imre Szeman. Baltimore: The Johns Hopkins University Press, 2005.

Senft, Teresa. *Camgirls: Celebrity and Community in the Age of Social Networks*. New York, NY: Peter Lang Publishing, 2008.

Shen, Dan. 'Unreliability in Autobiography vs. Fiction.' *Poetics Today* 28 (1), 2007: 43–87.

Skeggs, Bev. 'The Toilet Paper: Femininity, Class and Misrecognition.' *Women's Studies International Forum*, 24 (2–4), 2001: 295–307.

———. *Class, Self, Culture*. London: Routledge, 2003.

Skeggs, Beverley and Helen Wood. 'The Labour of Transformation and Circuits of Value 'Around' Reality TV.' *Continuum*, 22 (4), 2008: 559–72.

Smith, Daniel. 'Charlie Is so "English"-Like: Nationality and the Branded Celebrity Person in the Age of YouTube.' *Celebrity Studies*, 5 (3), 2014: 256–74.

Smith, Sidonie and Julia Watson. *Reading Autobiography: A Guide for Interpreting Life Narratives*. Minneapolis: University of Minnesota Press, 2001.

———. *Interfaces: Women, Autobiography, Image, Performance*. Ann Arbor: University of Michigan Press, 2002.

————. 'Virtually Me: A Toolbox About Online Presentation.' *Identity Technologies: Constructing the Self Online*, ed. by Anna Poletti and Julie Rak. Madison, Wisconsin: University of Wisconsin Press, 2013.

Smith, Sidonie. *Subjectivity, Identity and the Body: Women's Autobiographical Practices in the Twentieth Century*. Bloomington: Indiana University Press, 1993.

Sontag, Susan. 'Against Interpretation.' *Against Interpretation and Other Essays*. London: Eyre & Spottiswoode, I, 1967a.

————. 'Notes on Camp.' *Against Interpretation and Other Essays*. London: Eyre & Spottiswoode, 1967b.

————. *On Photography*. New York: Farrar, Straus, and Giroux, 1977.

Spicer, Jakki. 'The Author Is Dead, Long Live the Author: Autobiography and the Fantasy of the Individual.' *Criticism*, 47 (3), 2005: 387–403.

Spickard, Paul R. 'Race, Nation, Identity and Power.' *Race and Nation: Ethnic Systems in the Modern World*, ed. by Paul R. Spickard. New York: Routledge, 2004.

Stainforth, Elizabeth, and David Thom. 'Metadata: Walter Benjamin and Bernard Stiegler.' *Theorising Visual Studies*, ed. by James Elkins. New York: Routledge 2013.

Stuart, Avelie, and Ngaire Donaghue. 'Choosing to Conform: The Discursive Complexities of Choice in Relation to Feminine Beauty Practices.' *Feminism & Psychology*, 22 (1), 2012: 98–121.

Switaj, Elizabeth Kate. 'Lady Gaga's Bodies: Buying and Selling *The Fame Monster*.' *The Performance Identities of Lady Gaga*, ed. by R. J. Gray. Jefferson, NC: McFarland, 2012.

Tasker, Yvonne, and Diane Negra. 'In Focus: Postfeminism and Contemporary Media Studies.' *Cinema Journal*, 44 (2), 2005: 107–10.

————. *Interrogating Postfeminism: Gender and the Politics of Popular Culture*. Durham, N.C.: Duke University Press, 2007.

Tiidenberg, K. 'Bringing Sexy Back: Reclaiming the Body Aesthetic via Self-Shooting.' *Cyberpsychology: Journal of Psychosocial Research on Cyberspace*, 8 (1), 2014: 126.

Tolson, Andrew. 'A New Authenticity? Communicative Practices on YouTube.' *Critical Discourse Studies*, 7 (4), 2010: 277–89.

Torrusio, Ann T. 'The Fame Monster: The Monstrous Construction of Lady Gaga.' *The Performance Identities of Lady Gaga*, ed. by R. J. Gray. Jefferson, NC: McFarland, 2012.

Trilling, Lionel. *Sincerity and Authenticity*. London: Oxford University Press, 1972.

Tseëlon, Efrat. *The Masque of Femininity: The Presentation of Woman in Everyday Life*. London: Sage, 1995.

Tuchman, Gaye. 'The Symbolic Annihilation of Women in the Media.' *Health and Home: Images of Women in the Mass Media*, ed. by G. Tuchman, A. Daniels, and J. Benet. Oxford: Oxford University Press, 1978.

Turner, Graeme, Frances Bonner, and P. David Marshall. *Fame Games: The Production of Celebrity in Australia*. Cambridge: Cambridge University Press, 2000.

Turner, Graeme. 'Approaching Celebrity Studies.' *Celebrity Studies*, 1 (1), 2010: 11–20.

Tyler, Imogen and Bruce Bennett. '"Celebrity Chav": Fame, Femininity and Social Class.' *European Journal of Cultural Studies*, 13 (3), 2010: 375–93.

Tyler, Meagan. 'Sex Self-Help Books: Hot Secrets for Great Sex or Promoting the Sex of Prostitution?' *Women's Studies International Forum*, 31 (5), 2008: 363–72.

Urry, John. 'The Global Media and Cosmopolitanism.' 26 April 2001. Cited in José I. Prieto-Arranz. 'The Semiotics of Performance and Success in Madonna.' *The Journal of Popular Culture*, 45 (1), 2012.

Urry, John, and Jonas Larsen. *The Tourist Gaze 3.0*. London: Sage, 2011.

Van Dijk, Teun A. 'Critical Discourse Analysis.' *The Handbook of Discourse Analysis*, ed. by D. Schiffrin, D. Tannen, and H. E. Hamilton. Malden, MA: Blackwell Publishers, 2001.

Wallenberg, Louise. 'Fashion Photography, Phallocentrism and Feminist Critique.' *Fashion in Popular Culture: Literature, Media and Contemporary Studies*, ed. by Joseph H. Hancock, Toni Johnson-Woods, and Vicki Karaminas. Bristol: Intellect, 2013.

Watson, Julia. 'Towards and Anti-Metaphysics of Autobiography.' *The Culture of Autobiography: Constructions of Self-Representation*, ed. by Robert Folkenflik. Stanford, CA: Stanford University Press, 1993.

Williams, Linda, and Victoria L. Banyard. *Trauma and Memory*. London: Sage, 1998.

Williams, Linda. *Hard Core: Power, Pleasure, and the "Frenzy of the Visible."* Berkeley: University of California Press, 1989.

———. *Porn Studies*. Durham and London: Duke University Press, 2004.

Williams, Rebecca. 'From Beyond Control to In Control: Investigating Drew Barrymore's Feminist Agency/Authorship.' *Stardom and Celebrity*, ed. by Holmes and Redmond. Los Angeles: Sage, 2007.

Williamson, Milly. 'Female Celebrities and the Media: The Gendered Denigration of the "Ordinary" Celebrity.' *Celebrity Studies*, 1 (1) 2010: 118–20.

———. 'Celebrity, Gossip, Privacy, and Scandal.' *The Routledge Companion to Media and Gender*, ed. by Cynthia Carter, Linda Steiner, and Lisa McLaughlin. New York: Routledge, 2014.

Wilson, J. A. 'Star Testing: The Emerging Politics of Celebrity Gossip.' *The Velvet Light Trap*, 65, 2010: 25–38.

Wolf, Naomi. *The Beauty Myth: How Images of Beauty Are Used Against Women.* New York: Anchor Books, 1992.

Woods, Faye. 'Classed Femininity, Performativity, and Camp in British Structured Reality Programming.' *Television New Media*, 6 November 2012.

Yagoda, Ben. *Memoir: A History*. New York: Riverhead Books, 2009.

Yelin, Hannah and Laura Clancy. 'Doing Impact Work While Female: Hate Tweets, "Hot Potatoes" and Having "Enough of Experts."' *European Journal of Women's Studies*. https://doi.org/10.1177/1350506820910194.

Yelin, Hannah. '"I Am the Centre of Fame": Doing Celebrity, Performing Fame and Navigating Cultural Hierarchies in Grace Jones' I'll Never Write my Memoirs.' *Celebrity Studies* (2019). https://doi.org/10.1080/19392397.2019.1615967.

York, Lorraine. 'Star Turn: The Challenges of Theorizing Celebrity Agency.' *The Journal of Popular Culture* 46 (6) 2013: 1330–47.

Yunuen Lewis, Caitlin. 'Cool Postfeminism: The Stardom of Sofia Coppola.' *In the Limelight and Under the Microscope*, ed. by Holmes and Negra. New York: Continuum, 2011.

Zuberi. Nabeel, 'Worries in the Dance: Post-millennial Grooves and Sub-bass Culture.' *Britpop and the English Music Tradition*, ed. by Andy Bennet and Jon Stratton. Aldershot: Ashgate, 2010.

NON-ACADEMIC SOURCES

Anderson, Pamela, and Tommy Lee. 'Pamela Anderson and Tommy Lee Sex Tape,' 1995. www.pornhub.com/view_video.php?viewkey=467533263.

Barkham, Patrick. 'I'm Famous, Buy Me.' *The Guardian*, 15 January 2007. http://www.theguardian.com/books/2007/jan/15/biography.patric kbarkham.

Barns, Sarah. 'Who Is Zoella? The YouTube Star Is Probably the Most Famous Person You've Never Heard of,' mirror.co.uk, 18 February 2015. https://www.mirror.co.uk/3am/celebrity-news/zoe-sugg---most-famous-3671787.

Beach, Natalie. 'I Was Caroline Calloway. Seven Years After I Met the Infamous Instagram Star, I'm Ready to Tell My Side of the Story.' *The Cut*, 10 September 2019. https://www.thecut.com/2019/09/the-story-of-caroline-calloway-and-her-ghostwriter-natalie.html.

Bigg Boss. 2008. TV, Endemol. Series 2.

Bignell, Paul. 'Decline and Fall of the C-list Female Celebrity Memoirs.' *The Independent*, 23 December 2007. http://www.independent.co.uk/arts-ent ertainment/books/news/decline-and-fallof-the-clist-female-celebrity-mem oirs-766946.html.

Billboard Staff. 'Paris Hilton Signs with Cash Money; Second Album to Feature Lil Wayne.' *The Hollywood Reporter*, 2 May 2013. http://www.hollywoodrep orter.com/earshot/paris-hilton-signs-cash-money-532750.

Blackburn, Virginia. 'Katie Price's Life? It's a Price Worth Paying.' *The Guardian*, 17 January 2010. http://www.guardian.co.uk/commentisfree/2010/jan/ 17/jordan-celebrity-memoir.

Blow Up. 1966. Film. MGM. London: Michelangelo Antonioni.

Cadwalladr, Carole. 'All Because the Ladies Love Jordan.' *The Observer*, 12 February 2006. http://www.guardian.co.uk/theobserver/2006/feb/12/fea tures.review47.

Celebrity Big Brother, 2007. TV, Endemol. Series 5.

Chen, Adrian, 'Nasim Aghdam, the YouTube Shooting, and the Anxiety of Demonetization.' *The New Yorker*, 6 April 2018. https://www.newyorker. com/tech/annals-of-technology/nasim-aghdam-the-youtube-shooting-and- the-anxiety-of-demonetization.

Cohen, Nadia. 'Beep, Beep, Beep … It's Big Brother!' *The Daily Mail*, May 2002. http://www.dailymail.co.uk/tvshowbiz/article-117087/Beep- beep-beep---Big-Brother.html#ixzz2UiGGZpS9.

Crone, Jack. 'Are We Seeing the Death of the Celebrity Memoir? *Mail Online*, 20 December 2014. http://www.dailymail.co.uk/news/article-2881571/ End-chapter-celebrity-memoirs-Autobiographies-rich-famous-no-longer-sell- says-publishing-house.html#ixzz3icP5MsBk.

Dent, Susie. *Larpers and Shroomers: The Language Report.* Oxford: Oxford University Press, 2004.

Desborough, James. JADE: YES I DID GIVE PJ THE BJ! *The People*, 28 July 2002.

DiCaro, Julie. 'The Dangers of the "Cool Girl" Ideal,' *Medium.com*, 6 Jan 2017. https://medium.com/the-establishment/the-dangers-of-the-cool-girl- ideal-76e59cf0f6ec.

Ditum, Sarah. 'Against Cool Girl Feminism.' *newstatesman.com*, 10 March 2014. https://www.newstatesman.com/sarah-ditum/2014/03/against-cool- girl-feminism.

Dolby, Trevor. 'Publishing Confessions.' *Prospect Magazine*, 14 January 2007. http://www.prospectmagazine.co.uk/arts-and-books/publishingconfessions.

Douglas, Scott. 'Baffled Tony Marsh Gets a View from the Other End of the Lens,' 12 March 2008. https://scottdouglas.wordpress.com/tag/paparazzi/.

Eaton, Phoebe. 'Terry Richardson's Dark Room.' *The New York Observer*, 20 September 2004. http://observer.com/2004/09/terry-richardsons-dark- room/.

Foster, Olivia. 'From a 32C to a 32G, and Back Again! How 16 YEARS of Cosmetic Surgery Gave Katie Price the Most Famous Boobs in the Country.' *Daily Mail*, 8 December 2014. http://www.dailymail.co.uk/femail/article-

2865206/How-16-YEARS-cosmetic-surgery-gave-Katie-Price-famous-boobs-country.html.

Foster, Patrick. 'Media Scrum Continues after Jade Goody's Death, with Rehashed Book and a Film Plan.' *The Times*, 24 March 2009.

Gadsby, Hannah. *Nannette*, Netflix.com, 2018.

Gaga, Lady. Interview with Alison Stephenson, 29 November 2010. http://www.youtube.com/watch?v=eS5tq4F659Q.

Gavras, Romain. 'M.I.A.' *Interview Magazine*, 7 July 2010. http://www.interv iewmagazine.com/music/mia/#_.

Germanotta, Stefani. 'Assignment # 4: Reckoning of Evidence.' Reportedly written 2003 During Her Freshman Year at NYU Tisch, 1 November 2004. Posted in Jordan Carter, 'The Theory Monster,' 4 February 2010. http://students.brown.edu/College_Hill_Independent/?p=2481.

Glass, Katie. 'Zoella's Bestseller: The Plot Thickens.' *The Times*, 7 December 2014. https://www.thetimes.co.uk/article/zoellas-bestseller-the-plot-thickens-6xgwdg5hkc2#commentsStart.

Goodreads. 'Interview with Pamela Anderson,' February 2010. http://www.goo dreads.com/interviews/show/484.Pamela_Anderson.

Greg Sandoval. 'Morgan Stanley Values YouTube as a $160 Billion Entity.' *Business Insider*, 18 May 2018. https://www.businessinsider.com/morgan-sta nley-values-youtube-160-billion-dollars-2018-5?r=US&IR=T.

Haddow, Douglas. 'The Real Controversy of MIA's Video.' *The Guardian*, 1 May 2010. http://www.theguardian.com/commentisfree/2010/may/01/ mia-video-real-controversy.

Hanley, Lynsey. 'Reality Cheque.' *New Statesman*, 16 October 2008. http://www.newstatesman.com/books/2008/10/jade-goody-star-brother-life.

Harris, John. 'Why Celebrity Memoirs Rule Publishing.' *The Guardian*, 13 December 2010. http://www.guardian.co.uk/books/2010/dec/13/celebr ity-memoirs-bestsellers-autobiography-christmas#ixzz2UhtsjwCT.

Hilton, Perez. 'Katie Price Reveals Her Struggle to Conceive a Child With Alex Reid.' *Perezhilton.com*, 25 October 2010. http://perezhilton.com/2010-10-25-katie-price-reveals-her-struggle-to-conceive-a-child-with-alex-reid.

———. 'Katie Flashes the Photogs A Smile Her Panties!' *Perezhilton.com*. 11 February 2011. http://perezhilton.com/2011-02-11-katie-price-wardrobe-malfunction-london-panties-shot.

Hirschberg, Lynn. 'MIA's Agitprop Pop.' *New York Times*, 25 May 2010. www. nytimes.com/2010/05/30/magazine/30mia-t.html.

Hollingshead, Ian. 'Is It Curtains for the Celebrity Memoir?' *The Telegraph*, 9 December 2011. http://www.telegraph.co.uk/topics/christmas/8943536/ Is-it-curtains-for-the-celebrity-memoir.html.

Hunter Johnston, Lucy. 'Yes, Using a Ghostwriter Matters When Your Whole Brand Is Built on Being Authentic.' *The Independent*, 8 December 2014.

https://www.independent.co.uk/voices/comment/zoella-theres-nothing-wrong-with-hiring-a-ghost-writer-as-long-as-you-admit-it-9910453.html.
Jade: The Reality Star Who Changed Britain, 2019. Blast! Films, Channel 4.
Jeffries, Stuart. 'Beauty and the Beastliness: A Tale of Declining British Values.' *The Guardian*, 19 January 2007. http://www.guardian.co.uk/media/2007/jan/19/broadcasting.comment.
'Jen McAllister Net Worth and Earnings 2018,' 12 July 2018. https://eceleb ritymirror.com/youtuber/jean-mcallister-aka-jennxpenn-net-worth-merch-books-episode/.
'Jenna Jameson Hair Hot Trimmer Shaver,' *Amazon.com*. http://www.amazon.com/Jenna-Jameson-Hair-Trimmer-Shaver/dp/B00041MB2U.
'JennxPenn,' socialblade.com, 29 August 2019. https://socialblade.com/you tube/user/jennxpenn.
Kean, Danuta. 'Celebrity Memoirs: Bookshop Bingo!' *The Independent*, 24 September 2015. http://www.independent.co.uk/arts-entertainment/books/features/celeb-memoirs-bookshop-bingo-417361.html.
Lachno, James. 'Lady Gaga—Top 10 Controversies.' *The Telegraph*, 20 April 2011. http://www.telegraph.co.uk/culture/music/rockandpopmusic/8463228/Lady-Gaga-Top-10-Controversies.html.
'Lady Gaga X Terry Richardson,' *Amazon.com*. http://www.amazon.co.uk/Lady-Gaga-X-Terry-Richardson/dp/144474125X.
Ladygagaxterryrichardsonthebook.com, Lady Gaga X Terry Richardson. http://www.ladygagaxterryrichardsonthebook.com/.
Listology, melladior@ho, 'Paris Hilton: Rich White Trash.' http://www.listology.com/story/paris-hilton-rich-white-trash.
Manaton, Thomas. 'Thomas Manaton.' *LinkedIn*. Retrieved on 6 December 2013 from https://www.linkedin.com/profile/view?id=188954041&aut hType=name&authToken=yXgW.
Mayer, Jane. 'Donald Trump's Ghostwriter Tells All.' *The New Yorker*, 18 July 2016. https://www.newyorker.com/magazine/2016/07/25/don ald-trumps-ghostwriter-tells-all.
McNeal, Stephanie. Caroline Calloway Says She Is Releasing A Book Called "Scammer." *BuzzFeed News*, 15 January 2020. https://www.buzzfeednews.com/article/stephaniemcneal/caroline-calloway-books-scammer.
Medved, Matt. 'Paris Hilton Reveals Las Vegas Residency, Defends DJ Career.' *The Hollywood Reporter*, 31 March 2015. http://www.hollywoodreporter.com/news/paris-hilton-reveals-las-vegas-785656.
Miller, Matthew. 'The (Porn) Player.' *Forbes Magazine*, July 4 2005. http://www.forbes.com/free_forbes/2005/0704/124.html.
Morrison, Nick. 'What Can Schools Learn from Jade Goody?' *Times Educational Supplement*, 17 April 2009. http://www.tes.co.uk/article.aspx?storyc ode=6011978.

Morrow, Mandy. 'Celebrity Book Deals: The Latest, Highest-Paid Advances.' *The Richest*, 3 August 2014. http://www.therichest.com/expensive-lifestyle/money/celebrity-book-deals-the-latest-highest-paid-advances/.

Naughton, John. 'Celebgate: It's Not the Internet We Need to Fix but Men's Squalid Behaviour.' *Guardian Online*, 7 September 2014.

O'Donoghue, Anna. 'The Most Famous Girl You've Never Heard of.' *irishexaminer.com*, 7 August 2014. https://www.irishexaminer.com/breakingnews/entertainment/the-most-famous-girl-youve-probably-never-heard-of-zoe-sugg-638538.html.

O'Hagan, Sean. 'Good Clean Fun?' *The Observer*, 17 October 2004. http://www.theguardian.com/film/2004/oct/17/photography.art.

Obituary: 'Jade Goody.' *The Telegraph*, 22 March 2009. http://www.telegraph.co.uk/news/obituaries/5031343/Jade-Goody.html.

OED Online. "capture, n.", Oxford University Press, June 2015. http://www.oed.com/view/Entry/27659?rskey=86l3QA&result=1&isAdvanced=false#eid.

'Pamela Anderson Is the Shameless Ploy of the Week.' *Entertainment Weekly*, 16 July 2004.

Parkin, Simon. 'The YouTube Stars Heading for Burnout: "The Most Fun Job Imaginable Became Deeply Bleak."' *The Guardian*, 8 September 2018. https://www.theguardian.com/technology/2018/sep/08/YouTube-stars-burnout-fun-bleak-stressed?CMP=Share_iOSApp_Other.

Peck, Jamie. 'Terry Richardson Is Really Creepy: One Model's Story.' *The Gloss*, 16 March 2010. http://www.thegloss.com/2010/03/16/fashion/terry-richardson-is-really-creepy-one-models-story/2/#ixzz3CjasFCrY.

Petersen, Anne Helen, 'How Millenials Became the Burnout Generation.' *buzzfeednews.com*, 5 January 2019. https://www.buzzfeednews.com/article/annehelenpetersen/millennials-burnout-generation-debt-work.

Prasad, Suran. 'Zoella net worth.' *Spears*, 29 August 2019. https://www.spearswms.com/zoe-sugg-net-worth/.

Quart, Alissa. 'The Age of Hipster Sexism.' *New York Magazine*, 30 October 2012. http://nymag.com/thecut/2012/10/age-of-hipster-sexism.html.

Reynolds, Simon. 'Piracy Funds What?' *Village Voice*, 15 February 2005.

Roose, Kevin. 'The Making of a YouTube Radical.' *The New York Times*, 8 June 2019. https://www.nytimes.com/interactive/2019/06/08/technology/youtube-radical.html.

Runcie, Charlotte. 'Girl Online on Tour by Zoe Sugg, Review: "More Authentic."' *The Telegraph*, 20 October 2015. https://www.telegraph.co.uk/books/what-to-read/zoe-sugg-girl-online-on-tour-review/.

Sager, Mike. 'What I've Learned: Pamela Anderson.' *Esquire Magazine*, 31 December 2004. http://web.archive.org/web/20121217055346/http://www.esquire.com/features/ESQ0105-WIL_Anderson.

Sales, Nancy Jo. "Hip-Hop Debs." *Vanity Fair*, September 2000. Cited in Fahy, 'One Night in Paris Hilton': 75–98.

Sauers, Jenna. 'Meet Terry Richardson, the World's Most F—Ked Up Fashion Photographer.' *Jezebel.com*, 16 March 2010. http://jezebel.com/5494634/meet-terry-richardson-the-worlds-most-fked-up-fashion-photographer.

Shriver, Lionel. 'How Did Glamour Model Jordan Become a Bestselling Author When She Doesn't Even Write?' *Mail Online*, 4 September 2008. http://www.dailymail.co.uk/femail/article-1052243/How-did-glamour-model-Jordan-best-selling-author-doesnt-write.html#ixzz42EBvHip4.

Singer, Jill. 'So What Do You Do, Neil Strauss?' *MediaBistro.com*, 17 August 2004. http://www.mediabistro.com/So-What-Do-You-Do-Neil-Strauss-a2441.html.

Singh, Anita. "Jade Goody Represented Wretched Britain', says Sir Michael Parkinson.' *The Telegraph*, 7 April 2009. http://www.telegraph.co.uk/news/celebritynews/jade-goody/5114664/Jade-Goody-represented-wretched-Britain-says-Sir-Michael-Parkinson.html.

———. 'Zoella Breaks Record for First Week Book Sales.' *The Telegraph*, 2 December 2014. https://www.telegraph.co.uk/news/celebritynews/11268540/Zoella-breaks-record-for-first-week-book-sales.html.

Spanier, Gideon. 'Celebs Lose Their Sheen for Publishers as Gift-buyers Spurn Celebrity Biographies.' *The Independent*, 19 December 2014. http://www.independent.co.uk/news/business/news/celebs-lose-their-sheen-for-publishers-as-giftbuyers-spurn-celebrity-biographies-9937012.html.

Steinmetz, Katy. 'Top 10 Controversial Music' Videos.' *Time Magazine*, 6 June 2011. http://entertainment.time.com/2011/06/07/top-10-controversial-music-videos/.

Stern, Jane, and Michael Stern. '"How to Make Love like a Porn Star": Lovers and Other Strangers.' *The New York Times*, 5 September 2004. http://www.nytimes.com/2004/09/05/books/review/05STERNL.html?_r=0.

Stone, Philip. 'Jade Title Reaches Number One.' *The Oxford Editors*, 7 April 2009. http://www.theoxfordeditors.co.uk/?p=216.

Strang, Fay. 'EXCLUSIVE: "My Intention Was to Put Art Culture into Pop Music": Lady Gaga Reveals She Aimed to "Reverse Warhol" in New Record.' *Mail Online*, 4 November 2013. http://www.dailymail.co.uk/tvshowbiz/article-2486872/Lady-Gaga-reveals-aimed-reverse-Warhol-new-album-ARTPOP.html#ixzz3KqrUw8BQ.

Sugg, Zoe. 'Book Meeting, Date Night & Found The Missing Wallet,' 24 April 2015. https://www.youtube.com/watch?v=0-m_8d5No5k.

———. 'Finishing Book Two & Louise's Launch,' 21 July 2015. https://www.youtube.com/watch?v=95_xihbNMgw.

———. 'Writing with a Pug, Meetings & Doggy Box,' 15 May 2015. https://www.youtube.com/watch?v=N2WpZdTVTpU.

Sutherland, John. 'Among the Ghosts.' *Spectator*, 11 June 2011. http://www. spectator.co.uk/features/7009933/among-the-ghosts.

Taylor, Charles. '"How to Make Love Like a Porn Star" by Jenna Jameson.' *Salon.com*, 25 August 2004. http://www.salon.com/2004/08/ 25/jenna_6/.

The Daily Mail. 'Controversial Singer M.I.A. Fighting "Ridiculous" $1.5 Million Fine for Swearing and Making Rude Gesture During Madonna's 2012 Super Bowl Show,' 20 September 2013. http://www.dailymail.co. uk/tvshowbiz/article-2426878/MIA-fighting-1-5m-fine-controversial-appear ance-Madonnas-2012-Super-Bowl-show.html#ixzz3hqQRWnRi.

'The Year of the Chav.' *The Daily Mail*, 19 October 2004. https://www.dailym ail.co.uk/news/article-322501/The-year-Chav.html.

The Daily Star. 'Jermaine in Frame: New Big Bro Race Row,' 3 February 2007. http://www.dailystar.co.uk/posts/view/12423.

The Simple Life, 2003–2007. TV, 20th Century Fox.

The Telegraph. '"It Wasn't Rape or Anything" Says David Bailey of His Sexual Conquests,' 22 December 2012. http://www.telegraph.co.uk/culture/976 2530/It-wasnt-rape-or-anything-says-David-Bailey-of-his-sexual-conquests. html.

THR Staff. 'Paris Hilton on Her Global Tour and Drug Use in the EDM Scene.' *The Hollywood Reporter*, 8 October 2013. http://www.hollywoodreporter. com/video/paris-hilton-her-global-tour-645126.

Tonks, Owen. 'Jodie Marsh Predicts Katie Price's Fall from Showbiz as she Slams her Attention Seeking Ways.' *The Mirror*, 26 March 2013. http://www.mir ror.co.uk/3am/celebrity-news/jodie-marsh-predicts-katie-prices-1786469.

Urban Dictionary. 'White Trash,' posted by 'Your Mom.' http://www.urband ictionary.com/define.php?term=white%20trash.

Us Weekly. 'Lady Gaga's Craziest Stunts and Most Outrageous Controversies.' http://www.usmagazine.com/entertainment/pictures/lady-gagas-craziest-stunts-and-most-outrageous-controversies-2014273/36953.

Wadler, Joyce. 'Boldface Names.' *The New York Times*, 10 August 2004. http:// www.nytimes.com/2004/08/10/nyregion/boldface-names-582794.html.

Wallace, Benjamin. 'Is Terry Richardson an Artist or a Predator?' *New York Magazine*, 15 June 2014. http://nymag.com/thecut/2014/06/terry-richar dson-interview.html.

Weiner, Jonah. 'How Smart Is Lady Gaga?' *Slate*, 16 June 2009. http://www. slate.com/articles/arts/music_box/2009/06/how_smart_is_lady_gaga.html.

Williams, Zoe. 'Zoe Sugg: The Vlogger Blamed for Declining Teenage Literacy.' *The Guardian*, 24 February 2017. https://www.theguardian.com/culture/ 2017/feb/24/zoe-sugg-zoella-the-vlogger-blamed-for-declining-teenage-lit eracy.

Wyatt, Edward. 'Political but Not Partisan: A Publisher Has It Both Ways.' *The New York Times*, 13 October 2004. http://www.nytimes.com/2004/10/13/books/13bbox.html?_r=0.

Yelin, Hannah, and Jonathan Wise. 'Dave: Now Everyone Has a Mate Called Dave.' *Advertising Works 17: Case Studies from the IPA Effectiveness Awards 2008*, ed. by Neil Dawson. Henley-on-Thames: WARC 2009.

'YouTubers who died too soon,' *ranker.com*. https://www.ranker.com/list/you tubers-who-died-young/youtuber?page=4.

"Zalfie". Blog at *zoella.co.uk*, 11 August 2013.

'Zoella,' socialblade.com, 29 August 2019. https://socialblade.com/youtube/user/zoella280390.

Index

© The Editor(s) (if applicable) and The Author(s) 2020

H. Yelin, *Celebrity Memoir*,

https://doi.org/10.1007/978-3-030-44621-5

CPI Antony Rowe
Chippenham, UK
2021-02-01 11:12